Agent of Change

Agent of Change
The Deposition and Manipulation of Ash in the Past

Edited by
Barbara J. Roth and E. Charles Adams

berghahn
NEW YORK • OXFORD
www.berghahnbooks.com

First published in 2021 by
Berghahn Books
www.berghahnbooks.com

© 2021, 2025 Barbara J. Roth and E. Charles Adams
First paperback edition published in 2025

All rights reserved. Except for the quotation of short passages for the purposes of criticism and review, no part of this book may be reproduced in any form or by any means, electronic or mechanical, including photocopying, recording, or any information storage and retrieval system now known or to be invented, without written permission of the publisher.

Library of Congress Cataloging-in-Publication Data

A C.I.P. cataloging record is available from the Library of Congress

Library of Congress Cataloging in Publication Control Number: 2021930026

British Library Cataloguing in Publication Data

A catalogue record for this book is available from the British Library

ISBN 978-1-80073-036-6 hardback
ISBN 978-1-80539-755-7 paperback
ISBN 978-1-80539-929-2 epub
ISBN 978-1-80073-037-3 web pdf

https://doi.org/10.3167/9781800730366

Contents

List of Illustrations   vii

Introduction: The Deposition and Manipulation of Ash in the Past   1
E. Charles Adams and Barbara J. Roth

Part I. Ash as a Transformative Agent

1. Ash Matters: The Ritual Closing of Domestic Structures in the Mimbres Mogollon Region   15
Barbara J. Roth

2. Complex Closure Practices Involving Ash at a Small Pueblo in Northeastern Arizona   30
E. Charles Adams

3. Sequencing Termination Events: Preparing Hearths for the Ritual Decommissioning of Ancestral Pueblo Pit Structures in the Northern U.S. Southwest   45
Susan C. Ryan

4. Symbolic Associations: Assessing the Co-occurrence of Turquoise and Ash in the Ancient U.S. Southwest   61
Samantha G. Fladd, Saul L. Hedquist, E. Charles Adams, and Stewart B. Koyiyumptewa

5. Fire, Ash, and Sanctuary: Pyrotechnology as Protection in the Precolonial Northern Rio Grande   76
Michael A. Adler

6. Burned Roofs and Cultural Traditions: Renewing and Closing Houses in the Ancient Villages of the Middle Fraser Canyon, British Columbia   94
Anna Marie Prentiss, Alysha Edwards, Ashley Hampton, Ethan Ryan, Kathryn Bobolinski, and Emma Vance

7. Agentive Ash and Dispersed Power in the Cahokia
   Mississippian World   113
   Melissa R. Baltus and Sarah E. Baires

8. Townhouses, Hearths, Fire, Smoke, Ash, and Cherokee
   Towns in Western North Carolina   136
   Christopher B. Rodning

9. Ash as an Agent of Transformation in Iroquoian Society   156
   William Fox

Part II. Ash and Ritual

10. Ashes to Ashes, Dust to Dust in Caddoan Mortuary Ritual   173
    Marvin Kay

11. Ashes for Fertility   186
    Cheryl Claassen

12. Ashes, Arrows, and Sorcerers   196
    William H. Walker and Judy Berryman

13. Divine Food and Fiery Covenants: The Significance of Ash
    in Ancient Maya Religion   213
    James L. Fitzsimmons

Afterword   229
    Tammy Stone

Illustrations

Figures

1.1.	Lake Roberts Vista, Harris, and Elk Ridge site locations. Created by Russell Watters.	18
1.2.	Harris site map. Created by Russell Watters.	20
1.3.	Ash-filled hearth prior to excavation, Harris site Pithouse 48. Photo by Barbara J. Roth.	23
2.1.	Location of Brandy's Pueblo in the middle Little Colorado River valley. Image courtesy of Samantha G. Fladd.	31
2.2.	Map of Brandy's Pueblo and exterior workspaces. Image created by Richard C. Lange, Arizona State Museum.	32
2.3.	Wall fall from intentional collapse of pueblo wall. Photo courtesy of Vincent M. LaMotta.	36
3.1.	Location of study area in the central Mesa Verde region. Used with permission of the Crow Canyon Archaeological Center.	46
3.2.	Four two-handed manos placed side by side on cooled hearth ash, Albert Porter Pueblo. Used with permission of the Crow Canyon Archaeological Center.	54
3.3.	Hawk remains placed on cooled hearth ash, Castle Rock Pueblo. Used with permission of the Crow Canyon Archaeological Center.	57
4.1.	Map showing the location of the Homol'ovi Settlement Cluster. Created by Samantha G. Fladd (based on Adams 2002).	64
4.2.	Map of Homol'ovi I showing the location of turquoise, ash cones, and two rooms discussed in detail in the text. Based

	on maps produced by the Homol'ovi Research Program, Arizona State Museum.	66
4.3.	Profile of Structure 729 hearth, and photos of a sample of the associated turquoise. Photos by Saul L. Hedquist.	68
5.1.	Map of groups and sites. Figure by Michael A. Adler.	77
5.2.	Plan map of Pot Creek Pueblo. Figure by Michael A. Adler.	86
6.1.	Bridge River site in context. Figure by the authors.	95
6.2.	Stratigraphic sequence of Housepit 54 (not to scale). Figure by the authors.	101
6.3.	The roof deposits of Housepit 54. Figure by the authors.	103
7.1.	Sites referred to in this chapter. Figure by Melissa R. Baltus and Sarah E. Baires.	116
7.2.	Features with ash deposits. Figure by Melissa R. Baltus and Sarah E. Baires.	129
8.1.	Cherokee town areas. Created by Christopher B. Rodning.	142
8.2.	The Coweeta Creek site plan. Features 32 and 33 are located northeast of Structure 1. Features 34 and 35 are located southwest of Structure 1. Created by Christopher B. Rodning.	143
8.3.	Posthole patterns and central hearth associated with late stages of the Coweeta Creek townhouse (Structure 1). Image courtesy of the UNC Research Laboratories of Archaeology, Chapel Hill.	144
8.4.	Posthole patterns and central hearth associated with early stages of the Coweeta Creek townhouse (Structure 1). Image courtesy of the UNC Research Laboratories of Archaeology, Chapel Hill.	145
9.1.	The Novvelle France or Taunton map, describing predispersal tribal locations in the lower Great Lakes region and dating to c. 1641. Photo by William Fox.	158
9.2.	Floor plan of Cahiague North Village House 3. (Hatched features are hearths and black features are "ash pits"). Figure by William Fox.	160
9.3.	Eleventh-century longhouse hearth complex (House 7, Elliott Village II). Figure by William Fox.	160
9.4.	Elliott Village "ash pit" profiles (stippled areas are ash fill). Figure by William Fox.	161

List of Illustrations ix

9.5. Husk Face mask, produced by Yvonne Thomas, Wolf Clan Mohawk, at Six Nations, Ontario. 165

10.1. Mound complexes in the study area. Harlan-style charnel houses are at Harlan, Goforth-Saindon, and Huntsville. Norman, Spiro/Coates, and Clements site investigations illustrate complementary platform mound constructions or derived charnel houses. Reprinted with permission of *Southeastern Archaeology* from Kay and Sabo 2006: 30, fig. 1. 174

10.2. Schematic vertical profile B of Goforth-Saindon Mound 1 excavation showing, in its earliest platform mound stage, submound pit(see laminated silt and "pinched" A-horizon that may distinguish the Feature 821 pit) and its two charnel houses (Features 355 and 821) beneath truncated pits with characteristic zebra-stripe fills in the intermediate platform mound stage. Directly beneath the redeposited fill is a final compound platform mound surface, the beginning of the final platform mound stage, at an excavation elevation between 1.0 and 1.5 meters below datum. Adapted from Kay, Sabo, and Merletti 1989: 139, fig. 44B, and Kay and Sabo 2006: 36, fig. 5, and with permission of *Oklahoma Archaeological Survey Studies in Oklahoma's Past* and *Southeastern Archaeology*. 176

10.3. Schematic views of excavated portions of charnel house Feature 355 overlying Feature 821 wall posts and carbonized roof debris on its fired clay floor. The house pit contains the floors and south walls of both structures. Feature 355 extended entryway was repaired with a new surface and clay pedestal added at its throat. This sealed the original entryway footprint surface. The entryway borders two post trenches whereas wall posts were in individual sockets. The blocking post is the entryway's last construction detail. Adapted with permission of *Southeastern Archaeology* from Kay and Sabo 2006: 35, fig. 4 and Kay and Sabo 2006: 38, fig. 8. 177

10.4. Feature 355 charnel house excavation photographs. (a) The extended entryway above the orange burnt clay floor. The darker gray circular discoloration in the center of the clay pedestal is the blocking post mold. The white plaster jacket protects a charred wood beam. Note also on the left (north) wall the ash zone just above the floor. It was leveled out to conform with the original mound platform surface. (b) Thin zone of charcoal from collapse of interior walls and roof. (c) Left (west) entryway trench charred caps of posts above hollow voids that rotted out and comprised an oxygen-free zone (see *a*) where burning ceased. Note secondary white ash swirls within a fifty-centimeter grid square defined by lines of intersecting string. Photos by Marvin Kay. 179

10.5. Marker mound partially excavated. (a, b) Two views of the mound core and its truncated black clay beneath the next prepared mound platform surface. Note the ash is superior in the core area and similarly positioned in the mound exterior zone (c). The exterior zone is dominated by black clay. The platform surface is characteristic in its thick dark gray underlayer with a burnt upper surface of lighter oxidized orange color. This distinctive treatment likely has the same connotation as the dark charnel house pit beneath the burnt clay floor. Adapted from Kay, Sabo, and Merletti 1989: 145, fig. 47C line drawing, and with permission of *Oklahoma Archaeological Survey Studies in Oklahoma's Past*. 183

11.1. Cumberland and Allegheny Plateaus. Wikimedia, CC BY-SA 2.5. 188

11.2. Ash in Red-Eye Hollow. Reprinted from Funkhouser and Webb 1929: 46, with permission. 189

11.3. Danger Cave ash layer. Reprinted from Funkhouser and Webb 1929: 46, with permission. 191

12.1. Cottonwood Spring Pueblo, Areas A through F (Lekson and Rorex 1987: HSR Report, p. 10, fig. 3). Created by the Human Systems Research. 204

12.2. Cottonwood Spring Pueblo, Area A, Locus 2. Created by the authors. 205

12.3. Illustration of deposit sequence in Room 3 (Corl 2014: 185, fig. 3). Created by Kristin Corl, used with permission. 205

12.4. Sample of projectile points collected from Cottonwood Spring Pueblo (A: Durango; B: Pueblo Side-Notched; C: Side-Notched; D: Maljamar; E: Bull Creek; F: Cottonwood Triangular; G: Awatovi Side-Notched). Created by the authors. 206

13.1. Map of Maya area. Created by James L. Fitzsimmons. 214

Tables

0.1.	Manipulation of Ash Described by Authors.	3
2.1.	AMS Radiocarbon Dates for Brandy's Pueblo (AZ P:3:114 [ASM]).	32
3.1.	Artifact Type and Number of Hearths Where Artifact Type Is Present	52
3.2.	Total Counts of Grayware (Corrugated and Plain Gray), Whiteware, and Nonlocal Wares (Including Redwares) from Hearths by Site.	53
3.3.	Number of Individual Specimens (NISP) and Types of Burned Fauna.	56
5.1.	Summary of the Use of Ashes for Noncooking Practices by Nine Ethnographic Groups.	81
7.1.	Features Having Ash Deposits from Sites in the American Bottom.	119
12.1.	Projectile Point Distribution at Cottonwood Spring Pueblo Area A.	207

Introduction

The Deposition and Manipulation of Ash in the Past

E. Charles Adams and Barbara J. Roth

This volume focuses on the deposition of ash and its varying meanings as part of depositional processes across North America. Ash and its companion, fire, are often ubiquitous and can take many forms depending on the context and meaning associated with their deposition. The symbolic substitution of ash for fire often results in ash taking on multiple meanings in protection, ritual closure, and cleansing. Because ash is essentially inert, it persists in the archaeological record, a quality not lost on societies in the past. The transformative power of fire and ash documented ethnographically and ethnohistorically by many Native American cultures illustrates that ash played an important role in many domestic and ritual activities, which suggests it played a similar role in the past. The chapters in this volume examine the multiple contexts where ash can be found in the prehistoric record and explore the concomitant multiple roles that ash played. They highlight the importance of the patterned deposition of ash as a social practice.

Ash appears in the archaeological record in many forms, reflecting its many social roles (Adams and Fladd 2017). One approach to understanding the social role of ash deposition is that of social stratigraphy, an approach introduced by McAnany and Hodder (2009) that provides an alternative means to understanding the deposition of both materials and sediment. This theory emphasizes that individual deposits within a unit of deposition are related both physically and socially. Thus, social stratigraphy broadens the focus of analysis to include the order and association of the depositional content and placement as reflecting social decisions; what was deposited before and after affects the meaning and social understanding of any individual deposit. This allows for the investigation of variability in deposits as representations of different social practices mediating relationships among people, materials, and spaces (see also Pollard 1995).

Unlike object-agents that animate the material world of traditional societies past and present (Alberti and Bray 2009), and which are distinctive to those traditions (for example, objects of pottery, stone, or bone), ash and fire are universal elements of human society. Fire is used for cooking, heating, or transforming material from one state to another, such as clay to pottery or wood to ash. Ash is transformed by fire and in turn is seen as having transformative properties. Thus, ash can serve as an agent of change.

For example, in the Marakwet tribe of Kenya (Moore 1982), ash can be a metaphor or mnemonic for an actor (female) or action (cooking) and simultaneously represent destruction (burning) and life (female and birth). Due to its potential for harm—causing infertility or even death—ash is disposed in socially specified and structured ways. In contrast, a fertile woman can cover herself in ash to deny a suitor (Moore 1982: 78), providing object-agency to ash. Even in its prescribed disposal fifteen meters from the house, ash is an active agent in the lives of the Marakwet.

During winter ceremonies at Zuni Pueblo in New Mexico, ash may not be removed from any house for a period of ten days lest the family fields suffer from drought (Parsons 1939: 573). Following the ceremony, ash must be handled by a woman and sprinkled on the ground before refuse accumulated over the same period can be deposited (Parsons 1939: 516). All Pueblos in the Southwest pass embers along the walls of homes to cleanse them from trouble and witchcraft before discarding them outdoors (Parsons 1939: 517). In all instances, ash is the first line of defense against witchcraft among Pueblo groups (Parsons 1939: 464). Typically, the remains of burned witches are deposited in designated areas (Parsons 1939: 730). Some Pueblo groups have ash piles where spiritually contaminated objects or fluids are discarded. Ash is also a central element in exorcism (Parsons 1939). The central role of ash in causing or preventing harm yields the need for its careful disposal.

The act of introducing ash, almost certainly as an acknowledged byproduct of and metaphor for fire and its transformative properties, invokes agency of individuals or groups, as well as objects bundled with these ashy deposits (Pauketat 2013). The chapters that follow detail the cross-cultural occurrences of these practices (see table 0.1 below). Importantly, they also highlight the manipulation of ash distinctive to their circumstance and show that modification of deposits by the addition of ash is intentional and transformative. The addition of ash can symbolize transformation from the living to liminal world, intentional erasure or forgetting of the past, or be symbolic of events or places (Mills 2008; Plunket 2002; Twiss et al. 2008; Whiteley 1998). Ash can provide structure to social practices with its repeated occurrence in mounds, houses, features, or their filling (sensu Giddens 1984). Within such social structure, ashy deposits can also be modified through bundling with objects, humans, or even adjacent deposits (Ortmann and Kidder 2013).

Table 0.1. *Manipulation of Ash Described by Authors.*

Use of Ash	Ethnographic/Historical Examples	Archaeological Examples	Authors
Hearth ash	Pueblo, Ute, Zuni, Cherokee, Iroquois	Domestic, community, and ceremonial hearths	Adler, Fladd et al., Fox, Rodning, Roth, Ryan
Ash enlivens	Maya, Pueblo	Bundled with other objects or adjoining deposits – see bundling of ash below	Baltus & Baires, Claassen, Fitzsimmons, Fladd et al., Ryan, Walker & Berryman
Ash cures/heals	Pueblo (Hopi, Zuni, Tewa, Zia), Navajo, O'odham, Iroquois, Caddo, Aztec	Hearths, with turquoise, with projectile points	Adler, Fladd et al., Fox, Kay, Roth, Walker & Berryman
Ash transforms/renews	Maya, St'át'imc, Nlaka'pamux, Cherokee, Iroquois, Dakota, Aztec	Covers occupation surfaces, below surfaces where new communal structures are built, covers burnt offerings	Adams, Baltus & Baires, Claassen, Fitzsimmons Fladd et al., Fox, Prentiss et al., Rodning, Roth
Ash purifies	Pueblo, Ute, Maya, Hopi, St'át'imc, Tewa, Nlaka'pamux, Aztec	Cover burials, cover "bloody and filthy" objects, cover powerful objects	Adler, Claassen, Fladd et al., Fitzsimmons, Prentiss et al., Ryan, Walker & Berryman
Ash protects/closure	Pueblo (Acoma, Hopi, Zuni, Tewa, Zia, Laguna), Ute, Navajo, O'odham, W. Apache, St'át'imc, Nlaka'pamux, Cherokee, Iroquois, Caddo, Aztec	Cover burials, cover powerful objects or spaces, block entrances or exits of ritually powerful or mortuary spaces	Adams, Adler, Fladd et al., Fox, Kay, Prentiss et al., Rodning, Roth, Ryan, Walker & Berryman
Ash transitions	Pueblo, Cherokee	Cover burials, cover surfaces to be repurposed	Adler, Baltus & Baires, Kay, Prentiss et al., Rodning
Ash as fertility	Pueblo, Hopi, Cherokee, Dhegihan	Gendered areas such as rock shelters, hearths	Adler, Baltus & Baires, Claassen, Fladd et al., Rodning
Bundling of ash	Pueblo (Zuni, Hopi, Acoma), Navajo	Manos (corn grinding), animal bone, palettes, projectile points, pottery, turquoise, tobacco, red cedar	Adams, Baltus & Baires, Fladd et al., Roth, Ryan, Walker & Berryman,
And social memory	Hopi, Maya, Navajo	Destruction of objects associated with closure	Adams, Fitzsimmons, Fladd et al., Ryan
Ash as food	Zuni, Maya, Iroquois	Left in hearths – usually maize or animal bone	Baltus and Baires, Fitzsimmons, Fladd et al., Fox
Color symbolism	Iroquois, Caddo	Colors of ash important in Caddoan charnal houses, rock shelters used by women	Claassen, Fox, Kay
Gendered	Hopi, Cherokee, Dakota	Rock shelters, hearths	Claassen, Fladd et al.
Disposal outside village	Pueblo, Cherokee	Ashes usually associated with evil or witchcraft	Adler, Rodning

Ash Deposition

Archaeological ash is present as a result of human action. Ash can either be a byproduct of daily activities, such as cooking, or a ritually meaningful deposit, depending on where and with what it was deposited.

In general, ash is present as either primary or secondary deposition (sensu Schiffer 1976, 1987). Primary deposition means ash is located where it was initially created through fire. Common examples are ash within hearths, firepits, or other thermal features. Presumably this ash is a result of fires burned in the feature; however, hearth ash often exhibits other characteristics associated with its use in a more ritualized manner. For example, at a fourteenth-century ancestral Hopi village in northeastern Arizona, Miljour (2016: 127) has documented the purposeful filling of hearths, following cessation of their use, with multiple colors of ash. Hearth ash has a particularly meaningful role for many of the chapter authors as either a means of closing a structure or as a portal for accessing and sometimes feeding ancestors by leaving real or symbolic food (Adler, chapter 5; Baltus and Baires, chapter 7; Fladd et al., chapter 4; Fox, chapter 9; Rodning, chapter 8; Roth, chapter 1; Ryan, chapter 3).

Another source of primary deposition of ash is from structural fires, usually roofs made of combustible material. In the Pueblo Southwest, for example, roofs are made of wooden beams covered by brush and grass. When the fire is hot and of long duration, the smaller elements of the roof are reduced to ash. These primary deposits will occur on floor surfaces or within the fill of structures, usually associated with larger burned elements of the roof. With structural fires, there is a question of intentionality and purpose. Occasionally structural fires can be accidental or caused by nonhuman factors, such as forest or grass fires (Lally and Vonarx 2011). More often, fires were intentionally set for one of a host of reasons: (1) to rid the organic roofing of infestations of insects or rodents (and other practical motives) often resulting in reuse of the structure; (2) to burn in a hostile manner, via acts internally or externally derived; (3) to serve as closure due to social factors (migration is an example); (4) to provide physical safety (burning organic remains of abandoned buildings); or (5) to prepare ritualistic space for spiritual purposes due to a death in the family or religious practices concerned with ancestors. Discerning the reasons for structural fires is usually done using other elements of the archaeological record to contextualize the event; for example, objects may be placed on floors or within features prior to or after a structure is burned (Icove et al. 2016; Lally 2005; Lally and Vonarx 2011; Twiss et al. 2008). Ash, then, is usually perceived as a fiery byproduct of burning and is imbued with the transformational powers that fire brings (see Adler, chapter 5; Fitzsimmons, chapter 13; and Prentiss et al., chapter 6).

Ash associated with fires from primary sources, while common, is a minor element of the quantity and diversity of archaeological ash. The vast majority of ash is a result of secondary deposition, meaning ash has been moved from the site of its original production to another location. Secondary deposition can appear random and uniform, sometimes characterized as "ashy fill," but just as often it can be concentrated into lenses or layers (Adams and Fladd 2017). Critically, these ashy deposits may occur in only limited architectural spaces and with suites of other behaviors manifest in associated objects or non-ashy deposits. Thus, its context as well as its composition is critical to understanding the role ash plays in the creation of the deposits (McAnany and Hodder 2009; Miljour 2016; Ortmann and Kidder 2013). One underappreciated element is the color of ash, because color can be manipulated, appearing often in the same depositional sequence as yellow, green, gray, or black (Miljour 2016). The ability to control its color encouraged its use as a coloring agent in complex, often foundational, deposits (Ortmann and Kidder 2013) or as a coloring agent and nutritional additive to many maize-based recipes as described by Baltus and Baires (chapter 7) and Fox (chapter 9).

The secondary deposition of ash is rarely random or socially meaningless. Its removal from primary deposits implies intentional cultural practices important and meaningful to members of the society, and the manipulation of ash usually occurred in culturally prescribed ways. For example, during the Hopi New Fire Ceremony (Fewkes 1900), four powerful religious societies rekindle fire in their ceremonial structures and deposit the ash in the direction of ancestral homes to harken the start of a new ceremonial year while invoking social memory of the community's ancestral homes.

Ash as an Agent of Change

The use of ash in the transition and/or transformation of a variety of features is consistent across a wide variety of site types and locations. Its association with fire is the powerful subtext of ash's agency, and, as described below and in the chapters to follow, this association offers powerful protection, purification, transformation, and potential for renewal.

Globally, ash's association with fire inherently embodies it with transformative properties, which are often associated with purification and protection. Ash can therefore be used to transform spaces from one state of being to another (Grove and Gillespie 2002; Manzanilla 2002; Plunket 2002; Twiss et al. 2008; Whiteley 1998). The use of ash for transformation and purification is often linked to concepts of renewal or closure. Activities surrounding deposition of ash in these cases can result in the destruction of objects and areas that are considered to be spiritually contaminated or that pose a danger to the uninitiated who are not able to protect themselves (Titiev 1944: 106; Walker 1995). Ash can be used to seal or cover lower deposits containing dangerous objects—usually sacra discarded in decommissioned religious structures or in mortuary contexts within or outside structures. It can also be used as a means to cleanse and renew. Thus, fire and ash, as symbols of transformation, serve as agents of change. They are used to end one chapter and begin the next in the life history of a hearth, building, or community.

One final aspect of ash deposition is its association with social memory. Ash frequently appears multiple times in complex deposits associated with the repeated use of objects, signifying knowledge of previous practices associated with a particular space. For example, the burning of Neolithic structures dating back seven to nine thousand years in southeastern Europe and the Near East has been characterized as creating permanent memories materially manifested in deposits of ash and charcoal in important places, serving to strengthen community identity (Tringham 2005; Twiss et al. 2008).

The Chapters

The chapters in this book focus on the deposition of ash and its purposeful manipulation by societies across North America. All the cases presented here show that ash, whether associated with primary deposition and fire or manipulated secondary deposits, held deeper meaning beyond simply burning down an infested roof, cooking, or other uses connected to daily practice. Instead, ash served alternative functions usually associated with domestic or communal ritual.

The chapter authors rely on archaeological context, historical documents, ethnographic accounts, or first-person experiences to describe the use of ash to protect, close, transform, renew, and purify. These important uses of ash explain its presence in hearths; pits; domestic, community, and ceremonial structures; exterior spaces; burials; and more. Whether combined with artifacts or other deposits, ash alters the purpose or intent of the object(s), space, or event. Ash even has traits of color (Claassen, chapter 11; Kay, chapter 10), odor (Fitzsimmons, chapter 13), and gender (Claassen, chapter 11; Fladd et al., chapter 4) that influence its actions. It is the inscription of ash with the transformative power of fire that enables its animation and active engagement with human and nonhuman actors.

The chapters also highlight the use of ash as a protective agent in ritually closing domestic, community, and ceremonial structures, burials, pits, rock shelters, and mortuary spaces. Many of the authors note the importance of ash as an agent of renewal and transformation, such as from the mundane to the sacred or as regeneration. Related to this concept is ash, again symbolizing fire, used to purify spaces, features, or structures. This is particularly apparent in Claassen's (chapter 11) interpretation of the burning of bundled objects associated with women's menstruation and giving birth, resulting in "blood and filth," necessitating the use of white ash to cover and purify these deposits in rock shelters in the eastern and western United States.

Chapter Organization

The chapters are divided into two sections. Part I includes nine chapters that address the role of ash and fire as transformative agents used in ritual closure and transformation in the United States (Southwest, Midwest, Southeast), British Columbia, and Ontario.

In "Ash Matters: The Ritual Closing of Domestic Structures in the Mimbres Mogollon Region," Barbara Roth examines the role that ash played in the ritual closure of domestic structures using data from pithouse and pueblo sites in the Mimbres region of southwestern New Mexico. Her data show that ash was used to close the lower floors of superimposed houses, that ash-filled hearths represent the final closure of pithouses, and that ash was used in particular burials, generally those associated with important households in the community. She argues that the use of ash in these contexts represented both closure (ash-filled hearths) and renewal (ash layers between superimposed floors).

In "Complex Closure Practices Involving Ash at a Small Pueblo in Northeastern Arizona," E. Charles Adams argues that ash was essential in the transformation of a small village in northeastern Arizona from a living community to its afterlife. The integral role of exterior space to the life (and afterlife) of the pueblo documented in his chapter is a reminder that more of pueblo life was spent outside pueblo rooms than inside them, and that the manipulation of ash was not solely confined to structures.

In "Sequencing Termination Events: Preparing Hearths for the Ritual Decommissioning of Ancestral Pueblo Pit Structures in the Northern U.S. Southwest," Susan C. Ryan uses data from multiple ancestral Pueblo sites in the Mesa Verde region of southwestern Colorado to examine how kiva hearths were ritually prepared prior to termination of the structure. Ryan argues that burning was an esoteric, transformative process that converted matter from one form to another, making communication of a termination event visually potent.

In "Symbolic Associations: Assessing the Co-occurrence of Ash and Turquoise in the Ancient U.S. Southwest," Samantha Fladd, Saul Hedquist, E. Charles Adams, and Stewart Koyiyumptewa argue that ash provides a ritually meaningful medium through which to alter or close spaces. In the U.S. Southwest, the patterned deposition of ash in archaeological contexts has been linked to practices of purification and the preservation or suppression of social memory. Turquoise also carries important symbolic meanings in the region, with notable links to moisture, sky, and personal and familial vitality. In archaeological contexts of the Pueblo Southwest, turquoise is often associated with ash or related features like hearths, suggesting an intentional link. This material linkage may represent a broader North American pattern.

In "Fire, Ash and Sanctuary: Pyrotechnology as Protection in the Precolonial Northern Rio Grande," Michael Adler contextualizes the use of fire and ash as part of a larger suite of practices used to protect past, present, and future occupants of villages from malevolent "others" across the pre- and postcolonial northern Rio Grande region of New Mexico. Like Adams, Adler sees the use of fire and ash as a crucial aspect of the transition of domestic and ritual structures from the living to the afterlife.

In "Burned Roofs and Cultural Traditions: Renewing and Closing Houses in the Ancient Villages of the Middle Fraser Canyon, British Columbia," Anna Marie Prentiss, Ashley Hampton, Alysha Edwards, Ethan Ryan, Kathryn Bobolinski, and Emma Vance draw on multiple data sets to develop conclusions on the history of (re)roofing Housepit 54 at the Bridge River site in British Columbia. They suggest the large-scale burned roof deposits typically found at housepit villages in the mid-Fraser region are representative of rituals designed to close and renew the life of a house, which is considered a living entity.

In "Agentive Ash and Dispersed Power in the Cahokia Mississippian World," Melissa Baltus and Sarah Baires draw on indigenous knowledge and tradition to show that fire was a transformative agent in the midcontinental prehistoric city of Cahokia. The power of fire and the communicative abilities of smoke are used in reconstructing the meaning of burning events in various archaeological contexts at Cahokia. The authors argue that ash was an active transformative agent, specifically focusing on the "gathered" or "assembled" nature of ash in conjunction with other burned materials and spaces.

In "Townhouses, Hearths, Fire, Smoke, Ash, and Cherokee Towns in Western North Carolina," Christopher B. Rodning also examines the remnants of fire and smoke—including ash—which were substances handled with care and carefully emplaced at particular points within the built environment of Cherokee towns in the southern Appalachians. Rodning considers evidence from both oral tradition and archaeological sites in addressing the agency of fire, smoke, and ash.

Finally, in "Ash as an Agent of Transformation in Iroquoian Society," William Fox examines ethnographic and historically documented Iroquoian domestic and ritual activities involving ash. These groups associate ash with curing rituals, protection, and a means to connect the mundane to the sacred. He uses data from Ontario Iroquoian longhouse features to compare archaeological and ethnographic evidence from New York State and the Southeast.

Part II contains four chapters that examine the ritual use of ash more broadly, using examples from the Plains, Great Basin, U.S. Southwest, and Mesoamerica. In "Ashes to Ashes, Dust to Dust in Caddoan Mortuary Ritual," Marvin Kay considers Caddoan mortuary rituals where sediments of varied textures and colors, including ash, were used in sometimes complex ways. Ash was retained from deliberately burnt charnel houses and then layered with dense black clay or a black charcoal layer from a burnt thatch-and-cane roof in mound construction. Kay argues that smoke emanating from a fire and its ash signified the passage of souls to the upper world and of life resurrected from death, whereas the black underlayer was a metaphor of death.

In "Ashes for Fertility," Cheryl Claassen examines evidence from caves and rock shelters in the Southeast and the Great Basin, paying particular attention to the contexts of ash deposits found in them. She argues that because women's work groups used the caves, the inevitable objects resulting from menstruation and giving birth, which ethnographic groups associate with "blood and filth," had to be burned, and the association of white ash with purification, renewal, and transformation made it appropriate for covering these deposits, leading to the abundance of ash in these shelters.

In "Ashes, Arrows, and Sorcerers," William Walker and Judy Berryman argue that strata of ash and projectile points deposited on floors and in the fill of abandoned houses in pueblos in southern New Mexico may derive from protective magic in response to malevolent power. In the ethnographic record of the American Southwest, ash and projectile points offer protection against death and sickness caused by witchcraft and sorcery. The authors argue that perhaps the use of ash and arrow points in the ritual closure of pueblo rooms served prophylactic functions to protect these places and their former occupants from harm.

In "Divine Food and Fiery Covenants: The Significance of Ash in Ancient Maya Religion," James L. Fitzsimmons provides an overview of the use of ash in ancient Mesoamerica, particularly within the context of mortuary behavior. He notes that peoples of ancient Mesoamerica frequently engaged in fiery ceremonies, viewing fires as sources of heat and life, light and power. As a result, they used fire not only to purify but also to vivify places, including shrines and burials. They also opened, purified, and closed these spaces, leaving behind burned layers and deposits of ash. The ash deposits provided proof to subsequent visitors of prior religious practices and strengthened their connection to gods and ancestors.

Conclusions

This book explores the properties, uses, meanings, and cross-cultural patterns in the deposition and manipulation of ash as it relates to ritual closure, social memory, and cultural transformation. The chapters in this book document these practices in areas covering all of North America, paralleling the manipulation of ash in association with burning/fire in the Old World (Mentzer et al. 2017; Tringham 2005; Twiss et al. 2008). Thus, using ash in ritual practices and viewing it as an active agent in transformative behavior regarding humans, structures, features, and objects is a practice going back thousands of years, and includes hunting and gathering as well as farming communities and simply to complexly organized societies. This book is intended to highlight practices involving ash and to encourage archaeologists to be more aware of the active role ash deposition played in creating the archaeological record.

Acknowledgments

First and foremost we would like to thank the authors for their persistence and promptness in pulling together their chapters and making revisions based on reviewers' comments under tight timelines. We are also deeply indebted to the three anonymous reviewers who provided not only detailed suggestions for improving each chapter but also strong support and encouragement for the uniqueness and value of the subject matter.

E. Charles Adams is emeritus curator of archaeology, Arizona State Museum, University of Arizona. Prior to retiring in 2020, Adams taught in the School of Anthropology in addition to being museum curator for thirty-five years. Adams directed a thirty-year research program in the ancestral Hopi villages of Homol'ovi in northeastern Arizona and has solely authored or edited more than a dozen books/monographs describing this research. Adams directed the Walpi Archaeological Project for the Museum of Northern Arizona after receiving his PhD from the University of Colorado, Boulder, in 1975. Work at Walpi involved a transformative collaborative experience with the Hopi First Mesa community and launched his lifelong engagement with Hopi tribal members and the Cultural Preservation Office.

Barbara Roth is a professor in the Department of Anthropology at the University of Nevada, Las Vegas. She received her PhD from the University of Arizona. Her recent research has focused on changes in household and community organization that occur as groups become more sedentary and dependent on agriculture and move from pithouses to pueblos in the Mimbres Mogollon region of southwestern New Mexico. She is the recent author of *Agricultural Beginnings in the American Southwest* (Rowman and Littlefield) and editor (with Patricia Gilman and Roger Anyon) of *New Perspectives on Mimbres Archaeology: Three Millennia of Human Occupation in the North American Southwest* (University of Arizona Press).

References

Adams, E. Charles, and Samantha G. Fladd. 2017. "Composition and Interpretation of Stratified Deposits in Ancestral Hopi Villages at Homol'ovi." *Journal of Archaeological and Anthropological Science* 9: 1101–14.

Alberti, Benjamin, and Tamara L. Bray. 2009. "Introduction to Animating Archaeology: Of Subjects, Objects and Alternative Ontologies." *Cambridge Archaeological Journal* 19: 337–43.

Fewkes, Jesse Walter. 1900. "New Fire Ceremony at Walpi." *American Anthropologist* 2: 79–138.

Giddens, Anthony. 1984. *The Constitution of Society*. Berkeley: University of California Press.

Grove, David C., and Susan D. Gillespie. 2002. "Middle Formative Domestic Ritual at Chalcatzingo, Morelos." In *Domestic Ritual in Ancient Mesoamerica*, edited by Patricia Plunket, 11–19. Cotsen Institute of Archaeology Monograph 46. Los Angeles: University of California.

Icove, David J., J. R. Lally, A. J. Vonarx, and E. Charles Adams. 2016. "Modeling Prehistoric Structural Fires at Chevelon Pueblo." In *Chevelon: Pueblo at Blue Running Water*, edited by E. Charles Adams, 105–16. Arizona State Museum Archaeological Series 211. Tucson: University of Arizona.

Lally, J. R. 2005. "Reconstructing the Cause and Origin of Structural Fires in the Archaeological Record of the Greater Southwest." PhD diss., Albuquerque: University of New Mexico.

Lally, J. R., and A. J. Vonarx. 2011. "Fire: Accidental or Intentional? An Archaeological Toolkit for Evaluating Accident and Intent in Ancient Structural Fires." In *Contemporary Archaeologies of the Southwest*, edited by William H. Walker and Kathryn R. Venzor, 157–71. Boulder: University Press of Colorado.

Manzanilla, Linda. 2002. "Living with the Ancestors and Offering to the Gods: Domestic Ritual at Teotihuacan." In *Domestic Ritual in Ancient Mesoamerica*, edited by Patricia Plunket, 43–52. Cotsen Institute of Archaeology Monograph 46. Los Angeles: University of California.

McAnany, P. A., and Ian Hodder. 2009. "Thinking about Stratigraphic Sequence in Social Terms." *Archaeological Dialogues* 16: 1–22.

Mentzer, Susan M., David Gilman Romano, and Mary E. Voyatzis. 2017. "Micromorphological Contributions to the Study of Ritual Behavior at the Ash Altar to Zeus on Mt. Lykaion, Greece." *Journal of Archaeological and Anthropological Science* 9: 1017–43.

Miljour, Heather. 2016. "Homol'ovi I Pueblo: An Examination of Plant Remains within Ash Closure, Renewal, and Dedication Deposits." M.A. thesis, University of Arizona, Tucson.

Mills, Barbara J. 2008. "Remembering While Forgetting: Depositional Practices and Social Memory at Chaco." In *Memory Work: Archaeologies of Material Practices*, edited by Barbara J. Mills and William H. Walker, 81–108. Santa Fe, NM: School for Advanced Research Press.

Moore, Henrietta L. 1982. "The Interpretation of Spatial Patterning in Settlement Residues." In *Symbolic and Structural Archaeology*, edited Ian Hodder, 74–79. New York: University of Cambridge Press.

Ortmann, Anthony L., and Tristram R. Kidder. 2013. "Building Mound A at Poverty Point, Louisiana: Monumental Public Architecture, Ritual Practice, and Implications for Hunter-Gatherer Complexity." *Geoarchaeology* 28(1): 66–86.

Parsons, Elsie Clews. 1939. *Pueblo Indian Religion*. 2 vols. Chicago: University of Chicago Press.

Pauketat, Timothy. 2013. *The Archaeology of the Cosmos: Rethinking Agency and Religion in Ancient America*. New York: Routledge.

Plunket, Patricia. 2002. "Introduction." In *Domestic Ritual in Ancient Mesoamerica*, edited by Patricia Plunket, 1–9. Cotsen Institute of Archaeology Monograph 46. Los Angeles: University of California.

Pollard, Joshua. 1995. "Inscribing Space: Formal Deposition at the Later Neolithic Monument of Woodhenge, Wiltshire." *Proceedings of the Prehistoric Society* 61: 137–56.

Schiffer, Michael B. 1976. *Behavioral Archaeology*. New York: Academic Press.

———. 1987. *Formation Processes of the Archaeological Record*. Salt Lake City: University of Utah Press.

Twiss, Kathryn C., Amy Bogaard, Doru Bogden, Tristan Carter, Michael P. Charles, Shahina Farid, Nerissa Russell, Mirjana Stevanović, E. Nurcan Yalman, and Lisa Yeomans. 2008. "Arson or Accident: The Burning of a Neolithic House at Çatalhöyük, Turkey." *Journal of Field Archaeology* 33: 41–57.

Titiev, Mischa. 1944. *Old Oraibi: A Study of the Hopi Indians of Third Mesa*. Papers of the Peabody Museum of American Archaeology and Ethnology 22. Cambridge, MA: Harvard University.

Tringham, Ruth. 2005. "Weaving House Life and Death into Places: A Blueprint for a Hypermedia Narrative." In *(Un)settling the Neolithic*, edited by Douglass Bailey, Alasdair Whittle, and Vicki Cummings, 98–111. Oxford: Oxbow Books.

Walker, William H. 1995. "Ritual Prehistory: A Pueblo Case Study." PhD diss., University of Arizona, Tucson.

Whiteley, Peter. 1998. *Rethinking Hopi Ethnography*. Washington, DC: Smithsonian Institution Press.

Part I
ASH AS A TRANSFORMATIVE AGENT

CHAPTER 1

Ash Matters

The Ritual Closing of Domestic Structures in the Mimbres Mogollon Region

Barbara J. Roth

The chapters in this volume examine the important role that ash played within prehistoric societies in North America. Many of these studies highlight the use of ash in ritual contexts where its role was for renewal and rebirth, which was an important way to symbolize these processes. Ash was not just used in ritual contexts, however. In looking at different ways that ash was used ethnographically and prehistorically across the U.S Southwest, it is clear that ash also played an important role in retiring and dedicating domestic structures.

In this chapter I examine the role that ash played in the ritual closure of domestic pithouse and pueblo rooms during the Late Pithouse (AD 550–1000) and Classic Mimbres periods (AD 1000–1130) in the Mimbres region of southwestern New Mexico. This time span encompassed significant social and ideological changes, and yet the continuity in the use of ash described here implies some continuity in domestic ritual practices over time.

Burning and ash were significant components in the ritual retirement of great kivas toward the end of the Late Pithouse period in the Mimbres region. The largest great kivas, found at the largest villages, were ritually retired in very elaborate ways. Extreme burning of Late Pithouse period great kivas has been well-documented by Creel and Anyon (2003; Creel et al. 2015). They argue that the ritual retirement was initially planned from the time of construction. They see the kiva retirements as tied to broader social changes associated with a growing focus on irrigation in the valley and waning ties with Hohokam groups to the west.

The role of ash in kiva retirement is further illustrated by recent work at the Harris site, a Late Pithouse period village located in the central portion of the Mimbres Valley where evidence of the ritual retirement of a Three Circle phase (AD 750–1000) great kiva dating to the AD 800s documents the use of ash and targeted burning (Roth 2015). The structure (Pithouse 55) contained a large adobe-lined hearth filled with clean ash containing an arrow point and a shell bracelet fragment, which was then capped with fifteen centimeters of adobe and several large pieces of ochre (see Ryan, chapter 3, and Adler, chapter 5, for discussions of similar kiva hearth closures in the northern Southwest). The front portion of the kiva was then burned, with the roof falling directly onto the floor near the entryway. Sixteen projectile points were recovered from the burned roof fall, with several recovered from a lens of sand between the roof fall and floor near the entryway. The points have been interpreted as intentionally placed there either as part of the retirement of the structure or as dedicatory objects embedded in the roof when the structure was built. As detailed by Walker and Berryman (chapter 12), projectile points served ethnographically as symbols of power and protection, and their co-occurrence with ash deposits in pueblo kivas in the Jornada region to the east of the Mimbres Valley suggests a shared tradition that may be region-wide versus valley-wide, as discussed in this chapter.

Similarly, a pit filled with smashed ceramic vessels was found in the plaza outside the entryway of this great kiva. The use of this pit has been tied to a feasting event associated with the ritual retirement of the kiva (Roth 2015). A layer of ash was placed on top of the pile of smashed vessels, and two palette fragments were found in the ash layer. The ash is interpreted as representing the final closure of the kiva. Neither of these circumstances is surprising given the ethnographic association of ash with cleansing and renewal; this particular great kiva was replaced by a much larger great kiva after it was retired, and the larger great kiva was retired by burning in the late AD 900s (Creel et al. 2015). Other examples of the use of ash in ritual contexts are known from throughout the Mimbres region and, as documented by Ryan (chapter 3 and Fladd, Hedquist, Adams, and Koyiyumptewa (chapter 4), are similar to the use of ash in closing kivas across the Southwest.

The use of ash as part of domestic rituals has not been studied to the same degree that the use of ash in ritual structures like kivas has been (but see Adams and Fladd 2017). As will be illustrated in this chapter, ash was a component of domestic rituals in the Mimbres region, especially in "closing" houses after they were abandoned. Three examples from across the Mimbres Valley are presented here that highlight the use of ash for domestic closure. The significance of this practice in terms of concepts of cleansing and renewal and its association with other aspects of social behavior are also discussed.

Example 1: Ritually Closing Houses before Building Houses above Them

Several cases of closing a pithouse or pueblo room prior to building another structure above it within the same architectural footprint exist in the Mimbres region. Here I highlight three examples of the use of ash in closing houses using data from my excavations at both pithouse and pueblo sites in the region.

Lake Roberts Vista

The Lake Roberts Vista site (LRV) is located on a knoll above Sapillo Creek, a tributary of the Gila River (figure 1.1). The site contains both pithouse and pueblo components, although the pueblo component has been badly looted, so only limited data are available on it. The site contains a moderate-sized (twenty to twenty-five) pithouse occupation that extends from the knoll top and surrounding terraces above Sapillo Creek. A pueblo component, estimated to be eighteen to twenty rooms, is present on top of the pithouse component on the knoll but does not extend to the slopes below. During both periods, the site had kivas that were apparently used for local community ceremonies.

Portions of six pithouses (one of which was converted into a Classic period kiva) and five pueblo rooms were excavated at the site in the early 1990s, and a large Three Circle great kiva on the west side of the site was tested (Roth 2007; Roth, Romero, and Stokes n.d.). Data from these excavations indicate that the site was occupied from the Georgetown phase (AD 550–650) of the Late Pithouse period through the Classic Mimbres period. Groups appear to have been seasonally mobile during the Georgetown and San Francisco (AD 650–750) phases, with a relatively rapid shift to sedentism observed during the Three Circle phase. Subsistence data and terrace features found in drainages near the site indicate that agriculture was practiced, but it was supplemented with wild resources, including piñon and game. Given the increase in sedentism documented during the Three Circle phase in both architecture and artifact data (Roth 2007) and the fact that many surface depressions mapped at the site likely represent Three Circle phase pithouses suggesting that population increased, it can be reasonably inferred that agricultural production increased through time and increased in importance during the Classic period. The size and depth of the Three Circle phase great kiva is larger than would be expected for a pithouse site the size of LRV, so Stokes and Roth (1999; Roth 2007) have suggested that the kiva was placed on the knoll top to serve a larger community surrounding the LRV site.

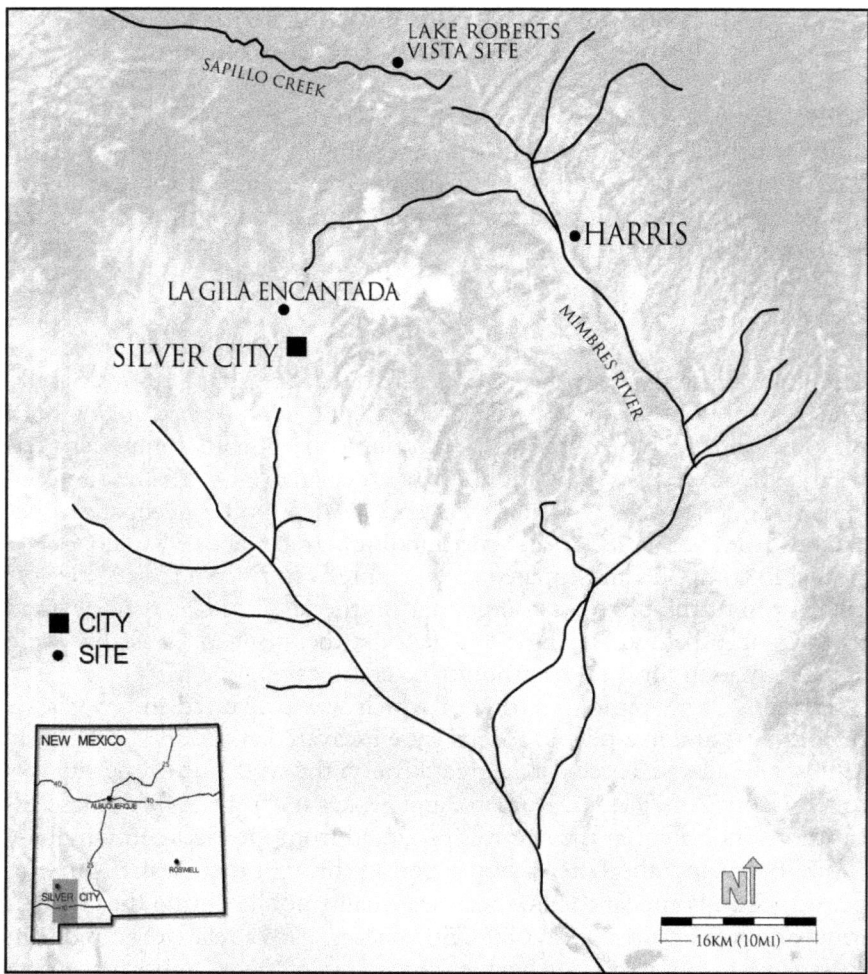

Figure 1.1. *Lake Roberts Vista, Harris, and Elk Ridge site locations. Created by Russell Watters.*

Pithouse 4 contained evidence of three separate occupation surfaces built within the same architectural footprint. The lower floor, which dated to the mid–AD 600s, was cleaned out before abandonment, and it had an ash-filled hearth (a topic to be returned to below). The second surface was directly above the roof fall of the lower floor and was initially interpreted as a "floor" representing a layer of ash with a bear mandible on it (Roth 2007). Another plastered habitation floor was built above this ash layer. Based on the nature of the ash layer, it is now apparent that it was not a floor but instead represented the ritual closure of the lower house prior to building the upper house. Bears are symbols of power in puebloan society, and although bear claws are more commonly represented than other parts of the animal, the purposeful placement of a bear mandible on top of the ash layer indicates that it was part of the closure of the lower floor.

Harris Site

A second case of domestic closure is documented at the Harris site, a large pithouse village located in the central portion of the Mimbres River Valley (figure 1.1). A total of fifty-four pithouses have been excavated at the site, along with a series of sequentially used great kivas (Haury 1936; Roth 2015). Roth (2019a) has discussed community development at the Harris site through the Late Pithouse period. The site was occupied beginning in the Georgetown phase (although an earlier Archaic period occupation may have been present) and continued through the late Three Circle phase. The initial Georgetown phase occupation was small relative to later periods, but the construction of a communal structure indicates that sedentism and perhaps population size was increasing. By the San Francisco phase, evidence for the presence of extended family groups represented by clusters of pithouses with shared traits is present (Roth 2015). Roth and Baustian (2015) see this development as tied directly to land tenure, and argue that these pithouse clusters represent landholding households. Evidence for both extended family groups (pithouse clusters with shared traits) and autonomous households is found during the Three Circle phase. Roth (2019a) argues that two of the extended family pithouse clusters found on opposite sides of the large central plaza were sponsoring rituals based on artifacts found within them. Unlike many other sites in the Mimbres River Valley, no pueblo was built on top of the pithouse village at the Harris site; it appears that groups dispersed from the site in the late AD 900s after the ritual retirement of the largest great kiva, and only a small population of autonomous households remained.

The example of domestic ritual closure at the Harris site involved extensive burning as well as the use of ash, but was similar to the Lake Roberts case in that the house floors were built within the same architectural footprint. At Harris, the lower house (Pithouse 54) was intentionally burned prior to the construction of the second floor (Pithouse 49). One unexcavated burial was found in the floor of Pithouse 54, and it is possible that the house was burned when this individual died. The intentional burning, like the ash deposit at the Lake Roberts site, appears to be related to ritually cleansing the house prior to the construction of Pithouse 49 (see also Adler, chapter 5). This structure has been interpreted as the residence of an important household in the village (Roth 2015), representing an extended family cluster located on the east edge of the large central plaza that the great kivas opened on to (figure 1.2). Pitting on jars found

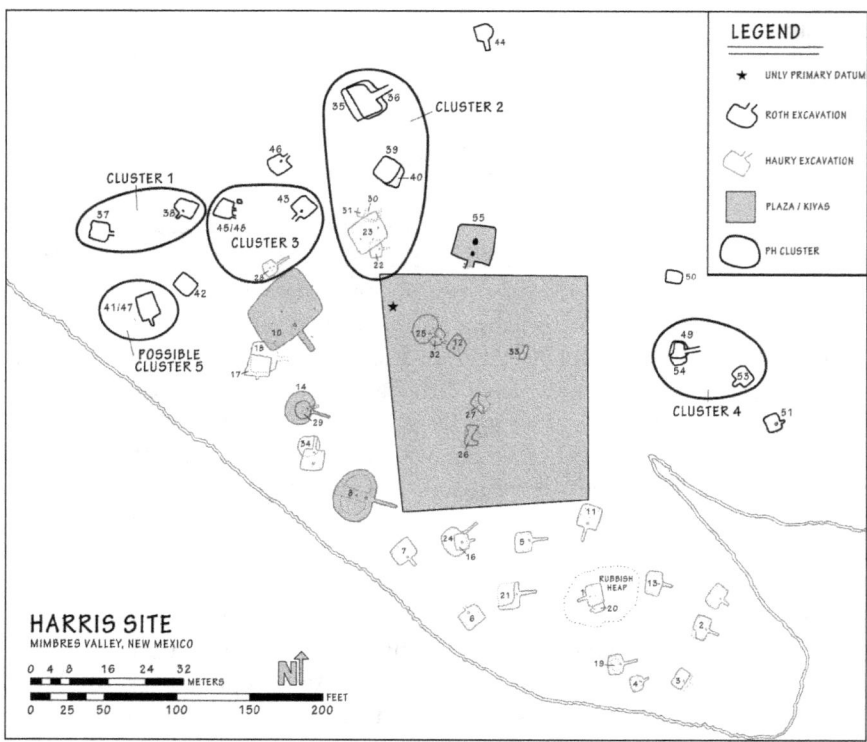

Figure 1.2. *Harris site map. Created by Russell Watters.*

within Pithouse 54 is similar to that found at NAN Ranch and in the Jornada Mogollon region to the west that is consistent with fermentation (Shafer 2003; Miller and Graves 2012). This and the recovery of a palette from another house in the cluster (Pithouse 53) have led Roth (2015) to posit that this household was sponsoring rituals in the associated Three Circle phase great kiva (Pithouse 55). This inference is drawn largely from the fact that smashed serving vessels, which are thought to have held corn beer, and two palette fragments were found in a pit outside the entrance to the kiva that was associated with a feasting event tied to the ritual retirement of that kiva. As noted above, the palettes were found in a layer of ash. Thus, burning and ash appear to have been used in multifaceted ways at Harris to signify closure and renewal, and the burning of Pithouse 54 was likely to have been part of these ritual activities.

Elk Ridge

A third case of closure is illustrated by another set of superimposed house floors within a pueblo room at the Elk Ridge site, a Classic period pueblo located in the northern portion of the Mimbres Valley (figure 1.1). The Elk Ridge site is the largest Classic Mimbres pueblo in this portion of the valley, with an estimated two hundred pueblo rooms, an underlying pithouse component, and several kivas, including a large unexcavated Late Pithouse period great kiva located in the southern portion of the site. The site sits on both U.S. Forest Service and private land, with a fence line dividing the two. The southern portion of the site, now owned by the Archaeological Conservancy, has been heavily looted, but the portion on Forest Service land is intact due in large part to the fact that it has been buried by alluvium.

Excavations conducted by the author along an arroyo cutting into the western part of the pueblo on Forest Service land has resulted in the excavation of fifteen pueblo rooms (including rooms with multiple floors), a late Three Circle phase pithouse, two extramural areas, a burned ramada, a turkey pen, a midden, six turkey burials, and forty human burials (Roth and Creel 2016, 2017; Roth 2018). The occupation of the pueblo spans the Late Pithouse through the Late Classic periods (late AD 900s to early 1000s). In addition to the Late Pithouse component, two pueblo components have been identified: an adobe pueblo component that apparently dates to the early Classic period and a cobble-adobe pueblo component typical of Classic period occupations across the valley that overlies the adobe pueblo component.

The example of the use of ash in ritually closing a lower house at Elk Ridge involves a structure with three separate floors representing temporally distinct occupations, starting with an early Classic adobe pueblo component (Room 112) and culminating in a cobble-adobe component (Room 105). Interconnected rooms (via doorways) associated with this particular room indicate that it was part of an extended family household. Multiple burials were found in the room floors, and this apparently represents a long-standing household at Elk Ridge. A layer of ash was found between the bottom adobe pueblo component (Room 112) and the second floor (Room 113). The ash layer is inferred to represent the ritual closure of the lowest structure prior to the construction of the second floor, as no evidence of structure burning was found. The previous roof fall was first removed, and then the layer of ash was apparently intentionally placed above the floor of Room 112 before Room 113 was built. A cache of four miniature vessels was found north of this ash layer. Fladd and Barker (2019) have recently documented the use of miniature vessels in the closure of ritual spaces at Homol'ovi in northern Arizona. Interestingly, no layer of ash was found between the second and third floors, but the lack of deposition between them indicates that the upper floor (Room 105) may represent more of a remodeling event that perhaps did not require the same form of ritual renewal.

Other examples of this practice have been documented in the Mimbres Valley, although past excavation strategies in the early 1900s, which often involved removing all fill to the floor, precluded identifying these kinds of depositional events. Despite the difficulties with the data base, it does not appear that all households were closed with ash. Thus, although the closure of domestic houses was apparently a common practice in the Mimbres region, the practice appears to have been limited to specific households. The data from Harris and Elk Ridge suggest that it may have been practiced by initial landholding households who played an important role in their respective villages. The fact that the use of ash to ritually close houses occurred from the Late Pithouse through the Classic period indicates a shared view of closure through time.

Example 2: Closing the House after Abandonment

The second example of the use of ash in domestic ritual closure is a more widespread phenomenon that occurred throughout the Mimbres region both spatially and temporally and involved the practice of leaving an ash-filled hearth when the house was abandoned (figure 1.3). In my experience, finding a purposefully abandoned structure without an ash-filled hearth is the exception. This practice appears as early as the Early Pithouse period (circa AD 200) and extends through the end of the Classic period. At the Harris site, a total of fifty-four houses have been excavated (thirty-four by Emil Haury in the 1930s and twenty by archaeologists from UNLV in the 2000s). Of those excavated by UNLV with hearths (n=18), the overwhelming majority (n=16; 89 percent) had ash-filled hearths. Interestingly, the two houses without ash-filled hearths were not part of extended family households.

This is not a phenomenon associated with just large pithouse sites. At La Gila Encantada, a relatively small Late Pithouse period site located along Walnut Creek outside Silver City, all but one of six excavated pithouses with hearths had ash-filled hearths; the exception was an early Georgetown phase structure that had an ephemeral hearth represented by an ash lens (Roth 2010; 2019b). The ritual retirement of both Three Circle phase great kivas at the Harris site also involved leaving an ash-filled hearth; although the circumstances differed, this indicates the practice of leaving ash-filled hearths in closing both ritual and domestic structures.

This practice also carries on into the pueblo period. At Elk Ridge, all but one of the excavated intact habitation room hearths dating from the Late Pithouse through the late Classic period were ash-filled. In contrast, none of the extramural hearths were ash-filled. Perusal of site reports from other excavated pueblos points to similar practices across the region, al-

Ash Matters

Figure 1.3. *Ash-filled hearth prior to excavation, Harris site Pithouse 48. Photo by Barbara J. Roth.*

though data are not available on the percentage of hearths that were ash-filled. As Ryan (chapter 3) notes, this practice extends to other portions of the Southwest as well.

Data from the Harris site sheds some light on the possible reason for closing houses. One excavated house provides data indicating that houses were embodied with meaning, possibly related to an animistic worldview, which is why it was so important to properly close the house upon abandonment. Pithouse 43, a San Francisco phase house that was part of an initial extended family pithouse cluster, was cleaned out before it was abandoned, leaving few in situ floor artifacts. The hearth (oval, adobe-lined, with a hearthstone) was filled with ash. This house had an Alma punched jar plastered into the floor behind the hearth. When the house was abandoned, the vessel was "killed" with a single kill hole and then a rock was placed over its opening. This was apparently part of the closing of the house, with the inferred intent to make sure that the house was properly retired. The widespread recovery of ash in the hearths of houses that were cleaned out and abandoned throughout the Pithouse and Classic Mimbres periods suggests that this view of proper closing stretched across time and remained an important cultural tradition throughout the region.

Example 3: Ash in Burials

The final example comes from the use of ash in burials associated with domestic structures. Several examples from my work at the Harris site are presented here. The Mimbres literature suggests that this practice was widespread in the valley but because of differences in recording methods, it is not possible to quantify the number or circumstances of ash in burials.

The shift to subfloor burial practices did not occur in the Mimbres region until the latter portion of the Late Pithouse period. At the Harris site, ash was found in burials in both extramural and in-floor contexts, but the practice was confined to specific individuals who were apparently important in the village. One example comes from San Francisco phase burials located in the central courtyard area of a pithouse cluster (Cluster 3) that has been interpreted as one of the initial extended family households at the site (Roth and Baustian 2015). Three burials were found in this area, including one adult male who was buried with what appears to have been a sash with shell beads, three *Glycymeris* shell bracelets stacked near his pelvis, a dart point, a pecking stone, and ash. A second male was buried with a *Glycymeris* shell bracelet on his left arm, a white chert arrow point, a piece of turquoise tesserae, and four pots, including two redware bowls filled with a mixture of ash and soil. A nearby burial of an older adult female also had four pots, two of which were filled with ash and soil. These burial data indicate that this extended family, which has been interpreted as one of the original landholding extended family households at the Harris site (Roth and Baustian 2015), was an important family in the village. The role of ash in signifying this is suggestive rather than definitive, but the context of the ash indicates that it played a different role than merely ritual cleansing.

The second case from the Harris site is one that Roth and Baustian (2015) have argued represents an important indication of social memory tied to land tenure and may be a practice that represents an outgrowth from the earlier San Francisco phase practice. This example comes from a Three Circle phase pithouse dating to the AD 800s with two superimposed floors and abundant trash fill. The burial of an older adult female was placed in the trash fill, with the burial pit excavated through the upper floor of the house so she was seated on the lower floor. This is thought to represent multigenerational household ties. A layer of ash approximately fifteen centimeters thick was placed on top of the burial pit, and the ash contained two palettes and several other artifacts that have been linked to dedicatory and retirement behaviors. The use of ash is again tied to ritual closure, but in this case it is tied to the closure of the physical house and the household. The woman was buried with four black-on-white pots, one of which was stylistically identical to a broken bowl recovered from a pit outside the entryway of the Three Circle phase great kiva that was associated with feasting when the kiva was ritually retired. As noted above, the feasting pit was covered with a layer of ash that contained two palette fragments. Thus we see that this particular burial was indicative of links between this woman's household and the broader community and that ash was an important component of the ritual acts involved in closing both her household and the associated great kiva.

Published data from Galaz (Anyon and LeBlanc 1984), NAN Ranch (Shafer 2003), and Swarts Ruin (Cosgrove and Cosgrove 1932; Creel n.d.) indicate that ash was used to cover some burials, but generally only a small percentage of excavated burials have ash (Creel, personal communication, 2017). This may reflect the significance of the individual and/or the individual's household and again reflects similar practices across the valley and over time.

Discussion: Cleansing and Renewal of Domestic Structures

The previous discussion illustrates that ash was used in the Mimbres region in several different ways in the closure of domestic contexts, serving as a complementary component to the use of ash in the ritual closure of great kivas. The earliest use of ash in closure appears to occur by AD 200 in the form of leaving ash-filled hearths when houses were abandoned (Diehl and LeBlanc 2001). This practice continued across the pithouse-to-pueblo transition into the Classic Mimbres pueblo-building period, illustrating a significant and long-term pattern of house closure lasting almost a millennium. Ethnographic data can inform on this to some degree, as Zuni groups would leave ash-filled hearths to ensure that evil spirits were not able to enter the house upon abandonment (see discussion in Walker and Berryman, chapter 12). The fact that the majority of the houses were cleaned out prior to abandonment indicates that groups were moving to another house, in most cases on the same site, and thus the closing of the house was likely to ensure that the house was protected in perpetuity. The killed ceramic vessel in the floor of Pithouse 43 at the Harris site indicates that the spirit of the house was essentially retired as the house was abandoned, and leaving clean ash in the hearth was apparently an important component of this closure practice.

A later component of what is probably an associated ritual practice began during the Late Pithouse period and involved using ash as a closing deposit between superimposed houses, with ash placed before the upper floor was built. This does not appear to have been as widespread a practice as the earlier one of leaving an ash-filled hearth, and it may have been confined to specific households, perhaps those with ties to ritual and/or communally integrative activities. In the cases described here, the superimposed houses that were closed with ash were important households in their respective villages. At the Harris site, the superimposed houses with ash were those that Roth and Baustian (2015) refer to as "anchor" households. They suggest that these were residences of heads of the major landholding extended family households in the village. At Elk Ridge, an ash layer was found in a superimposed house that has been interpreted as associated with one of the core landholding families (as initially described by Shafer 2003). This suggests that while ash-filled hearths represent a common form of closure shared among all Mimbres groups, the use of ash as a closure deposit between occupations was reserved for specific circumstances—and perhaps restricted to specific families. In two of the three cases described here, burials were present in the floors of the houses that were closed with ash (Room 112 at Elk Ridge and Pithouse 54 at Harris); in the third case at the Lake Roberts Vista site, only half of the house was excavated, so it is possible that burials were present in the unexcavated portion of the house. In these cases, it appears that rather than representing ritual closure of the structure, the ash layer between floors instead represents cleansing and renewal, a property associated ethnographically with burning and ash.

The use of ash in burials is more difficult to contextualize, in part because it is not as common as would be expected given that ash was apparently considered such an integral component of closure of domestic and communal ritual spaces. One would expect that ash would be found in most burials, but that is not the case. Of the forty burials excavated at

Harris during UNLV's work there, only four had ash, while only two of the burials excavated at Elk Ridge had it. Thus, it appears that only certain individuals were buried with ash. Unlike some of the other circumstances of the use of ash described in other chapters (cf. Walker and Berryman, chapter 12) however, ash does not appear to have been associated with witchcraft, although its use in burials may have served to both cleanse and protect.

Conclusion

As illustrated in this chapter and others in this volume, ash played an important role in the ritual closure of structures, both domestic and ritual, across North America. The significance of burning, ash, and its likely association with cleansing and renewal made it a significant element that was readily accessible for closure activities. In the Mimbres region, the use of ash for closure took several different forms, ranging from the common practice of closing houses by leaving an ash-filled hearth when the structure was abandoned to less inclusive practices of closing the lower house of superimposed structures and placement of ash in burials, possibly of important people at the site.

One final factor that should be considered in evaluating the significance of the use of ash at the sites described in this chapter and those discussed elsewhere in this volume is that modern excavation strategies are significantly enhancing our ability to address these forms of ritual activities involving ash. Although "ash lenses" might have been recorded in field notes of early excavations, ash was rarely mentioned in more than an aside, if at all. In the Mimbres region, early excavation strategies did not emphasize careful excavation of deposits above floors, where these layers of ash generally occur and could thus easily be missed. Ash matters—and it is now possible to see the different ways that the use of ash played out in different contexts in prehistory.

Acknowledgments

Work at the Harris Site was funded in part by a National Science Foundation grant (#1049434). Thanks are due to the many graduate and undergraduate students and volunteers from the Grant County Archaeological Society who participated in excavations at the Harris site, LRV, and Elk Ridge. My ideas about ash and ritual have benefitted greatly from discussions with Roger Anyon, Darrell Creel, Danielle Romero, and Beau Schriever.

Barbara Roth is a professor in the Department of Anthropology at the University of Nevada, Las Vegas. She received her PhD from the University of Arizona. Her recent research has focused on changes in household and community organization that occur as groups become more sedentary and dependent on agriculture and move from pithouses to pueblos in the Mimbres Mogollon region of southwestern New Mexico. She is the recent author of *Agricultural Beginnings in the American Southwest* (Rowman and Littlefield) and editor (with Patricia Gilman and Roger Anyon) of *New Perspectives on Mimbres Archaeology: Three Millennia of Human Occupation in the North American Southwest* (University of Arizona Press).

References

Adams, E. Charles, and Samantha G. Fladd. 2017. "Composition and Interpretation of Stratified Deposits in Ancestral Hopi Villages at Homol'ovi." *Archaeological and Anthropological Sciences* 9: 1101–14.

Anyon, Roger, and Steven A. LeBlanc. 1984. *The Galaz Ruin: A Prehistoric Mimbres Village in Southwestern New Mexico*. Albuquerque, NM: Maxwell Museum of Anthropology.

Cosgrove, H. S., and C. B. Cosgrove. 1932. *The Swarts Ruin: A Typical Mimbres Site in Southwestern New Mexico*. Papers of the Peabody Museum of American Archaeology and Ethnology 15. Cambridge, MA: Harvard University.

Creel, Darrell, and Roger Anyon. 2003. "New Perspectives on Mimbres Communal Pitstructures and the Implications for Ritual and Cultural Developments." *American Antiquity* 68: 67–92.

Creel, Darrell, Roger Anyon, and Barbara Roth. 2015. "Ritual Construction, Use and Retirement of Mimbres Three Circle Phase Great Kivas." *Kiva* 81: 201–19.

Diehl, Michael W., and Steven A LeBlanc. 2001. *Early Pithouse Villages of the Mimbres Valley and Beyond: The McAnally and Thompson Sites in Their Cultural and Ecological Contexts*. Papers of the Peabody Museum of Archaeology and Ethnology 83. Cambridge, MA: Harvard University.

Fladd, Samantha G., and Claire S. Barker. 2019. "Miniature in Everything but Meaning: A Contextual Analysis of Miniature Vessels at Homol'ovi I." *American Antiquity* 84:107–26.

Haury, Emil W. 1936. *The Mogollon Culture of Southwestern New Mexico*. Medallion Papers 20. Globe, AZ: Gila Pueblo.

Miller, Myles R., and Timothy B. Graves. 2012. "Sacramento Pueblo: An El Paso and Late Glencoe Phase Pueblo in the Southern Sacramento Mountains." Fort Bliss Cultural Resources 10–22. Fort Bliss, TX: Environmental Division.

Roth, Barbara J. 2007. "The Late Pithouse Period Occupation of the Lake Roberts Vista Site." In *Exploring Variability in Mogollon Pithouses*, edited by Barbara J. Roth and Robert Stokes, 5–11. Arizona State University Anthropological Research Papers 58. Tempe: Arizona State University.

———. 2010. "Engendering Mimbres Mogollon Pithouses." In *Engendering Households in the Prehistoric Southwest*, edited by Barbara J. Roth, 136–52. Tucson: University of Arizona Press.

———. 2015. "Archaeological Investigations at the Harris Site (LA 1867), Grant County, New Mexico." Report on file, Department of Anthropology. Las Vegas: University of Nevada.

———. 2018. "2017 Archaeological Investigations at the Elk Ridge Site (LA 79863), Mimbres Valley, Grant County, New Mexico." Report submitted to the U.S. Forest Service, Gila National Forest, Silver City, NM.

———. 2019a. "Pithouse Community Development at the Harris Site, Southwestern New Mexico." In *Communities and Households in the Greater American Southwest*, edited by Robert J. Stokes, 183–200. Boulder: University Press of Colorado.

———. 2019b. "Identifying Social Units and Social Interaction during the Pithouse Period in the Mimbres Region, Southwestern New Mexico." In *Interaction and Connectivity in the Greater Southwest*, edited by Karen G. Harry and Barbara J. Roth, 133–50. Boulder: University Press of Colorado.

Roth, Barbara J., and Kathryn M. Baustian. 2015. "Kin Groups and Social Power at the Harris Site, Southwestern New Mexico." *American Antiquity* 80: 1–22.

Roth, Barbara J., and Darrell Creel. 2016. "Report on 2015 Archaeological Excavations at the Elk Ridge Site (LA 79863), Mimbres Valley, Grant County, New Mexico." Report submitted to the U.S. Forest Service, Gila National Forest, Silver City, NM.

———. 2017. "2016 Archaeological Investigations at the Elk Ridge Site (LA 79863), Mimbres Valley, Grant County, New Mexico." Report submitted to the U.S. Forest Service, Gila National Forest, Silver City, NM.

Roth, Barbara J., Danielle Romero, and Robert Stokes. n.d. The Pithouse and Pueblo Occupations of the Lake Roberts Vista Site. Manuscript in preparation.

Shafer, Harry. 2003. *Mimbres Archaeology at NAN Ranch Ruin*. Albuquerque: University of New Mexico Press.

Stokes, Robert J., and Barbara J. Roth. 1999. "Mobility, Sedentism, and Settlement Patterns in Transition: The Late Pithouse Period in the Sapillo Valley, New Mexico." *Journal of Field Archaeology* 26: 423–34.

CHAPTER 2

Complex Closure Practices Involving Ash at a Small Pueblo in Northeastern Arizona

E. Charles Adams

Introduction

In 1984, Arizona State Museum (ASM), under Richard C. Lange's and my direction, began a long-term research program focused on the area of the middle Little Colorado River valley that the Hopi refer to as Homol'ovi (place of buttes or small hills/mounds), which today is in the vicinity of Winslow, Arizona. From 1984 through 2006, research focused on a group of ancestral Hopi villages that archaeologists call the Homol'ovi Settlement Cluster (HSC) (Adams 2002). This cluster of seven villages was occupied from AD 1260 to 1400. In conjunction with the excavations, Lange (1998) directed a full coverage survey of over 30 square miles that documented more than 500 loci and 222 sites, revealed occupation spanning more than 2,000 years, and recorded several small settlements with distinctive architectural and ceramic traditions indicating that groups from the north and south migrated into the area at various times between AD 600 and 1225. Interestingly, the area appears to have been completely depopulated when the large Homol'ovi villages were founded (Adams 2002).

To further explore the early occupation of the region and its relationship to the large pueblos, Adams and Lange established a University of Arizona School of Anthropology field school 8 kilometers south of Chevelon Pueblo, one of the eastern HSC villages, on the private Rock Art Ranch that lasted from 2011 to 2016. In addition to the full-coverage survey that documented 223 sites and loci on 6.65 square miles, two pueblos were partially excavated: Multi-kiva (MK) site and Brandy's Pueblo. This chapter focuses on Brandy's Pueblo (AZ P:3:114 [ASM]), which lies 500 meters east of Chimney Canyon (an ephemeral drainage that flows into the Little Colorado River) on top of a small knoll with excellent visibility of the surrounding region (figure 2.1).

The pueblo comprises four contiguous rooms constructed of shaped sandstone slabs (figure 2.2). Two hundred fifty meters south of the pueblo, an intact rectangular pit structure with a ramp entry, likely an isolated kiva, was excavated. It had been burned and its walls collapsed as closure practices with no objects left on the floor. By combining the six AMS radiocarbon dates recovered from excavations, occupation of the pueblo and kiva can be placed between AD 1225 and 1254 (University of Arizona, AMS Radiocarbon Laboratory, AA101448 to 101553) (table 2.1). Tree-ring-dated decorated ceramics from the Cibola tradition to the southeast and Little Colorado tradition to the north support the AMS dates. While decorated ceramics were uniformly imported, petrographic analysis of corrugated brown wares, which comprise 66 percent of the ceramic assemblage of eight thousand sherds, indicate up to 30 percent were made locally (Estes n.d.; Ownby 2016).

Four nearby pueblos of equal size lie within one kilometer of Brandy's Pueblo, and ceramics suggest they are contemporary. Similar clusters of contemporary small pueblos with brown corrugated assemblages have

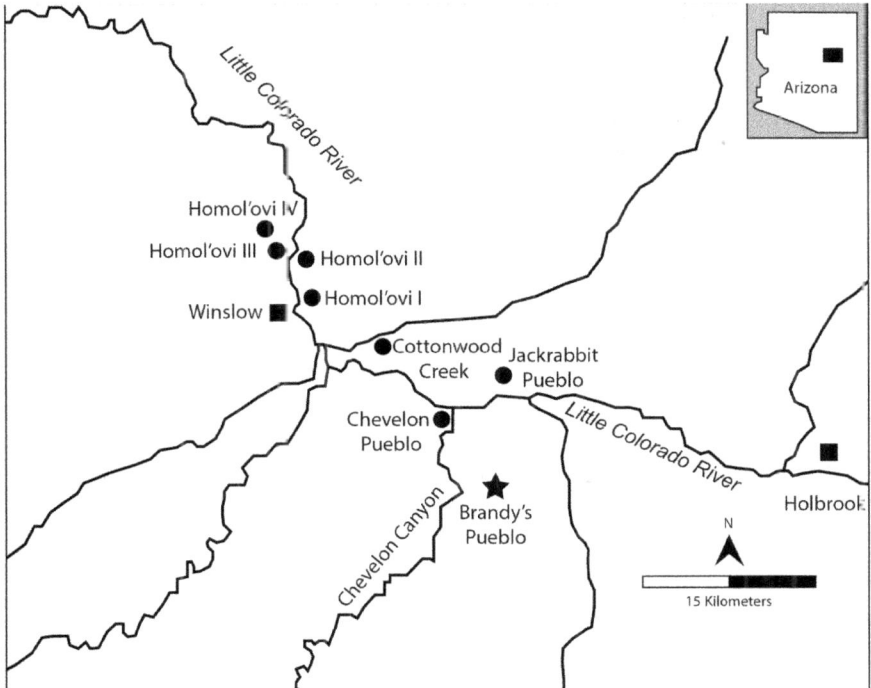

Figure 2.1. *Location of Brandy's Pueblo in the middle Little Colorado River valley. Image courtesy of Samantha G. Fladd.*

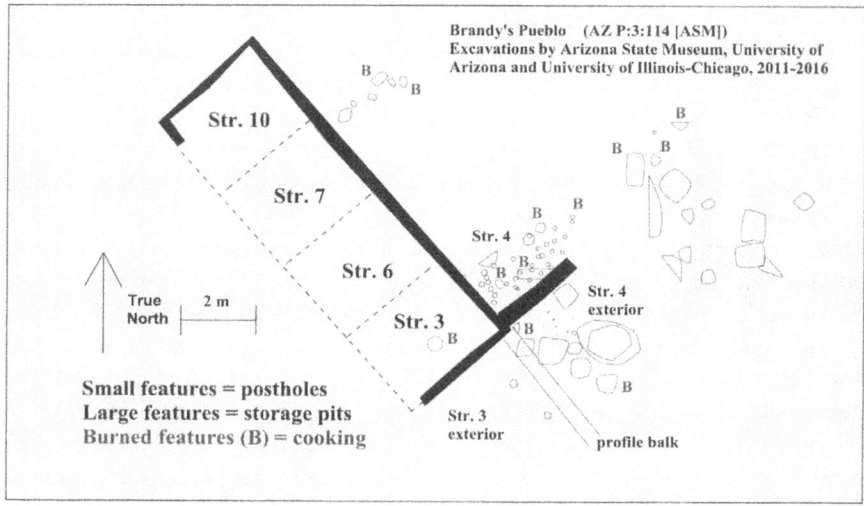

Figure 2.2. *Map of Brandy's Pueblo and exterior workspaces. Image created by Richard C. Lange, Arizona State Museum.*

Table 2.1. *AMS Radiocarbon Dates for Brandy's Pueblo (AZ P:3:114 [ASM])*[1]

AA	Context	Feature	Dated Material	14C age BP	d14C age	Age CE (95.4%)
AA101448	Extramural storage? pit (deep trash-filled pit)	8	Maize cob	801	38	1169–1277
AA101449	Structure 3 circular hearth	1	Maize kernel	806	38	1166–1276
AA101450	Extramural fire pit	11	Maize cob	756	38	1210–1295
AA101451	Extramural fire pit	14	Maize kernel	800	38	1170–1278
AA101452	Extramural fire pit (ephemeral, just below modern ground surface)	3	Maize kernel	693	39	1255–1325 (64.5%) 1345–1394 (30.9%)
AA101453	Structure 2 hearth	1	Wood charcoal-bark	768	39	1186–1290

[1]Calibrated by Vincent M. LaMotta using OxCal 4.2 online (IntCal 09 calibration curve), 20 September 2013.

been documented in the area, suggesting a migration of pueblo groups from twenty to forty kilometers south, where dense clusters of earlier brown ware producing pueblos are known (Solometo 2004). The reasons for this movement are not known, although violence in these earlier southern villages has been argued to be prevalent (Solometo 2001, 2004) Another possibility is that they were attracted by the abundance of water at or slightly below the surface of Chimney and other nearby canyons as well as the Little Colorado River (K. Adams and Smith n.d.) that is not available in the higher southern locales. The dominance of corrugated brown wares in the assemblage at Chevelon Pueblo and its average of a quarter of utility wares in other Homol'ovi pueblos (Cutright-Smith and Barker 2016; Barker 2017) suggest that occupants of the small pueblos or their descendants settled in the large, late villages. In addition to ceramic and architectural connections to Homol'ovi villages, occupants of Brandy's Pueblo used ash as an important element in closure, which is the focus of the remainder of this chapter. Extensive closure practices involving ash from many HSC villages are detailed in Adams (2016) and Adams and Fladd (2017).

Previous Work and Archaeological Details

Although the pueblo was heavily disturbed by backhoeing in the 1980s, enough standing walls remain to determine the total size and number of rooms (figure 2.2). Due to the backhoeing, only one-third of a floor in one room and one-tenth in a second remained undisturbed. A slab-lined hearth with several refittable sherds was on the floor of the first room. Wood from this hearth dated to AD 1221 (1166–1276, calibrated at two sigma; AA101449) (table 3.1). In contrast to the pueblo, the exterior work areas were virtually untouched, and more than 130 features were documented (figure 2.2). All were cut into the caliche layer thirty centimeters below the surface, with the deeper ones cut into the underlying sandstone. These can be classified into two groups. Those within two meters of the pueblo are generally small and shallow, with most being remains of postholes and others shallow fire pits or associated activity pits. Burned corncobs and kernels are ubiquitous in thermal features and provided five of the six radiocarbon dates. Many postholes are in linear arrangements and suggest the exterior to the entire four-room-long east side of the pueblo was covered with a ramada. Outside this area are twenty large storage pits, some over one meter deep and nearly as wide. Their size and location suggest that all were built by prior occupants of the site, most likely during the preceramic Basketmaker II (BMII) occupation of the hill, which includes a pithouse located four meters northeast of the pueblo.

Features and Surfaces

For the purposes of this chapter, I will focus on the features and surfaces associated with the pueblo occupation. As noted, most features are preserved in the underlying caliche; however, the tops of these features originate in at least three definable surfaces, each covered in ash. The earliest surface is the caliche layer, with ash and ash stain of the white caliche concentrated in areas near thermal features. It is probable that the ash covering this surface is a result of natural scatter from the ever-present winds of the region and periodic cleaning. In contrast, the upper two surfaces are covered with ash layers that are not near thermal features and in fact are upwind from them. Therefore, these ash layers are most likely purposely deposited. The lower of the two ash layers is about ten centimeters above the caliche layer. It lies on the middle surface, extends beneath the top surface described below, and lies beneath a massive fifty-centimeter-high wall constructed as an extension of the south wall of the pueblo. The wall clearly demarcates space and separates the area east of the pueblo, which has a high density and variety of features, from an area with two large storage pits and thermal features. The wall would have provided an effective wind barrier to activities under the ramada. Beneath the wall and lying on top of the ash layer is a brown corrugated jar broken into numerous pieces. Similar associations of ceramics and ash occur on the upper surface described below. Thus, the two- to five-centimeter-thick ash layer and brown corrugated jar used to cover the surface prior to construction of the dividing wall appear to be associated with closure of the surface and dedication of the dividing wall (Adams 2016).

The top activity surface is about five centimeters above the second surface. The most intact portion of this surface lies along the full three-and-a-half-meter length of the southeast wall of the pueblo, extending at least four meters southeast, which was the extent of excavations. The distribution of the two- to three-centimeter-thick ash layer covering the top surface appears to avoid outdoor activity areas under the ramada. This surface and associated ash layer is distinctive from the earlier surfaces due to four attributes. First, it covers a much larger area, fully fifteen square meters. Second, it has only three features—two postholes and a shallow pit. Although the features look like postholes, given their isolation, they probably served a different purpose. For example, one "posthole" feature was filled with sherds and capped with a shaped obliterated corrugated brown ware sherd. Also on the top surface, two *Glycymeris* sp. shell beads were recovered from the shallow pit. The placement of objects in both features likely resulted from ritual acts of closure. Third, artifacts—almost all partially reconstructible vessels—are ubiquitous either on the top surface or in the ash covering the surface. Most ceramic artifacts are contemporary with the pueblo's occupation; however, about 20 percent predate or date to the beginning of the pueblo's occupation, suggesting they could be heirloom pieces. A Western Triangular–style projectile point—a style contemporary with the occupation of the pueblo—was also deposited on the top surface. In chapter 12, Walker and Berryman describe the complementary role of arrow points and ash in providing protection from witches. A fragment of a *Glycymeris gigantea* shell bracelet was recovered from the lower ash-covered surface in this area. It is possible the shell in the feature on the top surface was referencing this earlier shell. Contemporary Pueblo people associate shells with water (Hedquist 2017).

Fourth, the pueblo walls were collapsed directly on top of the upper ash-covered surface as well as on top of the last use surface under the ramada. These walls were intact when they collapsed. The two preserved standing walls are the southeast wall, three and a half meters long, and the northeast wall, which is ten and a half meters long. These walls are thirty-five to forty centimeters or four to five courses high. There is no evidence of roofing. When roofs are in place and collapse, they almost always pull standing walls inward. All walls at Brandy's Pueblo collapsed outward. Therefore, the roofs were likely dismantled prior to overturning the walls.

The Walls

The walls to Brandy's Pueblo are substantial. They are constructed of moderately shaped, preselected slabs of Moenkopi sandstone quarried from an exposure five hundred meters west in Chimney Canyon. The compound walls, which average thirty-five centimeters wide, are two courses of stone that interlock to strengthen the wall. Wall fall ranges from two to three meters in extent and consists of twenty-five to thirty rows of stones (figure 2.3). Standing walls at four to five courses and thirty-five to forty centimeters high suggest the walls were at least two meters high when standing. Given their construction, these walls were not likely to totally collapse immediately after the occupants left. The most logical conclusion is they were pushed over, something requiring a coordinated effort, possibly involving tools, given the width and height of the walls. The undeniable conclusion is that the pueblo was purposely destroyed, an event involving complex preparations—including ash and placement of objects—to dedicate the exterior spaces for closure. The practices recorded

Figure 2.3. *Wall fall from intentional collapse of pueblo wall. Photo courtesy of Vincent M. LaMotta.*

at Brandy's Pueblo suggest that the exterior spaces were prioritized over interior spaces, perhaps because they were the focus of activities and the hub of social life at the pueblo.

The Artifacts

More than three hundred sherds were documented in the ash fill or lying directly on the upper occupation surface southeast of the pueblo, representing 4 percent of total analyzed ceramics. More than 45 percent of sherds on the top occupation surface are decorated, almost entirely jars, while the site average is only 24 percent. No painted pottery was produced at the pueblo, nor is production of painted pottery known within a fifty-kilometer radius of Brandy's Pueblo (Douglass 1987). Two-thirds of painted ceramics were exchanged from production areas more than seventy kilometers southeast—part of the Cibola Whiteware tradition (Triadan 1997; Van Keuren 1999; Zedeño 1994). Nearly all the decorated sherds are large with many refitting, although from multiple locations on the surface, suggesting that large decorated storage jars and corrugated cooking vessels were broken and placed across the ash-covered surface as dedication and closure, or placed intact and scattered due to wall collapse. Sacrifice of vessels of such value to the community could be a display of prestige and social power among the pueblo's inhabitants. Its association with destruction of the pueblo itself indicates that the community was actively forgetting life at the pueblo (Adams 2016; Mills 2008; Walker 1995). The inclusion of a Western Triangular arrow point to the assemblage is consistent with this interpretation (see Walker and Berryman, chapter 12).

The Ash

Given the color and makeup of the ash used to cover the top two exterior surfaces, it was likely obtained from nearby thermal features and not by special preparation. Because ash results from complete combustion of its organic source material, micro-charcoal fragments derived from ash deposits must be used to identify the source materials. Because organics combust differently, identified fragments may not accurately reflect the original makeup of organic material. Charcoal fragments recovered from the pueblo's ash are dominated by local bushes and trees growing in and around Chimney Canyon and include cottonwood, sage, cliffrose, juniper, and willow; corn kernels and cobs, which were common in thermal features, were also recovered as fragments from the ash deposit. The use of corncobs in shallow features to close surfaces was also noted in nearby Homol'ovi pueblos dating to the late 1300s (Adams 2016). All plants in the ash at Brandy's Pueblo grow within one kilometer of the pueblo today, and together they may have been intended to commemorate the organic landscape or place of the pueblo (Bowser 2004; Zedeño and Bowser 2009). Contemporary Hopi clean hearths once a year as part of ritual practices associated with renewal of the physical and social community (Parsons 1936, 1939). Ash from these hearths is collected by participants in associated ceremonies and disposed in specified areas short distances from the villages. Ash in general is used by Hopi and other Pueblo groups to purify and close areas to control potential harmful energy (Parsons 1939: 364, 462–64).

Comparisons

Adams (2016) reports similar purposeful breakage of ceramics on the last occupation levels in rooms at Homol'ovi I and relates it to Hopi oral histories of closure practices as part of leaving "footprints" or physical indicators of social memory tying the villages to migration routes. In contrast to Brandy's Pueblo, the vessels at Homol'ovi I were whole bowls with clear impact fractures on their exteriors. These were not noted on the jars at Brandy's Pueblo. It seems unlikely that this was the intent by occupants of Brandy's Pueblo because collapsing the walls over the surface and artifacts would have obscured their presence.

Lange (2015, n.d.) documented similar wall collapse scenarios at the Multi-kiva site (AZ P:3:112[ASM]) about fifteen kilometers south of Brandy's Pueblo dating roughly twenty five to fifty years earlier based on ceramic cross-dating and calibrated radiocarbon dates. Only four of about twenty-five rooms at Multi-kiva Pueblo were excavated; however, wall clearing documented many more walls, and where disturbance was minimal, large exterior wall collapse was present. Because the Multi-kiva site was two stories in places, wall fall exceeded four meters in some cases and invariably rested on surfaces exposed during the village's occupation. In addition, the three intact excavated rooms all had indications of purposeful burning likely related to site closure, a pattern noted at the kiva associated with Brandy's Pueblo and at the Homol'ovi villages (Adams and Fladd 2017). One of the burned rooms at Multi-kiva Pueblo was a ceremonial structure and was unique in having a small floor assemblage, including almost half a Walnut Black-on-white bowl and ash covering its heavily plastered surface. Although the ash was a product of the combustion of the grass and brush components of the roof, its presence directly connects ash to fire in closure of this room. The extreme disturbance of the rooms could have hidden this practice at Brandy's Pueblo, although ash was likely used to symbolize fire and transformation.

Other excavations in the region involving pueblos include mitigation work thirty kilometers south of Brandy's Pueblo along the Cholla Power Plant power line from Joseph City to Phoenix in the late 1970s (Reid 1982). Impacted sites ranged from one hundred years earlier than Brandy's Pueblo to those contemporary with it. Only four involved architecture, and none identified similar closure patterns, although exterior workspaces were not reported. Excavation work from 1971 to 1974 and 1997 to 2001 by UCLA/University of Virginia in upper Chevelon Canyon (Solometo 2004) on numerous pueblos thirty kilometers south and contemporary with or predating Brandy's Pueblo also did not document these closure practices, although structure burning was common. Solometo (2004) associated the burning with warfare, not closure. Limited excavations at Creswell Pueblo (AZ J:14:282 [ASM]) in Homolovi State Park twenty kilometers northwest of Brandy's Pueblo uncovered a nearly identical four-room pueblo with similar masonry walls that ceramics indicate is contemporary (Barker and Young 2017). Unfortunately, testing focused in associated pit structures (likely kivas), and virtually no testing of potential work areas adjacent to the pueblo or within the pueblo rooms was conducted. Wall fall is not visible; however, occupants of nearby Homol'ovi II, a 1,000-room pueblo occupied 150 years later, likely removed most of the wall stone for their own pueblo and used some to build a small farming structure on top of the rubble mound of the pueblo (Adams

2002: 36). One kiva was decommissioned through burning, but additional closing practices at Creswell Pueblo remain to be investigated.

Excavations of several small pueblos associated with great kivas sixty kilometers south of Brandy's Pueblo reveal interesting patterns of burning (Herr et al. 1999). The associated pueblos are comparable in number of structures and construction techniques to Brandy's Pueblo, although occupation was one hundred years earlier. Of the three great kivas excavated, only Hough's Great Kiva (AZ P:16:112 [ASM]) was burned (Herr et al. 1999: 59–60). Only rooms associated with Hough's and Cothrun's Kiva site (AZ P:12:277 [ASM]) were excavated, and nearly every excavated pueblo room was burned. In all instances, burning was associated with site abandonment and structure closure. For the most part, little was left on the floors (Herr et al. 1999). Although remains of fallen walls were common, in no instance was there evidence of intentional collapse comparable to Brandy's Pueblo or the Multi-kiva site.

Only one pueblo in the same area was contemporary. Pottery Hill (AZ P:12:12 [ASM]), seventy kilometers south of Brandy's Pueblo, is much larger at forty-five to fifty rooms. Its rectangular kiva is larger and deeper than that at Brandy's Pueblo. The Pottery Hill kiva was burned, and a thin ash layer was included in its closure (Mills et al. 1999: 135–37). Thus, the practice of burning to close ceremonial and habitation structures was widespread in the region by the early 1100s, with ash introduced to closure practices by the early 1200s. It would be worth exploring whether some of the burning attributed by Solometo (2001, 2004) to conflict in upper Chevelon Creek is in fact also part of room or village closure (see Adler, chapter 5).

Interpretations

In recent years, the interpretation of intentional burning and destruction of ancestral Pueblo communities on the Colorado Plateau, many with human remains on floors of pithouses or kivas, as a product of conflict (LeBlanc 1999; Solometo 2001), has been revisited (Darling 1998; Walker 1999; also see Adler, chapter 5). In part, this is due to the persistence of these patterns for hundreds of years, suggesting they are structural components of important practices of appropriate behaviors when one individual (or more) within a community dies (Cameron 1990; Hedquist and Miller 2013; Wilshusen 1986). Cultural practices worldwide underscore the diversity and intentionality of how to respond to these situations (HRAF 2018). In the Southwest United States alone, numerous historic indigenous groups employ closure practices that include burning or abandonment of houses, placement of objects within these structures, and veneration and revisitation or avoidance of these places as products of social memory, i.e., remembering or forgetting (Cameron 1990; Lightfoot 1994; Mills and Walker 2008; Walker 1995; also refer to Adler, chapter 5; Fladd et al., chapter 4; Roth, chapter 1; Walker and Berryman, chapter 12). For example, Diné (Navajo) avoid homes where an occupant has died. The home, or hogan, is left standing, burned, or torn down, and the remains serve as a visible reminder to all in the community as a place to be avoided. Generally, no new dwellings are constructed within a kilometer of the hogan for decades (Jett and Spencer 1981: 28). For Brandy's Pueblo, there is no evidence of buried or unburied human remains, although their presence within the highly disturbed pueblo rooms cannot be ruled out and extramural burials have been reported by the landowner. There is also evidence, described in more detail below, that in later times among Ancestral Pueblo groups the remains of deceased individuals were not left in the structure, yet the structure could still be considered to be spiritually contaminated, necessitating closure and relocation of the remaining occupants. This may explain the treatment of Brandy's Pueblo.

Thus, Ancestral Pueblo community practices of leaving the deceased in place and destroying the associated structure through fire were replaced with rituals that do not include, for the most part, entombing human remains or the use of fire. These newer practices may have evolved as pueblos grew in size and number of occupants, meaning everyone was not related and moving was costly in resources. For example, in nearby fourteenth-century Homol'ovi villages, only very young humans, possibly those who had yet to go through naming rituals, were interred in already decommissioned rooms associated with extensive depositional practices, including objects and ash (Adams 2016; Fladd 2018).

The widespread practice of burning ceremonial and habitation structures in the region near Brandy's Pueblo suggests that fire was an essential component of structure and community closure (Herr et al. 1999). This is likely derived as a general practice of purification and protection from spiritual contamination, as deceased were interred nearby, not necessarily within the structure itself. Adams and Fladd (2017) and Adams (2016) have documented extensive substitution of ash for actual burning of structures, implying that ash is symbolic and represents the transformation of an object or space from one material state to another in these pueblo communities. Ash was added to complement or replace fire in the area by the early 1200s (Mills et al. 1999). Thus, the use of ash to cover surfaces at Brandy's Pueblo is consistent with practices of using ash to avoid spiritual contamination.

Similar uses of ash as a transformative agent have continued in most Pueblo communities during the twentieth century and to the present. More specifically, in Hopi tradition, fire and ash are used to end one chapter and begin another in the life history of inalienable objects, hearths, buildings, or a community (Whiteley 1998). Burning is transformative from one state to another, with ash symbolizing the altered and used-up state (Parsons 1939). In terms of closure, then, ash represents the transformation of Brandy's Pueblo from the living material state to the liminal state or afterlife, and, for reasons previously discussed, it was focused on exterior spaces.

Items associated with the deposition of ash in the Homol'ovi pueblos are complex and likely represent identity, memory, and objects used in transformational rituals (Adams 2016). Those used at Brandy's Pueblo, with their focus on large storage and cooking jars from the present and recent past, may represent the femaleness of the space/pueblo or the identity of past and present members of the household, and they may also have established social memory for descendants. Their association with ash suggests that it was the transformative agent in this negotiation. The laying of ash on exterior occupation surfaces followed immediately by the intentional collapse of the pueblo walls, resulting in their covering the ash-covered surfaces, may represent a different component of social memory—purposeful forgetting (Kuchler 1999; Meskell 2008; Mills 2008). In this sense, ash is an important element to an elaborate set of practices designed to protect any who later encounter the pueblo. Destruction through wall collapse is evidence of whatever danger lies within.

Therefore, ash is ambivalent—used as an agent of change and transformation by social groups wishing to either commemorate or forget their history. Likely it is the objects associated with ash that provide clues as to its intended purpose. Is pottery associated with the ash being sacrificed or commemorated? Because the pottery is hidden by the collapsed wall at Brandy's Pueblo, its intent or even existence would be known only by the social group who built, occupied, and destroyed the pueblo. If destruction of the pueblo is related to a death in the family occupying it, then objects destroyed by collapsing its walls may belong to this individual. The last act of closure, collapse of the pueblo's walls, may be the most salient clue, as its meaning likely extended well beyond Brandy's Pueblo or even the small group of pueblos of which it is a part. This is suggested by use of the same practices at the Multi-kiva Pueblo fifteen kilometers away—burning/ash as a transformative agent followed by purposeful destruction of the village. Lack of reoccupation of either pueblo, or even the prominent hills on which they are situated, suggests these highly visible acts of destruction signaled to later travelers that reoccupation was dangerous. Therefore, as in Hopi society, burning and ash protect against ritual forces deemed harmful and relate to beliefs in the natural order of decay, morally and materially, requiring protection and purification (Whiteley 1998). The goal in all cases is protection from spiritual contamination.

Acknowledgments

The University of Illinois, Chicago, under the direction of Vincent M. LaMotta, PhD, cosponsored the Rock Art Ranch field school during the 2011 and 2012 field seasons. Dr. LaMotta directed excavations at Brandy's Pueblo during this time. Partial funding for the field school was provided through NSF-REU Grant No. 1262184.

E. Charles Adams is emeritus curator of archaeology, Arizona State Museum, University of Arizona. Prior to retiring in 2020, Adams taught in the School of Anthropology in addition to being museum curator for thirty-five years. Adams directed a thirty-year research program in the ancestral Hopi villages of Homol'ovi in northeastern Arizona and has solely authored or edited more than a dozen books/monographs describing this research. Adams directed the Walpi Archaeological Project for the Museum of Northern Arizona after receiving his PhD from the University of Colorado, Boulder, in 1975. Work at Walpi involved a transformative collaborative experience with the Hopi First Mesa community and launched his lifelong engagement with Hopi tribal members and the Cultural Preservation Office.

References

Adams, E. Charles. 2002. *Homol'ovi: An Ancient Hopi Settlement Cluster*. Tucson: University of Arizona Press.
———. 2016. "Closure and Dedication Practices in the Homol'ovi Settlement Cluster, Northeastern Arizona." *American Antiquity* 81: 42–57.
Adams, E. Charles, and Samantha G. Fladd. 2017. "Composition and Interpretation of Stratified Deposits in Ancestral Hopi Villages at Homol'ovi." *Archaeological and Anthropological Sciences* 9: 1101–14.
Adams, Karen R., and Suzanne J. Smith. n.d. "Modern Plant Studies: Insights into Ancient Plant Communities and their Resources at Rock Art Ranch." In *13,000 Years of History at Rock Art Ranch, Northeastern Arizona*, edited by E. Charles Adams. Submitted to The Arizona Archaeologist. Phoenix: Arizona Archaeological Society.
Barker, Claire S. 2017. "Inconspicuous Identity: Using Corrugated Pottery to Explore Social Identity within the Homol'ovi Settlement Cluster, A.D. 1260–1400." PhD diss., University of Arizona, Tucson.
Barker, Claire S., and Lisa C. Young. 2017. "Networks of Ceramic Exchange: Comparing Homol'ovi Pueblo III Pithouse and Pueblo Communities." *Kiva* 83: 183–202.
Bowser, Brenda J. 2004. "Prologue: Toward an Archaeology of Place." *Journal of Archaeological Method and Theory* 11(1): 1–3.
Cameron, Catherine. 1990. "Pit Structure Abandonment in the Four Corners Region of the American Southwest: Late Basketmaker III and Pueblo I Periods." *Journal of Field Archaeology* 17: 27–37.
Cutright-Smith, Elisabeth, and Claire S. Barker. 2016. "Pottery." In *Chevelon: Pueblo at Blue Running Water*, edited by E. Charles Adams, 117–54. Arizona State Museum Archaeological Series 211. Tucson: University of Arizona.

Darling, Andrew. 1998. "Mass Inhumation and the Execution of Witches in the American Southwest." *American Anthropologist* 100: 732–52.

Douglass, Amy A. 1987. "Prehistoric Exchange and Sociopolitical Development: The Little Colorado White Ware Production-Distribution System." PhD diss., Arizona State University, Tempe.

Estes, Byron. n.d. "Ceramics." In *13,000 Years of History at Rock Art Ranch, Northeastern Arizona*, edited by E. Charles Adams. Submitted to The Arizona Archaeologist. Phoenix: Arizona Archaeological Society.

Fladd, Samantha G. 2018. "Access, Accumulation, and Action: Social Identity at Homol'ovi." PhD diss., University of Arizona, Tucson.

Hedquist, Saul L. 2017. "A Colorful Past: Turquoise and Social Identity in the Late Prehispanic Western Pueblo Region, A.D. 1275–1400." PhD diss., University of Arizona, Tucson.

Hedquist, Saul L., and Kye Miller. 2013. "Reach 12A Sites and Ritual Deposition in a Regional Context." Paper presented at the 79th Annual Meeting, Society for American Archaeology, Austin, TX.

Herr, Sarah, Elizabeth M. Perry, and Scott Van Keuren. 1999. "Excavations at Three Great Kiva Sites." In *Living on the Edge of the Rim: Excavations and Analysis of the Silver Creek Archaeological Research Project 1993–1998*, edited by Barbara J. Mills, Sarah A. Herr, and Scott Van Keuren, 53–115. Arizona State Museum Archaeological Series 192(1). Tucson: University of Arizona.

HRAF. 2018. Human Relations Area Files. New Haven, CT: Yale University.

Jett, Stephen C., and Virginia E. Spencer. 1981. *Navajo Architecture: Forms, History, and Distributions*. Tucson: University of Arizona Press.

Kuchler, Steven. 1999. "The Place of Memory." In *The Art of Forgetting*, edited by A. Forty and S. Kuchler, 53–73. Oxford: Berg.

Lange, Richard C. 1998. *Prehistoric Land-Use and Settlement of the Middle Little Colorado River Valley: The Survey of Homol'ovi Ruins State Park, Winslow, Arizona*. Arizona State Museum Archaeological Series 189. Tucson: University of Arizona.

———. 2015. "Preliminary Report on Excavations at Multi-kiva Site (AZ P:3:112 [ASM])." Report on file, Arizona State Museum. Tucson: University of Arizona.

———. n.d. "Report on Excavations at the Multi-kiva Site (AZ P:3:112 [ASM])." In *13,000 Years of History at Rock Art Ranch, Northeastern Arizona*, edited by E. Charles Adams, 165–200. Submitted to The Arizona Archaeologist. Phoenix: Arizona Archaeological Society.

LeBlanc, Steven A. 1999. *Prehistoric Warfare in the American Southwest*. Salt Lake City: University of Utah Press.

Lightfoot, Ricky R. 1994. *The Duckfoot Site: Archaeology of the House and Household*. Occasional Paper 4. Cortez, CO: Crow Canyon Archaeological Center.

Meskell, Lynn. 2008. "Memory Work and Material Practice." In *Memory Work: Archaeologies of Material Practices*, edited by Barbara J. Mills and William H. Walker, 233–44. Santa Fe, NM: School for Advanced Research Press.

Mills, Barbara J. 2008. "Remembering while Forgetting: Depositional Practices and Social Memory at Chaco." In *Memory Work: Archaeologies of Material Practices*, edited by Barbara J. Mills and William H. Walker, 81–108. Santa Fe, NM: School for Advanced Research Press.

Mills, Barbara J., Sarah A. Herr, Eric J. Kaldahl, Joanne M. Newcomb, Charles R. Riggs, and Ruth Van Dyke. 1999. "Excavations at Pottery Hill." In *Living on the Edge of the Rim: Excavations and Analysis of the Silver Creek Archaeological Research Project 1993–1998*, edited by Barbara J. Mills, Sarah A. Herr, and Scott Van Keuren, 117–48. Arizona State Museum Archaeological Series 192(1). Tucson: University of Arizona.

Mills, Barbara J., and William H. Walker. 2008. "Introduction: Memory, Materiality, and Depositional Practice." In *Memory Work: Archaeologies of Material Practices*, edited by Barbara J. Mills and William H. Walker, 3–24. Santa Fe, NM: School for Advanced Research Press.

Ownby, Mary F. 2016. "Petrographic Analysis of Mogollon Brown Ware from Northern Arizona." Petrographic Report 2016-05. Tucson, AZ: Desert Archaeology, Inc.

Parsons, Elsie Clews. 1939. *Pueblo Indian Religion*. 2 vols. Chicago: University of Chicago Press.

Parsons, Elsie Clews, ed. 1936. *The Journals of Alexander M. Stephen*. 2 vols. New York: Columbia University Press.

Reid, J. Jefferson, ed. 1982. *Cholla Project Archaeology, the Chevelon Region*. Arizona State Museum Archaeological Series 161(2). Tucson: University of Arizona.

Solometo, Julia. 2001. "Tactical Sites of the Chevelon and Clear Creek Drainages." In *The Archaeology of Ancient Tactical Sites*, edited by J. Welch and T. Bostwick, 21–36. Phoenix: Arizona Archaeological Council.

———. 2004. "The Conduct and Consequences of War: Dimensions of Conflict in East-Central Arizona." PhD diss., University of Michigan, Ann Arbor.

Triadan, Daniela. 1997. *Ceramic Commodities and Common Containers: Production and Distribution of White Mountain Red Ware in the Grasshopper Region, Arizona*. Anthropological Papers of the University of Arizona 61. Tucson: University of Arizona Press.

Van Keuren, Scott. 1999. *Ceramic Design Structure and the Organization of Cibola White Ware Production in the Grasshopper Region, Arizona*. Arizona State Museum Archaeological Series 191. Tucson: University of Arizona.

Walker, William H. 1995. "Ritual Prehistory: A Pueblo Case Study." PhD diss., University of Arizona, Tucson.

———. 1999. "Where Are the Witches of Prehistory?" *Journal of Anthropological Method and Theory* 5: 245–308

Whiteley, Peter. 1998. *Rethinking Hopi Ethnography*. Washington, DC: Smithsonian Institution Press.

Wilshusen, Richard. 1986. "The Relationship between Abandonment Mode and Ritual Use in Pueblo I Anasazi Protokivas." *Journal of Field Archaeology* 13: 245–54.

Zedeño, María N. 1994. *Sourcing Prehistoric Ceramics at Chodistaas Pueblo, Arizona: The Circulation of People and Pots in the Grasshopper Region*. Anthropological Papers of the University of Arizona 58. Tucson: University of Arizona Press.

Zedeño, María N., and Brenda J. Bowser. 2009. "The Archaeology of Meaningful Places." In *The Archaeology of Meaningful Places*, edited by Brenda Bowser and María Nieves Zedeño, 1–14. Salt Lake City: University of Utah Press.

Chapter 3

Sequencing Termination Events
Preparing Hearths for the Ritual Decommissioning of Ancestral Pueblo Pit Structures in the Northern U.S. Southwest

Susan C. Ryan

Introduction

With the development of a detailed understanding of formation processes, we have gained the ability to identify how termination behaviors were related by subtle linkages in time and space. Individual actions that took place within the various portions of a structure were temporally distinct events yet related through ultimate decommissioning objectives. Each individual behavior qualified the meaning of those that preceded or followed it. Utilizing data collected from multiple ancestral Pueblo sites in the central Mesa Verde region (figure 3.1) dating to the Basketmaker III–Pueblo III periods (AD 500–1280), this chapter examines how pithouse and kiva hearths were intentionally decommissioned prior to the termination of the structure as a whole. Various preparatory behaviors identified include hearths to fill completely with ash, the placement of material culture on and within hearth ash, the placement of fauna offerings, and the placement of hatch covers over hearths prior to roof collapse. The timing of these events is an important factor in determining the duration of the termination activities within the structure as well as the order and nature of decommissioning events.

As Adams and Roth note in the introduction to this volume, the transformative power of fire and ash have been documented ethnographically and ethnohistorically throughout many Native American cultures and illustrate the important role ash played in domestic and ritual activities. Among Pueblo groups, ash has been noted to seal or protect individu-

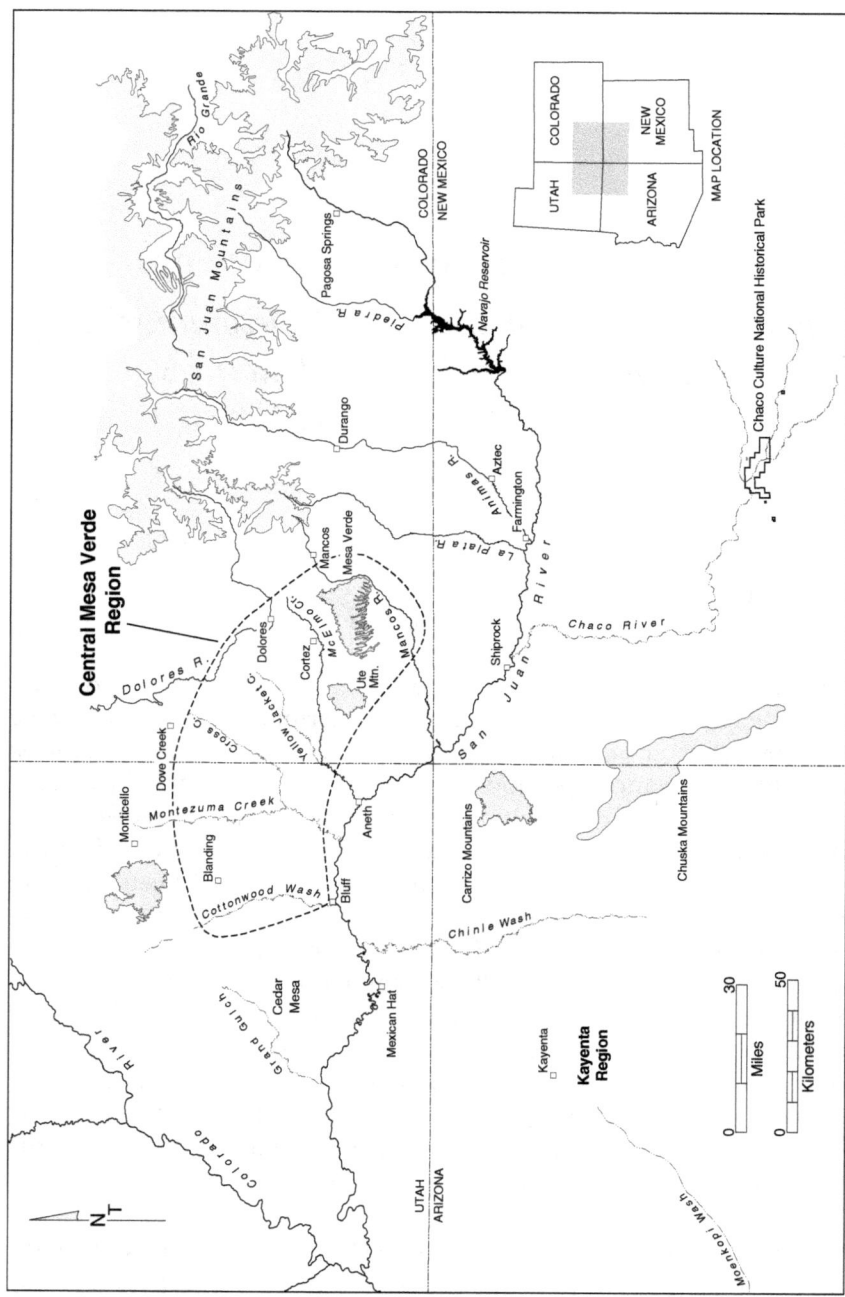

Figure 3.1. Location of study area in the central Mesa Verde region. Used with permission of the Crow Canyon Archaeological Center.

als or areas from danger or disease resulting from spiritual contamination (Parsons 1939: 364, 462–64; Titiev 1944: 106). Burning objects, such as structures, personal items, and ritual paraphernalia, into ashes has also been documented for purification purposes (Parsons 1939: 462–64; Walker 1998; Whiteley 1998). In the Hopi tradition, fire and ash are/were used to signal the termination and renewal of cyclical events, such as those during the New Fire Ceremony (Fewkes 1900) when household members cleaned out their hearths and deposited the remains in a designated area in order to start a new fire, marking the beginning of the ceremonial calendar. At the Pueblo of Acoma, Parsons (1939: 364) noted,

> The practice of sprinkling a line or half-circle or full circle of ashes or meal around the kiva or in front of the house or chamber where a ceremony is going on is also an act of closure, although it may be described merely as a form of "trapping." For example, at the Acoma Fire society's solstice ceremony, when people were eager to get the good seats, they had to wait on the roof of the chamber until the society sang their welcoming song and a member came up and scraped away the line of ashes with his arrowpoint.

Although burning has been recognized and studied in the recent past by archaeologists with respect to protection and purification, the role of ash in decommissioning spaces has gone largely unrecognized (see Adams and Fladd 2017). In this chapter, ash deposits found within hearths are considered to be deliberate depositions related to termination events within a household structure. Drawing from Parsons (1939: 364), I suggest that ash served to "trap" or seal hearths and that the objects placed within the ash were a means to provide the hearth, and the overall structure, with honorary, dedicatory materials prior to structure decommissioning.

Hearths

Scholars in the U.S. Southwest are just beginning to recognize the extent of termination behaviors associated with the deliberate closing of structures. The most commonly recognized termination event in the U.S. Southwest was the dismantling and/or burning of structure roofs (see also Adams, chapter 2; Fladd et al., chapter 4; Prentiss et al., chapter 6; and Roth, chapter 1, for additional examples of structure decommissioning events associated with burning). Often, decommissioned structures had intentionally placed vessels, tools, or foodstuffs located on the structure floor or bench, or within features. The placement of these objects suggests that the termination of a structure involved multiple, preparatory steps prior to the final act of removing, collapsing, or burning the roof. I suggest that we often overlook the treatment of features within these related activities. Features, including hearths, sipapus, niches, ventilator shafts, and floor vaults also received decommissioning treatments, and the remains of these behaviors provides researchers with the abilities to gain a deeper understanding of termination events. The interpretation of formation processes within structures indicates that termination activities were indeed multidimensional and often took place in diverse ways at distinct times, spanning hours to multiple days. This research supports the notion that structure termination was by no means a simple, one-dimensional event but rather multiple, sequentially integrated events.

For this study, I focus specifically on the decommissioning of hearths, or formally constructed pits that frequently show signs of thermal alteration. In the Mesa Verde region, hearth fires were used for light, heat, and cooking, and were round, oval, D-shaped, or square (Ryan 2013). Additionally, adobe and/or sandstone slabs or masonry may have been used to line the feature. Based on archaeobotanical remains recovered from hearth ash flotation samples, juniper (*Juniperus osteosperma*), piñon pine (*Pinus edulis*), and sagebrush (*Artemisia*; *A. tridentata*) were the most common fuel woods utilized during the Basketmaker III–Pueblo III periods (Crow Canyon Archaeological Center 2003). The ethnographic record for flora use among Native peoples in the American Southwest also confirms that juniper, pine, and sagebrush were the most utilized resources for fuel (Rainey and Adams 2004). It is inferred that each domestic household had one or more hearths mainly for utilitarian, domestic purposes. However, hearths had functions beyond utilitarian needs. For example, in modern Pueblo societies, such as Zuni Pueblo, hearths are "fed" each day with bits of food to nourish ancestors and to maintain a sense of balance and well-being for household members (Dan Simplicio, personal communication 2018). Moreover, in modern Pueblo and Ute cultures, ash from hearths is a powerful element that can be used to "absorb" impurities from the body and mind or to "cloak" flaws that are not wished to be transferred to those who might be prone to negative energy, such as newborns (Rebecca Hammond and Dan Simplicio, personal communication 2018). Although we are unable to detect feeding or cloaking behaviors from the archaeological record at this point in time, we are able to detect the contexts where ancestral people intentionally transformed a space used primarily for utilitarian needs to set the stage for terminal events associated with structure decommissioning.

Methods and Data

The Crow Canyon Archaeological Center Research Database (Crow Canyon Archaeological Center 2003) contains over thirty-five years of data collected from numerous research projects on ancestral Pueblo sites dating to the Basketmaker III–Pueblo III periods in the central Mesa Verde region (figure 3.1). For the purposes of this study, Basketmaker III period (AD 500–750) pithouse hearths and Pueblo I (AD 750–950), Pueblo II (AD 950–1150), and Pueblo III (AD 1150–1300) period kiva hearths were examined to analyze final decommissioning behaviors associated with structure termination. Careful attention was paid to stratigraphy, omitting overlying roof sediments from each hearth during excavation to ensure that data were representative of the primary refuse, or hearth ash, and associated contents.

There are 206 hearth records with associated data from the central Mesa Verde region in the Crow Canyon Archaeological Center Research Database (Crow Canyon Archaeological Center 2003). Of these, only nine have comments noting that the primary refuse, or ash, was cleaned out prior to structure depopulation or significantly disturbed by bioturbation activities. The overwhelming majority of hearths were documented as having been full or nearly full of primary refuse when uncovered by the excavator. It is critical to note that occupants intentionally chose to not clean out pit structure or kiva hearths prior to structure depopulation. I interpret this behavior as an intentional termination event associated with multistaged preparation activities leading to structure decommissioning (see Roth, chapter 1, for a similar example from the Mimbres region).

Timing and Experimental Archaeology

In the phenomenological sense, burning is an esoteric, transformative process that converts matter of one form to another, mainly a solid into smoke, charcoal, and ashes. Any material having undergone the burning process will be visibly transformed, and it is this transformation that makes the communication of the decommissioning performance visually and emotionally potent. There are three causes of fires: providential, or fires ignited by natural causes such as lightning or volcanic activity; accidental fires, or fires resulting from human carelessness with either fire or fuel for fire; and incendiary, or fires that are the result of intentional human action (Lally and Vonarx 2011). For the purposes of this study, I assume that all hearth fires were of the incendiary type, as they were the result of actions taken by a structure's occupants.

The accumulation rate of hearth ash is a necessary factor in determining the timing and sequencing of termination activities. We may draw from accumulation observations in the use of modern wood-burning stoves that utilize the same types of fuel wood as did those of the ancestral Pueblo people, mainly piñon and juniper. Most wood-burning stoves require ash to be cleaned out every twenty-four hours following continual use, such as in the winter months. Given that their volume is roughly that of ancient hearths, perhaps even larger, it can be assumed that hearth ash recovered from pithouses and kivas represents the final twenty-four to forty-eight hours of use within a given structure, possibly up to a week, depending on the amount of use and the given season.

In order to test this hypothesis—that the ash remaining in ancient hearths represents the final twenty-four- to forty-eight-hour period prior to structure decommissioning, and not the weeks or months leading up to a termination event—an experimental study was conducted utilizing a replica Basketmaker III–period pithouse constructed on the Crow Canyon Archaeological Center's campus. The replica structure contains an adobe-lined hearth constructed from local, undisturbed native sediment and has a fifteen–liter volume capacity. The adobe has been hardened and fire-reddened from over two decades of use by Crow Canyon's staff, providing experiential education programs demonstrating fire-making and other lifeways of Basketmaker III–period peoples. Also present in the replica pithouse are a single, sandstone-slab deflector located immediately south of the hearth and a roof hatch located immediately above the hearth, allowing for ventilation.

To remain consistent with utilized ancient fuel types, only dry juniper wood was selected as fuel from the surrounding landscape. Each piece was individually weighed until precisely five pounds was collected. On a late November afternoon (1:39 P.M., forty-three degrees Fahrenheit, 25 percent humidity, and nine miles-per-hour wind speed) a fire was started in the replica hearth using a match to ignite a small "nest" of juniper bark crafted from the weighed fuel. Pieces of juniper wood were placed in the hearth for the next sixty-six minutes until the fuel wood was expended and the flames were no longer visible. Charcoal smoldered in the hearth for approximately the next forty-five minutes until embers became inactive. When cool, the hearth contents—composed of ash and charcoal—were collected, measured, and weighed. Interestingly, 271.6 grams of charcoal and ash were recovered—the conflagration having reduced the juniper wood from the initial 2267.96 grams, or five pounds, to 11.98 percent of its original weight and 1.1 liters by volume. Given that the replica hearth holds 15 liters by volume, the fuel wood remnants occupied 7.3 percent of the hearth following an approximately one-hour conflagration. Given these calculations, it would only take approximately fourteen hours of burning juniper wood at a low to moderate rate to completely fill the hearth with charcoal and ash.

The results of this experiment are noteworthy for multiple reasons. First, it provides information on the final termination behaviors associated with structure hearths, not the day-to-day domestic activities of the months or weeks leading up to structure depopulation. Hearth ash and charcoal recovered from the archaeological record represents a very short duration of time, less than a twenty-four-hour period in some instances. Because of this, researchers must be careful not to make inferences from flotation or faunal samples recovered from pit structure hearths regarding everyday domestic activities, as they more likely represent termination activities. Second, this experimental study illuminates the timing in which material objects were intentionally placed within hearth deposits as part of termination activities. As will be discussed below, the majority of material culture collected from hearths does not exhibit burning, indicating that objects were placed in hearths when burning ceased and ashes were cool. Finally, this study provides insights into the nature and timing of holistic structure termination, as events were indeed sequenced and planned. Based on the law of superposition, hearth treatment activities took place prior to roof decommissioning events and subsequent to domestic needs for light, heat, and cooking.

The Placement of Material Culture

Material culture collected and analyzed from hearth contents was examined for this study. Table 3.1 lists all material types present and the number of hearths from which a particular material type was found (see the Crow Canyon Archaeological Center Laboratory Manual, Volume I [2005] for definitions of artifact types and categories). The most common artifact types to appear in pit structure hearths dating from the Basketmaker III–Pueblo III periods include chipped stone (N=68); fauna, or nonhuman bone (N=63); pottery, or sherds (N=95); gizzard stones (N=21); tree-ring samples (N=20); adobe (N=13); minerals/stone samples (N=11); and eggshell (N=10). For the purposes of this study, only pottery, ground stone, and fauna will be discussed in detail.

When considering the function of pottery, it is inferred that graywares were used for cooking directly over hearths, whereas white- and nonlocal wares (including redwares) were used for storage and serving. Because of this, it may be assumed that grayware vessels were deposited in hearths when a vessel accidentally broke; however, if white- and nonlocal wares were found in hearths, it is inferred they were either swept into the feature as refuse or intentionally placed as part of termination activities. Of the seventy hearths containing pottery data in the Crow Canyon Research Database (2003), graywares represent 73 percent (corrugated and plain graywares), whitewares represent 26 percent, and nonlocal wares (nonlocal and redwares) represent less than 1 percent of the recovered sherds (table 3.2). However, graywares should not be excluded from termination

Table 3.1. *Artifact Type and Number of Hearths Where Artifact Type Is Present.*

Artifact Type	Number of Hearths Artifact Type Present
Chipped Stone	68
Nonhuman Bone	63
Bulk Sherds	48
Bulk Sherds Large	26
Groundstone*	24
Bulk Sherds Small	21
Gizzard Stones	21
Tree-Ring Sample	20
Adobe	13
Mineral/Stone Sample	11
Egg Shell	10
Other Ceramic Artifact	9
Other Modified Stone/Mineral	9
Micro-Debitage	8
Bead	6
Core	6
Peckingstone	6
Projectile Point	6
Bone Awl	5
Unfired Sherds	5
Modified Flake	4
Other Modified Bone	4
Pebbles	4
Biface	3
Polishing Stone	3
Shell	3
Bone Tube	2
Pendant	2
Polishing/Hammerstone	2
Shaped Sherd	2
Unmodified Stone	2
Effigy	1
Hammerstone	1
Modified Sherd	1
Polished Igneous Stone	1
Single-Bitted Axe	1

*Note: Groundstone category includes Two-Hand Manos (N=6), Slab Metates (N=5), Bulk Indeterminate Groundstone (N=3), Indeterminate Groundstone (N=3), Manos (N=3), Abraders (N=2), Metates (N=1), and One-Hand Manos (N=1).

Table 3.2. *Total Counts of Grayware (Corrugated and Plain Gray), Whiteware, and Nonlocal Wares (Including Redwares) from Hearths by Site.*

Site Number	Site Name	Corrugated	Non-Local	Plain Gray	Red Ware	White Ware	Total Pottery Count
42SA22760	Hedley Site Complex	0	0	0	0	2	2
5MT10246	Lester's Site	6	0	0	0	2	8
5MT10647	Dillard Site	0	0	39	0	2	41
5MT10684	Dry Ridge Site	0	0	1	0	6	7
5MT10709	Portulaca Point	0	0	1	0	0	1
5MT10736	5MT10736	0	0	3	0	0	3
5MT11338	G & G Hamlet	34	0	4	0	19	57
5MT11842	Woods Canyon Pueblo	6	0	1	0	0	7
5MT123	Albert Porter Site	48	0	3	0	57	108
5MT16790	Meadow View	2	0	0	0	1	3
5MT16803	Pinyon Place	0	0	1	0	1	2
5MT16805	Harlan Great Kiva	7	0	0	0	18	25
5MT16808	Monsoon House	6	0	1	0	3	10
5MT1825	Castle Rock Pueblo	180	0	2	1	40	223
5MT2032	Switchback Site	0	0	2	0	1	3
5MT3807	Shields Pueblo	106	1	20	0	146	273
5MT3868	Duckfoot	0	0	336	15	30	381
5MT3901	Green Lizard Site	4	0	0	0	1	5
5MT3918	Shorlene's Site	0	0	1	0	0	1
5MT3936	Lillian's Site	4	0	0	0	2	6
5MT3951	Troy's Tower	1	0	0	0	2	3
5MT3967	Catherine's Site	1	0	1	0	1	3
5MT5	Yellow Jacket Pueblo	6	0	0	0	34	40
5MT5152	Kenzie Dawn Hamlet	4	0	0	0	0	4
5MT604	Goodman Point Pueblo	244	0	0	0	45	293
5MT765	Sand Canyon Pueblo	252	1	0	0	54	307
	Total	911	2	416	16	467	1816

placement activities since dedicatory objects would most likely be represented by complete or nearly complete vessels. This assumption proves to be correct in that there are numerous cases where whole grayware vessels were placed on the hearth and were subsequently crushed when the roof collapsed onto the structure floor. Artifact context and association are another indicator of termination activities associated with hearths containing pottery vessels. For example, in a Pueblo III–period kiva at Shields Pueblo, a mano was placed next to corrugated and black-on-white vessels. The mano, a grinding tool, has no direct relationship to activities that took place within the hearth. Moreover, neither the mano nor the vessels exhibited thermal alteration; they were positioned on the hearth after it was full of ash and the ashes were completely cooled. Thus, it should be assumed that both the vessels and the ground stone were carefully selected objects placed in the hearth as part of termination activities.

Ground stone, particularly manos and metates, is another artifact class worthy of examination in termination activities. In another example, this one from a Pueblo III–period kiva at Albert Porter Pueblo, four unburned manos, once originally used for grinding, were purposely placed on top of the kiva's cooled hearth ash as part of termination behaviors (figure 3.2). Interestingly, there were nineteen unique instances of manos having been placed in hearths in the Crow Canyon Research Database and six instances of intentional metate placement.

Likewise, the placement of hatch covers over hearth features as termination acts is notable. In these instances, the hatch covers, or shaped sandstone slabs, were in direct contact with hearth ash and exhibited no

Figure 3.2. *Four two-handed manos placed side by side on cooled hearth ash, Albert Porter Pueblo. Used with permission of the Crow Canyon Archaeological Center.*

thermal alteration. During excavation, hatch covers were typically found in shattered fragments due to the weight of the collapsed roof. Like ground stone, hatch covers have no primary relationship to the hearth, but were placed in hearth contexts as part of termination events. At this time, there is no possibility of quantifying the relative frequency of purposeful hatch cover placement using the Crow Canyon Research Database (2003), as the records are inconsistent in noting these occurrences; excavators often concluded that hatch covers fell onto the hearth prior to roof collapse instead of being deposited as the result of intentional activities. Thus, it is critical for future excavators to carefully assess these contexts to determine if roof sediments are found between hearth ash and the hatch cover—if so, then they were likely deposited when the roof collapsed. If not, then they were likely placed over the hearth to seal it as part of termination activities preparing the structure for decommissioning.

Faunal Remains in Hearths

Because a pit structure hearth is intended for use mainly as a thermal feature, it is expected that objects placed within it, such as fuel wood, fauna, and artifacts, indicate evidence of thermal alteration. According to Driver (2005), one index that fauna were cooked within a hearth is the appearance of localized burning. Localized burning occurs when a bone is partially exposed during roasting; the exposed portion of the bone is charred but the remainder, which is covered by meat, is unburnt. Localized burning, or roasting, is defined by a blackened area of burning, usually quite sharply defined, and is often surrounded by a dark-brown zone grading into the normal color of unburnt bone. Such areas are seen most often on mandibles and long bones, but these can occur on other elements. Burning over the entire specimen, such as that seen on fauna coded as "burnt black," is not a good indicator of cooking or roasting but instead is associated with prolonged exposure to thermal alteration beyond what is needed for consumption leading to carbonization. Bones burnt uniformly black are known to have been defleshed and exposed to heat at around six hundred degrees Celsius. Elements coded as burnt white, gray, or blue/gray have been thermally altered beyond the burnt black stage into calcification. Bones that were burnt white are generally understood to have been exposed to temperatures upwards of seven hundred degrees Celsius. Thermal alteration that produces calcined bones goes beyond what is required for consumption. Fauna remains that do not exhibit thermal modification were most likely deposited after the hearth fire went out—when the ashes were cool—or by natural taphonomic processes that moved the bones into position at a later time. Although Badenhorst and Driver (2015) note that squirrels, wood rats, pocket gophers, and even smaller rodents such as mice and voles found in hearths were most likely consumed, this study omitted the following small rodents from the dataset due to the possibility that they were natural, postoccupational intrusions: deer mice, kangaroo rats, mice, prairie dogs, pocket gophers, rodents, squirrels, voles, and wood rats.

In sum, 2,311 individual elements, or Number of Individual Specimens (NISP), from 20 sites were represented in hearths in the Crow Canyon Research Database (2003). However, this total was reduced to 490 by excluding possible postoccupational fauna intrusions (listed above, N=144) and the sum of unidentified elements (N=1677). The most commonly represented fauna collected from hearths dating from the Basketmaker III–Pueblo III periods included cottontails (N=133), small mammals (N=54), turkey (N=53), large birds (N=44), and jackrabbits/hares (N=20). Of the counts listed above, turkey remains were found in 26 distinct hearths, cottontails in 23, large birds in 19, small mammals in 9, and jackrabbits/hares in 4. Thus, turkeys and cottontails were the most common fauna type cooked or intentionally placed in hearths during the Basketmaker III–Pueblo III periods. To determine if faunal remains were deposited during consumptive events or if they were placed during termination activities, each element was assessed for thermal alteration.

Of 147 elements, 119 were coded as burnt white/gray/blue, 22 were burnt black, and 6 exhibited localized burning (table 3.3). In all cases, cottontail (N=48), jackrabbits/hares (N=40), and turkeys (N=24) were the most common fauna types burned, suggesting that they represent food elements that were initially roasted, then turned black, and finally white the longer they were exposed to prolonged heat. Only 31 percent of the elements were thermally altered, further suggesting that only a limited amount of food preparation behaviors were taking place in pithouses and kivas during the final days of structure depopulation.

Table 3.3. *Number of Individual Specimens (NISP) and Types of Burned Fauna.*

Fauna Type	NISP Burned White	NISP Burned Black	NISP Localized Burning	NISP Total
Cottontail	43	4	1	48
Small Mammal	37	3	0	40
Large Birds	11	2	1	14
Turkey	9	11	3	23
Jackrabbit/Hare	9	2	1	12
Rabbit/Hare	7	0	0	7
Small Carnivore	1	0	0	1
Small Bird	1	0	0	1
Large Carnivore	1	0	0	1

Surprisingly, the majority of fauna (69 percent) analyzed from hearths exhibited no thermal alteration, suggesting they were deposited after the hearth fire went out and ashes were cool, or by natural taphonomic processes that moved the bones into position at a later date. The most common unburned fauna type by NISP was cottontail (N=83), followed by dogs/wolves (N=82), small mammals (N=71), large birds (N=28), turkeys (N=27), hawks (N=22), jackrabbits/hares (N=8), rabbits/hares (N=3), deer (N=2), perching birds (N=2), and small carnivores (N=1).

Given that structure roofs were often intentionally collapsed and/or burned soon after hearth termination, it seems highly unlikely that fauna such as turkey, rabbits, jackrabbits, and large birds would have moved into hearths following structure collapse as part of natural, postdepositional processes.

The unburnt fauna data provide one of the greatest insights into hearth termination behaviors, as these are most likely fauna that were intentionally placed within the hearth as dedicatory objects as opposed to having been consumed for food. Although there is some overlap between consumptive and dedicatory fauna, such as cottontails, small mammals, large birds, turkeys, jackrabbits, and hares, there are five types of fauna that stand out as solely dedicatory (i.e., exhibiting no thermal alteration). These include dogs, wolves, hawks, deer, perching birds, and small carnivores. In most cases, these offerings represent only portions of the entire animal or bird; however, in some cases the entire body was placed in the hearth, such as the example of a hawk laid on top of cooled hearth ash in a Pueblo III–period kiva at Castle Rock Pueblo (figure 3.3).

Figure 3.3. *Hawk remains placed on cooled hearth ash, Castle Rock Pueblo. Used with permission of the Crow Canyon Archaeological Center.*

Conclusions

As Appadurai (1986:3–4; 13–16) notes, objects have different values and meanings depending on their contexts, and the same object can endure changes in both depending on its biography. The topic of artifact biographies, or life histories, is now encountered in a number of works by archaeologists. As Schiffer and Reid (2017:3–6) note, the life histories of artifacts are based on the concept of behavioral chains, which link different activities to all stages of artifact use. Context is everything in our discipline and, in order to understand behavioral chains, it is important to differentiate depositional processes produced as part of human behaviors from those produced through natural means. The content, form, frequency, and distribution of materials should be assessed because objects may be utilized for purposes that they were not originally produced for.

The importance of recording precise architectural and feature stratigraphy, and the nuances of termination behaviors as identified in these strata, allows for insight into termination sequencing behaviors. This chapter highlights several important points to consider when interpreting termination activities associated with structures. First, termination behaviors were temporally distinct events yet were related via ultimate decommissioning objectives. These events most likely took place over a period of one to several days, highlighting preconceived plans and actions as part of decommissioning objectives. Second, features in particular received termination treatments apart from the most recognized treatments given to structure roofs. The depositional processes and material culture found in association with these features needs to be carefully examined. Hearths in particular received termination treatments that included: (1) allowing the hearth to fill completely with ash (i.e., not cleaning the hearth out); (2) dedicatory offerings of material culture and fauna, with the possibility that artifact biographies and context may have been intentionally altered during this process; and (3) sealing or capping the hearth with hatch covers prior to roof decommissioning. Finally, it is essential to stress that a hearth's contents represent the final day, or days, leading to structure depopulation and that the majority of material culture contents are not indicative of activities associated with everyday, domestic household behaviors. These deposits are suggestive of pre-planned termination events leading to the final use and closure of households as practiced by numerous generations from the Basketmaker III–Pueblo III periods.

Architecture is socially produced, resulting in a built landscape that reflects cultural schemas and ideologies through its design, construction, and intended use (Hegmon 1989). The reproduction of social systems would not be possible without the action of individuals or actors. Giddens

(1984: 9) defines "agency" as the choices made by individuals as they take action. Actors possess knowledge of rules, or schemas, and the ability to mobilize resources; this serves as the foundation for their social action and agency (Sewell 1992). Pit structure and kiva residents had the ability to transpose schemas from one social context to another, which resulted in the transformation of the very structures that give them the ability to act, allowing for change, transformation, and/or repetition of social systems through time (Sewell 1992: 8). The actors, or residents, involved in structure decommissioning were emotionally and physically tied to the structure—they were most likely the individuals who constructed, inhabited, and maintained the structure during its use-life. They had intimate knowledge of how the interior of the structure looked, smelled, and felt and how it tied into their overarching cosmology. In this way, their agency was used to intentionally transform household features used primarily for domestic purposes, including light, heat, and cooking, into entities that were terminated with respect.

This practice was instituted in various ways for centuries in the central Mesa Verde region, starting with the first, permanent, full-time pithouses constructed in the AD 500s until regional depopulation at the end of the AD 1200s. The act of decommissioning a household hearth with precision and care indicates the acknowledgment of the importance of this feature and its function within the structure, within everyday human life, and within the cycles of birth and death. The items that were placed within the hearth and its ash were selected as dedicatory offerings, acknowledging the life force and service that these incredibly important features provided to its residents over generations. In this chapter, ash deposits within hearths are interpreted to be deliberate depositions related to termination events within a household structure. Ash served as a powerful medium to seal off a hearth from continued use. The objects placed within hearth ash were a means to provide these ritually significant features, and their overall structures, with honorary, dedicatory materials prior to structure decommissioning.

Susan C. Ryan received her PhD from the University of Arizona. She is currently the director of archaeology at the Crow Canyon Archaeological Center in Cortez, Colorado. She directed two major excavation projects from 1998 to 2004 and is currently the principal investigator for the Northern Chaco Outliers Project. As director of archaeology, Ryan aligns the center's mission with ongoing field, laboratory, and report publication activities. Her research interests include public archaeology, the nature and extent of Chaco influence in the Mesa Verde region, the AD 1130–1180 drought, and the built environment.

References

Adams, E. Charles, and Samantha G. Fladd. 2017. "Composition and Interpretation of Stratified Deposits in Ancestral Hopi Villages at Homol'ovi." *Archaeological and Anthropological Sciences* 9: 1101–14.

Appadurai, Arjun. 1986. "Introduction: Commodities and the Politics of Value." In *The Social Life of Things: Commodities in Cultural Perspective*, edited by Arjun Appadurai, 3–63. New York: Cambridge University Press.

Badenhorst, Shaw, and Jonathan C. Driver. 2015. "Faunal Remains." In *The Archaeology of Albert Porter Pueblo (Site 5MT123): Excavations at a Great House Community Center in Southwestern Colorado*, edited by Susan C. Ryan. Retrieved 15 March 2017 from www.crowcanyon.org/albertporter.

Crow Canyon Archaeological Center. 2005. *The Crow Canyon Archaeological Center Laboratory Manual, Version 1*, edited by Scott Ortman, Erin L. Baxter, Carole L. Graham, G. Robin Lyle, Lew W. Matis, Jaime A. Mereweather, R. David Satterwhite, Jonathan D. Till. Retrieved 13 December 2018 from https://www.crowcanyon.org/ResearchReports/LabManual/LaboratoryManual.pdf.

———. 2003. *The Crow Canyon Archaeological Center Research Database* [HTML Title]. Retrieved 4 March 2018 from http:/www.crowcanyon.org/researchdatabase.

Driver, Jonathan C. 2005. "Manual for Description of Vertebrate Remains." 7th ed. On file. Cortez, CO: Crow Canyon Archaeological Center.

Fewkes, Jesse W. 1900. "The New-Fire Ceremony at Walpi." *American Anthropologist* 2(1): 80–138.

Giddens, Anthony. 1984. *The Constitution of Society: Outline of the Theory of Structuration*. Berkeley: University of California Press.

Hegmon, Michelle. 1989. "Social Integration and Architecture." In *The Architecture of Social Integration in Prehistoric Pueblos*, edited by W. D. Lipe, R. Slickman, and R. Paul, 5–14. Occasional Papers 1. Cortez, CO: Crow Canyon Archaeological Center.

———. 2003. "Setting Theoretical Egos Aside: Issues and Theory in North American Archaeology." *American Antiquity* 68(2): 213–43.

Lally, Joe, and A. J. Vonarx. 2011. "Fire: Accidental or Intentional? An Archaeological Toolkit for Evaluating Accident and Intent in Ancient Structural Fires." In *Contemporary Archaeologies of the Southwest*, edited by William H. Walker and Kathryn R. Venzor, 157–72. Boulder: University Press of Colorado.

Parsons, Elsie Clews. 1939. *Pueblo Indian Religion*. Vol. 1, pt. 2. Chicago: University of Chicago.

Rainey, Katharine D., and Karen R. Adams. 2004. "Plant Use by Native Peoples of the American Southwest: Ethnographic Documentation." Retrieved 26 November 2018 from http://www.crowcanyon.org/plantuses.

Ryan, Susan C. 2013. *Architectural Communities of Practice: Ancestral Pueblo Kiva Production During the Chaco and Post-Chaco Periods in the Northern Southwest*. PhD diss, University of Arizona, Tucson.

Schiffer, Michael B. and J. Jefferson Reid. 2017. "The Strong Case Approach." In *The Strong Case Approach in Behavioral Archaeology*, edited by Michael B. Schiffer, Charles Riggs, and J. Jefferson Reid., 1–11. Salt Lake City: University of Utah Press.

Sewell, William H., Jr. 1992. "A Theory of Structure: Duality, Agency, and Transformation." *American Journal of Sociology* 98(1): 1–29.

Titiev, Mischa. 1944. *Old Oraibi: A Study of the Hopi Indians of Third Mesa*. Papers of the Peabody Museum of American Archaeology and Ethnology 22. Cambridge, MA: Harvard University.

Walker, William H. 1998. "Where Are the Witches of Prehistory?" *Journal of Archaeological Method and Theory* 5: 245–308.

Whiteley, Peter. 1998. *Rethinking Hopi Ethnography*. Washington, DC: Smithsonian Institution.

CHAPTER 4

Symbolic Associations
Assessing the Co-occurrence of Turquoise and Ash in the Ancient U.S. Southwest

Samantha G. Fladd, Saul L. Hedquist,
E. Charles Adams, and Stewart B. Koyiyumptewa

Introduction

Ash holds a unique place in the archaeological record. As the byproduct of fire, whose uses include cooking, warmth, and firing pottery, it is a ubiquitous and renewable resource that has largely been linked to domestic and mundane practices of the past. However, archaeologists are increasingly critiquing the imposition of a sacred-secular divide to studies of ancient societies (e.g., Bell 1992; Brück 1999; Fogelin 2008; Leach 1968; Stahl 2008). Fowles (2013) specifically questions whether the establishment of such a division in research contexts accurately represents Pueblo worldviews. In such discussions, explanations for and analyses of the distribution of common but symbolically significant materials such as ash come to the forefront. Although ash may be created by practices involved with a range of thermal activities, how does its deposition in the archaeological record articulate with its well-understood cultural significance among modern Pueblo communities?

While a common material throughout the Pueblo world, ash is symbolically linked to concepts of purification and renewal as seen through its use in numerous ceremonial practices ethnographically (e.g., Adams and Fladd 2017; Fewkes 1900; Roth and Schriever 2015; Van Keuren and Roos 2013). On the other end of the spectrum, turquoise is considered to be a rare material throughout the region whose use and distribution is often tightly restricted. The symbolic use and importance of turquoise, which is tied to its association with moisture, is widely acknowledged in archaeological discussions (e.g., Hedquist 2016, 2017; Mathien 2001;

Plog 2003). In this chapter, we explore the significance of the intersection of ash and turquoise in the archaeological record of the Pueblo Southwest. The combination of ash and turquoise in archaeological deposits may hold symbolic meaning that remains understudied to date. For example, the context of merged deposits that contain both ash and turquoise may help clarify the enduring social role or importance of the associated architectural spaces. Drawing on contemporary Hopi insights regarding the significance and utility of ash as relayed by our coauthor Stewart Koyiyumptewa, we test for potential patterning by examining the co-occurrence of ash and turquoise in deposits from Homol'ovi I (AZ J:14:3 [ASM]), an ancestral Hopi village dating to the fourteenth century.

Symbolism of Ash and Turquoise at Hopi

Uses of ash abound in the ethnographic record of the Pueblo Southwest, specifically from the Hopi. Some of its more common uses include serving as an integral component of piiki bread, helping to remove husks from corn, and rubbing on babies after birth. Symbolic associations all point to the importance of fire and ash as an agent of renewal, purification, and protection (Adams and Fladd 2017). As recounted by Fewkes (1900), the New Fire Ceremony in Hopi villages includes the annual cleaning of hearths and the removal of ash to specific locations within the village in order to prepare the community. In this case, the cleaning and removal of ash marks the emergence of the new year, the ash itself acting as a transformative agent in this process.

Ash is also often used in various contexts to distinguish the living and protect individuals from spiritual contamination during important ceremonial rites (Adams and Fladd 2017: 1105; Parsons 1939: 364, 464; Titiev 1944: 106). It is associated with witchcraft and clown societies, being used to demarcate their "houses" from others within a village (Parsons 1939: 464). The burning of important ritual paraphernalia associated with witchcraft provides a means to neutralize or terminate the threat of evil or corruption to the community (Adams and Fladd 2017: 1105; Walker 2008; Whiteley 1998). Many materials and spaces in Hopi culture are deemed potentially dangerous to women, children, and uninitiated or unprotected members of society. Ash and the act of burning serves to neutralize this danger through its deposition into rooms and to protect individuals or objects with which it comes into contact (see also Walker 1995a, 1995b). Thus, large or dense concentrations of ash uncovered in the archaeological record, like the occurrence of structural burning (e.g., Adams and Fladd 2017; Icove et al. 2016), may signal efforts to protect, purify, or renew an area or associated individuals and materials.

In contrast to ash, turquoise as a material is rare and often restricted in space and utility. Despite its relative scarcity, however, turquoise remains a highly valued component of Pueblo society and is present in all major ceremonies in Hopi culture (e.g., Hedquist 2017; Waters 1977; Whiteley 2004, 2012). Ethnographically, turquoise holds a prominent place in myth, ritual, aesthetics, and cosmology. The acquisition and use of this material has been traced to the time of migrations to the Hopi Mesas and the development of important ceremonies (Hedquist 2017: 251–53). Turquoise still serves as an important offering, deposited in shrines and decorating objects like prayer sticks and adornments (e.g., Hedquist 2016, 2017; Mathien 2001; Plog 2003). Forms, such as beads, pendants, and tesserae, important in Hopi society today, have also been encountered in the archaeological record (Hedquist 2016, 2017). Archaeological occurrences of turquoise in contexts such as caches, structural foundations, and burials demonstrate its important, perhaps ritually oriented, role in pre-Hispanic Pueblo practices and the potential resemblance between its past and present symbolism.

Symbolic associations for turquoise vary. It is linked with the winter season and masculinity, thus being tied to war and hunting practices (Whiteley 2012: 148–49). Most notably, turquoise is symbolic of moisture, as well as what moisture provides in the arid Southwest region—lush vegetation, corn and other crops, health and prosperity—elements critical today, and which have been critical for Pueblo ancestors over the course of millennia (Hedquist 2017: 253–55). Furthermore, the color of turquoise is linked to the southwest direction. Nuvatukya'ovi (the San Francisco Peaks) are located to the southwest of the Hopi Mesas and are homes to the katsinas, who are tied to rain and thunderclouds (e.g. Adams 1991, 1994, 2002; Hedquist 2017: 255). Drawing on this extensive symbolism, turquoise acts as a crucial component of the Hopi worldview, providing "a symbolic connection to life-sustaining moisture" (Hedquist 2017: 249).

Homol'ovi I and the Homol'ovi Settlement Cluster

Occupied from AD 1260 to 1400, the Homol'ovi Settlement Cluster (figure 4.1) was composed of seven villages located along the middle Little Colorado River in northeastern Arizona (Adams 2002; LaMotta 2006). This period in Pueblo history, the early Pueblo IV period, was marked by increased settlement size, as a limited number of large clusters were formed across the landscape, although the nature and shape of those settlement clusters varied and remains debated (e.g., Adams and Duff 2004). Constructed by migrants to the region (e.g., Barker 2017; Lyons 2001, 2003), each of the villages of the Homol'ovi Settlement Cluster was unique in terms of size and occupation span.

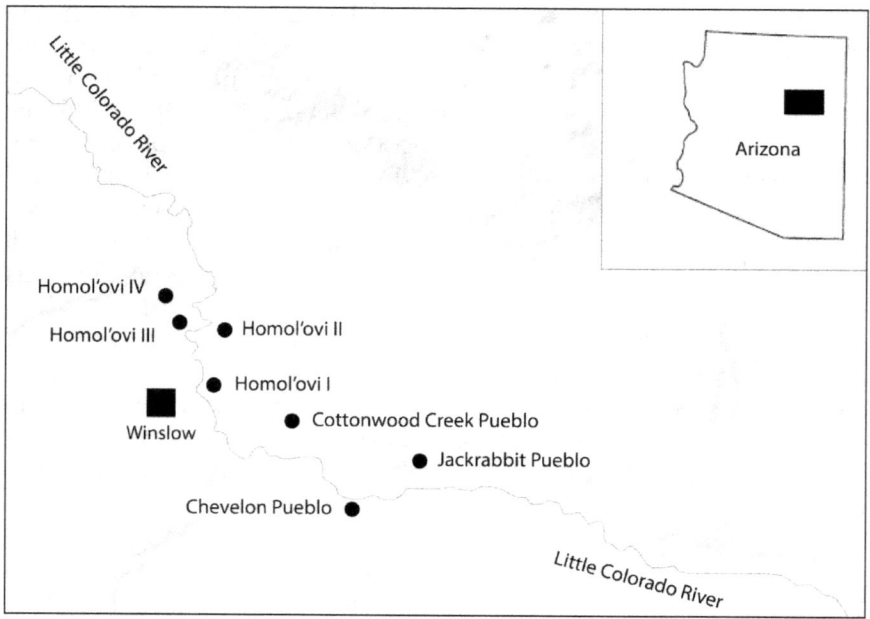

Figure 4.1. *Map showing the location of the Homol'ovi Settlement Cluster. Created by Samantha G. Fladd (based on Adams 2002).*

Located in the widest portion of the floodplain, Homol'ovi I was one of the largest of the villages and among the longest occupied. Initial construction occurred in the AD 1290s through the gradual addition of stonemasonry room blocks at the north end of the site. The pueblo underwent several episodes of remodeling before it took its final eleven-hundred-room nucleated form with four plazas prior to the residents moving to the Hopi Mesas around AD 1400. Most notably, a large enclosed southern plaza built primarily of adobe brick room blocks was added to the pueblo around AD 1360 (Adams 2002; LaMotta 2006). These spatial alterations corresponded temporally with the construction of the nearby village of Homol'ovi II, an addition of a similar large plaza to the existing village of Chevelon Pueblo, and the adoption of the katsina religion (e.g., Adams 1991, 1994, 2004, 2016a). Excavations at the site resulted in the documentation of seventy structures following a deposit-oriented methodology inspired by behavioral archaeology (Adams 2002).

Uniquely strong chronological control exists for the Homol'ovi Settlement Cluster. LaMotta (2006) divided the occupation of Homol'ovi into four phases of roughly twenty to thirty years each. These phases can be identified in individual deposits using the percentage of Jeddito Yellow Ware in comparison to other decorated ceramics. Corroboration of this method was achieved through the use of dendrochronology and radiocarbon dating, as well as ceramic seriation at Chevelon Pueblo (Cutright-Smith 2007; Cutright-Smith and Barker 2016; LaMotta 2006). This system, in consort with detailed reconstructions of architectural construction patterns (Gann 2003), allows for the synchronic and diachronic analysis of intravillage occupation and closure patterns.

Use of space within Homol'ovi I was flexible and constantly changing, resulting in clear evidence for ritualized foundation and closure practices (Fladd 2018). As defined by Adams (2016b: 43), closure refers to "a suite of practices with material manifestations that ends the occupation of a structure or settlement with the added intent of either remembering or forgetting associated people, groups, or events." These practices have been extensively studied, in large part due to the ability to parse depositional details. For example, Walker (1995a) used data from Homol'ovi II to underscore the singular nature of the fill of kivas, particularly the unique object types deposited within them, leading to the definition of several discrete types of ritual disposal. The distinctive closure practices have been linked to nonresidential crosscutting social groups, such as sodalities (Adams 2016a; Walker 1995a; Ware 2014). Building upon these ideas, Adams and LaMotta (2006: 59) defined and analyzed "enriched deposits" that include a "higher frequency of complete objects, exotic goods, or non-subsistence fauna." Within the Homol'ovi Settlement Cluster, these principles have been used to define a temporal shift in the ritual exploitation of animals (LaMotta 2006), the deposition and meaning of turquoise (Hedquist 2016, 2017), four distinct depositional practices involving ash (Adams and Fladd 2017), the variable use of fire as a means of kiva closure (Adams 2016b), the use of distinct suites of plants in closure deposits (Miljour 2016), the ritualized deposition of miniature vessels (Fladd and Barker 2019), and a variety of foundation and closure practices associated with features, structures, and communities (Adams 2016b). These previous studies on the practices of construction and deposition at the Homol'ovi Settlement Cluster provide the basis for our current investigation of the intersection of ash and turquoise at Homol'ovi I.

Ash and Turquoise at Homol'ovi I

An examination of the intersection of ash and turquoise at Homol'ovi I revealed several interesting patterns. Ash was a common inclusion in depositional practices across the village, forming a portion of 20 percent of the deposits recorded during excavation of the structures (Fladd 2018). Turquoise was encountered much less frequently, being found in forty-seven discrete occurrences (2 percent of the total deposits excavated) within structures (figure 4.2)—one additional deposit was located in an

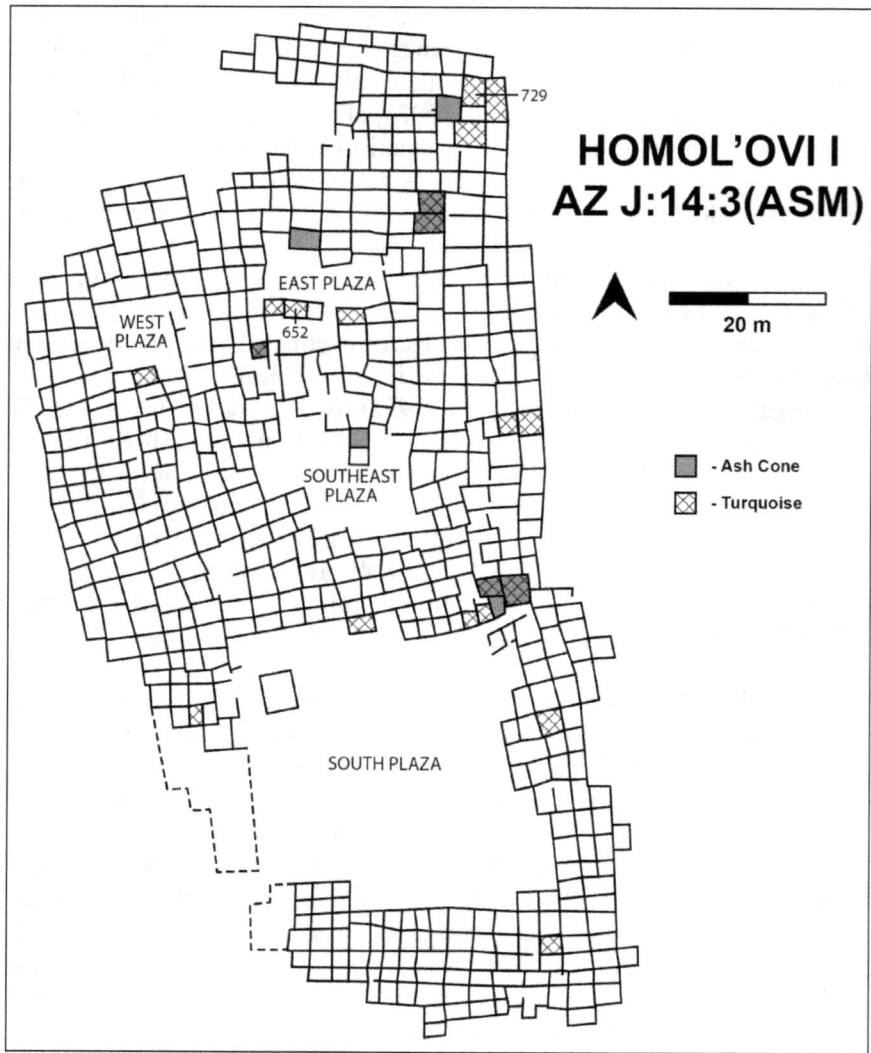

Figure 4.2. *Map of Homol'ovi I showing the location of turquoise, ash cones, and two rooms discussed in detail in the text. Based on maps produced by the Homol'ovi Research Program, Arizona State Museum.*

extramural midden context (Hedquist 2017). Locations of turquoise varied in terms of the types of rooms and deposits, ranging from sealed contexts in clear ritual spaces to offerings found in collapsed roofs of habitation rooms. While turquoise was found in association with three of the four excavated kivas (75 percent), it also occurred in 40 percent of habitation rooms and 45 percent of storage rooms. Of specific interest here, thirty of the forty-seven instances of turquoise or 64 percent were found in deposits containing ash. The ubiquity of their association at the village suggests this pairing was not accidental, instead representing an intentional and accepted relationship between the two materials.

The turquoise that occurred with ash at Homol'ovi I was generally found in cultural deposits within rooms. Previous research at the Homol'ovi Settlement Cluster identified four distinct types of ash deposits, three of which were found in association with turquoise (Adams and Fladd 2017). The most common type of ash deposition within these villages, accounting for 39 percent of the total ash recorded at the site, was in the form of thick and dense ash layers intermixed with large quantities of artifacts. These ashy strata represented over one-third of the turquoise and ash deposits at Homol'ovi I. Deposits of this type were associated with closure practices as they served to quickly bury the room, thus sealing its contents and potentially providing spiritual protection to the spaces and materials as well as later visitors to the village. The second form of ash, discrete pockets, has been linked to possible hearth-cleaning activities, and it accounted for 18 percent of the ash deposits recorded at Homol'ovi I. The only subfloor occurrence of turquoise was located within a deposit characterized by ash pockets. This turquoise may have been placed in a hearth prior to its cleaning or added to the ash as an offering to spiritually sanctify the area for the subsequent construction of the habitation room that it underlay.

The third type of ash deposit noted at the Homol'ovi villages was the ash cone, accounting for 18 percent of the ash deposits at the site. These conical formations were formed through the repeated deposition of materials through a roof hatchway or other opening and often consist of alternating layers of ash with sand and/or clay, which resulted in a distinctive striped pattern being created in the fill. When artifacts were included in these layers, they appeared to be carefully selected, generally consisting of rare or whole objects. An analysis of the types of artifacts located within ash cones at the three largest Homol'ovi Settlement Cluster villages suggests that shared knowledge of the proper creation of these forms crosscut pueblos in the settlement cluster spatially and temporally (Fladd 2018: 214–17). Ash cones themselves were infrequent occurrences, appearing in only ten of the seventy excavated structures (14 percent) at Homol'ovi I (figure 4.2). These distinctive forms were found mainly in spaces tied to male ritual practices, including kivas and ritual rooms. The symbolic associations with these spaces and the links they provide to the spirit world may have required a more complex and measured closure practice. Interestingly, at Homol'ovi I, ash cones also appeared in a habitation structure and a mealing structure, suggesting control over these ritual forms was not entirely restricted to male ritual spaces. In addition to ash, turquoise was found within three of the cones formed in rooms associated with male ritual practices. In these cases, turquoise may have served as an offering to the memories tied to the room, perhaps viewed as an important act to ensure vitality of the associated sodality group by properly acknowledging and honoring its past.

The final type of ash deposition defined for the Homol'ovi Settlement Cluster consisted of discrete ash lenses, which comprised only 6 percent of the total deposits relating to ash and did not occur with turquoise. The remainder of the deposits associated with ash at Homol'ovi I consisted of either ash created through the deliberate burning of structures, ash found within features, or minor deposits of ash intermixed with cultural deposition. These contexts represent the remaining overlap between turquoise and ash within the pueblo.

Two particularly interesting contexts for the convergence of ash and turquoise deserve additional attention. Structure 729 (figure 4.2), which was one of the earliest constructions at the village, was the center of a large ritual complex in the northern portion of the site and may have served as a clan house (Adams 1983, 2002). Nearly 150 tesserae of turquoise were placed into the ashy contents of the hearth on the highest floor level, which was then sealed with a layer of orange clay (figure 4.3). The multiple stages of closure in the hearth were mirrored in the later treatment of the room, which included the burying of the floor through the deposition of cultural materials prior to the structure being dismantled and the roof burned. The placement of turquoise within the ashy deposits in the hearth may have served as an offering to the feature and associated (perhaps former) community members, while also preserving the symbolic significance of the turquoise itself. The decision to later burn this structure suggests that efforts to symbolically seal the space occurred at

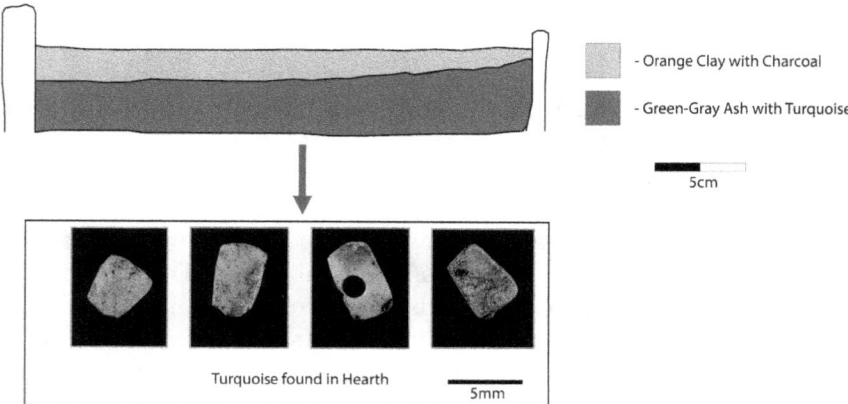

Figure 4.3. *Profile of Structure 729 hearth, and photos of a sample of the associated turquoise. Photos by Saul L. Hedquist.*

multiple levels and involved several discrete but related practices involving the repeated use of ash and burning as well as the singularized deposition of turquoise (see also Hedquist 2016).

Structure 652 (figure 4.2) was a storage room that was razed in order to construct a small, enclosed plaza partway through the occupation of Homol'ovi I. The materials used to fill this structure represent the repeated placement of unique and valuable objects. Five pieces of turquoise tesserae were located within this dense and ashy fill, along with a turtle shell, ladle handle, two projectile points, and a miniature pinch pot (Fladd and Barker 2019). Additionally, a neonate was buried within the fill of the room. The placement of this child altered the later deposits into the room fundamentally, which included the addition of blue-green minerals (Adams 2002: 20; Hedquist 2016: 217). Ash in this context could have been used to purify and symbolically prepare the area in order to construct the overlying plaza. The practices and materials underlying the plaza surfaces may have been spiritually dangerous for later residents, and the ash may have served to neutralize those dangers. Alternatively, the centrality of plazas to katsina religious activities, which arrived at the village partway through occupation, may have necessitated practices to sanctify the area prior to its use by important spirits (see also Fladd et al. 2019).

While turquoise was recovered in a wide variety of contexts at Homol'ovi I, depositional patterns, as well as contemporary Pueblo insights that affirm the material's value, allude to the intentional placement of individual deposits. Furthermore, turquoise was exceedingly rare at Homol'ovi I, and analyses of individual artifacts clearly showed efforts to rework and conserve the material throughout occupation of the village (Hedquist 2016, 2017). As such, the deposition of turquoise, which removed the items from circulation, likely warranted special consideration. Many were likely "sacrificed" as ritual offerings, perhaps to commemorate ancestral locations (sensu Walker 1995a, 1995b).

In reviewing the association of ash and turquoise at Homol'ovi I, M. Koyiyumptewa noted that the ash could serve to purify or protect the sacrificed turquoise. Thus, their association in room closure deposits suggests that the residents of Homol'ovi I used ash to protect and purify both spaces and objects throughout the village. When combined, ash and turquoise served as a particularly potent symbolic offering that evoked protection and renewal through the proper honoring of the past.

Ash and Turquoise throughout the Pueblo World

Our discussion to this point has focused on Hopi symbolism. However, while the nuances and specific meanings differ, the overarching significance of ash and turquoise extend to Pueblo culture more broadly. At Acoma, for example, ashes are used to draw a circle around the kiva prior to the fire society's solstice ceremony. Other members of the pueblo cannot cross this line of ash until it is scraped away by an initiated member of the society (Parsons 1939: 364–65). While its specific place in this ceremony is distinct, ash, when serving to demarcate space and protect individuals, resembles its use in closure practices observed at Homol'ovi I (see also Adams 2016b; Adams and Fladd 2017). Additionally, spirits known as "ash boys" are believed to reside in village middens in Tewa pueblos, and offerings, such as crystals, are regularly made to them (Hays-Gilpin and Ware 2015). These offerings appear to take the form of rare objects and could have included materials such as turquoise as well.

At Zuni, embers are rubbed over the walls to "cleanse" houses and remove troubles during the winter solstice ceremony (Parsons 1939: 464). Ashes also play an important role during the *Itiwana* ceremony, at which time a fire taboo is observed for ten days that restricts the use of hearths and the disposal of ashes. Parsons (1939: 573) summarizes the meaning behind this practice—"As the house is full of ashes so will it be full of corn"—emphasizing the association of ash with renewal and fertility. Turquoise, as a symbol of moisture and vitality, overlaps with the meanings attributed to ashes and hearths in this context. Additionally, hearths at Zuni are closely tied to ancestors, providing a portal through which they can be fed. As such, the placement of turquoise in hearths provides spiritual nourishment while also protecting the place itself (Hedquist 2017: 239). At Rattlesnake Point, an ancestral Zuni community dating to the fourteenth century, a hearth in a habitation room contained a turquoise pendant embedded into the clay foundation of the feature. Additional cultural turquoise—in this case likely malachite—was placed within the fill of the hearth. The recovery of turquoise in these contexts suggests it was used to dedicate and close the feature, possibly indicating a similar symbolic association as is seen at Zuni today (Hedquist 2017: 131). A similar practice may explain the turquoise found in the hearth of Room 729 at Homol'ovi I.

An important component of the significance of these materials is their color. Color symbolism is a central organizing principle, with certain colors associated with specific, albeit different, directions for Pueblo groups. Blue-green and black are two of the most frequently used colors in this system, communicating layered and nuanced meanings to community members (Plog 2003; Riley 1963; Reyman 1971; Stephen 1898). Each color has symbolic associations with cardinal directions, types of beans, males, and specific katsina figures (e.g., Heib 1979: 578; Parsons 1939: 99; Stephen 1898: 260; Stephen 1936: 345). Ornaments and paraphernalia, including mosaics and prayer sticks, frequently incorporate black, blue-green, white, and red in various forms and combinations (e.g., Bunzel 1932; Parsons 1939: 279; Voth 1912). While the nuances of these relationships vary by Pueblo, their aesthetic properties may have also influenced the combination of the often-black ash and blue-green turquoise in the archaeological record. Further consideration of the color of ash, which has been noted as varying at Homol'ovi I (Miljour 2016), found in association with turquoise would provide greater insights into the significance of color symbolism in these contexts.

Discussion and Conclusion

As outlined in this chapter, the intersection of ash and turquoise occurred frequently in deposits throughout Homol'ovi I. The redundancy of their co-occurrence—two-thirds of the turquoise deposits at the site also contain ash—suggests that this association was widely practiced and accepted as an appropriate combination of materials by society. These deposits took a variety of forms indicative of differing degrees of restricted knowledge and social memory. However, they shared a broader symbolic association, speaking to the importance of turquoise as a symbol of moisture and a highly valued material and the role of ash as a transformative and protective substance. The inclusion of ash with turquoise served the dual purpose to protect this highly valued material and enhance its role as an offering to significant spaces, individuals, and memories at Homol'ovi I.

While this chapter has focused explicitly on identifying the link between ash and turquoise using Hopi and Pueblo perspectives, there is reason to believe that the articulation of turquoise and representations of fire, such as ash, was a more widespread phenomenon in the Americas. In Navajo creation mythology, a fire drilled through a turquoise disk is believed to have created the sun, associating fire and turquoise with the beginning of time (Taube 2000: 318). Aztec mythology also links the birthplace of the sun with the "turquoise enclosure" or turquoise hearth (Taube 2000: 309). Turquoise mirrors are used to signify the central hearth and birthplace of the sun, which is often identified with a blue turquoise disk (Taube 2000: 317, 319). Links between the sky, celestial beings, and turquoise are also apparent in Nahuatl, where the same word can be used to mean "turquoise," "meteor," or "year" (Taube 2000: 294).

The physical comingling of ubiquitous ash and singular turquoise in archaeological deposits results in the symbolic convergence of the layered and complex meanings associated with these two materials. In the Pueblo Southwest, these meanings are clearly tied to practices of purification, renewal, and vitality as ensured through proper offerings to ancestors. Beyond the Southwest, associations with mythic origins and the sky are apparent. While we may never fully understand the complexity of these relationships, further research into the co-occurrence of ash, hearths/burning, and turquoise will help to clarify the nuances of these symbols and their meanings both individually and in concert with one another.

Acknowledgments

Funding for this research was generously provided by numerous sources, including the School of Anthropology at the University of Arizona, the Homol'ovi Research Program at the Arizona State Museum, and two National Science Foundation Dissertation Improvement Grants (BCS-1440452 and BCS-1616907). Additionally, this work would not have been possible without the numerous granting agencies (Wenner Gren Foundation, Earthwatch Institute, and the Arizona State Museum) that supported the excavations at the Homol'ovi Settlement Cluster and the numerous scholars, students, and volunteers who participated in the project over the years. It was an honor to start this project with our coauthor and friend, Saul Hedquist. His doctoral work on the Homol'ovi sites was central to the paper's initial conception. While his input on the final version would have undoubtedly improved the quality, we drew extensively from his insights on the topic, and we hope he would be happy with its current form.

Samantha G. Fladd is an assistant professor of anthropology and curator of archaeology at the University of Colorado Boulder. She formerly served as the supervisory archaeologist for the Northern Chaco outliers project at Crow Canyon Archaeological Center. Her research focuses on the articulation of social and spatial organization in the Pueblo Southwest.

Saul L. Hedquist was senior archaeologist and ethnographer with Logan Simpson. He received his PhD from the University of Arizona in 2017. His research integrated provenance studies, depositional analyses, and indigenous collaboration in a groundbreaking analysis of turquoise in the northern Southwest. Hedquist's research interests included Pueblo ethnography, landscape anthropology, and American Southwest archaeology, particularly that of northern Arizona. His work with the Hopi Tribe began in 2010 and continued through multiple projects. Hedquist passed away in November 2018, a huge personal loss for his family, friends, and all who knew him, and a professional loss for the discipline of archaeology.

E. Charles Adams is emeritus curator of archaeology, Arizona State Museum, University of Arizona. Prior to retiring in 2020, Adams taught in the School of Anthropology in addition to being museum curator for thirty-five years. Adams directed a thirty-year research program in the ancestral Hopi villages of Homol'ovi in northeastern Arizona and has solely authored or edited more than a dozen books/monographs describing this research. Adams directed the Walpi Archaeological Project for the Museum of Northern Arizona after receiving his PhD from the University of Colorado, Boulder, in 1975. Work at Walpi involved a transformative collaborative experience with the Hopi First Mesa community and launched his lifelong engagement with Hopi tribal members and the Cultural Preservation Office.

Stewart B. Koyiyumptewa is the program manager for the Hopi Cultural Preservation Office and also serves at the Tribal Historic Preservation Officer for the Hopi Tribe. He has worked for the Hopi Tribe for the past twenty years and has worked on a variety of Cultural Resource projects within the Four Corners region. He is also from the village of Hotevilla and is a member of the Badger Clan.

References

Adams, E. Charles. 1983. "The Architectural Analogue to Hopi Social Organization and Room Use, and Implications for Prehistoric Northern Southwestern Cultures." *American Antiquity* 48: 44–61.

———. 1991. *The Origin and Development of the Pueblo Katsina Cult*. Tucson: University of Arizona Press.

———. 1994. "The Katsina Cult: A Western Pueblo Perspective." In *Kachinas in the Pueblo World*, edited by Polly Schaafsma, 35–46. Albuquerque: University of New Mexico Press.

———. 2002. *Homol'ovi: An Ancient Hopi Settlement Cluster*. Tucson: University of Arizona Press.

———. 2004. "Homol'ovi: A 13th-14th-century Settlement Cluster in Northeastern Arizona." In *The Protohistoric Pueblo World A.D. 1275–1600*, edited by E. Charles Adams and Andrew I. Duff, 119–27. Tucson: University of Arizona Press.

———. 2016b. "Closure and Dedication Practices in the Homol'ovi Settlement Cluster, Northeastern Arizona." *American Antiquity* 81: 42–57.

Adams, E. Charles, ed. 2016a. *Chevelon: Pueblo at Blue Running Water*. Arizona State Museum Archaeological Series 211. Tucson: University of Arizona.

Adams, E. Charles, and Andrew I. Duff, eds. 2004. *The Protohistoric Pueblo World: A.D. 1275–1600*. Tucson: University of Arizona Press.

Adams, E. Charles, and Samantha G. Fladd. 2017. "Composition and Interpretation of Stratified Deposits in Ancestral Hopi Villages at Homol'ovi." *Archaeological and Anthropological Sciences* 9: 1101–14.

Adams, E. Charles, and Vincent M. LaMotta. 2006. "New Perspectives on an Ancient Religion: Katsina Ritual and the Archaeological Record." In *Religion in the Prehispanic Southwest*, edited by C. S. VanPool, T. L. VanPool, and D. A. Phillips Jr., 73–94. Walnut Creek, CA: AltaMira Press.

Barker, Claire S. 2017. "Inconspicuous Identity: Using Everyday Objects to Explore Social Identity within the Homol'ovi Settlement Cluster, A.D. 1260–1400." PhD diss., University of Arizona, Tucson.

Bell, Catherine. 1992. *Ritual Theory; Ritual Practice*. Oxford: Oxford University Press.
Brück, Joanna. 1999. "Ritual and Rationality: Some Problems of Interpretation in European Archaeology." *European Journal of Archaeology* 2: 313–44.
Bunzel, Ruth L. 1932. "Introduction to Zuñi Ceremonialism." In *Forty-Seventh Annual Report of the Bureau of American Ethnology, 1929–1930*, 473–544. Washington, DC: Government Printing Office.
Cutright-Smith, Elisabeth M. 2007. "Modeling Ancestral Hopi Agricultural Landscapes: Applying Ethnography to Archaeological Interpretations." MA thesis, University of Arizona, Tucson.
Cutright–Smith, Elisabeth, and Claire S. Barker. 2016. "Pottery." In *Chevelon: Pueblo at Blue Running Water*, edited by E. Charles Adams, 165–209. Arizona State Museum Archaeological Series 211. Tucson: University of Arizona.
Fewkes, Jesse Walter. 1900. "Tusayan Migration Traditions." In *Annual Report of the Bureau of American Ethnology for the Years 1897–1898*, 573–634. Washington DC: Government Printing Office.
Fladd, Samantha G. 2018. "Access, Accumulation, and Action: Social Identity at Homol'ovi." PhD diss., University of Arizona, Tucson.
Fladd, Samantha G., and Claire S. Barker. 2019. "Miniature in Everything but Meaning: A Contextual Analysis of Miniature Vessels at Homol'ovi I." *American Antiquity* 84: 107–126.
Fladd, Samantha G., Claire S. Barker, E. Charles Adams, Dwight C. Honyouti, and Saul L. Hedquist. 2019. "To and From Hopi: Negotiating Identity through Migration, Coalescence, and Closure at the Homol'ovi Settlement." In *The Continuous Path: Pueblo Movement and the Archaeology of Becoming*, edited by Samuel Duwe and Robert Preucel, 124–46. Tucson: University of Arizona Press.
Fogelin, Lars, ed. 2008. *Religion, Archaeology, and the Material World*. Carbondale, IL: Center for Archaeological Investigations.
Fowles, Severin. 2013. *An Archaeology of Doings: Secularism and the Study of Pueblo Religion*. Santa Fe, NM: School of Advanced Research Press.
Gann, Douglas. 2003. "Spatial Integration: A Space Syntax Analysis of the Villages of the Homol'ovi Cluster." PhD diss., University of Arizona, Tucson.
Hays-Gilpin, Kelley, and John Ware. 2015. "Chaco: The View from Downstream." In *Chaco Revisited: New Research on the Prehistory of Chaco Canyon, New Mexico*, edited by Carrie Heitman and Stephen Plog, 322–45. Tucson: University of Arizona Press.
Hedquist, Saul L. 2016. "Ritual Practice and Exchange in the Late Prehispanic Western Pueblo Region: Insights from the Distribution and Deposition of Turquoise at Homol'ovi I." *Kiva* 82: 209–31.
———. 2017. "A Colorful Past: Turquoise and Social Identity in the Late Prehispanic Western Pueblo Region, A.D. 1275–1400." PhD diss., University of Arizona, Tucson.
Heib, L. A. 1979. "Hopi World View." In *Southwest*, edited by Alfonso Ortiz, 577–80. Handbook of North American Indian, vol. 9, edited by William C. Sturtevant. Washington, DC: Smithsonian Institution Press.
Icove, David J., J. R. Lally, A. J. Vonarx, and E. Charles Adams. 2016. "Modeling Prehistoric Structural Fires at Chevelon Pueblo." In *Chevelon: Pueblo at Blue Running Water*, edited by E. Charles Adams, 105–16. Arizona State Museum Archaeological Series 211. Tucson: University of Arizona.
LaMotta, Vincent M. 2006. "Zooarchaeology and Chronology of Homol'ovi I and Other Pueblo IV Period Sites in the Central Little Colorado River Valley, Northern Arizona." PhD diss., University of Arizona, Tucson.
Leach, Edmund R. 1968. *Pul Eliya: A Village in Ceylon; A Study of Land Tenure and Kinship*. Cambridge: Cambridge University Press.
Lyons, Patrick D. 2001. "Winslow Orange Ware and the Ancestral Hopi Migration Horizon." PhD diss., University of Arizona, Tucson.
———. 2003. *Ancestral Hopi Migrations*. Anthropological Papers of the University of Arizona 68. Tucson: University of Arizona Press.

Mathien, F. Joan. 2001. "The Organization of Turquoise Production and Consumption by the Prehistoric Chacoans." *American Antiquity* 65: 103–18.
Miljour, Heather. 2016. "Homol'ovi I Pueblo: An Examination of Plant Remains within Ash Closure, Renewal, and Dedication Deposits." MA thesis, University of Arizona, Tucson.
Parsons, Elsie Clews. 1939. *Pueblo Indian Religion*. 2 vols. Chicago: University of Chicago Press
Parsons, Elsie Clews, ed. 1936. *Hopi Journal of Alexander M. Stephen*. 2 vols. Columbia University Contributions to Anthropology 23. New York: Columbia University Press.
Plog, Stephen. 2003. "Exploring the Ubiquitous through the Unusual: Color Symbolism in Pueblo Black-on-White Pottery." *American Antiquity* 68: 665–95.
Reyman, J. E. 1971. "Mexican Influence on Southwestern Ceremonialism." PhD diss., Southern Illinois University, Carbondale.
Riley, C. L. 1963. "Color-Direction Symbolism: An Example of Mexican-Southwestern Contacts." *America Indigena* 23: 49–60.
Roth, Barbara J., and Bernard Schriever. 2015. "Pithouse Retirement and Dedication in the Mimbres Mogollon Region of Southwestern New Mexico." *Kiva* 81: 179–200.
Stahl, Ann B. 2008. "Dogs, Pythons, Pots, and Beads: The Dynamics of Shrines and Sacrificial Practices in Banda, Ghana, 1400–1900 CE." In *Memory Work: Archaeologies of Material Practices*, edited by Barbara J. Mills and William H. Walker, 159–86. Santa Fe, NM: School of Advanced Research Press.
Stephen, Alexander M. 1898. "Pigments in Ceremonials of the Hopi." *Archives of the International Folk-lore Association* 1: 260–65.
Taube, Karl. 2000. "The Turquoise Hearth: Fire, Self Sacrifice, and the Central Mexican Cult of War." In *Mesoamerica's Classic Heritage: From Teotihuacan to the Aztecs*, edited by D. Carrasco, L. Jones, and S. Sessions, 269–40. Boulder: University of Colorado Press.
Titiev, Mischa. 1944. *Old Oraibi: A Study of the Hopi Indians of Third Mesa*. Papers of the Peabody Museum of American Anthropology and Ethnology 22. Cambridge, MA: Harvard University.
Van Keuren, Scott, and Christopher I. Roos. 2013. "Geoarchaeological Evidence for Ritual Closure of a Kiva at Fourmile Ruin, Arizona." *Journal of Archaeological Science* 40: 615–25.
Voth, H. R. 1912. *Brief Miscellaneous Hopi Papers*. Anthropological Series XI (2). Chicago: Field Museum of Natural History.
Walker, William H. 1995a. "Ritual Prehistory: A Pueblo Case Study." PhD diss., University of Arizona, Tucson.
———. 1995b. "Ceremonial Trash?" In *Expanding Archaeology*, edited James M. Skibo. William H. Walker, and Axel E. Nielsen, 67–79. Salt Lake City: University of Utah Press.
———. 2008. "Practice and Nonhuman Social Actors: The Afterlife Histories of Witches and Dogs in the American Southwest." In *Memory Work: Archaeologies of Material Practices*, edited by Barbara J. Mills and William H. Walker, 75–91. Santa Fe, NM: School for Advanced Research.
Ware, John A. 2014. *A Pueblo Social History: Kinship, Sodality, and Community in the Northern Southwest*. Santa Fe, NM: School for Advanced Research Press.
Waters, Frank. 1977 [1963]. *Book of the Hopi*. London: Penguin Books.
Whiteley, Peter M. 1998. *Deliberate Acts: Changing Hopi Culture through the Oraibi Split*. Tucson: University of Arizona Press.
———. 2004. "The Southwest "Painterly" Style and Its Cultural Context." In *Totems to Turquoise: Native North American Jewelry Arts of the Northwest and Southwest*, edited by K. Chalker, 148–55. New York: American Museum of Natural History.
———. 2012. "Turquoise and Squash Blossom: A Pueblo Dialogue of the Long Run." In *Turquoise in Mexico and North America: Science, Conservation, Culture, and Collections*, edited by J. C. H. King, Max Carocci, Caroline Cartwright, Colin McEwan, and Rebecca Stacey, 148–54. London: Archetype Publications.

CHAPTER 5

Fire, Ash, and Sanctuary
Pyrotechnology as Protection in the Precolonial Northern Rio Grande

Michael A. Adler

Introduction

As is detailed throughout the chapters in this volume, humans have incorporated ash and other fire-generated materials into a variety of behaviors and associated contexts for millennia. In this chapter I focus on the integration of ash into depositional contexts across the northern Southwest, specifically in Ancestral Pueblo settlements in the northern Rio Grande region. In order to understand the variety of potential reasons for ash use in these prehistoric contexts, I turn first to ethnographic reports of ash use among indigenous groups in the larger Southwest and Great Basin regions to compare and contrast ash use practices. This cross-cultural survey documents that ash and associated fire-generated materials were widely used in ethnographically recorded activities among indigenous groups in the Southwest. I then turn to archaeological data to explore the extensive use of fire, ash, and other pyrotechnic products across indigenous communities in the region. I focus on excavated architectural and mortuary contexts from Pot Creek Pueblo, supplemented with archaeological data from nearby Picuris Pueblo, to detail the temporal and spatial utilization of fire and ash. I argue that these fire-related actions and products are part of a larger set of behaviors addressing transitional and liminal conditions faced by indigenous individuals and social groups in the northern Rio Grande region during pre- and postcolonial time periods. Ash, a material transformed by fire from its original living state to a purified dust, is a substance that serves several purposes among the living, including the shielding of the living and associated "living" spaces from malevolent forces and spirits.

Relatedly, I argue that the act of burning creates a pathway to protection, supporting the successful transition from one lived space to another.

Ethnographic Perspectives on Ash Use in the American Southwest

The American Southwest has one of the richest ethnographic records of indigenous New World societies, having been the focus of anthropological observations since the infancy of social sciences. The focus of most early anthropology was on salvaging cultural information and materials before the then-impending end of indigenous lifeways, providing extensive descriptions of beliefs, rituals, technologies, and architectural contexts. At the same time, early archaeology, particularly that focusing on Ancestral Pueblo contexts, was busy exposing large swaths of uninhabited village contexts in order to detail the cultural historical foundations of native groups across the region.

It would be impossible to summarize the voluminous ethnohistoric literature on ash use by Native American indigenous groups, so I start here with a survey of nine ethnographically recorded groups in the Human Relations Area Files (HRAF) Collection of Ethnography that are part of the sample of groups in the American Southwest (figure 5.1). The purpose of this survey is to assess a sufficiently large sample of groups in the region to narrow down the range of strategies, beliefs, and symbolic behaviors

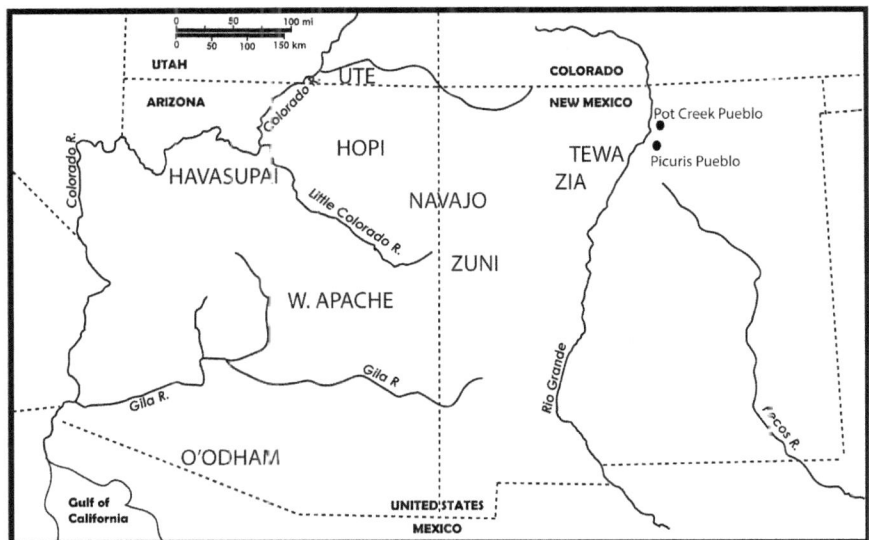

Figure 5.1. *Map of groups and sites. Figure by Michael A. Adler.*

associated with ash use both prior to and after colonization. The HRAF Collection of Ethnography is not encyclopedic in its coverage of all of the pertinent literature for any one region, but I have always found it to be a strong starting point for studying a focal topic like this one.

This is not a statistically meaningful survey for several reasons. First, it is regionally specific to nine cultural groups occupying what is now the southwestern region of the United States, and we are well aware of the contacts, continuities, and interactions between the groups of this area and those from surrounding regions, particularly Plains groups as well as those now living south of the international border with Mexico. As such, it is limited to groups with histories of shared interactions, traditions, and migrations. It is this same nexus of shared traditions, as well as heterogeneity, in ash use that is the focus of this study.

This survey is explicitly not an attempt to find causal linkages between other cultural variables (subsistence practices, household organization, sociopolitical organization, etc.) and the presence/absence of practices involving ash and fire products. A search for explanatory linkages between ash use and cultural variations on a larger, global scale would be interesting, but such a truly cross-cultural study would need to begin with a sample that avoids Galton's problem, one of the oldest critiques in the discipline of anthropology. Following Tylor's famous lecture "On a Method of Investigating the Development of Institutions Applied to Laws of Marriage and Descent" (Tylor 1889), one of anthropology's first cross-cultural studies, Galton pointed out that "full information should be given as to the degree in which the customs of the tribes and races which are compared together are independent. In might be, that some of the tribes had derived them from a common source, so that they were duplicate copies of the same original" (Tylor 1889: 270).

The basic premise of Galton's problem is that meaningful analytical comparisons of the role of a cultural practice should differentiate causal relationships that are due to functional regularities across cultures from those due to historical relationships, often typified as "diffusion." As Naroll (1961) summarized later, Galton's problem is essentially that of "discriminating so-called 'historical' from 'functional' associations in cross-cultural surveys." This perspective assumes that culture should be understood as two parts: one that is historical, unpredictable, and contingent, and the other characterized by regular, predictable functional associations between adaptive human behaviors. This dichotomous perspective that Naroll and others propose as the basis for Galton's problem implies that specific associations between cultural behavioral patterns are either functional, and likely evolutionarily or biologically determined, or they are historical, resulting from contingent, unpredictable interactions such as migration and acculturation. As emphasized by Vermeulen and de

Ruijter (1975), the explanatory nature of these two dichotomous perspectives, one historical, inductive, and contingent, and the other functional, deductive, and generalizing, became even more polarized by philosophers of science such as Popper (1968) who degraded the explanatory nature of inductivist approaches relative to the explanatory strength of nomothetic deductivist perspectives.

My approach here relies intentionally on an inductivist approach because I am interested in the history of certain cultural practices that social groups have used across several centuries to better understand both the continuities and differences in these practices. This approach directly engages the theoretical perspectives of scholars including Ware (2014), Whiteley (2016, 2018), and others arguing for a more robust engagement of sociocultural theory and the rich ethnographic record in the American Southwest. A central argument in Ware's research is that the perceived challenges of relying on ethnographic analogy in archaeology have, over the past fifty years, turned archaeologists away from integrating what we know of the historic societies of the Southwest into archaeological explanations. While the potential problems of strict analogy are well-trodden grounds in archaeological theory, Ware (2014) and others contend that studies integrating the ethnographic record and archaeological perspectives in explanatory partnership are essential. I agree that our inclusion of ethnographic comparative information does not end with simple ethnographic analogies. Instead, the simultaneous consideration of ethnographic and archaeological information allows us to approach the more recent Southwestern societies as ethnological homologies that descend, with modification, from their ancestral foundations. Whiteley, Ware, and others point out that these homologies coexist with substantive heterogeneities, including language differences, variant social organization, and shifts in geographical distribution, population density, and settlement scale over time. Likewise, my interest here is not simply what similarities cohere between the archaeological uses of ash and fire and the ethnographic observations of the same, but also what is different between these contexts and what these heterogeneities might tell us about social changes over the past centuries in the region.

A second reason for cautious use of this cross-cultural sample is the fact that there is no objectively testable way to numerically compare ethnographic descriptions and observations of ash across the entire corpus of ethnographic literature for the Southwest, because the HRAF sample includes only a selection of those publications deemed to be most representative of the ethnographic record for the region. By definition, this sample does not include the entire corpus of oral traditions that have been collected and translated. Neither does it have associated field notes and records that form the basis for these publications. Each case is a qualitative survey that focuses on textual references that include the words "ash" or "ashes" and as such is not a metric of defined behaviors. Ethnographic descriptions may focus on a range of behaviors associated with ash and burned materials, or they might simply address a class of behaviors with no reference to related materials, so there is no strict objective comparability across and between ethnographies.

A final caution rests in the reality that this is a temporally expansive sample of ethnographic information. This means that information from these nine groups in my sample spans many decades, so there may well be some element of cultural "sharing" over time between these groups that could, for example, result in ash-related behaviors shared between groups in the twentieth century that may not have been shared by these groups in the nineteenth century.

In sum, this sample is designed to provide some general empirical information on ash-related practices across a range of social groupings from the American Southwest, generating possible traditions of shared beliefs that may well have historical depth in the region. The sample cannot be used to posit causal relationships between ash use and, for example, belief systems in the region. This is a sample providing inspiration for future research that controls for time, space, subsistence practices, and other variables.

Ethnographic Insights on the Use of Ash

The eHRAF sample of Southwestern and Great Basin cultures contains ethnographic information from thirteen groups, including Eastern Apache, Western Apache, Mescalero Apache, Hopi, Tewa Pueblos, Zuni, Navajo, O'odham, Maricopa, Northern Paiute, Havasupai, Zia, and Ute. Of these thirteen, only nine had sufficient information on ash and fire product use to be included in this study (figure 5.1). As such, the sample includes a wide range of primary subsistence strategies, including foragers, mixed foraging and food-producing groups, and intensive food-producing groups. Settlement strategies range from seasonally mobile groups to sedentary village-based societies. Linguistic diversity includes groups speaking Uto-Aztecan, Kiowa Tanoan, and other language families. Kinship structure is equally diverse.

Within the sample of nine groups, there are a total of 1,207 paragraphs of ethnographic description in 167 publications that mention either ash or ashes, and thousands more that mention fire. Within these ash descriptions, nearly half describe ashes associated with cooking practices and food recipes. I have not included cooking-related references in the sample but instead focus on the other half of the sample. Table 5.1 summarizes the types of practices that include ashes in noncooking behaviors.

Table 5.1. *Summary of the Use of Ashes for Noncooking Practices by Nine Ethnographic Groups.*

	Hopi	Zuni	Navajo	Tewa	O'od-ham	W. Apache	Zia	Ute	Hava-supai
Witchcraft Protection	X	X	X	X	X	X	X	X	
Infant Protection	X	X	X	X	X	X	X	X	
Healing Ceremonies	X	X	X	X	X		X		
Infant Beauty	X	X							
Human Burial			X	X					
War Medicine Protection	X		X						
Scalp Ceremony Protection			X						
Luck in Hunting	X								X
Crop Fertility	X								
Ceremony Completion	X								

There are several commonalities in the ethnographic data, most importantly the roles of ash in protecting from malevolent forces and dangerous situations, curing illnesses, increasing fertility, and performing rituals of purification. These patterns are augmented by ethnographic examples elsewhere in this volume for groups that are not included in the HRAF sample (see Walker and Berryman, chapter 12).

Ash as Protection from Malevolent Spirits

The most important trope in the Southwestern literature is the use of ash as a barrier or prophylactic against both visible and invisible evils applicable across all ages and sexes. Large numbers of descriptions by informants and anthropologists identify ash as a medium transformed by the most purifying of all transformations: fire.

Ash protects against those forces that are not, and may never be, purified. The most common force requiring a protective barrier is the sorcery delivered through witchcraft by those practicing some form of the dark arts. Within this sample, eight of nine cultures utilize ash as a protectant from witchcraft and sorcery. Descriptions include the smearing of ash on faces and bodies to serve as a barrier to the spells and evils wrought by witches and other malevolent spirits. The ashy barrier also commonly symbolizes a cloudy disruptive veil, one that disorients ghosts and hides the innocents from their harmful view and intentions. Those practicing the healing arts commonly utilized ash to place on the bodies of the ill, to rid the area of illness-causing spirits, and to disorient any malevolent spirits in the area with the clouds of ash dispersed by the healers. Ash is also embodied in spiritual beings. Among the Tewa, one of the most benevolent of these is "Ash Youth," a deity that protects the living from some of the dangers of the spiritual world (Ortiz 1969).

Ash, then, can be either a protecting barrier or the potentially dangerous product of removing and burning the items placed or shot into the victim by malevolent witches. One common difference between the use of ash as healing and the destruction of the burned evil items taken from a victim is that the latter often involves the deposition of the evil-laden ash outside of the physical boundaries of the village. Parsons (1929: 225) notes that, among the Tewa,

> ashes of witch-related illness materials, taken from captured "witches," are burned and these ashes are discarded by the curer to the west, outside the village, the direction where all evil is discarded.

Parsons (1939: 424) goes on to detail that

> ashes are everywhere associated with magic or witchcraft, both as a means to magic and in prophylaxis. In the Santa Clara tale of the Witch wife, ashes are thrown into the witch medicine of boiling piñon gum, to make the jars crack and spill out the bad medicine. In curing, at Nambé, what is taken out of the body of the patient, is dropped into a circle of ashes, and then itself reduced to ashes and "blown" away.

Among the most vulnerable to witchcraft are infants and children. The protective use of ash against witchcraft specifically targets the young in eight of the nine cases in the survey. For example, among the Hopi (Beaglehole 1970: 9),

> infants and young children are carefully watched that witches may not work spells over them. . . . extra precautions against sorcery are also taken during the December moon (G ia''mï''ia'', "danger moon"). Ashes and piñon gum are rubbed or stuck on a child's forehead, piñon gum on an adult's, whenever either goes outside the house.

Sanctification of ceremonial contexts and acts commonly involves ash being sprinkled or dispersed by certain ritual implements. During Zuni initiation ceremonies, Stevenson (1904: 561) recorded ritual leaders

> lifting ashes with his plumes, and returning to the altar they sprinkle it with the ashes. Again lifting the ashes, they skip to the outer door, which is on the south side of the room, and throw the ashes out. Gathering more ashes, they throw them to the north of the room, and continue the same operation for the west, south, and east. Returning to the altar, they dance for a while, and then repeat the gathering and sprinkling of ashes toward the four regions; and returning to the outer entrance they repeat the sprinkling. Once more gathering ashes, they place them in a little heap in front of the altar by the food which was deposited previous to the afternoon meal. Each time the ashes are thrown (which is for physical purification) the men exclaim, "Sh-u -u."

The strong association between ash, healing, and witchcraft protection is supported by Jorgenson's (1980) extensive study of Western North American indigenous groups. His research summarizes 292 variables, including ceremonialism, shamanism, and other cultural behaviors across 172 tribal groups. The research includes 32 groups from the Southwestern United States and 20 from the Great Basin region. In his summary of the 52 Southwestern and Great Basin groups, all but three (Cocopa, Yuma, and Mojave), or 94 percent of the groups, identify supernatural sources and/or evil shamans/sorcerers as the source of intrusive foreign objects that cause illness or death. This association stretches far outside of these regions, comprising one of the most commonly shared beliefs across indigenous groups in the Western United States. Thus, the protective role of ash, helping to shield the living from intrusive evil objects and disperse any burned products of these intrusions, is a strong pattern across the western part of the continent.

Ash as Protection from Violence and Warfare

The prophylactic powers of ash also extend from the spiritual violence wrought by witches into the realm of violence between warring groups. Hopi war chiefs would signal the end of battles with outside groups by placing ashes and hair inside a reed arrow and shooting the arrow toward the territory of the enemy or in the direction where the enemy had retreated (Beaglehole 1970: 24). It is not clear whether the hair being shot was from enemy captives or casualties, or whether it came from the Hopi. Given the widespread belief among many Southwestern and Great Basin groups that witches could do damage to the living by taking hair or clothing from their victims, it would be surprising if this protective act involved sending the hair of one's own community.

The protective nature of ash is limited, however, to those contexts controlled and understood by the living. For example, the ash from a ghost's hogan can be fatal to Navajo who are not aware of its origin. Hearth ash disposed of during the Zuni ceremony when the War Gods are being returned to their shrine can be similarly debilitating to those who are not aware of this liminal ceremonial period (Bunzel 1932: 535).

Ash and Funerary Ceremonies

Ash use in contexts involving the transition from the world of the living to that of the ancestors is also part of transitional ceremonies across the indigenous Southwest. Among the Tewa, Ortiz (1969: 54–55) describes the role of ash in sanctifying the home of a deceased member of the community:

> As the lead elder reenters he picks up the hand broom once again, pokes it into the fireplace to get ashes, and blows in an outward motion over the people, and at each of the corners of the house. This final symbolic act is intended to protect the house itself, first by invoking the protection of the *xayeh* (soul-associated objects) which are buried under the floor at each corner of Tewa homes. Secondly, the ashes are intended to invoke the protection of Ash Youth, a benevolent spirit of Category 6, who lives in ashes.

Ash and Good Fortune

Among the Hopi and Havasupai, ash also plays a role in ensuring productivity in both the hunt and agriculture. Beaglehole (1970: 6) states that

> the women and men left behind in the villages might help the hunters to secure good fortune by rubbing ashes from the cooking fires behind their ears after the men left the village and further, by thinking no evil thoughts while the men were away.

Summary: Ethnographic Use of Ash

In sum, ash is a powerful material that can heal, protect, sanctify, and sometimes pollute, depending on the context. Though we must always be cognizant of the pitfalls of ethnographic analogy that can simply overwrite the historic past onto our interpretations of the deep past, the strong commonalities in the ethnographic observations across various groups with a range of linguistic, subsistence, and historical differences bespeak strong symbolic undercurrents in the roles played by ash, fire, and other fire-related materials.

Of the many roles played by ash, two major themes are consistent across Southwestern and Great Basin ethnographic groups. First, ash is an active part of liminal contexts within major transitions. The birth of a child, initiation of new members to social groups, the passage from living to deceased, all commonly involve ash as a protective medium in transitional acts. Ash not only coats the newly born, it also assists with the travels of deceased spirits so that the spirits do not remain among the living.

A second consistent active role for ash is in the healing of those afflicted with a range of maladies. Common within this small HRAF sample, as well as across Jorgenson's (1980) more comprehensive survey, is the association between fire, ash, and the healing of witchcraft victims. While we might easily subsume the healing role of ash within the category of liminal and transitional contexts, the very specific curative powers of ash need special mention. Next, I turn to specific archaeological examples exhibiting patterns of ash use in the northern Rio Grande region over the past several centuries.

Ash in Archaeological Contexts in the Northern Rio Grande Region

There is clearly a large class of behavioral contexts involving important roles for ash in the ethnographic record, but here I focus on two: ash found in mortuary and architectural contexts in the northern Rio Grande region, specifically those in the Taos and Picuris areas. Extensive excavations in Pot Creek Pueblo (figure 5.2) and Picuris Pueblo have, over the past several decades, provided substantial information on both pre- and postcontact village occupations in these two Tiwa communities (Adler 2010; Adler and Dick 1999; Fowles 2004, 2013). Both site occupations exhibit patterns of ash use, burning, and other pyrotechnically related activities that inform on some of the cross-cultural observations in the first part of this chapter.

Ash and Mortuary Contexts in the Northern Rio Grande

Throughout the diversity of human cultures, mortuary activities are intensely transformative and liminal. A wide variety of ceremonies address the final transformation from living to deceased, a journey that often requires the living to provide guidance, protection, and support, all of which can put the living and deceased in harm's way.

Thanks to the recent summaries of mortuary contexts from Pot Creek Pueblo, Catrina Whitley (2009, 2011, 2013) has documented strong patterning in burial contexts in the region during the Valdez Phase (AD 1000–1200) and later the Talpa Phase (AD 1250–1325). My discussions

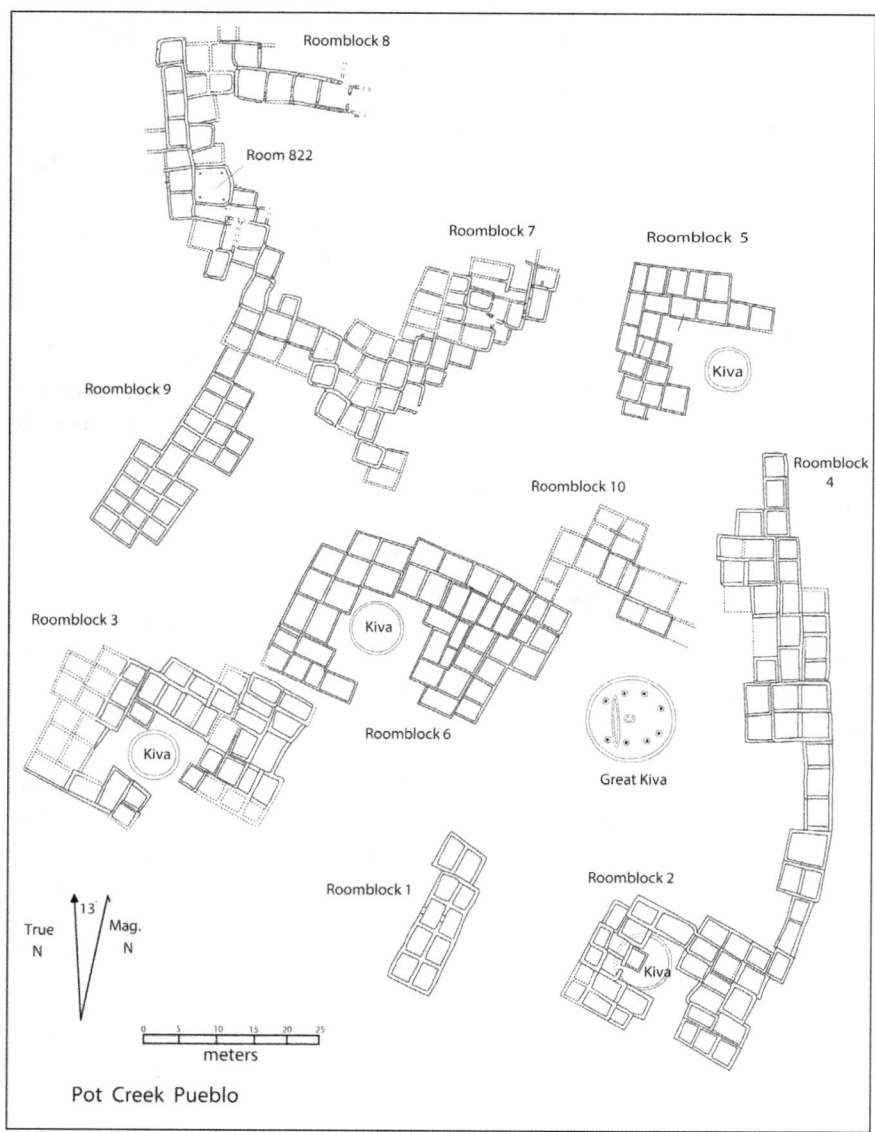

Figure 5.2. *Plan map of Pot Creek Pueblo. Figure by Michael A. Adler.*

here focus primarily on the Talpa Phase burials from Pot Creek Pueblo, the primary source of excavated data from this period. Pot Creek Pueblo's primary occupation was relatively short, between AD 1260–1320 based on over 400 tree-ring dates from across the settlement. At the height of the site occupation in the early fourteenth century, Pot Creek Pueblo contained 350–450 surface rooms spread across ten-room blocks (figure 5.2).

Of the thirty-two burial contexts that Whitley analyzed, twenty-nine were placed in burial pits resting on sterile soil in areas that subsequently were used as middens. The other three burials were in pits dug through existing midden deposits, again resting on sterile soil. The burials were uniformly covered with a coating or layer of ash, and the pit was then filled with a mixture of ash, charcoal, and soil. The use of ash and charcoal is consistent with the protective nature of ash recorded throughout the ethnographic accounts, with a layer of stone slabs and cobbles capping the burial in nearly all excavated examples. The association of the burials and ash with subsequent utilization of the area as a midden location is consistent with ethnographic reports from Taos Pueblo (Parsons 1929) that identifies these middens as "ash piles," which are sacred in their own right as places where things that are "all used up" are placed to return to the earth for later regeneration and reincarnation as living things. As with the descriptions by Ortiz (1969) and others, ash accompanies and protects those entities experiencing the transition from living to deceased.

Kiva Contexts and Ash at Pot Creek Pueblo

A recurrent pattern in Pot Creek Pueblo archaeological contexts is the filling of kiva hearths with ash in association with the disuse of kiva structures. As I have detailed elsewhere, the occupants of Pot Creek Pueblo purposefully decommissioned surface and subsurface architectural spaces at the end of the site occupation around AD 1320 (Adler 2010; Adler forthcoming). Kiva spaces were prepared for decommissioning by placing a variety of stone, antler, and ceramic materials in ventilator shafts and covering the kiva floor with combustible fuels, including tree branches and *Artemisia*. Prior to the burning of the kiva roof, the kiva floor hearth was filled with completely combusted wood ash. This is no small amount of ash, as this and other hearths are up to 0.6 meters (2 feet) deep and 0.6 meters (2 feet) in diameter. In those kivas with good documentation, a clay layer sealed the top of the ash deposit (see Roth, chapter 1, for a similar example from the Mimbres region). The roofing was then set on fire, as indicated by the differential burning in roofing areas across the site.

One example of a burned kiva is located in the plaza of Roomblock 6. The structure has clear evidence of preparation prior to burning. A range of partial and intact artifacts, including whole ceramic vessels, deer antlers, shaped stone balls, and bone awls, were placed in the ventilator shaft of the structure. Several whole projectile points were placed on the floor of the southern half of the kiva. The central hearth was filled with compact white ash, which was then capped with a layer of packed adobe to completely seal the hearth. Placed on the ash pit, a regionally distinctive floor feature appended to the east side of the hearth, were two stacked deer skulls—one facing north, the other facing south. Large chunks of adobe, presumably part of the kiva roofing material, littered the floor in the excavated portion of the kiva, indicating that the roof had been partially dismantled to allow fire spread. Fuel, in the form of sagebrush and small branches, covered the floor. The fire appears to have been purposefully set consuming the western side of the kiva roof and support beams.

The kiva was subsequently filled with over seven feet of finely laminated silt and clay layers, clearly the result of a long period of deposition of aeolian and water-lain sediments that were almost completely devoid of any artifacts. This indicates that the kiva was destroyed and left to fill with little to no postdestruction deposition of trash or other habitation-related debris. In other words, kiva destruction coincided with the disuse of the surrounding surface rooms of Roomblock 6, and perhaps was associated with the termination of the village occupation altogether.

Similar patterns of kiva termination were encountered in three other kivas excavated at Pot Creek Pueblo in Roomblocks 2, 3, and 5. Each of these kivas has similar sets of antler, bone, and stone artifacts left on the floor. Central to the discussion here, each of the kiva hearths was completely filled with white ash and then capped with an adobe seal.

The practice of sealing hearths with ash is one aspect of what I argue to be the use of fire and its products to produce protectant sealants for these structures that are transitioning from living to the afterlife. Subterranean kivas in the northern Rio Grande serve as deep soundings into the underworld, the subsurface home of ancestors, spirits, and ultimately the origin of Pueblo peoples. Kivas in this region are also the houses of the ancestors, structures that carry on the tradition of subterranean housing that precedes the use of surface architecture by hundreds of years in the northern Rio Grande. These portals into the underworld provide access to the spirits and forces of Pueblo forebearers, and they are powerful, liminal spaces used by the living and those that have passed from the present-day world. Hearths are the deepest perforations through the floor of Rio Grande–region kivas, and as such were likely considered to be equivalent to sipapus, spirit portals that serve as providing connections between the underworld and the present world.

Protection of these spiritual access points by filling them with ash and capping deposits ensured that these previously lived and living spaces would not be accessible to those spirits and forces that could despoil spaces that were no longer protected by the village occupants. The possibility that malevolent actors, namely witches, could gain access to these important spiritual places was countered by filling the hearth with the most effective protectant available: ash. After the access points to the underworld were sealed, the Pot Creek Pueblo occupants then burned these structures to rid them of any evil or potential for ingress by those seeking to do harm to the living and the dead. As explained by a Taos Pueblo elder who visited Pot Creek Pueblo when the Mound 6 kiva was under excavation, "a witch getting into a kiva to cast spells will make the living ill, it will make the children not yet born ill, and it will make the ancestors long past ill as well" (identity withheld, 1996). Ash and fire protect the living, the deceased, and those not yet alive.

Exceptions to the Rule: Unburned Kivas at Pot Creek and Picuris Pueblos

The role of burning, paired with the strategic placement of ash in hearth contexts, is strengthened when we add information from Picuris Pueblo. Picuris and Taos Pueblos both have ancestral ties to Pot Creek Pueblo. Archaeological evidence indicates that all three settlements likely had earlier occupations into the eleventh and early twelfth centuries, but all certainly had significant Talpa Phase occupations during the thirteenth and early fourteenth centuries. Pot Creek Pueblo's occupation ended in the early fourteenth century, and Taos and Picuris are both around today and claim ancestral ties to the Pot Creek Pueblo village and surrounding landscape.

We have no excavated kiva contexts from Taos Pueblo, but the work of Herbert Dick in Picuris nearly fifty years ago has provided excavation data from twelve partially or completely excavated kiva contexts. Dick and others (1999) report that eleven of these kivas were unburned, three of which still contained painted murals. The reporting on hearth fill is spotty for the kivas, since several of the kivas at Picuris were trenched but not completely excavated to expose the central hearth. Kiva roofs were either left intact or, in some cases, appear to have been dismantled prior to the filling of the kiva depression through cultural and natural deposition. What's clear, however, is that all of the kiva features were allowed to decompose under the care and protection of the surrounding community, which, apart from a short visit to Cuartelejo in the late seventeenth and early eighteenth centuries, was occupied for the last nine to ten centuries. This practice continues today. Two kivas in use in the 1960s when Dick mapped the entire village are not presently in use. Both have their roof access doors closed and secured with wooden covers and are slowly decomposing under the watchful gaze of community members.

The one Picuris exception to the practice of kiva disuse and decomposition is Kiva D, known to Picuris occupants in the 1960s as the "Cochiti Witch Kiva." Dick was allowed to excavate the Cochiti Witch Kiva, and according to information given to Dan Wolfman and Herbert Dick by Picuris elders, this kiva had been constructed by a person or group from Cochiti Pueblo (Dick et al. 1999). Trouble within the Picuris community, long before the elders were present, led to the departure of the Cochiti person or group and the destruction of the kiva. The archaeological manifestations of the destruction include the plugging of all the wall niches with stones and mud plaster, the sealing of the ash-filled hearth with plaster, a final coat of plaster over the entire kiva wall, and the cleaning of the kiva floor. Only a small cluster of artifacts was left on the floor under an eastern shelf on the wall, and the kiva was burned. This structure was sealed with plaster, ash, and fire to ensure that no access, in or out, would be possible. This most closely approximates the evidence of purposeful sealing and decommissioning of kivas at Pot Creek Pueblo, a practice employed by ancestors of the Taos and Picuris peoples over seven hundred years ago.

One final note about kivas, ash, and exceptions: There are two kivas at Pot Creek Pueblo that are not burned. The first is the unique D-shaped surface kiva, Room 822, a large room with a central hearth and ventilator shaft that fronts a likely plaza and an unexcavated large kiva at the site. Though Room 822 was not burned, Fowles (2004) documented burned offerings in the form of seeds and other agriculturally related materials that were left on the floor on the south side of the structure. Cobbles had been jammed down the ventilator shaft, common to other kivas at the site, and a deer antler was also wedged into the vent shaft. The central hearth had a thick lower layer of consolidated ash. This structure is the only one with human remains at Pot Creek Pueblo, with the remains of a year-old infant missing a cranium. Fowles (2004) attributes the decommissioning of the Room 822 structure to this potential act of violence and proposes that the structure was collapsed in on itself well before the disuse of the surrounding village, though there are no tree-ring dates or other means of establishing when this unique aboveground structure was decommissioned.

In his analysis of the ash in the central hearth of Room 822 at Pot Creek Pueblo, Fowles notes that the predominant species in the thick ash deposit comes from Cottonwood (*Populus spp.*). Cottonwood grows in water-rich environments and was likely to have been far less common than the piñon, juniper, and Ponderosa pine in the uplands around Pot Creek Pueblo. He proposes that the water symbolism of the cottonwood may have been one reason for the choice of this wood. He also notes, however, that cottonwood burns cleanly and produces a pure white ash, the type smeared on Tiwa men during ritual relay, dances, and other public rituals, so its presence in the kivas could have ties to its uses in body decoration as well.

The other unburned kiva is the oversized or "Great Kiva" at Pot Creek Pueblo. According to Wetherington (1968), who excavated this large feature in 1961, the kiva was not completed—he based this on his observation that the central hearth had never been fired, as indicated by a lack of ash and no blackening of the hearth wall.

My explanation for these two features, neither of which were destroyed by fire, is part of a longer discussion involving the decommissioning of Pot Creek Pueblo. The short answer to the differential treatment of these two ritual spaces is that they were part of an architectural tradition brought to Pot Creek Pueblo by migrants, likely from the Tewa Basin to the south, during the latter portion of the Pot Creek occupation. As such, I think that these structures were not decommissioned in ways similar to those described above, which were part of the tradition of feature use and decommissioning associated with the autochthonous occupants of the Taos region for the past two centuries or more.

Conclusions

Ash, charcoal, fire, and the interplay of these forces and materials serve significant roles in many ethnographic descriptions of ceremony, symbolism, belief, and community throughout Southwestern and Great Basin ethnographic groups. The ethnographic survey of groups in the HRAF sample, as well as that by Jorgenson (1980), support two major active roles for ash. First, ash is an active part of liminal contexts within major transitions, including the birth of a child, the initiation of society members, and the journey from the land of the living to that of the ancestors. The symbolic use of a material that has been transformed by fire, one of the strongest sacralizing forces shared across cultures, undergirds the powerful relationships between fire, life, and continuity. A second active role for ash is in the healing of those afflicted with a range of maladies. There is a consistently strong association between fire, ash, and the healing of witchcraft victims.

These more recent anthropological observations inform on and illuminate archaeological contexts that contain ash, charcoal, and the application of fire to living spaces. In the northern Rio Grande, where indigenous Tiwa-speaking community members consider all things, including buildings and kivas, to be alive, there is firm evidence that their ancestors sought to protect these life-endowed places with ash and fire. Kiva hearths are filled with ash as a final act of sealing these important portals into the supernatural underworld. Fire is the final cleansing act that provides eternal protection from the witches and others "of a different breath" (Ortiz 1969), who, throughout the existence of the Pueblo people, have sought to sow evil and harm to others. Ash blanketed the ancestral Tiwa who were interred as a final act of the funerary ritual at Pot Creek Pueblo, protecting their spirits from any possible harm. The ashy veil continues to connect the living and the ancestors across this ancient part of the indigenous world, hopefully shielding those of the past, present, and future from harm and misdeeds.

Michael Adler is associate professor of anthropology at Southern Methodist University and serves as the William P. Clements Endowed Executive Director of the SMU-in-Taos Program. His primary research focus is the complex ancestries of Pueblo communities in the American Southwest, specifically the concepts of ancestry and cultural identity, as well as how communities constitute that complicated concept called "the past." He has also worked with traditional acequia irrigation cooperatives in northern New Mexico to document ancestral land and water use systems. He considers collaborative indigenous archaeology to be an important intellectual legacy that hopefully inspires future generations of scholars.

References

Adler, Michael. 2010. "You're Fired: Abandonment Signatures in Ancestral Pueblo Village Contexts." Paper Presented at the 75th Annual Meeting. St. Louis, MO: Society for American Archaeology.
———. Forthcoming. "Resting the Ancestors: The Life History of an Ancestral Northern Tiwa Community." Monograph draft in possession of the author.
Adler, Michael, and Herbert Dick. 1999. *Picuris Pueblo through Time: Eight Centuries of Change at a Northern Rio Grande Pueblo*. William P. Clements Center for Southwest Studies. Dallas, TX: Southern Methodist University.
Beaglehole, Ernest. 1970. *Hopi Hunting and Ritual*. New Haven, CT: Human Relations Area Files Press.
Bunzel, Ruth L. 1932. "Introduction to Zuni Ceremonialism." *Annual Reports of the American Bureau of Ethnography* 47: 467–544.
Dick, Hebert W., D. Wolfman, C. Schaafsma, and M. Adler. 1999. "Prehistoric and Early Historic Architecture and Ceramics at Picuris." In *Picuris Pueblo through Time: Eight Centuries of Change at a Northern Rio Grande Pueblo*, edited by M. Adler and H. Dick, 43–100. William P. Clements Center for Southwest Studies. Dallas, TX: Southern Methodist University.
Fowles, Severin M. 2004. "The Making of Made People: The Prehistoric Evolution of Hierocracy among the Northern Tiwa of New Mexico." PhD diss., University of Michigan, Ann Arbor.
———. 2013. *An Archaeology of Doings: Secularism and the Study of Pueblo Religion*. Santa Fe, NM: School for Advanced Research Press.
Jorgenson, Joseph. 1980. *Western Indians: Comparative Environments, Languages, and Cultures of 172 Western American Indian Tribes*. San Francisco, CA: Freeman.
Naroll, Raoul. 1961. "Two Solutions to Galton's Problem." *Philosophy of Science* 28: 15–39.
Ortiz, Alfonso. 1969. *The Tewa World: Space, Time, Being and Becoming in a Pueblo Society*. Chicago: University of Chicago Press.
Parsons, Elsie Clews. 1929. *The Social Organization of the Tewa of New Mexico*. Memoirs 36. Washington, DC: American Anthropological Association.
Popper, Karl. 1968. *The Logic of Scientific Discovery*. London: Routledge and Kegan Paul.

Stevenson, Matilda C. 1904. "The Zuni Indians." *Annual Reports of the American Bureau of Ethnography* 23: 13–608.

Tylor, E. B. 1889. "On a Method of Investigating the Development of Institutions: Applied to Laws of Marriage and Descent." *Journal of the Royal Anthropological Institute of Great Britain and Ireland* 18: 245–72.

Vermeulen, C., and A. de Ruijter. 1975. "Dominant Epistemological Presuppositions in the Use of the Cross-Cultural Survey Method (and Comments and Reply)." *Current Anthropology* 16: 29–52.

Ware, John A. 2014. *A Pueblo Social History: Kinship, Sodality, and Community in the Northern Southwest*. Santa Fe, NM: School for Advanced Research Press.

Whiteley, Peter M. 2016. "Dualism and Pluralism in Pueblo Kinship and Ritual Systems." *Structure and Dynamics* 9: 252–72.

———. 2018. "Introduction: Homology and Heterogeneity in Puebloan Social History." In *Puebloan Societies: Homology and Heterogeneity in Time and Space*, edited by Peter M. Whiteley, 1-24. Santa Fe, NM: School for Advanced Research.

Whitley, Catrina Banks. 2009. 'Body Language: An Integrative Approach to the Bioarchaeology and Mortuary Practices of the Taos Valley." PhD diss., Southern Methodist University, Dallas, Texas.

———. 2011. "Ash and Smoke: Classic and Coalition Mortuary Ritual in the Northern Rio Grande." Paper presented at the 76th Annual Meeting. Sacramento, CA: Society for American Archaeology.

———. 2013. "Female Kiva Societies in the Taos Valley: Mortuary and Bioarchaeological Evidence." Paper presented at the 78th Annual Meeting. Sacramento, CA: Society for American Archaeology.

Wetherington, Ronald. 1968. *Excavations at Pot Creek Pueblo*. Publication 6. Taos, NM: Fort Burgwin Research Center.

Wolfman, Daniel. 1962. "Report on Excavations at Picuris Pueblo, 1962 Field Season.' On file, Department of Anthropology, Southern Methodist University, Dallas, TX.

CHAPTER 6

Burned Roofs and Cultural Traditions

Renewing and Closing Houses in the Ancient Villages of the Middle Fraser Canyon, British Columbia

Anna Marie Prentiss, Alysha Edwards, Ashley Hampton, Ethan Ryan, Kathryn Bobolinski, and Emma Vance

Introduction

Archaeologists have long recognized the deep roof deposits associated with housepits in the ancient villages of the Mid-Fraser Canyon, British Columbia (figure 6.1) (Hayden 1997; Prentiss and Kuijt 2012; Stryd 1973). These are complex deposits of burned sediments, artifacts, faunal remains, charcoal, and ash, often considered the consequence of routine burning to eliminate problems associated with wood rot, insect and rodent infestations, and odor of accumulated household refuse (Alexander 2000; Hayden 2000). However, this scenario does not fully explain why houses would be burned upon abandonment when they could be vacated without the extra work of creating and tending a large fire. This raises the possibility that burned roofs in the Mid-Fraser may also be the consequence of a cultural tradition requiring the burning of house roofs at select times, including upon abandonment of the house.

Until recently, we have not had the data to explore in depth such scenarios in the Mid-Fraser context. However, recent excavations at the Bridge River site, a large housepit village in the Mid-Fraser Canyon area, have revealed lengthy multifloor and roof sequences that provide new insight into household histories (Prentiss, Foor, and Hampton 2018; Prentiss, Foor, Hampton, et al. 2018). More specifically, excavations of the deeply stratified Housepit 54 have identified a discontinuous sequence of thin, spatially isolated roof deposits representing localized thermal events capped

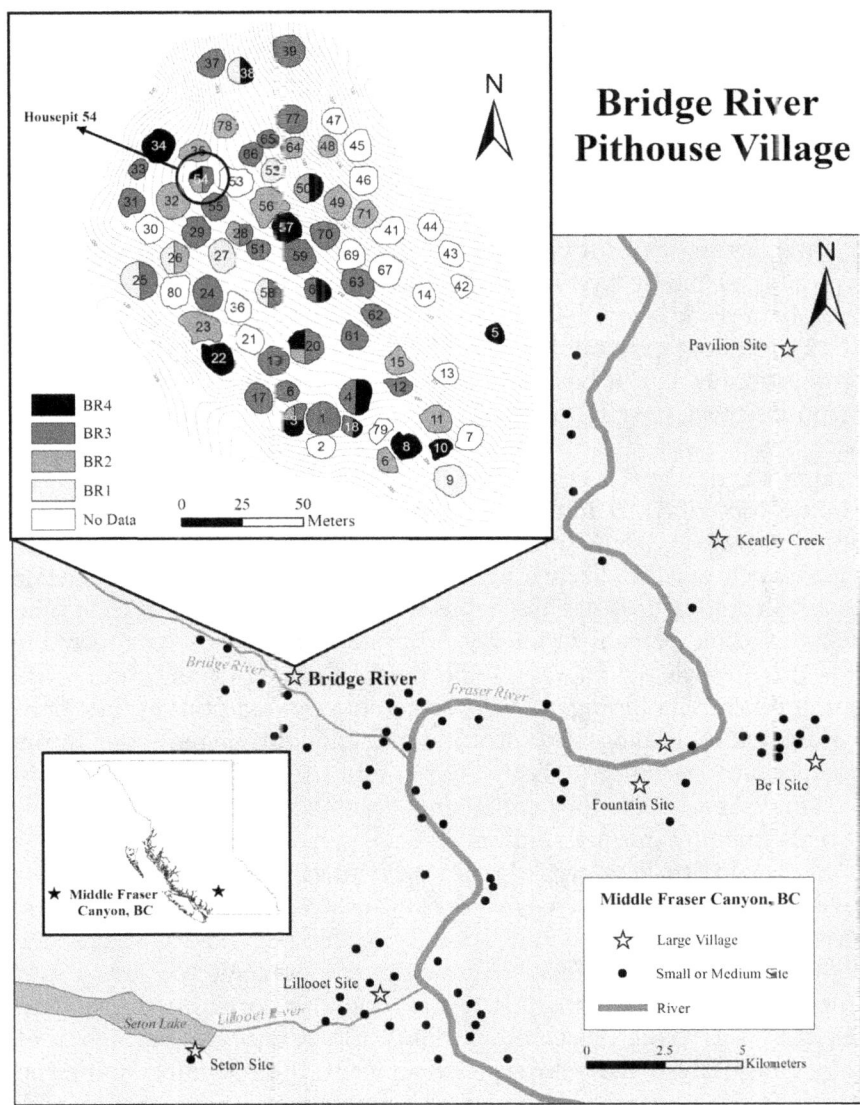

Figure 6.1. *Bridge River site in context. Figure by the authors.*

by later floors. Drawing on multiple data sets, we develop conclusions on the history of (re)roofing at Housepit 54. From there we propose a new model for Mid-Fraser household history suggesting that the burned roof deposits typically found are representative of cultural practices designed to renew and/or close the life of a house, similar to those described by Adams (chapter 2), Adler (chapter 5), and Roth (chapter 1) for the Southwest.

We consider the social implications of this conclusion and reflect on house burning as a ritual tradition in select regions of the globe.

Burned Roofs as Ritual Traditions

We recognize that roofs on Mid-Fraser pithouses were substantial architectural features that included thick support posts and substantial beams, typically covered by layers of vegetation or woven mats and further insulated by a thick layer of sediments (Alexander 2000; Prentiss and Kuijt 2012). Ethnography offers some insight into variability in the practice of disassembly and/or burning of these features. James Teit (1906: 273) mentions the Upper Lillooet (St'át'imc) tradition of burning houses of deceased persons. Teit (1900: 331) notes that lodges of the deceased among the nearby Thompson (Nlaka'pamux) people were also burned. Fire was described to Teit (1906: 283) as "mysterious," and smoke was noted as sacred (Teit 1900: 350; 1906: 250). Indeed, winter pithouses were ritually purified, likely using smudge fires in the spaces where the deceased slept (Teit 1900). Discussions with contemporary elders and other knowledgeable persons in today's St'át'imc communities (conducted by Edwards) reveals the ongoing importance of smudging as cleansing and burning as ritual offering. Specific contemporary traditions include burning food and clothing at cemeteries and smudging living space during occupational transitions. Clearly, the careful use of fire, ash, and smoke remain essential tools for maintaining clean and safe living spaces while also maintaining spiritual traditions.

Archaeologists have argued that roof removal, whether by burning or disassembly, could be seen as a practical process associated with the removal of rotten wood and infestations of vermin (e.g., insects) (Alexander 2000; Hayden 2000). This is affirmed in ethnographic contexts, for example by Laforet and York (1981) who note that concern with insect infestations was so high that among some Nlaka'pamux groups house roofs were disassembled and reconstructed annually. If disassembly and reconstruction was routinely associated with reoccupied houses, then it could make equally good economic sense for people to simply walk away from houses slated for permanent abandonment after salvaging any useful (i.e. not insect-infested) and accessible items (Hayden 2000). The latter did occur sometimes as documented by the Fur Trade floor at Housepit 54, where roof deposits were extensive but unburned and lacking in timbers (Prentiss 2017a). Yet despite these practical considerations, roofs on older houses were routinely burned (Prentiss and Kuijt 2012), which leads us to hypothesize that such burnings might also have served to implement important cultural and even spiritual protocols. Such traditions are recognized in a number of other contexts around the world.

Case studies provide affirmation that house-closing rituals by burning were a routine practice in many contexts particularly associated with village scale aggregations of food-producing peoples. Probably the best-known archaeological record of burned roofs is found in the Early to Middle Neolithic of southeastern Europe (Burdo et al. 2013; Chapman 2000; Souvatzi 2008; Stevancvić 1997, 2002; Tringham 1991, 2000, 2005). Here, house walls were built from mud brick or wattle and daub with wood frame roofs. Fires were apparently kindled with extra fuel and set at floor level before spreading upward through house rafters. This led to orderly but complete collapse of the roof and portions of walls, particularly if the house was constructed from wattle and daub. There is evidence that in some cases houses were filled with artifacts, food items, and, more rarely, collections of human remains prior to burning (Burdo et al. 2013). The origin of this tradition may have its roots in the Neolithic of the nearby Near East, where there is evidence from Çatalhöyük for purposeful and possibly ritual-related incidences of selective house burning (Cessford and Near 2005). Tringham (2005) sees the burning of structures as domicide or a process of "killing" houses but also simultaneously as creating permanent memories, materially manifested in deposits of ash and charcoal, of important places and thus strengthening community identity. Thus, Tringham does not see burning of Neolithic structures as permanent abandonment rituals but rather as activities of groups reaffirming the traditions associated with these long-lived spaces.

There is abundant evidence for the burning of structures in the American Southwest associated with the Anasazi, Mogollon, and Mimbres cultures (Adams, chapter 2; Montgomery 1993; Roth, chapter 1; Schlanger and Wilshusen 1993; Wilshusen 1986). Schlanger and Wilshusen (1993) outline four strategies for the abandonment of houses in the Dolores area of southwest Colorado that include short-distance move with anticipated return, long-distance move with anticipated return, short-distance move with unlikely return, and long-distance move with unlikely return. It is within the latter two contexts that they expect burning to most likely play a role, potentially linked to ritual activities and burial practices. Wilshusen (1986) argues that it is not easy to burn an Anasazi earth-covered structure. Thus, the high frequency of such ruins could indicate a pattern of purposeful engagement with this kind of ritual destruction. Gordillo and Vindrola-Padrós (2017) describe a similar context in the late precolonial archaeological record of northwestern Argentina. Many rooms at the site La Rinconada, filled by burned roof material, also contain abundant fragmentary ceramic vessels, leading the authors to conclude that these items were placed in these positions immediately prior to burning. Diverging from arguments by Wilshusen (1986) and Tringham (2005), they suggest that while burning was indeed ritual in nature, it was more likely associated with the process of symbolic release attached to permanent departure from the site.

As recognized in the interior British Columbia examples, disassembly and burning of old roof superstructures was also accomplished for many practical reasons. Cameron (1991) draws upon ethnographic information to suggest a number of reasons by which structures would be abandoned, including deterioration and decay, change in the function of structures, social and demographic changes, social change, and disease and death (including concerns about ghosts). Pawnee groups made annual decisions whether or not to repair or to disassemble and rebuild an earth lodge given the adverse effects of water from melting snow and rain on house timbers (Weltfish 1965). Siberian groups routinely abandoned and deconstructed pithouses when they were no longer fit for human occupation (Levin and Potapov 1956). Abandonment and reconstruction of houses on the Northwest Coast often occurred in response to demographic and social changes (e.g. Ames 2006; de Laguna 1972; Marshall 2006). Houses were also burned involuntarily as associated with warfare (e.g. Rice and LeBlanc 2001 [and chapters therein]) and accidents (e.g. Bankoff and Winter 1979; LaMotta and Schiffer 1999). Many groups burned the houses of the deceased, including the Navajo (Kent 1984), the St'át'imc (Teit 1906), and the Nlaka'pamux (Teit 1900).

This brief survey of variation in the ethnographic and archaeological records indicates that we should have sufficient grounds to develop frames of reference to recognize variability in the treatment of roof superstructures, particularly as associated with ritual abandonments. We propose five potential scenarios. First, it is obvious that some roofs were cleared without recourse to burning. Within this scenario, we would not expect to find evidence for in situ burning. Wooden architectural elements could be either missing or still in place depending upon whether wood was salvaged during or after abandonment. If roofs were insulated with sediments, then we could expect sediments to have at least partially sloughed back into the house depression. Assuming that abandonment was at least to some degree a planned process, house floor assemblages could be expected to be typically cleared of usable tools and furniture (Stevenson 1982). Second, unintended burning could have occurred as a part of abandonment. Such events might have resulted from accidents or been associated with warfare. However, with earth-covered pithouses, it seems unlikely that either scenario would have been a regular occurrence given the difficulties in burning such structures (Wilshusen 1986). Indicators of accidental or warfare-related burns could include at least partial burning of roof timbers and oxidation of any associated sediments. Burned architectural elements should be present, and given the likelihood of catastrophic abandonment, still-usable artifacts and furniture should remain on floors. Within the warfare scenario, we might also find indicators of conflict in the form of weapons and remains of deceased persons showing signs of violent death. Ash and charcoal in the latter scenario represent little more than reminders of unfortunate events.

The next three scenarios concern intended burning. First, burning could be a practical solution to a variety of problems, including wood rot, vermin infestation, disease, and ghosts. Such scenarios would include indicators of purposeful firing as shown by accumulation of tinder and the clearing of roof sediments (though the same could subsequently slump back into house depressions). In situations where timber rot and insects were of major concern, we could expect some salvaging of any timbers with remaining utility. Where associated with disease and death, salvage of roof timbers would not be likely. Likewise, burnings of houses associated with disease and death would not likely include cleanout of furniture and useable tools. Second, burning could be associated with ritual renewal of a house. If so, we would expect select or total burning of roof timbers or other materials with little evidence for practical engagement in wood salvage for future uses. There could also be evidence for accumulation of tinder prior to the fire. We would expect associated house floors to have been prepared for abandonment at least in the form of removal of still-usable items. Then we would also expect subsequent reoccupation of the house. A final scenario would be burning as a house-closing tradition. Here we would expect preparation for a major fire that might include accumulated tinder and a complete roof-wide burning process leading to a massive accumulation of ash and charcoal. We would expect roof sediments on earthen-roofed housepits to have been swept back, but then to slump into the depression postfire. We cannot preclude the possibility that usable timbers might still have been taken for applications elsewhere. However, the house floor still should have been prepared for abandonment without planned return (i.e. Stevenson 1982), though ritual items could have been placed within the house prior to burning.

The Roofs of Housepit 54, Bridge River Site, British Columbia

The Bridge River site (EeRl4) is one of several large housepit villages in the Mid-Fraser Canyon of southern interior British Columbia (figure 6.1). The large aggregate villages of the Mid-Fraser developed in the centuries after ca. 2000 cal. B.P., reached peak sizes by approximately 1300 cal. B.P., and were largely abandoned at ca. 500–1000 cal. B.P. (Prentiss and Kuijt

2012). They were subsequently reoccupied in the final centuries of the precolonial period with final abandonments of individual houses during the late Fur Trade period of the mid-nineteenth century (Prentiss 2017a, 2017b). Dramatic fluctuations in human populations over the past two thousand years appear to be due to variation in returns on salmon fishing combined with effects of human predation on populations of other keystone resources, particularly deer and geophytes (plants with edible roots) (Prentiss et al. 2014; Prentiss, Foor, and Hampton 2018). Complex social organization developed by ca. 1300 cal. B.P., during which material wealth-based social inequalities emerged and were negotiated in relationship to membership in lineage-like house groups and clans (Prentiss et al. 2012; Prentiss, Foor, and Murphy 2018).

Housepit 54 is one of eighty houses at Bridge River (figure 6.1) and contains the longest fully documented, continuously occupied sequence of floors and associated roofs of any house in the interior Pacific Northwest region. Housepit 54 was excavated in four 4-by-4-meter excavation blocks identified as Blocks A (southwest), B (southeast), C (northwest), and D (northeast) (Prentiss 2017a; Prentiss, Foor, Hampton, et al. 2018). As detailed by Prentiss, Foor, and Hampton (2018), Housepit 54 contains an uninterrupted sequence of fifteen floors with five associated roof deposits dating in the range of ca. 1,100 to 1,460 years ago (figure 6.2). This suggests that on average each floor was occupied for about twenty-four years or a single generation. We designate floor deposits as stratum II and roofs as stratum V. Where there are multiple variants in the stratigraphic sequence, we add additional letter and sometimes number designations. Thus, the floor sequence of interest here is IIa to IIo. Floors IIm to IIo are associated with the earliest variant of Housepit 54, interpreted to represent space for a single family. Floors IIf to IIh reflect a larger (about thirteen-by-five-meter maximum diameters) rectangular house able to hold at least two extended families. Finally, floors IIa to IIe were created after the house expanded to its full thirteen-meter diameter oval shape with space for at least four family groups. Later reoccupation floors (II and IIa1) and roofs (V and Va1) are discussed elsewhere (Prentiss 2017a, 2017b; Prentiss, Foor, and Hampton 2018). Radiocarbon dating places the IIi to IIo floors within the late Bridge River (BR) 2 period (ca. 1300–1450 cal. B.P.) and the IIa to IIh floors in BR 3 (ca. 1100–1300 cal. B.P.). During BR 2 times, occupants created what appears to be a circular arrangement of houses (Prentiss et al. 2008). Late in BR 2 the village was nearly abandoned, likely due to subsistence stresses largely brought on by poor salmon runs (Prentiss et al. 2014; Prentiss, Foor, and Hampton 2018; Prentiss, Foor, and Murphy 2018). However, subsistence conditions subsequently improved and populations spiked upward, and two circular arrangements of houses were constructed during early to mid–

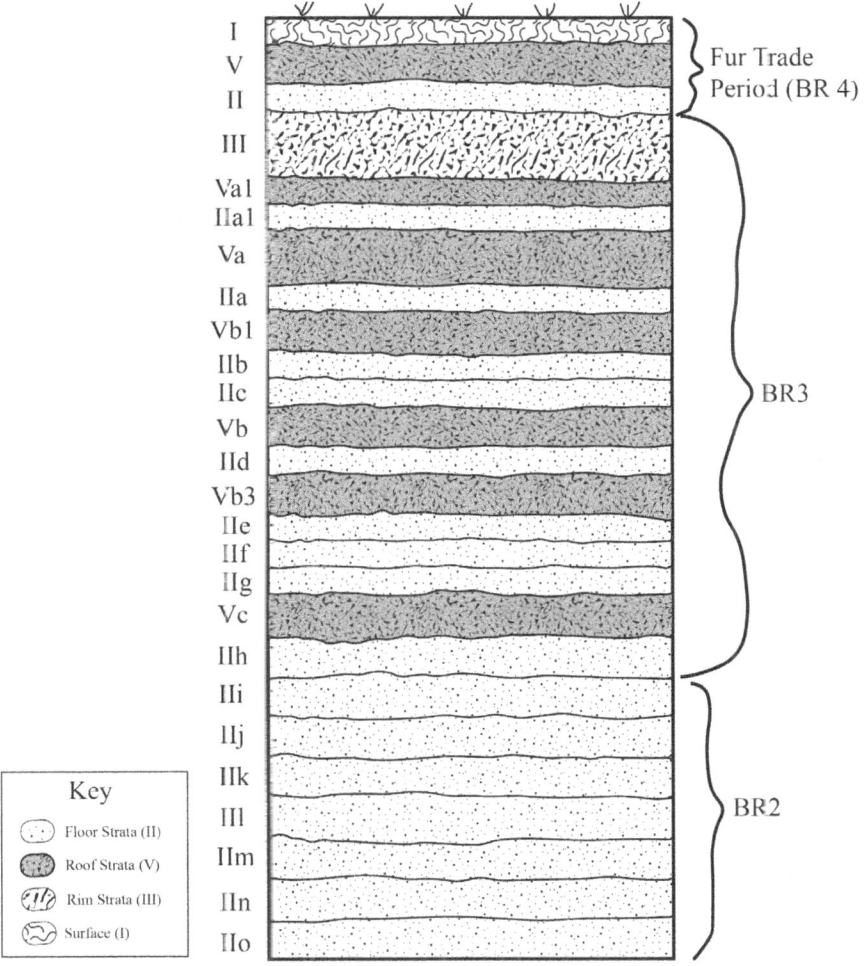

Figure 6.2. *Stratigraphic sequence of Housepit 54 (not to scale). Figure by the authors.*

BR 3 (ca. 1200–1300 cal. B.P.) times (Prentiss et al. 2008; Prentiss and Walsh 2016). Current evidence suggests that material wealth-based social inequality developed on inter- (Prentiss et al. 2012; 2014) and intrahouse (Prentiss, Foor, Hampton, et al. 2018; Prentiss, Foor, and Murphy 2018) bases during peak population in BR 3. The village was abandoned at the end of BR 3, ca. one thousand years ago. Housepit 54 was reoccupied during the British Columbia Fur Trade period (Prentiss 2017b).

The roof sequence associated with the IIa–IIo floors of Housepit 54 consists of five strata termed Va, Vb1, Vb, Vb3, and Vc (figure 6.3). These roofs are associated respectively with floors IIa, IIb, IId, IIe, and IIh, and all show signs of burning in the form of ash and charcoal deposits. Thus, we find at least partial burned roofs on four of the five floors (IIa, IIb, IId, IIe) occupied when the house was at maximum size late in its history, while only one was created and burned in association with one of the rectangular house floors (IIh).

In the following discussion we review evidence for variation in the archaeological manifestations of the Housepit 54 roofs with a focus on spatial extent, depth of strata, content in charcoal and ash reflecting structural elements, color of oxidized sediment (as a marker of burning temperature per Stevanović [1997]), and variation in animal bones. Animal bones were routinely discarded on rooftops during winter occupations and thus were often burned in fires (Williams-Larson et al. 2017). Bones left in situ during burn events are more likely to have been burned to some degree, while those removed from roof contexts are less likely to have been burned. We might also expect variation in bone densities assuming that final roofs could accumulate more bone per unit of sediment due to recycling of roof sediments containing bones discarded during previous occupations compared to roofs of earlier occupations. Higher frequencies of faunal remains would normally also accumulate greater taxonomic diversity (Grayson 1984). In the case of Housepit 54, taxonomic richness (measured as N taxa per roof) strongly correlates with sample size ($r=0.986$, $p=0.002$).

Ratios of burned to unburned lithic debitage derived from roofs did not demonstrate any significant differences to those derived from associated floors. Thus, we did not consider those items sensitive to the effects of burning. We also note at the outset that all associated floors appear to have been prepared for abandonment. It is apparent that no sweeping occurred, as hearth-centered activity areas are evident on each floor and indicated by clusters of faunal remains and lithic artifacts (particularly debitage). Lithic tools recovered from these floors are heavily retouched and often broken. Thus, it appears that tools with possibilities for further use were selectively removed from each floor upon abandonment. One exception is a large grinding stone that was apparently in continuous use from its establishment on floor IId through the close of IIa, a period of about one hundred years. This item likely reinforced social memories across multiple generations.

Stratum Va, associated with floor IIa, is the most extensive roof deposit of the deeper floor sequence. Spatially, it covers nearly the entire excavated area (figure 6.3). The northeast corner of Block A lacks Va deposits because they were apparently removed by excavators from the Fur Trade

Burned Roofs and Cultural Traditions 103

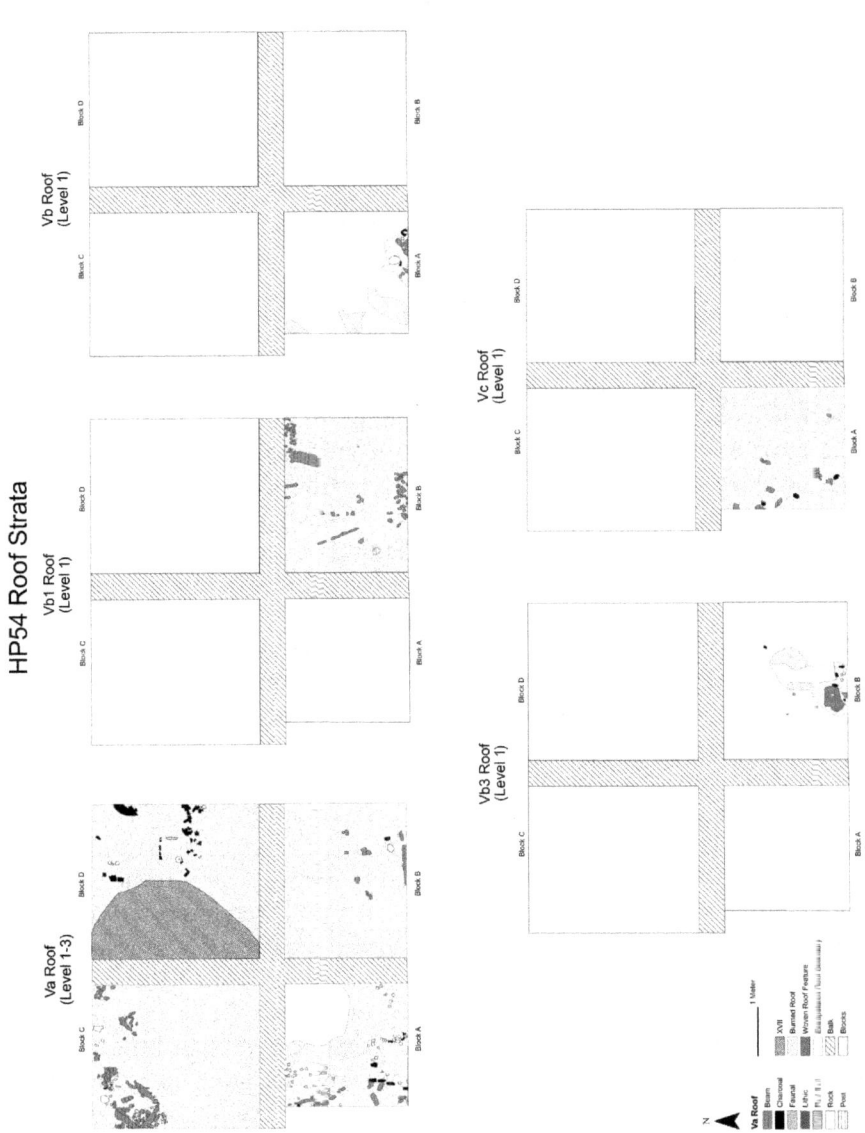

Figure 6.3. *The roof deposits of Housepit 54. Figure by the authors.*

floor (II) during creation of the fire-cracked rock midden in that context (Prentiss 2017a). Stratum Va is also the thickest roof layer in the deep floor sequence, with deposits varying from ten to twenty centimeters in the middle of the floor to over sixty centimeters on some margins, particularly in northwest Block C (Prentiss, Foor, and Hampton 2018; Prentiss, Foor, Hampton, et al. 2018). Burned timbers occur in all blocks but are particularly dense and complexly layered with ash deposits in northwest Block C. Sediment oxidation is present in all blocks and Munsell colors include 7.5YR 5/6 and 10YR 4/4, 4/6, and 5/8. Comparing these outcomes to experimental burning of clays by Stevanović (1997), it would appear that Va burned at temperatures ranging from four or five hundred degrees Celsius, recognized on the west profile of Block A and north profile of Block C, to seven or eight hundred degrees Celsius, registering on the south and east walls respectively of Blocks B and D. A relatively large and dense assemblage of faunal remains was collected from Va contexts (NISP=1284; Richness=8; Density=380 per cubic meter), of which only 21 percent showed evidence for burning. Given that 16 percent of faunal remains (NISP=387) from the associated floor (IIa) are burned, this seems to suggest that the burning occurred in contexts mostly independent of areas that contained disposed faunal remains. Thus, it is likely that insulating roof sediments (containing discarded bones from the floor) were largely removed before the burning event and subsequently slumped back into the house depression after the fire.

Stratum Vb1 is a roof deposit found only in Block B and associated with floor IIb (figure 6.3). Vb1 contains a series of burned timbers oriented approximately perpendicular to the south rim of Housepit 54 and are thus best interpreted as roof beams. There is evidence for one in situ roof post. The deposit is very thin, no more than ten centimeters at the thickest, and consists primarily of charcoal, burned timbers, and thin lenses of ash and oxidized clay. The Munsell color for the oxidized clay on the south wall of Block B is 10YR 5/6 implicating a burning temperature in the seven-to-eight-hundred-degree-Celsius range as compared to results of experiments by Stevanović (1997). All faunal remains (NISP=46) are burned, whereas only 37 percent of those from the associated floor (NISP=1768) are burned. Faunal density is also much lower (92 per cubic meter) than Va, as is taxonomic richness (3). Thus, it is possible that these bones were largely in place during the firing event and can reflect on burning temperature, drawing on data from Gifford-Gonzalez (2018: 321). About 65 percent of bones are brown to red-brown, indicating lower temperature (285–525 degrees Celsius). However, the other 35 percent are blue to white indicating high temperatures (600–1,200 degrees Celsius). This generally confirms projections drawn from soil color that a somewhat variable but in places extremely hot fire took place on Vb1.

Stratum Vb is a sparse roof deposit covering portions of the western and southern sides of Block A (figure 6.3). This is also a thin deposit (less than ten centimeters maximum) made up of four discontiguous patches of charcoal-stained sediment containing a small collection of burned timbers along the south wall of the block. While the collection of timbers likely represents fragmentary roof beams, it is impossible to say anything more about roof architecture from these materials. No oxidized sediment was recognized either on the horizontal surface Block A or on the associated wall profiles. Thus, we are unable to assess burning temperatures from sediment characteristics. The lack of oxidized sediments implies that heat might not have been extreme and that all burning was completed before sediments became associated with collapsed roof materials. As on Vb1, all faunal remains (NISP=32) from Vb are burned, raising the possibility that they were exposed to high heat during the actual burning event. However, only 4 percent of the bones (NISP=2286) from the associated floor (IId) are burned. Degree of burning is relatively similar between the two contexts. Bones from the roof context are entirely white, implying extremely high heat (six to twelve hundred degrees Celsius), while those from the floor context are 94 percent blue or white, similarly implicating high heat. Despite similarities in the degree of burning, the discrepancy between percentages of burned bones in the roof versus floor contexts does seem to imply that bones on the roof must have been largely in place during the burn event. Bone density is higher than other deeper (below Va) roofs (305 per cubic meter), but this may be the result of sampling error given the very low volume of excavated sediments associated with Vb1 (0.105 cubic meters). Nonetheless, it is still well below the numbers evident on Va. Taxonomic richness is very low (2).

Stratum Vb3 is another sparse roof deposit, in this case located in Block B covering floor IIe (figure 6.3). Vb3 materials occur as a thin (average of about five centimeters in thickness) cluster in the south-central portion of the block and include ash, charcoal staining, patchy oxidized sediment, and highly fragmentary burned timbers. One small patch along the south wall of Block B consists of a dense array of burned interwoven twig-sized timbers that may reflect an aspect of roof architecture not previously encountered in the archaeological record. However, as with Vb it is hard to extrapolate anything further regarding roof architecture, and there is no evidence for house posts. The Munsell color of the oxidized sediment is 10YR 5/6, again appearing to represent a very hot fire, potentially in the seven-to-eight-hundred-degree-Celsius range. Faunal remains from Vb3 are present in low densities (seventy-three per cubic meter), with low taxonomic richness (2), and are all burned (NISP=17). In comparison, the faunal remains (NISP=4756) of the associated floor (IIe) are only 2 percent burned. Bone colors from the roof context are dominated by browns

(88 percent), supporting lower temperatures, though an additional 12 percent are white and indicative of high heat. In contrast, 88 percent of burned bones from the IIe floor are blue or white, reflecting impacts of high heat. Distinctions between burned/unburned and variation in degrees of heating combined with low densities appear to imply that bones were largely in place during the roof burn event but that they were embedded in enough sediment as to prevent severe burning.

Stratum Vc is the deepest of the roof deposits in Housepit 54, associated with the IIh floor (Prentiss, Foor, Hampton, et al. 2018) and exclusively found in Block A (figure 6.3). This is another very thin layer (consistently less than ten centimeters maximum thickness) consisting of charcoal- and ash-stained sediment, patchy oxidized clay, and highly fragmentary burned timbers. Given sparse materials, it is impossible to reconstruct roof architecture, and there is no evidence for roof posts. The oxidized sediment has a Munsell reading of 10YR 5/6, suggesting another relatively hot fire. Like the other deep strata roofs, faunal remains from Vc are not taxonomically rich (2), they occur at lower density (182 per cubic meter) as compared to those of Va, and all (NISP=77) are burned. In contrast, those of associated floor IIh (NISP=1660) are largely unburned (93 percent). Similar to Vb3, the large majority of the Vc faunal remains (82 percent) were altered at comparatively low temperatures, whereas 18 percent were burned at high temperatures. Burned faunal remains from the IIh floor are dominated by white and blue (77 percent) with lesser numbers of brown (22 percent) and gray (1 percent). Thus, we conclude that as recognized on other roofs below Va, bones must have been in place on the roof during the burn event but were partially insulated from the highest heat.

In summary, we recognize a distinction between the Va and the deeper roof deposits. The Va roof was apparently insulated with a thick layer of sediments containing large quantities of faunal remains likely deposited by IIa occupants but probably also having accumulated through recycling of sediments used during many earlier generations. The Va roof also appears to have been substantially cleared of those sediments before burning in its entirety at moderate to high temperatures. After the fire, sediments likely slumped and washed back into the basin associated with the burned roof materials. The complexity of roof materials in northwestern Block C also raises the possibility that human groups may have played a role in moving redeposited roof sediments into the house depression. All deeper roofs burned at equally high temperatures with sediments still at least partially in place. Given the spatially limited nature of each of these roof deposits, we suggest that in each case (Vb, Vb1, Vb3, and Vc) only portions of each roof were burned intact, thus implying that the rest of the superstructures and associated sediments were removed before the burning event occurred.

The substantial differences in the treatment of the final (Va) versus older roofs raise the possibility that these events had quite different meanings.

The final roof was more likely an act of closing, in which an entire roof was burned and the house not reoccupied. In contrast, we propose that the burning of all deeper roofs may have been related to renewal where burning was not necessary for closing an old floor or reflooring and building a new roof. Perhaps the smaller-scale burning events marked the close of important generational cycles, with the expectation of new beginnings within the same structural context. The permanent deposition of ash along with charcoal, burned artifacts, and calcined remains thus would have become a sacred residue in much the same way that ash from a smudge is regarded in today's St'át'imc society. It may be significant that these smaller-scale burning events also came at the start of the BR 3 period (IIh floor), and at significant junctures during BR 3 period (closing of nearly all floors [IIe, IId, and IIb] associated with Housepit 54 at full size; the lack of a burned roof over floor IIc is an interesting anomaly).

Discussion

The Housepit 54 sequence provides our first direct insights into variation in roof-related rituals involving ash in the Mid-Fraser context. This in turn offers a number of implications for our understandings of the histories of long- and short-lived houses in the Mid-Fraser. Finally, it lends credence to some prior interpretations of burned house traditions in other regions of the globe.

The roofs on Mid-Fraser pithouses were substantial affairs, with substantial post and beam architecture and typically capped by a layer of sediment acting as insulation against winter cold and summer heat (Alexander 2000; Prentiss and Kuijt 2012). Some form of roof collapse always accompanied the abandonment of houses. We have learned that most though not all final roofs were burned, as was the case with the Housepit 54 Fur Trade period roof (Prentiss 2017a). The history of Housepit 54 suggests that transforming wooden architectural elements to deposits of ash and charcoal could be a marker of renewal and of closure. There are many other long-lived houses at Bridge River, including Housepits 1, 3, 4, 11, 16, 20, 23, and 58 (Prentiss et al. 2008, 2012), and all have substantial final roof deposits. However, there are also many houses with single floors and associated roofs (Housepits 24, 25, and 34 are good examples), implicating shorter occupation spans (Prentiss et al. 2008, 2012). The fact of large-scale burned roofs in short and long-lived houses pre-dating Fur Trade times suggests that regardless of actual longevity, house groups retained a concept of House as a sociopolitical entity (e.g. Lévi-Strauss 1979) that required a formal closing process when the structure was permanently abandoned. To date, we have found only limited evidence of other possible closing or renewal traditions at Bridge River. Our best example comes from Housepit 25, where we found a stack of minimally butchered deer bones lying on a floor and enveloped in burned roof deposits. However, these remains could represent a food-related ritual (e.g. feast or potlatch) held immediately prior to the closing of the house but not specifically part of the abandonment process. Hayden (1997; Crellin and Heffner 2000) found a canid skull placed in the center of the Housepit 7 floor at Keatley Creek, directly buried by burned roof deposits more strongly implying some other form of closing ritual.

The burned roof tradition in the Mid-Fraser has clear similarities to traditions of house burning documented as far back as the Early Neolithic of southeastern Europe. For Mid-Fraser peoples the conversion of wooden roof superstructures to deposits of charcoal and ash no doubt invoked conceptions of cleanliness and safety along with practice of spiritual traditions. This lends credence to Tringham's (2005) thoughts regarding the uses of fire and its byproducts to reify the importance of traditions and places. The placement of animal parts prior to major burns could also affirm processes of spiritual release as suggested by Gordillo and Vindrola-Padrós (2017). While the St'át'imc people of today no longer burn down houses, charcoal and ash remain critical components of many rituals. Smoke from smudge fires purifies, and burned offerings connect people to the spirit world. Thus, archaeologists would do well to consider the role of ash deposits in archaeological contexts as the consequence of important cultural phenomena whether associated with small features or entire burned living structures.

Acknowledgments

The Bridge River Archaeological Project is a collaborative partnership between the University of Montana and Xwísten, the Bridge River Indian Band. We thank Susan James, Bradley Jack, and Gerald Michel. Funding for the Housepit 54 project derives from generous support by the National Endowment for the Humanities (Grants RZ-51287-11 and RZ-230366-1). Any views, findings, conclusions, or recommendations expressed in this article do not necessarily represent those of the National Endowment for the Humanities. We thank Barbara Roth and Chuck Adams for their kind invitation to join such an interesting book project. We thank all students and colleagues who contributed time in the field and lab. Finally, we thank Matt Walsh and the editors for their comments on the manuscript.

Anna Marie Prentiss is regents professor of anthropology at the University of Montana, Missoula. She received her PhD in archaeology at Simon Fraser University in 1993. Her research focuses on the archaeology of fishing, hunting, and gathering peoples on North America's Rocky Mountains, Pacific Northwest, and Western Arctic. Her recent books include *The Last House at Bridge River* (University of Utah Press) and the *Handbook of Evolutionary Research in Archaeology* (Springer).

Alysha Edwards is an undergraduate student in the Department of Anthropology, University of Northern British Columbia. She is also a member of the Ts'kw'aylaxw First Nation. Her interests include archaeology and ethnology of the St'át'imc people (Middle Fraser Canyon area of British Columbia), heritage management, and indigenous archaeology. She has engaged in archaeological research in British Columbia, Canada, and Wyoming, United States.

Ashley Hampton is a doctoral candidate in anthropological archaeology at the Department of Anthropology, University of Montana, Missoula. She holds an MA degree from Florida Atlantic University and is interested in identity, social relations, and economic strategies in household contexts among fishing, hunting, and gathering societies of California and British Columbia. Her doctoral dissertation research focuses on these issues at Housepit 54, Bridge River Site.

Ethan Ryan is a doctoral student in anthropological archaeology at the Department of Anthropology, University of Montana, Missoula. He holds an MA degree in anthropology from the same department. He is an active participant in tribal archaeology in Montana with specializations in GIS, remote sensing, and UAV survey. His interests include hunter-gatherer socioeconomic adaptations and household archaeology in North America's Rocky Mountains, Pacific Northwest, and Western Arctic.

References

Alexander, Diana. 2000. "Pithouses on the Interior Plateau of British Columbia: Ethnographic Evidence and Interpretation of the Keatley Creek Site." In *The Ancient Past of Keatley Creek*. Vol. 2: *Socioeconomy*, edited by Brian Hayden, 29–66. Burnaby, BC: Archaeology Press.

Ames, Kenneth M. 2006. "Thinking about Household Archaeology on the Northwest Coast." In *Household Archaeology on the Northwest Coast*, edited by Elizabeth A. Sobel, D. Anne T. Gahr, and Kenneth M. Ames, 16–36. International Series 16, Ann Arbor: International Monographs in Prehistory.

Bankoff, H. Arthur, and Frederick A. Winter. 1979. "A House-Burning in Serbia: What Do Burned Remains Tell an Archaeologist?" *Archaeology* 32: 8–14.

Burdom, Natalia, Mikhail Videiko, John Chapman, and Bisserka Gaydarska. 2013. "Houses in the Archaeology of the Tripillia-Cucuteni Groups." In *Tracking the Neolithic House in Europe: Sedentism, Architecture, and Practice*, edited by Daniela Hoffman and Jessica Smith, 95–116. New York: Springer.

Cameron, Catherine M. 1991. "Structure Abandonment in Villages." *Archaeological Method and Theory* 3: 155–94.

Cessford, Craig, and Julie Near. 2005. "Fire, Burning, and Pyrotechnology at Çatalhöyük." In *Perspectives: Reports from the 1995–1999 Seasons*, edited by Ian Hodder, 171–82. British Institute at Ankara Monograph 40. Cambridge: McDonald Institute.

Chapman, John. 2000. *Fragmentation in Archaeology: People, Places, and Broken Objects in the Prehistory of South-Eastern Europe*. London: Routledge.

Crellin, David F., and Ty Heffner. 2000. "The Cultural Significance of Domesticated Dogs in Prehistoric Keatley Creek Society." In *The Ancient Past of Keatley Creek*. Vol. 2: *Socioeconomy*, edited by Brian Hayden, 151–64. Burnaby, BC: Archaeology Press.

De Laguna, Frederica. 1972. *Under Mount Saint Elias: The History and Culture of the Yakutat Tlingit, Part One*. Contributions to Anthropology 7. Washington, DC: Smithsonian Institution.

Gordillo, Inés, and Bruno Vindola-Padrós. 2017. "Destruction and Abandonment Practices at La Rinconada, Ambata Valley (Catamarca, Argentina)." *Antiquity* 91: 155–72.

Gifford-Gonzalez, Diane. 2018. *An Introduction to Zooarchaeology*. New York: Springer International Publishing.

Grayson, Donald K. 1984. *Quantitative Zooarchaeology: Topics in the Analysis of Archaeological Faunas*. New York: Academic Press.

Hayden, Brian. 1997. *The Pithouses of Keatley Creek*. Fort Worth, TX: Harcourt Brace College Publishers.

———. 2000. "Site Formation Processes at Keatley Creek." In *The Ancient Past of Keatley Creek*. Vol. 1: *Taphonomy*, edited by Brian Hayden, 299–336. Simon Fraser University, Burnaby: Archaeology Press.

Hayden, Brian, and Aubrey Cannon. 1982. "The Corporate Group as an Archaeological Unit." *Journal of Anthropological Archaeology* 1: 132–58.

Kent, Susan. 1984. *Analyzing Activity Areas: An Ethnoarchaeological Study of the Use of Space*. Albuquerque: University of New Mexico Press.

LaForet, Andrea, and Annie York. 1981. "Notes on the Thompson Winter Dwelling." In *The World Is as Sharp as a Knife: An Anthology in Honour of Wilson Duff*, edited by Donald N. Abbott, 95–104. Victoria: British Columbia Provincial Museum.

LaMotta, Vincent M., and Michael B. Schiffer. 1999. "Formation Processes and House Floor Assemblages." In *The Archaeology of Household Activities*, edited by Penelope M. Allison, 19–29. London: Routledge.

Levin, M. G., and L. P. Potapov. 1956. *The Peoples of Siberia*. Chicago: University of Chicago Press.

Lévi-Strauss, Claude. 1979. "Nobles Sauvages." In *Culture, Science et Développement: Contribution à une histoire d l'homme*. Mélanges en l'honneur de Charles Morazé, edited by Charles Morazé and Raymond Aron, 41–55. Toulouse: Privat.

Marshall, Yvonne. 2006. "Houses and Domestication on the Northwest Coast." In *Household Archaeology on the Northwest Coast*, edited by Elizabeth A. Sobel, D. Ann Trieu Gahr, and Kenneth M. Ames, 37–56. International Monographs in Prehistory Archaeological Series 16. New York: Berghahn Books.

Montgomery, Barbara Klie. 1993. "Ceramic Analysis as a Tool for Discovering Processes of Pueblo Abandonment." In *Abandonment of Settlements and Regions*, edited by Catherine M. Cameron and Steve A. Tomka, 157–64. Cambridge: Cambridge University Press.

Prentiss, Anna Marie. 2017a. "The Archaeology of the Fur Trade Occupation at Housepit 54." In *The Last House at Bridge River: The Archaeology of an Aboriginal Household in British Columbia during the Fur Trade Period*, edited by Anna Marie Prentiss, 42–66. Salt Lake City: University of Utah Press.

Prentiss, Anna Marie, ed. 2017. *The Last House at Bridge River: The Archaeology of an Aboriginal Household in British Columbia during the Fur Trade Period*. Salt Lake City: University of Utah Press.

Prentiss, Anna Marie, Hannah S. Cail, and Lisa M. Smith. 2014. "At the Malthusian Ceiling: Subsistence and Inequality at Bridge River, British Columbia." *Journal of Anthropological Archaeology* 33: 34–48.

Prentiss, Anna Marie, Guy Cross, Thomas A. Foor, Dirk Markle, Mathew Hogan, and David S Clarke. 2008. "Evolution of a Late Prehistoric Winter Village on the Interior Plateau of British Columbia: Geophysical Investigations, Radiocarbon Dating, and Spatial Analysis of the Bridge River Site." *American Antiquity* 73: 59–82.

Prentiss, Anna Marie, Thomas A. Foor, Guy Cross, Lucille E. Harris, and Michael Wanzenried. 2012. "The Cultural Evolution of Material Wealth Based Inequality at Bridge River, British Columbia." *American Antiquity* 77: 542–64.

Prentiss, Anna Marie, Thomas A. Foor, and Ashley Hampton. 2018. "Testing the Malthusian Model: Population and Storage at Housepit 54, Bridge River, British Columbia." *Journal of Archaeological Science: Reports* 18: 535–50.

Prentiss, Anna Marie, Thomas A. Foor, Ashley Hampton, Ethan Ryan, and Matthew J. Walsh. 2018. "The Evolution of Material Wealth-Based Inequality: The Evidence from Housepit 54, Bridge River, British Columbia." *American Antiquity* 83: 598–618.

Prentiss, Anna Marie, Thomas A. Foor, and Mary-Margaret Murphy. 2018. "Testing Hypotheses about Emergent Inequality (Using Gini Coefficients) in a Complex Fisher-Forager Society at the Bridge River Site, British Columbia." In *Ten Thousand Years of Inequality: The Archaeology of Wealth Differences*, edited by Timothy A. Kohler and Michael E. Smith, 96–129. Tucson: University of Arizona Press.

Prentiss, Anna Marie, and Ian Kuijt. 2012. *People of the Middle Fraser Canyon: An Archaeological History*. Vancouver: University of British Columbia Press.

Prentiss, Anna Marie, and Matthew J. Walsh. 2016. "Was There a Neolithic '(R)evolution' in North America's Pacific Northwest Region? Exploring Alternative Models of Socio-Economic and Political Change." In *The Origins of Food Production*, edited by Nuria Sans, 276–91. Paris: World Heritage Papers (HEADS 6) UNESCO.

Rice, Glen E., and Steven A. LeBlanc, eds. 2001. *Deadly Landscapes: Case Studies in Prehistoric Southwestern Warfare*. Salt Lake City: University of Utah Press.

Schlanger, Sarah H., and Richard H. Wilshusen. 1993. "Local Abandonments and Regional Conditions in the North American Southwest." In *Abandonment of Settlements and Regions*, edited by Catherine M. Cameron and Steve A. Tomka, 85–98. Cambridge: Cambridge University Press.

Souvatzi, Stella G. 2008. *A Social Archaeology of Households in Neolithic Greece*. Cambridge: Cambridge University Press.

Stevanović, Mirjana. 1997. "The Age of Clay: The Social Dynamics of House Construction." *Journal of Anthropological Archaeology* 16: 334–95.

———. 2002. "Burned Houses in the Neolithic of Southeast Europe." In *Fire in Archaeology*, edited by D. Gheorghiu, 55–62. Oxford: British Archaeological Reports.

Stevenson, Mark G. 1982. "Toward an Understanding of Site Abandonment Behavior: Evidence from Historic Mining Camps in the Southwest Yukon." *Journal of Anthropological Archaeology* 1: 237–65.

Stryd, Arnoud H. 1973. "The Later Prehistory of the Lillooet Area, British Columbia." PhD diss., University of Calgary.

Teit, James. 1900. *Jesup North Pacific Expedition: The Thompson Indians of British Columbia*. Memoirs I: 63–392. New York: American Museum of Natural History.

———. 1906. *Jesup North Pacific Expedition: The Lillooet Indians*. Memoirs II (V): 93–300. New York: American Museum of Natural History

Tringham, Ruth. 1991. "Households with Faces: The Challenge of Gender in Prehistoric Architectural Remains." In *Engendering Prehistory: Women and Prehistory*, edited by Joan M. Gero and Margaret W. Conkey, 93–131. Oxford: Blackwell.

———. 2000. "The Continuous House: A View from the Deep Past." In *Beyond Kinship: Social and Material Reproduction in House Societies*, edited by Rosemary A. Joyce and Susan D. Gillespie, 115–34. Philadelphia: University of Pennsylvania Press.

———. 2005. "Weaving House Life and Death into Places: A Blueprint for a Hypermedia Narrative." In *(Un)settling the Neolithic*, edited by Douglass Bailey, Alasdair Whittle, and Vicki Cummings, 98–111. Oxford: Oxbow Books.

Weltfish, Gene. 1965. *The Lost Universe: Pawnee Life and Culture*. Lincoln: University of Nebraska Press.

Williams-Larson, Alexandra, Kristen D. Barnett, Pei-Lin Yu, Matthew Schmader, and Anna Marie Prentiss. 2017. "Spatial Analysis of the Fur Trade Floor and Roof at Housepit 54." In *The Last House at Bridge River: The Archaeology of an Aboriginal Household during the Fur Trade Period*, edited by Anna Marie Prentiss, 182–208. Salt Lake City: University of Utah Press.

Wilshusen, Richard H. 1986. "The Relationship between Abandonment Mode and Ritual Use in Pueblo I Anasazi Protokivas." *Journal of Field Archaeology* 13: 245–54.

CHAPTER 7

Agentive Ash and Dispersed Power in the Cahokia Mississippian World

Melissa R. Baltus and Sarah E. Baires

Introduction

Elsewhere (Baltus and Baires 2012) we have described the significance of burning in the context of Cahokian Mississippian religious politics. Specifically, we identified the intentional use of fire as a means of transubstantiating and mitigating the power embodied within places and paraphernalia used in Cahokian politico-religious practices. Additionally, Baltus and Wilson (2019) have enumerated burned buildings in the American Bottom region, demonstrating their increasingly restricted contexts during the formative eleventh-century years of Cahokia. The restricted use of burning as a means of cleansing architectural space becomes more formalized during the twelfth century, a period recognized as the peak of Cahokian political and religious centralization, and returns to a more widespread use following the decentralization of the thirteenth century (Baltus and Wilson 2019). While these studies have focused on the practices of burning, there has been less focus on the deposition of the material remains of these practices, specifically that of ash. As fire has been recognized as a powerful element that was increasingly bundled (sensu Pauketat 2013a) with other materials, spaces, elements, and actions in Cahokian religious-politics, we consider whether ash is likewise recognized as a potent material or is simply a byproduct of a variety of practices. We explore the depositional contexts of ash over the course of history in the American Bottom region to note trends in deposition and consider changing relations between ash, practices of burning, and significant spaces and objects.

Transformation, Vibrancy, and Powerful Deposits

Ethnographically, fire has been documented to be a transformative agent, a powerful force of life (as well as death) (Frazer 1911–15; Grantham 2002; Judson 2000; La Flesche 1995). Archaeologists have discussed the use of fire as an agent of transformation, transubstantiation, and termination of a variety of media, from food to pottery, human bodies to houses (Baltus and Baires 2012; Hall 1997; Tringham 2005). Like fire, smoke is also considered active and agentic. Smoke acts as both messenger (La Flesche 1939; Radin 1970 [1923]) and cleanser or purifier (Grantham 2002).

Given the recognized power and potency of fire and smoke as social agents, it may be the case that other byproducts of fire, especially ash, would likewise be considered agentic or powerful. These materials may be considered "vibrant matter" (Bennett 2010), materials that have some inherent potency (or in this case, potency that emerges from relations between fire, fuel, and air). This vibrant matter has the ability to enliven or transform other objects and elements through relational engagement, for example, through their deposition in a shared context or as part of an assemblage (Deleuze and Guattari 1987). This assemblage, or bundling (after Pauketat 2013a, discussed further below) of vibrant matter, brings forth something new; it is transformative of places and things.

Past discussion of deposition has typically focused on intentionally placed objects and soils or "structured deposits" (see Garrow 2012 for history of the concept). From its initial use, however, the focus of structured deposition has been to identify the symbolic or structural meaning represented by the deposit. Whether deposition results from "ritual" or "everyday" use (if this distinction is necessarily tenable, see Baires and Baltus 2017), recent explorations of the concept take a more relational perspective. In this manner, objects, places, materials emerge as social beings in relation to each other. Agency comes from the relationship between things or, according to Bennett (2010: 117), from the "diverse assemblage energies and bodies." Pauketat (2013a) describes the emerging qualities of Mississippian Cahokia as a process of bundling specific things, practices, bodies, and beings together. In this manner, we describe the assembling or bundling of ash deposits in relation to other features in the American Bottom landscape during the emergence of Cahokia as a city. We consider this process of bundling to include particular substances (material objects in addition to fuel) as well as places (location of burning to location of deposition), temporal events (e.g., building termination, feasting), and social beings (human and other-than). As such, what is bundled is at once similar and never the same—meaning patterns of ash deposition unite similar substances and perhaps cite (and therefore bundle in) prior events and participants but in ever-transforming assemblages.

Case Study

The Native American city of Cahokia, located near modern-day East St. Louis, Illinois, was a locus of intensive political-religious gatherings during the mid-eleventh through mid-fourteenth centuries AD (Dalan et al. 2003; Emerson 1997; Pauketat 2004, 2013a). A population swelling to more than fifty thousand in the wide floodplain of the Mississippi River (known as the American Bottom) was concentrated largely in three precincts that comprise the central administrative complex: St. Louis, East St. Louis, and Cahokia (figure 7.1) (Brennan et al. 2018; Emerson et al. 2018; Pauketat 2004, 2013a; Pauketat and Lopinot 1997). Early coalescence in this administrative complex coincided with the initiation of earthen pyramid construction (Dalan et al. 2003; Schilling 2014) and a wide-scale reorganization of urban and rural space (Emerson 1997). The rural reorganization created hamlets and farmsteads interconnected through ceremonial and administrative "nodal" sites (Emerson 1997) while the urban reorganization followed a "Cahokia Grid" (Fowler 1997). Additional spatial transformations included the creation of public ceremonial spaces near Monks Mound and the Grand Plaza, replacing formerly domestic structures of the Terminal Late Woodland (AD 900–1050) village that originally stood there (Pauketat 2013b). Specialized L-, T-, and circular buildings (small sweat lodges and large rotundas) were embedded into the landscape, both at Cahokia and at outlying "nodal" sites (Emerson 1997) during the early growth of the city (ca. AD 1050), and persisted through the late twelfth century.

During the late twelfth century, a palisade was constructed around the core of "downtown" Cahokia, and a series of storage structures surrounded by walls in the East St. Louis precinct were burned (Iseminger et al 1990; Pauketat 2005). Following this, a broader suite of transformations occurred, including the addition of large clay caps to many mounds, the termination of specialized T-, L-, and circular political-religious buildings, and the replacement of highly iconographic pottery (Ramey Incised) with undecorated jars (Cahokia Cordmarked) and novel plate forms (Wells Incised) (Baltus 2014; Pauketat et al. 2013). Populations at East St Louis and Cahokia proper declined steeply after this point (Emerson et al 2018; Pauketat and Lopinot 1997), though new sites were founded in the floodplain and surrounding uplands, mound construction continued at some of these surrounding sites, and commensal practices increased (Baltus 2014;

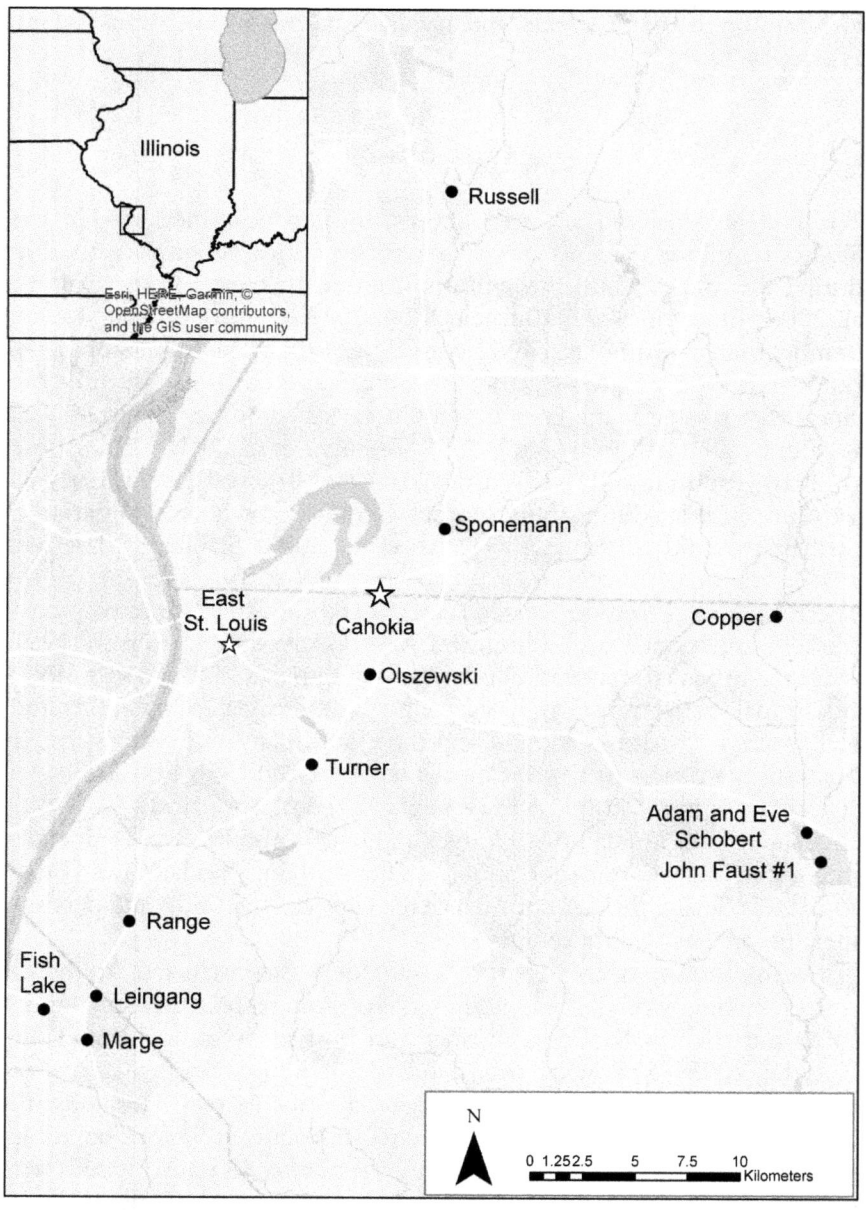

Figure 7.1. *Sites referred to in the chapter. Figure by Melissa R. Baltus and Sarah E. Baires.*

Pauketat 2013b). This thirteenth-century revitalization (see Baltus 2014) included a changed relationship with fire (see Baltus and Baires 2012 and Baltus and Wilson 2019) and, as described below, a changed relationship with ash.

Data Set

The American Bottom region benefits from a plethora of fully or partially excavated sites due to numerous highway-construction-related survey and mitigation projects. Most notable is the FAI-270 project, which yielded extensive data sets ranging from the Archaic period to the post-Cahokian Oneota occupation of the river valley (Bareis and Porter 1984). Additional large-scale CRM and salvage projects, alongside research-driven archaeological excavations, contribute to a broad understanding of patterns of deposition in the American Bottom and eastern uplands (see figure 7.1). By considering the centuries prior to the emergence and expansion of the city of Cahokia, starting with the Late Woodland Period (ca. AD 500–900) and the Terminal Late Woodland (ca. AD 900–1050), we can consider the ways in which the deposition of ash has changed in relation to the dynamics of Cahokia's emergence and the attendant transformations in ontological relations through practices of earthen mound construction, large-scale ceremony, and structured depositional practices.

As demonstrated elsewhere, Cahokians transformed their politico-religious landscape using fire as a transubstantiating element (Baltus and Baires 2012; Baltus and Wilson 2019). Baltus and Baires (2012) establish that Cahokians utilized fire to release or mitigate the power embedded within specific political-religious objects and spaces. Meanwhile, Baltus and Wilson (2019) describe the temporal transformations of building-specific burning practices in the American Bottom region. They show that what was likely a folk practice related to cleansing the landscape of defunct buildings became increasingly concentrated in specific contexts (e.g., politico-religious buildings and mound structures) at Cahokia during the eleventh and twelfth centuries. The burning of buildings was bundled (after Pauketat 2013a) first with offerings of nuts, then corn, then increasingly with deposits or offerings of objects, most often complete or broken stone tools. By the late twelfth and into the thirteenth centuries, practices of engaging fire in the termination of specific buildings differed on the basis of whether the building was completely cleaned out with the addition of a few broken objects, whether a building was completely cleaned with the addition of offerings of complete stone tools, or whether a building was burned with the entirety of its material assemblage included (Baltus and Wilson 2019).

The documented instances of ash deposits in the American Bottom region (using the same data drawn from by Baltus and Wilson [2019]), are notably fewer than those of burned buildings and burned deposits. Those reported, however, demonstrate a similar transformation from seemingly "domestic" or mundane associations to fewer, circumscribed locations from the Late Woodland to the Mississippian periods. These changes in the context of ash deposition are considered here in relation to other transformations taking place within the region, including areas in the eastern uplands. Additionally, we offer possible explanations as to why there are fewer deposits of ash in relation to the amount of burning demonstrated at Cahokia and in the American Bottom region. Our descriptions of ash deposition below reference "deposits," "lenses," and "zones." These terms are roughly interchangeable, though regional parlance tends to use "lens" to describe thinner deposits and "zones" for thicker or larger deposits; we try to use the same terms as the initial reporters. Specific details of ash deposits (including presence of intermixed materials or soils) are described in table 7.1; these data are dependent upon initial reporting and are therefore inconsistent in the amount of detail available. Only features where the presence of ash is clearly described by the initial reporters are included in our analysis.

The Late Woodland period in the American Bottom region is one of maize horticulturalists living in dispersed homesteads to small villages (Fortier and Jackson 2000; Kelly 1990). Hunting and fishing are common, and some sites (e.g., Range) suggest periodic large-scale gatherings (figure 7.1). During the Late Woodland period, ash deposits were present, but not prevalent, in the American Bottom region. There were nine features recorded at four sites that contained depositional lenses or zones of ash (table 7.1). Most of these features consisted of earth ovens or hearth features, the exceptions being a nonstructural post pit that contained an ash zone near the top of its fill and two structures with ash zones or lenses in their fill. The ash recorded in these two structures is interpreted by the initial reporters as secondary deposition (Kelly et al. 1987), while the other features suggest in situ burning with attendant ash.

The subsequent Terminal Late Woodland period continues with larger village occupations by maize farmers with increasing regionalization of pottery production styles (hinging largely on differences in temper type: grit in the northern American Bottom and limestone in the southern American Bottom) (Fortier et al. 2006; Kelly 1990). These material differences demonstrate trends of intervillage gatherings, which likely included ceremonial events (Fortier and McElrath 2002). Platform mounds were constructed at a small number of sites in the region, including Washausen, Pulcher (both sites located some twenty to forty kilometers south of Cahokia), and Morrison (located three kilometers northwest of Cahokia) (Betzenhauser 2011; Betzenhauser et al. 2017; Kelly 1993). Ash deposits were identified in thirty-three features at five sites throughout the American Bottom region (see Table 7.1). The greatest concentration of these are the earth ovens, hearths, and exterior pits at the Range site—a large village that appears to have been a gathering place throughout the Late Woodland and Terminal Late Woodland. In addition to the typical hearths and

Table 7.1. *Features Having Ash Deposits from Sites in the American Bottom.*

Site	Temporal Affiliation	Feature #	Feature type	Context Notes	Additional Notes	Citation
Adam and Eve Schobert site	LW	F145	earth oven	basal zone with charcoal and ash and an upper zone disturbance	deepest LW pit at the site	Holley et al. 2001a
Leingang	LW		interior pit (hearth)	ashy soil over compact fired soil	two fill areas of brown and dark greyish brown ashy fill w/burned clay and charcoal; interior pit re-excavated and used for hearth?	Bentz et al. 1988
Leingang	LW		post pit	Monumental marker post with ash zone near top		Bentz et al. 1988
Range	LW	F4907	structure	ash lens in fill	structure also had dog burial	Kelly et al. 1987
Range	LW		exterior pit (earth oven)	pit with limestone floor, ash fill on portion of floor		Kelly et al. 1987
Range	LW	F1083	hearth	ash lens above oxidized base		Kelly et al. 1987
Fish Lake	LW/TLW	F43	exterior pit	deep outslanted pit with limestone ash lenses	LS used to line pits - indirect cooking	
Fish Lake	LW/TLW	F72	exterior pit	shallow inslanted pit with limestone ash lens	LS used to line pits - indirect cooking	
Sponemann	TLW	F815	earth oven	ash zone recorded in at least one earth oven		Fortier et al. 1991
Range	TLW		structures	five structures with ash lenses on floors of burned structures		Kelly et al. 1987

(continued)

Table 7.1. Continued

Site	Temporal Affiliation	Feature #	Feature type	Context Notes	Additional Notes	Citation
Range	TLW	F2647	structure	thin areas of ash on floor	no oxidation on floor - separate unit of fill deposited post abandonment	Kelly et al. 1987
Range	TLW	F3948	structure	thin areas of ash on floor	no oxidation on floor - separate unit of fill deposited post abandonment	Kelly et al. 1987
Range	TLW	F4844	hearth	three ash zones in multizone pit		Kelly et al. 1987
Range	TLW	F1801	hearth	concentration of charcoal with some ash and limestone slab in fill	pit hearth	Kelly et al. 2007
Range	TLW	F5110	hearth	ashy area in structure with ~70% B burned clay and >100 pieces of burned limestone on oxidized floor	surface hearth in largest structure in occupation area;	Kelly et al. 2007
Range	TLW	F821	hearth	ash lens at base	charcoal, BC, oxidation	Kelly et al. 1990
Range	TLW	F5195	earth oven	ash zones		Kelly et al. 1987
Range	TLW	F3687	earth oven	ash zones		Kelly et al. 1987
Range	TLW	F3800	earth oven	ash zones		Kelly et al. 1987
Range	TLW	F3813	earth oven	ash zones		Kelly et al. 1987
Range	TLW	F4059	earth oven	ash zones	one of four central pits	Kelly et al. 1987
Range	TLW	F4844	earth oven	ash lens	no in situ oxidation or firing of walls/floors	Kelly et al. (#20)

Agentive Ash and Dispersed Power   121

Site	Temporal Affiliation	Feature #	Feature type	Context Notes	Additional Notes	Citation
Range	TLW	F3427	exterior pit	four ash lenses interspersed throughout multizone pit		Kelly et al. 1987
Range	TLW	F36110	exterior pit	ash lens		Kelly et al. 2007
Range	TLW	F1018	exterior pit	ash lens		Kelly et al. 2007
Range	TLW	F1232	exterior pit	ash lens	located in center top and center middle; thin and basket-load-like	Kelly et al. 2007
Range	TLW	F2521	exterior pit	ash lens	located in center top and center middle; thin and basket-load-like	Kelly et al. 2007
Range	TLW	F877	exterior pit	ash lens	located in center top and center middle; thin and basket-load-like	Kelly et al. 2007
Range	TLW	F2335	exterior pit	ash lens	located in center top and center middle; thin and basket-load-like	Kelly et al. 2007
Range	TLW	F2437	exterior pit	ash lens in center to bottom		Kelly et al. 1990
Range	TLW	F4948	exterior pit	ash lens in center to bottom		Kelly et al. 1990
Range	TLW	F4946	exterior pit	ash lens in center to bottom		Kelly et al. 1990
Marge	TLW	F15	exterior pit	two ash zones	ash zones in upper center of pit; upper ash zone heavily laden with animal bone, ash is completely combusted limestone; also three refuse zones and two burned limestone hearth accumulations in pit	Fortier 1996

(continued)

Table 7.1. Continued

Site	Temporal Affiliation	Feature #	Feature type	Context Notes	Additional Notes	Citation
Marge	TLW	F16	exterior pit	ash zones in middle and lower of seven zones		Fortier 1996
Marge	TLW	F17	exterior pit	ash and charcoal zones in center/middle of lower fill		Fortier 1996
Marge	TLW	F61	exterior pit	ash in lower center of pit		Fortier 1996
Cahokia 15B	TLW	F159/172	exterior pit	inner ash zone (F172)	in rectangular belled pit with flat base; lower vegetal fiber lining on floor	Pauketat 2013b
Cahokia 15B	TLW	F161	exterior pit	ash and sand mixture zone and black soil/ash mixture zone		Pauketat 2013b
Cahokia 15B	TLW	F65	exterior pit	3.5 cm thick ash zone at base of pit	rectangular-oval pit with vertical walls and flat floor (possible earth oven)	Pauketat 2013b
East St. Louis/ MRB	TLW		exterior pit	two exterior restricted pits with ash lenses		Brennan et al. 2018
East St. Louis/ MRB	Lohmann	F1071	hearth	hearth with one ash zone	two zones total	Brennan et al. 2018
East St. Louis/ MRB	Lohmann	F0622	Marker post pit	exterior post pit with one ash zone	29 zones total	Brennan et al. 2018
East St. Louis/ MRB	Lohmann	F0455	Marker post pit	exterior post pit with two ash zones	37 zones total	Brennan et al. 2018

Site	Temporal Affiliation	Feature #	Feature type	Context Notes	Additional Notes	Citation
Range	Lohmann	F2770	exterior pit	ash lens in center, middle of deep multizoned pit	largest Mississippian pit feature and one of the largest at site regardless of temporal affiliation; large amount of diversity of material interpreted as a community pit - ceremonial and community activities	Hanenberger et al. 2003
Range	Lohmann	F620	roasting pit	ash in middle-edge of feature	lots of bone, located in large community structure	Hanenberger et al. 2003
Range	Lohmann	F2566	roasting pit	top zone of feature		Hanenberger et al. 2003
Olszewski	Lohmann		earth oven?	deep pit w/burned zone at base with greasy ashy texture	carbonized wood, grass, nuts, maize, squash, red cedar, tobacco	Jackson and Hanenberger 1990
East St. Louis Southside	Lohmann	F418	submound discard deposit	pockets of ash ~2-10 cm thick surrounded by burned zones with charcoal, debris, gumbo	separated from lower soils with fine sand deposit and from above mound by series of fills that are potentially flood deposits (or intentionally laid silts)	Pauketat 2005
Cahokia 15A	Lohmann	F184	exterior pit	upper ash zone		Pauketat 1998
Cahokia 15A	Lohmann	F171	ditch	ash lens in profile	meandering ditch feature	Pauketat 1998
Turner	Lohmann-Stirling	F140	smudge pit	possible lens of ash above burned corn, wood, seeds	ash not described for feature, but suggested by photo	Milner 1983

(continued)

Table 7.1. Continued

Site	Temporal Affiliation	Feature #	Feature type	Context Notes	Additional Notes	Citation
Cahokia Murdock Mound	Lohmann-Stirling	V3	Mound pits	three shallow refuse and ash pits	found during excavation of 15 inches of village loess deposit - above V2 and below V4	Smith 1969
Cahokia Murdock Mound	Stirling	P8	Mound Marker post pit	monumental marker post with ash zone near top	covered only by gumbo fill (mound fill); post on final platform surface; "bathtub pit half filled with ash"	Smith 1969
Cahokia Murdock Mound	Stirling	P8	Mound Ash pit	"enormous rectangular ash pit"	located on final platform surface about 5 feet east of the marker post; ash pit and marker post within enclosure on summit of mound	Smith 1969
Cahokia Kunnemann Mound	Stirling	F85	Mound hearth	white ash base lens with reddish cinder "ash" above	lower two zones of hearth; hearth on floor of F72	Pauketat 1993
Cahokia Kunnemann Mound	Stirling	F110	Mound hearth	thin layer of ash on bottom of hearth fill	directly above red plastered surface; hearth on floor of F74 (rotunda)	Pauketat 1993
Cahokia Kunnemann Mound	Stirling	F117	Mound hearth	1 cm of white ash directly above red plastered surface, lense of ash, charcoal, BC, sherds and bone directly above that	hearth on floor of F74 (rotunda)	Pauketat 1993
Cahokia Kunnemann Mound	Stirling	F92	Mound structure	ashes on floor near F123/F123A hearth feature	F123 had groove around it in square enclosing hearth; structure on mound layer; structure had red plastered floor	Pauketat 1993

Site	Temporal Affiliation	Feature #	Feature type	Context Notes	Additional Notes	Citation
Range	Stirling	F648	hearth	ash lens at base below charcoal laden lens and oxidation on upper walls	interior of circular single post structure F46 (**sweatlodge**)	Hanenberger et al. 2003
John Faust #1 (11S237)	Stirling	F493	hearth	center zone an ash lens with moderate mottles of black silty loam and BC inclusions	three zones total; 55 cm diameter, 6 cm deep; interior hearth of structure F415 in Locale E; structure is **largest domestic structure** in Faust south locality and largest Stirling domestic structure in the project	Holley et al. 2001b
East St. Louis/ MRB	Stirling/ Moorehead	F4422	hearth	hearth with one ash zone	two zones total	Brennan 2018a
Russell	Moorehead	F9	exterior pit	ash zone in center-middle of pit	pit located **near edge of plaza/ courtyard** with four points	Brennan 2018b
Copper	Moorehead	M3	Mound base	2-8 cm thick ash lens mixed with charcoal, silt, deer bone and large pottery sherds	above 1-1.5 cm thick burned material and grey water sorted silts; ash covered by thin (1-2 cm) layer of grey ashy silt, then by packed mottled yellow zone	Baltus 2014
East St. Louis/ MRB	General Mississippian	F4335	hearth	hearth with one ash zone	four zones total	Brennan 2018a

earth ovens where ash was likely a byproduct of in situ burning, we see five structures (all at the Range site) with thin ash deposits on their floors. None of these structures have additional evidence for in situ burning (e.g., oxidized soils), which suggests these deposits of ash were made at or after abandonment of the buildings and before their basins were filled with refuse and soil. Additionally, this is the first time we see lenses of ash layered between soil and refuse zones in exterior pits. This is noted in numerous examples at the Range and Marge sites, with a few pits with ash recorded in the downtown precinct and East St. Louis precinct of Cahokia (see table 7.1, figure 7.1). Some of these zones are the result of completely combusted limestone, a byproduct of hot-rock cooking in earth ovens.

A sudden growth in population in the Cahokia precinct, corresponding with a surge in mound and plaza construction activities, marks the beginning of what is recognized as the early Mississippian period in the American Bottom. During the Lohmann phase (AD 1050–1100), populations coalesced at Cahokia, and the surrounding floodplain was reorganized into isolated farmsteads and nodal sites (Emerson 1997). Public ceremonial facilities (e.g., rotundas and council houses) replaced residential buildings in "downtown" Cahokia. Ash deposits decrease during this period, recorded in just twelve features at five sites throughout the American Bottom region. In addition to deposits in hearths, roasting pits, and a single earth oven, we find ash in new contexts—specifically in former locations of monumental marker posts, submound deposits in the East St. Louis and downtown Cahokia precincts, and an anomalous ditch feature in the downtown Cahokia precinct (see table 7.1). Additionally, a single exterior pit at the Range site contains an ash deposit; this deep multizoned pit was the largest Mississippian pit feature and contained a large amount and diversity of material. This feature was interpreted by the researchers as a community pit utilized for ceremonial activities (Hanenberger et al. 2003). The ash deposition patterns are similar to those of structure burning during the early Mississippian period where burned structures are increasingly incorporated into mound or submound deposits or are found in association with specialized structures.

The Stirling phase (AD 1100–1200) is an era during which numerous mounds were constructed and maintained, the Circle Post Monument (or woodhenge) in downtown Cahokia was built and rebuilt, and other politico-religious structures were built, used, and terminated (sometimes through fire) throughout the region. People moved into and out of the American Bottom, and, during the later twelfth century, a palisade was built around the core of downtown Cahokia, a compound was built to the west of this fortified core, and a wall around a series of storage structures in the East St. Louis precinct was built and burned (Iseminger et al. 1990; Pauketat 2013b; Pauketat et al. 2013).

The number of sites at which ash deposits are found decreases again during the Stirling phase; just eight features at three sites contain ash (see table 7.1). The majority of ash deposits recorded during the Stirling phase were incorporated into mound layers and mound structures. Cahokia's Murdock Mound contained a monumental marker post pit with an ash zone near the top and a large rectangular ash pit on the same mound surface (Smith 1969). The Kunnemann Mound likewise contained a series of hearths on the floors of mound-surface structures, including two hearths on the floor of a rotunda structure and a prepared hearth in a mound-surface structure with a red-plastered floor (Pauketat 1993). Ash zones were recorded in these hearths within these specialized structures and were typically juxtaposed against either red plaster floors below or oxidized deposits above (Pauketat 1993). The three ash-containing features outside of mound contexts dating to the Stirling phase consist of hearths; one is the interior hearth of a circular sweat lodge at the Range site, the second an interior hearth of the largest domestic structure at the upland Faust #1 site, and the third a hearth in the East St. Louis precinct that dates to the Stirling or Moorehead phase (see figure 7.1) (Brennan et al. 2018; Hanenberger et al. 2003; Holley et al. 2001a, 2001b). These patterns of ash deposition during the Stirling phase continue to mirror patterns of structural burning, with a greater concentration associated with specialized structures (L-, T-, circular) and mound-top structures (Baltus and Wilson 2019). With the exception of the single hearth at East St. Louis, which may postdate the Stirling phase, all ash deposits are seemingly related to powerful politico-religious spaces.

The Moorehead phase (AD 1200–1300) typically marks a dramatic change in Cahokian religious-politics (Baltus 2014; Emerson 1997; Pauketat et al. 2013; Trubitt 2000). Population in downtown Cahokia declined, while the East St. Louis precinct was all but depopulated (Brennan et al. 2018; Dalan et al. 2003; Pauketat and Lopinot 1997). Seemingly only minimal mound construction and mound-summit buildings continued through the Moorehead phase in East St. Louis, and large clay caps were added to a number of mounds in the Cahokia precinct, effectively terminating their construction (Dalan et al. 2003; Pauketat 2004). Baltus (2014) refers to the changes we see in the Moorehead phase as part of a Cahokian revitalization movement, including the large-scale termination of specialized politico-religious buildings (L-, T-, and circular structures), the rapid discontinuation of specialized pottery (Ramey Incised), and a renewed focus on feasting events.

Ash deposits during the Moorehead phase are few: a single exterior pit at the upland nodal site of Russell contained an ash zone in the center, and a lens of ash and bone was deposited at the base of a mound at the upland Copper site (see figure 7.1) (Baltus 2014; Brennan 2018). The pit at the Russell site was located near the edge of the site's small plaza and contained four complete projectile points (Brennan 2018). In some ways, this pit shares similarities with the early Mississippian "community pit" at the Range site (discussed above); given its proximity to the plaza and its potential offering of completed stone tools, the ash deposit in the Russell site pit may have been active in community-building, extra-domestic practices. The roughly two- to eight-centimeter-thick ash lens at the base of the Copper mound contained large pottery sherds and animal bone suggestive of commensal activities corresponding with the initial construction of the mound. This ash lens caps an anthropogenic deposit of water-sorted silts and was subsequently capped by packed yellow silt (Baltus 2014). This shares similarities with the Lohmann and Stirling phase burned buildings encapsulated within mound layers, though there is no structural evidence (e.g., wall trenches or posts) for a submound building in the Copper mound.

No ash deposits are recorded for Sand Prairie phase (AD 1300–75) sites in the American Bottom, despite continued practices of structural burning (see Baltus and Wilson 2019). Given the decline of ash deposition during the preceding Moorehead phase, this may indicate a longer-term process in which ash is no longer specially deposited in particular contexts.

Discussion

Practices of burning are notably important during the Mississippian period at and around Cahokia, as documented by the increased number of burned buildings during the Terminal Late Woodland period and the increasingly circumscribed nature of building burning associated with the establishment and growth of Cahokian religious-politics (see Baltus and Wilson 2019). Ash deposits, while present in the American Bottom region, are notably few compared to the number of features with evidence for burning, including burned structures but also hearths, earth ovens, smudge pits, roasting pits, interior and exterior pits, and posts. This disparity between episodes of burning and deposits of ash—the byproduct of burning—will be discussed further below.

The ash deposits that are documented shift in number and context from the Late Woodland through the Mississippian period in the American Bottom, though the number of sites at which ash deposition occurs are few in number throughout (figure 7.2). During the Late Woodland and Terminal Late Woodland, the majority of ash deposits are typically associated with features defined as cooking or heating facilities; ash is therefore considered to be a byproduct of in situ burning practices. At least two features dating to the Late Woodland and 23 features dating to

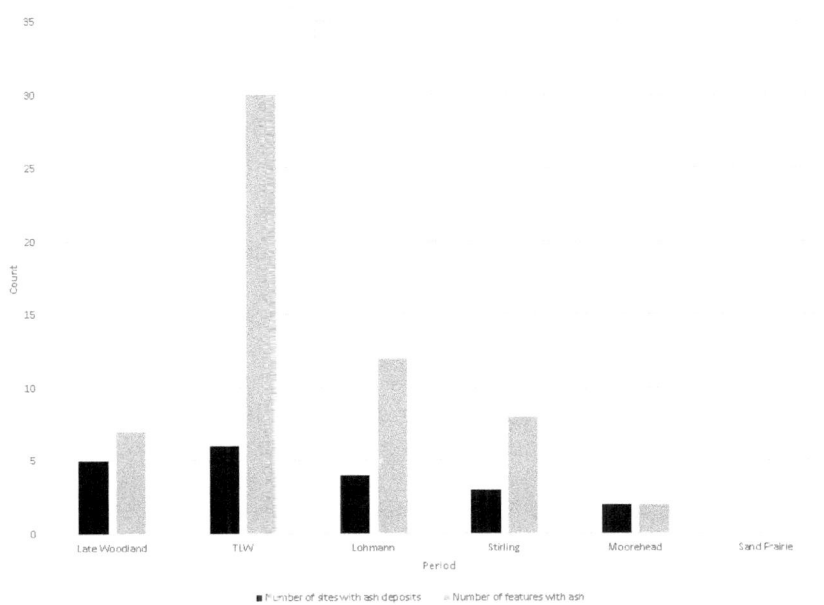

Figure 7.2. *Features with ash deposits. Figure by Melissa R. Baltus and Sarah E. Baires.*

the Terminal Late Woodland period contain lenses of ash that have been deposited as part of the in-filling process of those features. These include ash deposited on the floors of structures, potentially as part of their termination, and what appear to be basket-loads of ash deposited in the center of refuse pits. While the number of features with ash deposits increases dramatically during the Terminal Late Woodland period, the number of sites remains fairly consistent. Considering the importance of intravillage commensality during the Terminal Late Woodland and the likelihood that sites like Range and Marge, which had a number of cooking facilities, were gathering places at which these activities took place, it is possible that the ash deposits at these sites originated in early political-religious burning events. Seemingly, ash takes on a new meaning during the Terminal Late Woodland period, affording more intentional deposits of the material as compared to the preceding Late Woodland.

The associations between burning practices, ash, and specific contexts intensifies during the early Mississippian Lohmann phase. The number of sites at which we find ash deposits declines slightly with the greater number of deposits concentrated in the Cahokia and East St. Louis precincts. Range continues to be an important site on the landscape, but ash deposits are clearly restricted to community features rather than individual residential structures. Ash deposits are increasingly incorporated into early mound deposits and other special features like marker posts or are associated with additional evidence of commensality (large amounts of bone) or ceremony (red cedar, tobacco). The bundling together of ash with increasingly specific political-religious contexts suggests recognition of the potency of this material at specific moments or resulting from particular burning practices.

This restriction intensifies during the subsequent Stirling phase; all ash deposits are found in mound-associated features or in hearths located within specialized architecture. The ash deposits in hearth features are likely the byproduct of in situ burning; however, there is seemingly a significance to leaving the ash in place in these particular buildings rather than cleaning it out (as we see in hearths elsewhere during this time period).

The late Mississippian period in the American Bottom demonstrates a significant decrease in ash deposits; only two features containing ash date to the penultimate Moorehead phase, while no ash deposits have been recorded for the final Sand Prairie phase. The Moorehead phase deposits include a single specialized mound-related context and one basket-loaded deposit in a pit that arguably could have been utilized in extradomestic deposition given its proximity to the plaza and its offering of completed projectile points. Both of these deposits are located at important mound and/or mortuary sites in the uplands outside of Cahokia, demonstrating continuity of practices of isolating ash from specific practices to be bundled with other significant materials or locations. Simultaneously, given the increased importance of commensality (which would logically include large-scale cooking) at and around Cahokia during the thirteenth century, the decrease in ash deposits overall seems surprising.

As noted above, the number of ash deposits in the American Bottom in general seems low compared to the amount of burning documented in the region. There are a number of potential explanations for this overall lack of ash, though many of these suggestions may be difficult if not impossible to demonstrate given the amount of modern disturbance that these sites have endured. Ash is recognized as a fertilizing agent (Guttmann 2005; Hejcman 2011; Woodward 1994). As maize became increasingly utilized in the American Bottom region, people from the Late Woodland through Mississippian period may have gathered the ash from most hearths, roasting pits, and earth ovens to spread in their fields to increase fertility.

Additionally, practices of nixtamalization, or alkali processing of maize, may include the use of hardwood ash or limewater to make the alkali solution (Lovis et al. 2011). Nixtamalization helps release necessary amino acids and other nutrients to make maize a more nutritious food source (Upton et al. 2015). As maize became increasingly important in the diet of people living in the American Bottom, especially before the introduction of the common bean after the fourteenth century (Lovis et al. 2011;

Simon and Parker 2006), the processing of maize may have included the use of burned limestone (which we find in abundance in the region) and ash collected from hearths and other in situ burning.

These seemingly "functional" uses of ash do not preclude their relational "vibrancy" however. If burning was considered a powerful transformative, renewing, and potentially life-giving process, then the products of that burning—namely ash—may be considered imbued with that same power. Ash bundled together with soil, water, and corn in varying manners may likewise be considered transformative, life-giving, or renewing through fertilizing fields and making maize.

Conclusion

The shift from ash deposits largely in the context of in situ burning in hearths and earth ovens to specialized and restricted spaces like mounds and political-religious buildings certainly suggests a shift in significance associated with this material over the course of the Mississippian period in the American Bottom. The bundling of ash—a byproduct of burning—with mound layers and important buildings is similar to the larger pattern of burned buildings in the region. This similarity in patterns of deposition suggest (1) that the ash deposits reported for features dating to the Mississippian period are likely intentional; (2) that ash is considered to be a significant—or "vibrant"—material given its associations with the transformative power of fire; and (3) the decreased number of features containing ash deposits throughout the course of the Mississippian period indicate the use of ash in other practices, though this does not necessarily indicate the decreased potency of ash as a transformative agent.

Melissa Baltus is an assistant professor of anthropology at the University of Toledo. Her research focuses on processes of urbanization and deurbanization in the context of the Native North American city of Cahokia. She studies how social-political change and community-identity transformations are embedded within the practices and choices of daily life. Baltus has authored or coauthored various book chapters and articles on ritualized practices of burning and deposition, as well as mound and nonmound architecture, and Mississippian warfare.

Sarah Baires is an assistant professor of anthropology at Eastern Connecticut State University. Her research focuses on the emergence of cities, with a particular focus on how people create community in new urban space. She focuses her research on the ancient Native American city of Cahokia. Baires is the author of *Land of Water, City of the Dead: Religion* *and Cahokia's Emergence* (University of Alabama Press, 2017), and has published articles on the topics of Mississippian mortuary practice, ritual and religious depositional practice, and the layout of the City of Cahokia. She has also been featured in the PBS series *Native America*.

References

Baires, Sarah E., and Melissa R. Baltus. 2017. "Matter, Places, and Persons in Cahokian Depositional Acts." *Journal of Archaeological Method and Theory* 24: 974–97.

Baltus, Melissa R. 2014. "Transforming Material Relationships: 13th Century Revitalization of Cahokian Religious-Politics." PhD diss., University of Illinois, Urbana-Champaign.

Baltus, Melissa R., and Sarah E. Baires. 2012. "Elements of Ancient Power in the Cahokian World." *Journal of Social Archaeology* 12: 167–92.

Baltus, Melissa R., and Gregory D. Wilson. 2019. "The Cahokian Crucible: Burning Ritual and the Emergence of Cahokian Power in the Mississippian Midwest." *American Antiquity* 84: 438–70.

Bareis, Charles J., and James W. Porter. 1984. *American Bottom Archaeology: A Summary of the EAI-270 Project Contribution to the Culture History of the Mississippi River Valley*. Urbana: University of Illinois Press.

Bennett, Jane. 2010. *Vibrant Matter: A Political Ecology of Things*. Durham, NC: Duke University Press.

Bentz, Charles, Dale L. McElrath, Fred A. Finney, and Richard B. Lacampagne. 1988. *Late Woodland Sites in the American Bottom Uplands*. Illinois Transportation Archaeological Research Reports 18. Urbana: University of Illinois.

Betzenhauser, Alleen. 2011. "Creating the Cahokian Community: The Power of Place in Early Mississippian Sociopolitical Dynamics." PhD diss., University of Illinois, Urbana-Champaign.

Betzenhauser, Alleen, Timothy R. Pauketat, Elizabeth Watts Malouchos, Neal Lopinot, and Daniel Marovitch. 2017. "The Morrison Site: Evidence for Terminal Late Woodland Mound Construction in the American Bottom." *Illinois Archaeology* 27: 6–32.

Brennan, Tamira K., ed. 2018a. *East St. Louis Precinct (11S706) Mississippian Features: Data Summary*. Illinois State Archaeological Survey Research Report 43. Urbana-Champaign: Prairie Research Institute, University of Illinois.

———. 2018b. *Mund and Moorehead Phase Occupations at the Russell Site*. Illinois State Archaeological Survey Research Report 128. Urbana-Champaign: University of Illinois.

Dalan, Rinita A., George R. Holley, William I. Woods, Harold W. Watters Jr., and John A. Koepke. 2003. *Envisioning Cahokia: A Landscape Perspective*. DeKalb: Northern Illinois University Press.

Deleuze, Gilles, and Félix Guattari. 1987. *A Thousand Plateaus: Capitalism and Schizophrenia*. Translated by Brian Massumi. Minneapolis: University of Minnesota Press.

Emerson, Thomas E. 1997. *Cahokia and the Archaeology of Power*. Tuscaloosa: University of Alabama Press.

Emerson, Thomas E., Brad H. Koldehoff, and Tamira K. Brennan. 2018. *Revealing Greater Cahokia, North America's First Native City: Rediscovery and Large-Scale Excavations of the East St. Louis Precinct*. Illinois State Archaeological Survey Studies in Archaeology No. 12. Urbana: University of Illinois.

Fowler, Melvin L. 1997. *The Cahokia Atlas: A Historical Atlas of Cahokia Archaeology*. Illinois Transportation Archaeological Research Program Studies in Archaeology No. 2. Urbana: University of Illinois.

Fortier, Andrew C. 1996. *The Marge Site: Late Archaic and Emergent Mississippian Occupations in the Palmer Creek Locality (11-Mo-99)*. Illinois Transportation Archaeological Research Program, American Bottom Archaeology FAI-270 Site Reports 27. Urbana: University of Illinois.

Fortier, Andrew C., Thomas E. Emerson, and Dale L. McElrath. 2006. "Calibrating and Reassessing American Bottom Culture History." *Southeastern Archaeology* 25: 170–211.
Fortier, Andrew C., and Douglas K. Jackson. 2000. "The Formation of a Late Woodland Heartland in the American Bottom, Illinois cal A.D. 650–900." In *Late Woodland Societies: Tradition and Transformation across the Midcontinent*, edited by Thomas E. Emerson, Dale L. McElrath, and Andrew C. Fortier, 139–48. Lincoln: University of Nebraska Press.
Fortier, Andrew C., Richard B. Lacampagne, and Fred A. Finney. 1984. *The Fish Lake Site*. Illinois Transportation Archaeological Research Program, American Bottom Archaeology FAI-270 Site Reports 8. Urbana: University of Illinois.
Fortier, Andrew C., Thomas O. Maher, and Joyce A. Williams. 1991. *The Sponemann Site: The Formative Emergent Mississippian Sponemann Phase Occupations*. Illinois Transportation Archaeological Research Program, American Bottom Archaeology FAI-270 Site Reports 23. Urbana: University of Illinois.
Fortier, Andrew C., and Dale L. McElrath. 2002. "Deconstructing the Emergent Mississippian Concept: The Case for the Terminal Late Woodland in the American Bottom." *Midcontinental Journal of Archaeology* 27 172–215.
Frazer, James G. 1911–15. *The Golden Bough*. London: Macmillan.
Garrow, Duncan. 2012. "Odd Deposits and Average Practice: A Critical History of the Concept of Structured Deposition." *Archaeological Dialogues* 19: 85–115.
Grantham, Bill. 2002. *Creation Myths and Legends of the Creek Indians*. Gainesville: University Press of Florida.
Guttmann, E. B. A. 2005. "Midden Cultivation in Prehistoric Britain: Arable Crops in Gardens." *World Archaeology* 37: 224–39.
Hall, Robert. 1997. *An Archaeology of the Soul: North American Indian Belief and Ritual*. Urbana: University of Illinois Press.
Hanenberger, Ned H., George R. Milner, Stevan C. Pullins, Richard Paine, Lucretia S. Kelly, and Kathryn E. Parker. 2003. *The Range Site 3: Mississippian and Oneota Occupations*. Illinois Transportation Archaeological Research Reports 17. Urbana: University of Illinois.
Hejcman, Michael. 2011. "Ancient Waste Pits with Wood Ash Irreversibly Increase Crop Production in Central Europe." *Plant and Soil* 339: 341–50.
Holley, George R., Kathryn E. Parker, Julie N. Harper, and Jennifer E. Ringberg. 1990. *Selected Early Mississippian Household Sites in the American Bottom*. Illinois Transportation Archaeological Research Program, American Bottom Archaeology FAI-270 Site Reports 22. Urbana: University of Illinois.
———. 2001a. "The Faust North Locality, Scott Joint-Use Archaeological Project." Edwardsville: Office of Contract Archaeology, Southern Illinois University.
———. 2001b. "The Prehistoric Archaeology of the Faust South Locality, Scott Joint-Use Archaeological Project." Edwardsville: Office of Contract Archaeology, Southern Illinois University.
Iseminger, William R., Timothy R. Pauketat, Brad Koldehoff, Lucretia S. Kelly and Leonard Blake. 1990. *The Archaeology of the Cahokia Palisade: The East Palisade Investigations, Part I*. Illinois Cultural Resources Study No. 14. Springfield: Illinois Historic Preservation Agency.
Jackson, Douglas K., and Ned H. Hanenberger, Katharine B. Judson, eds. 2000. *Native American Legends of the Great Lakes and the Mississippi Valley*. DeKalb: Northern Illinois University Press.
Judson, Katharine B., ed. 2000. *Native American Legends of the Great Lakes and the Mississippi Valley*. DeKalb: Northern Illinois University Press.
Kelly, John E. 1990. "The Emergence of Mississippian Culture in the American Bottom Region." In *The Mississippian Emergence*, edited by B. D. Smith, 113–52. Washington, DC: Smithsonian Institution Press.
———. 1993. "The Pulcher Site: An Archaeological and Historical Overview." *Illinois Archaeology* 5: 434–51.
Kelly, John E., Andrew C. Fortier, Steven J. Ozuk, and Joyce Williams. 1987. *The Range Site: Archaic through Late Woodland Occupations*. Illinois Transportation Archaeological Research

Program, American Bottom Archaeology FAI-270 Site Reports 16. Urbana: University of Illinois Press.

Kelly, John E., Steven J. Ozuk, and Joyce A. Williams. 1990. *The Range Site 2: The Emergent Mississippian Dohack and Range Phase Occupations (11-S-47)*. Illinois Transportation Archaeological Research Program, American Bottom Archaeology FAI-270 Site Reports 20. Urbana: University of Illinois Press.

———. 2007. *The Range Site 4: Emergent Mississippian George Reeves and Lindeman Phase Occupations*. Illinois Transportation Archaeological Research Program, Research Reports 18. Urbana: University of Illinois.

La Flesche, Francis. 1939. *War Ceremony and Peace Ceremony of the Osage Indians*. Smithsonian Institution, Bureau of American Ethnology Bulletin 101. Washington, D.C.: United States Government Printing Office.

———. 1995. *The Osage and the Invisible World: From the Works of Francis La Flesche*. Edited and introduced by Garrick A. Bailey. Norman: University of Oklahoma Press.

Lovis, William A., Gerald R. Urquhart, Maria E. Raviele, and John P. Hart. 2011. "Hardwood Ash Nixtamalization May Lead to False Negatives for the Presence of Maize by Depleting Bulk $\delta^{13}C$ in Carbonized Residues." *Journal of Archaeological Science* 38: 2726–30.

Milner, George R. 1983. *The Turner and DeMange Sites*. Illinois Transportation Archaeological Research Program, American Bottom Archaeology FAI-270 Site Reports 4. Urbana: University of Illinois.

Pauketat, Timothy R. 1993. *Temples for Cahokia Lords: Preston Holder's 1955–1956 Excavations of Kunnemann Mound*. University of Michigan Museum of Anthropology Memoirs 26. Ann Arbor: University of Michigan.

———. 1998. *The Archaeology of Downtown Cahokia: The Tract 15A and Dunham Tract Excavations*. Illinois Transportation Archaeological Research Program Studies in Archaeology 1. Urbana: University of Illinois.

———. 2004. *Ancient Cahokia and the Mississippians*. Cambridge: Cambridge University Press.

———. 2005. *The Archaeology of the East St. Louis Mound Center Part I: The Southside Excavations*. Illinois Transportation Archaeological Research Program Research Report 21. Urbana: University of Illinois.

———. 2013a. *An Archaeology of the Cosmos: Rethinking Agency and Religion in Ancient America*. New York: Routledge.

———. 2013b. *The Archaeology of Downtown Cahokia II: The 1960 Excavation of Tract 15B*. Illinois State Archaeological Survey Studies in Archaeology 8. Urbana: University of Illinois.

Pauketat, Timothy R., Andrew C. Fortier, Susan M. Alt, and Thomas E. Emerson. 2013. "A Mississippian Conflagration at East St. Louis and Its Political-Historical Implications." *Journal of Field Archaeology* 38: 210–26.

Pauketat, Timothy R., and Neil H. Lopinot. 1997. "Cahokian Population Dynamics." In *Cahokia: Domination and Ideology in the Mississippian World*, edited by T. R. Pauketat and T. E. Emerson, 103–23. Lincoln: University of Nebraska Press.

Radin, Paul. 1970 [1923]. *The Winnebago Tribe*. 37th Annual Report of the US Bureau of Ethnology to the Secretary of the Smithsonian Institution, 1915–1916, 35–560. New York: Johnson Reprint Corporation.

Schilling, Timothy. 2014. "The Chronology of Monks Mound." *Southeastern Archaeology* 32: 14–28.

Simon, Mary, and Kathryn Parker. 2006. "Prehistoric Plant Use in the American Bottom: New Thoughts and Interpretations." *Southeastern Archaeology* 25: 212–57.

Smith, Harriet M. 1969. "The Murdock Mound." In *Explorations into Cahokia Archaeology*. Illinois Archaeological Survey Bulletin 7, edited by Melvin L. Fowler, 49–88. Urbana: University of Illinois.

Tringham, Ruth. 2005. "Weaving House Life and Death into Places: A Blueprint for a Hypermedia Narrative." In *(Un)settling the Neolithic*, edited by D. Bailey, A. Whittle, and V. Cummings, 98–111. Oxford: Oxbow Books.

Trubitt, Mary Beth. 2000. "Mound Building and Prestige Goods Exchange: Changing Strategies in the Cahokia Chiefdom." *American Antiquity* 65: 669–90.

Upton, Andrew J., William A. Lovis, and Gerald R. Urquhart. 2015. "An Empirical Test of Shell Tempering as an Alkaline Agent in the Nixtamalization Process." *Journal of Archaeological Science* 62: 39–44.

Woodward, D. 1994. "Gooding the Earth." In *The History of Soils and Field Systems*, edited by S. Foster and T. C. Smout, 1–110. Aberdeen: Scottish Cultural Press.

CHAPTER 8

Townhouses, Hearths, Fire, Smoke, Ash, and Cherokee Towns in Western North Carolina

Christopher B. Rodning

Many Native American groups recognize that the forces that animate and enliven people also animate and enliven elements of the landscape and some forms of material culture. From this perspective, some elements of landscape and material culture possess agency. Fire and smoke are also elements of the material world that possess such animacy and agency. Fire transforms wood and earth, and smoke moves between earth and sky. One material outcome of these transformations by fire is ash. Deposits of and receptacles for ash are found at many archaeological sites, and they offer clues about the role of fire and smoke within past cultural landscapes.

Within Native American cultural traditions of the Mississippian Southeast, fire is an earthly manifestation of the sun. Sacred fires were kept in the hearths of temples built on the summits of Mississippian mounds, and fire played an important role in Mississippian ritual (Corkran 1953, 1955; Knight 1986, 2006). Sacred fire is represented in Mississippian iconography by cross-in-circle motifs, including those depicted on engraved marine shell and on painted pottery, although the same symbol may instead—or, probably, may additionally—represent the four cardinal directions, the earth, the center of the cosmos, a community layout, a large town marker post, or all of the above (Cobb and King 2005; King 2011; Lankford 2007, 2011; Muller 1989, 2007).

Archaeological sites and oral traditions associated with Cherokee culture and Cherokee towns in the southern Appalachians shed light on the animacy and agency associated with fire and related elements of smoke and ash. At the point of European contact in the Americas, there were dozens of Cherokee towns in the southern Appalachians (Dickens 1978, 1979, 1986; Chapman 1985, 2009; Goodwin 1977; Hally 1986; Hudson 1986; Rodning 2001b, 2002b, 2002c; Schroedl 1986, 2000, 2001, 2009; Smith 1979). The community centers of Cherokee towns were public structures known as townhouses, which were large earth-and-wood structures built beside plazas and sometimes on earthen mounds (Rodning 2002a, 2010a, 2013, 2015b). Household dwellings and domestic activity areas were situated around townhouses and plazas, and some farmsteads were located in rural areas between towns. Townhouses were community centers, monuments and landmarks for the towns associated with them, containers for sacred fire, and portals to other cosmological domains.

Cherokee Townhouses and "Constant Fire"

Townhouses generated smoke and ash from sacred fires that were kept burning constantly in townhouse hearths—probably, often, by eligible male elders selected for this task (Gearing 1958, 1962)—and from practices of periodically burning townhouses themselves, after which point the structures were rebuilt in place, marking episodes of community renewal, perhaps following generational cycles (Rodning 2009a, 2015a). Columns of smoke emanating upward from townhouse hearths would have been visible from inside these public structures, of course, and from plazas adjacent to them, as well as from houses, gardens, fields, paths, peaks, and other towns and farmsteads nearby. These columns of smoke were visible symbols of the vitality of towns themselves, and, probably, were *axes mundi* connecting towns to the sky, and conduits for communications between people and the cosmos. Smoke generated from burning townhouses were visible symbols of moments in the life histories of communities, marking endpoints, of sorts, when towns may have moved elsewhere or, often, when a town would rebuild its townhouse and rekindle its fire, enacting the renewal of the community and the place at which it became anchored to its landscape and its history.

Fire and smoke do not preserve archaeologically in and of themselves, of course, but there are material remnants of burning and of ash deposits at archaeological sites in the southern Appalachians, and references to the transformative powers and spiritual properties of fire, smoke, ash, and the places and architectural spaces associated with them. One important source of Cherokee oral tradition from the late 1600s to early 1700s is the extant postscript to the journal kept by Alexander Longe of his life as an English trade agent in Cherokee towns (Corkran 1969). Another source is the vast compendium of Cherokee oral tradition compiled by James Mooney, an ethnologist affiliated with the Smithsonian Institution, during the course of his interactions with Cherokee elders in western North Carolina during the late nineteenth century (Mooney 1900).

Longe wrote about many aspects of Cherokee life, including religion and belief systems, ritual, naming, marriage and kinship, leadership and politics, trade and exchange, dances and feasts, subsistence practices, and human interaction and intervention in the natural world. Longe spent time in Cherokee townhouses speaking with Cherokee town leaders, and in several instances, as Longe recalled, after he had lit his pipe with embers from the fire in the townhouse hearth, his hosts would not let him leave the townhouse before putting out the flame in his pipe (Corkran 1969: 36). Fire and ashes from the townhouse hearth were not allowed outside the townhouse, except for once per year, when those involved in carrying ashes from the townhouse hearth fasted and drank medicine before removing "old" ashes and, presumably, rekindling the "new" fire for the town and townhouse. There were other instances when taking townhouse fire outside the townhouse would have been allowed, including, for example, when townhouse fire was carried by warriors setting out on warpaths; when townhouse hearths were periodically cleaned, renovated, rebuilt, and rekindled; and when fire was taken from townhouse hearths to kindle or rekindle fires in the hearths of household dwellings or the hearths of townhouses in neighboring towns (Mooney 1900: 396). Those instances, though, must have been carefully choreographed and conducted, reflecting the power and symbolism of fire, smoke, embers, and ashes from townhouse hearths. Longe noted that the ashes from townhouse hearths were periodically emplaced at carefully selected points outside townhouses, and that those points within the built environment of Cherokee towns were known as *Skeona*, which Longe translated as "the spirits" or "place of the spirits" (Corkran 1969: 36). Longe indicated that there were rules about who could approach those ash emplacements, and rules about when and how. Children who did approach them apparently needed scarification, for purposes of healing and purification. It is tempting to connect *Skeona*, as Longe recorded it, to historic and modern iterations of *Skeona*, including Skeenah Creek in the upper Little Tennessee Valley and Skeenah Creek in the Georgia Blue Ridge.

Another reference to ash within the Cherokee landscape comes from the Cherokee town name of Kâsdu′yĭ, which Mooney (1900: 524) translates as "ashes place," through the combination of *kâsdu*, meaning ashes, and *yĭ*, the locative, referring to the place where the modern city of Asheville, North Carolina, is located. This placename makes a reference to a different name for the same place, Unta′kiyasti′yĭ, which translates as "where they race" (Mooney 1900: 544). This version of the placename is also thought to refer generally to an area along the French Broad River near Asheville (Mooney 1900: 408). There were not major Cherokee towns located along the French Broad River during the eighteenth century or, apparently, during the period of early and intermittent Spanish explorations of the southern Appalachians during the sixteenth century (Beck 1997, 2013; Hudson 1986; Moore 2002b), but there were many settlements in this area during the prehistoric period (Dickens 1976, 1978; Keel 1976; Moore 2002a). This section of the French Broad River encompasses the Swannanoa River and its intersection with the French Broad near Asheville, and the name, Swannanoa, derives from the Cherokee word for the trail that connected Cherokee town areas in southwestern North Carolina with the people farther east known to the Cherokee as the Ani′-Suwa′lĭ (Mooney 1894), which is a reference to the province and the community known as Xuala and Joara in the sixteenth century, situated in the uppermost reaches of the Catawba River Valley along the eastern edge of the Blue Ridge Mountains (Mooney 1900: 380, 409, 509, 532).

Mooney noted the symbolism of fires kept in Cherokee townhouse hearths, practices of keeping those fires burning constantly, and the role of fire from townhouse hearths in rekindling fires in the hearths of household dwellings, and, sometimes, the transport of fire from the townhouse hearths of large and old Cherokee towns—like Keowee, Nequassee, Cowee, and Kituhwa, for example, all known as "Mother Towns" and all important points within the Cherokee landscape in the past and still in the present—to outlying settlements. His rendering of a historical tradition, "The Mounds and the Constant Fire" (Mooney 1900: 395–97), describes the practice of a male elder (known as a "firekeeper") keeping the sacred fire inside a townhouse hearth burning perpetually. Another historical tradition, "The Spirit Defenders of Nikwasi" (Mooney 1900: 336–37), focuses on mythical warriors coming to the aid of the Cherokee town of Nequassee in an attack by an "enemy from the south" (perhaps English colonists from Carolina), but the oral tradition also makes reference to a story of smoke emanating from the Kituhwa mound at a time when a contingent of Cherokee warriors was encamped nearby during the U.S. Civil War.

Mooney (1889: 168–69) characterizes the process of building townhouses and mounds as follows, including references to the roles of firekeepers in maintaining the fires kept in townhouse hearths.

> The practice of building mounds originated with the *Ani'ntsi* and was kept up by the *Ani-Kitu'hwagi*. They were built as sites for town-houses . . . and some were low, while others were as high as small trees. In building the mound a fire was first kindled on the level surface. Around the fire was placed a circle of stones, outside of which were deposited the bodies of seven prominent men, one from each gens, these bodies being exhumed for the purpose from previous interments. With the bodies was placed an *ulast'ti* stone (a talismanic crystal), the horn, tooth, or scale of an *uktena* (an enormous horned serpent with magic powers), a feather from the right wing of the *su'ndwa* (a mythic hawk, the ancestor of the present pigeon hawk), a similar feather from the golden eagle, and beads of seven colors—red,

blue, black, white, yellow, purple, and gray-blue. Through shamanistic rites these articles were invested with such fatal magic properties that should an invader ever penetrate to the town-house, to which all the people of the settlement fled on every occasion of alarm, he would inevitably die before he could reach his own country. A hollow cedar log to serve as a chimney or air hole was then fixed perpendicularly above the fire, and the earth was built up around this so as to form a mound. Upon this mound the town-house was built, so that the mouth of the fire-pit was in the middle of the town-house floor. The fire was in charge of a "fire-maker" and was never allowed to go out, but was always smouldering at the bottom of the hole, the opening being covered over with ashes until wanted on the occasion of a dance, when long stalks of the *tsilsû'ti* ("fire-builder," *Erigeron Canadaense*) weed were thrust down the cedar shaft, tinder was placed over the opening, and after some magic ceremonies the fire ascended by means of the dry stalks, the wood was piled on and all was ready for the dance. All the fire in the different houses of the settlement was obtained from the fire-maker at the town-house.

The reference here to the seven men from each gens is a reference to the seven matrilineal clans, whose members lived in each of the major Cherokee towns. The reference to beads of varying colors is a reference to glass beads acquired from English colonists and traders. An *uktena* is a powerful mythic snake in Cherokee cosmology and mythology (Hudson 1976; Mooney 1900). The *uktena* scale noted in this oral tradition is probably symbolized by a marine shell pendant known as a gorget, many of which have rattlesnake designs engraved on them (Muller 2007; Rodning 2012).

Mooney (1889: 171) adds the following about cycles of building and rebuilding townhouses in place, as well as cases in which townhouses burned (accidentally, perhaps, at least in some cases) and were then buried.

On account of the sanctity attached to the location in the minds of the people, a new town-house was usually built upon the site of the old, as was the case in this instance, and as destruction by fire must have been a common accident, each successive burning causing a deposit of a layer of earth a foot or so in depth from the falling roof, it follows that this cause alone would in time result in raising the floor of the town-house considerably above the surrounding surface, even if built originally upon the natural level, as was probably the case after the old Indian ways were modified by contact with the whites. In the case of a town-house erected upon an ancient mound built as described in the tradition, such an accident would, of course, add the same proportion to the height of the original mound. In this way the height of the mound would serve to roughly indicate comparative length of occupancy of the site, and the stratification of the earth and ashes would represent successive burnings and new erections.

It is interesting to note Mooney's reference here to "a layer of earth a foot or so in depth" accumulating above the burned and buried remnants of an old townhouse before a new townhouse was built. Earth was an important element of embankments and roof material for houses and townhouses in the greater southern Appalachians. Fire and earth were both important elements in renewing Cherokee townhouses, according to Mooney's description. There are many archaeological examples of the importance of burning and burying structures associated with earthen mounds in the Southeast (Kay and Sabo 2006; Krause 1996; Lewis and Kneberg 1946; Lewis et al. 1995; Perttula 2009; Perttula and Rogers 2007; Schambach 1996; Trubitt 2009), and examples from the Southwest of burning kivas in association with "ritual retirement" or termination of those ceremonial structures (Creel and Anyon 2003, 2007; Creel et al. 2015; Crown and Wills 2003; Walker 1995).

From these references in oral tradition and translations of Cherokee names for particular places and groups of people, it is evident that fire and ash were important elements of the Cherokee cultural landscape. Fire and ash were emplaced at townhouses and earthen mounds, which themselves formed important landmarks and community centers. Although not directly visible archaeologically, columns of smoke emanating upward from fires kept in townhouse hearths, and columns of smoke generated from cycles of burning townhouses before burying and rebuilding them, were likely important elements of the landscape as well.

The Coweeta Creek Site

The Coweeta Creek site in southwestern North Carolina demonstrates interesting parallels to aspects of townhouse mounds, hearths, and ash accumulations as described by Mooney, Longe, and others (figure 8.1; Rodning 2015a). The site is located close to the confluence of the eponymous stream and the Little Tennessee River, within the area of the historic Middle Cherokee towns, and not far from the area of the Cherokee Out towns (Dickens 1976, 1978, 1979; Keel 1976; Rogers 2009; Smith 1979; Steere 2015; Waselkov and Braund 1995). The former group of towns includes Cowee and Nequassee, and the latter includes Kituhwa, whose name refers to the place, the mound, and the people of Kituhwa, or the "Ani-Kitu'hwagi" (Duncan and Riggs 2003; Goodwin 1977; Mooney 1900).

The Coweeta Creek site dates largely from the 1400s through the early 1700s, and it includes a townhouse mound, an adjacent plaza, and an area around the plaza where household dwellings and related structures were placed (figure 8.2; Rodning 2015a). The relatively compact spacing of domestic structures has been seen as an indication that a log stockade surrounded the settlement, but there is no direct evidence of such a stockade (Rodning 2001b; Ward and Davis 1999). Sequences of hearths are

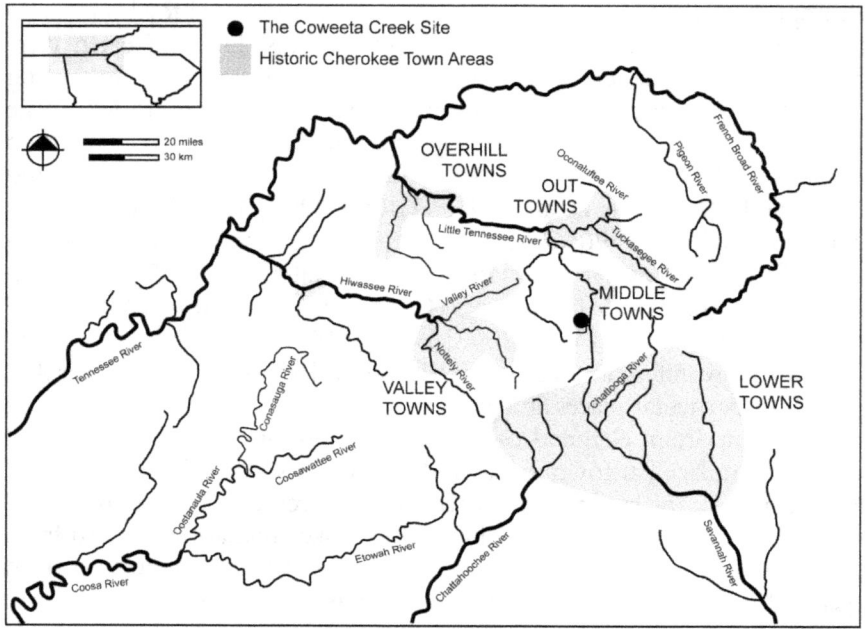

Figure 8.1. *Cherokee town areas. Created by Christopher B. Rodning.*

present within public and domestic structures at the site, and dozens of pits and burials are present inside and beside structures (Rodning 2001a, 2011a; Sullivan and Rodning 2001, 2011). During the 1400s or 1500s, several domestic structures were present at the site, and those houses were rebuilt in several iterations each, but in an offset pattern, in which the central hearths—and, therefore, the structures surrounding them—shifted somewhat from one stage to another (Rodning 2007, 2009b). After an apparent episode of abandonment, perhaps lasting several decades or even several generations, the site was reestablished in the seventeenth century as a town with a more formal settlement plan, including the townhouse, the town plaza, and the domestic structures in areas around the plaza (Rodning 2007, 2009a). Notably, the townhouse and dwellings all adhere to the same axis and alignment, and at this point houses were built and rebuilt in place rather than in the offset pattern seen earlier (Rodning 2009b). Eventually most, if not all, of the houses were abandoned, and the last stage of the townhouse was abandoned during the early eighteenth century (Rodning 2002a, 2008, 2010b).

At least six—and probably seven or more—iterations of the townhouse were built and rebuilt in place at a single point within the town plan (figure 8.3; Rodning 2015a: 72–82). Pairs of entrance trenches represent foundations for passageways that cut through earthen embankments sur-

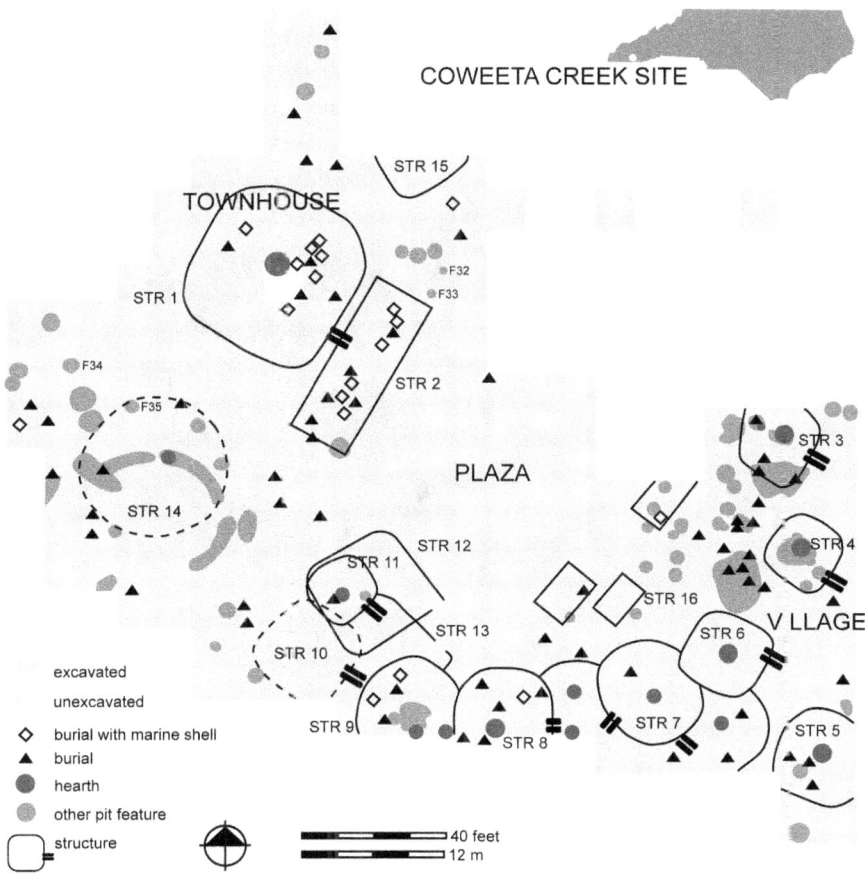

Figure 8.2. *The Coweeta Creek site plan. Features 32 and 33 are located northeast of Structure 1. Features 34 and 35 are located southwest of Structure 1. Created by Christopher B. Rodning.*

rounding the outer edges of the townhouse. The original entryway was present along the southeastern wall of the townhouse, and later it was moved to the southernmost corner, although the entryway maintained the original alignment—opening toward the southeast—throughout the history of the townhouse. Outside the entryway, between the townhouse and the plaza, was a rectangular ramada, visible archaeologically as an array of postholes. This ramada represents the kind of structure (roofed but without walls) described in written accounts from the 1700s as a "summer townhouse," and the square structure with rounded corners is analogous to what in the 1700s was often called a "winter townhouse."

Much like Mooney's description indicates, the first stage of the townhouse was built by clearing off some ground and placing a hearth at a

Figure 8.3. *Posthole patterns and central hearth associated with late stages of the Coweeta Creek townhouse (Structure 1). Image courtesy of the UNC Research Laboratories of Archaeology, Chapel Hill.*

center point for the eventual structure (figure 8.4). Several burials are associated with early stages of the townhouse—perhaps all, and certainly most, associated with its first stage (figure 8.2; Rodning 2011a). Some burials include items such as shell beads, shell pins, shell pendants, and smoking pipes made of carved stone or clay. One burial of an adult male, placed in the ramada (Structure 2) and outside the original entryway into the townhouse, included a quiver of seven arrows—perhaps a reference to the seven Cherokee clans? Another burial nearby, with another adult male, included a marine shell gorget with an engraved rattlesnake motif—perhaps a material symbol of the *uktena* scale that Mooney noted? Interestingly, on top of this burial was a hearth, and a receptacle of fire that may have been closely associated with the person buried here, and the items placed in the ground with him. Meanwhile, the placement of burials in the ramada seem to make reference to pathways for the movement of people into and out of the townhouse. At some point, the first stage of the townhouse was burned down, it was buried with sand and architectural rubble, and it was then rebuilt in place, replicating the original. This cycle was repeated, and while the temporal intervals between stages are not known with certainty, it may have been once every fifteen to twenty-five years following generational succession of town leadership. The last stages of the townhouse were slightly larger than the original, and slightly more round in shape, perhaps in part to accommodate larger numbers of people.

Several pits outside the townhouse were filled with ash and charcoal (figure 8.2; Rodning 2015a: 82–83). Features 32 and 33 are circular pits situated northeast of the ramada (Structure 2) outside the main townhouse (Structure 1). Features 34 and 35 are circular pits southwest of the townhouse. I interpret these deposits as emplacements of ash and other charred material from the townhouse hearth, broadly comparable to the ash heaps outside townhouses that Longe described as *Skeena*. It is possible that Structure 15, just north of the townhouse (Structure 1) and the rectangular ramada (Structure 2) between the townhouse and plaza, might represent the dwelling of firekeepers, the male elders noted by Mooney (1900: 395–97) and Gearing (1962: 22–23) whose responsibility it was to keep the townhouse fire going (Rodning 2015a: 83). This "honored or sacred fire" is known as *atsi'la gălûṅkw`ti'yu* (Anderson et al. 2010: 48; Mooney 1900: 511; Rodning 2015a: 41). Another example of even more substantial ash heaps outside a public structure is the Mississippian site of Ledford Island, along the Hiwassee River, in eastern Tennessee (Sullivan 1987). This site dates to the 1400s or 1500s, and the spatial layout of the town—townhouse, plaza, village area, and log

Figure 8.4. *Posthole patterns and central hearth associated with early stages of the Coweeta Creek townhouse (Structure 1). Image courtesy of the UNC Research Laboratories of Archaeology, Chapel Hill.*

stockade—closely resembles the settlement layout at the Coweeta Creek site (Schroedl 1998). I suggest—somewhat speculatively—that such emplacements of ash were probably common in areas surrounding Cherokee townhouses, that they were probably carefully chosen and remembered by Cherokee townspeople and firekeepers, and that the movement of ash from townhouse hearths to these emplacements was probably carefully scripted, at least in some cases.

Mooney and Longe indicate that ashes were removed from townhouse hearths and disposed nearby once per year. Some pits outside the Coweeta Creek townhouse were receptacles for ash, probably including ashes removed from the townhouse hearth. Given the sacred status of the fires kept in Cherokee townhouse hearths, emplacements of ash beside the Coweeta Creek townhouse—and, probably, similar ash heaps beside other townhouses—were and are elements of Cherokee sacred landscapes.

Although speculative on my part, it is possible that there was some amount of color symbolism associated with ash. For the Cherokee and other Native American groups in the American South, the color white was and is associated with peace, purity, balance, and age; the color red with warfare and blood; and the color black with death (Cobb and Drake 2008; Cobb and Giles 2009: 92; Dye 2009: 160; Gearing 1962; Hudson 1976: 234–37; Mooney 1891: 342–43, 1900: 207, 485, 496; Pursell 2004; Welch 2005: 152–53, 155, 162–70, 257–58). The process of burning wood involves all those colors—fire and flames are red, charred wood is black, and ash and embers are white. Ash is an endpoint—as a substance that is white or grayish white, perhaps it had a symbolic association with the color white, and as an outcome of burning, perhaps ash had an association with the transformative powers of fire itself, as well. The emplacement of ash beside Cherokee townhouses, the practice of keeping fire burning constantly within townhouse hearths, and generational episodes of burning and burying remnants of townhouses themselves may have drawn upon color symbolism and may have embedded that color symbolism within the landscape (Rodning 2010a, 2015a).

Earth, Wood, Smoke, and Ash

The sequence of townhouses at Coweeta Creek dates to the 1600s and early 1700s, the ash heap at Ledford Island likely dates to the 1400s or early 1500s (Sullivan 1987), and the architectural form of Cherokee townhouses likely dates back to the fourteenth century in eastern Tennessee (Sullivan 2018). The patterns of ash emplacements described here therefore likely date back at least to the middle to late Mississippi period in the southern Appalachians. There are also ash deposits associated with

Mississippian mounds in the Yazoo Basin of northwestern Mississippi (Nelson 2019) and with Late Woodland-period Coles Creek-culture mounds in the Natchez Bluffs area of southwestern Mississippi (Kassabaum and Nelson 2016; Nelson and Kassabaum 2014), hinting that associations between ash and monumental architecture may have been widespread in the Native American South. The importance of sacred fire, as evident from hearths inside temples and from cross-in-circle motifs in Mississippian iconography, is definitely widespread in the Mississippian Southeast.

Perhaps the potency of ash goes back even further into the past, and can be traced at least as far back as the Middle Woodland or even Early Woodland period, and to Hopewell and Adena mortuary practices and charnel houses evident at earthworks in the Ohio Valley and elsewhere in the Eastern Woodlands. Many Hopewell burial mounds in Ohio, northern Mississippi, western Tennessee, and northeastern Louisiana cover the burned and buried remnants of charnel houses, which were settings for cremations and in some cases for pits containing the cremated remains of the dead and burials emplaced within ashes and other charred remnants of burned charnel houses (Brown 1979; Mainfort 2013; Seeman 1979; Seeman and Soday 1980; Walling et al. 1991). In these settings, the transformative forces of fire were associated with the treatment of the dead, the mortuary practices associated with conducting them during rites of passage to the afterlife, and the construction of mounds during the late first millennium BC and early first millennium AD. Similar evidence, on a somewhat smaller scale in most cases, is present at mound sites in the Ohio River Valley associated with Adena ceremonialism from the Early Woodland period, during the early first millennium BC (Clay 1998; Mainfort 1998). Charnel houses associated with Adena and Hopewell traditions of the Woodland period, Mississippian mounds, and Cherokee townhouses are separated by temporal distances and regional differences, and I am not suggesting there are clear historical ties connecting them, but I also do find it meaningful that in each of these settings, and in each of these periods, fire and ash (and, probably, smoke) were closely associated with ceremonialism and monumentality.

Another manifestation of ash in Cherokee towns—and at sites dating to the Mississippi and Woodland periods in the Southeast—was the ash generated from smoking tobacco in pipes made of clay or carved stone. According to Cherokee oral tradition and medicinal practice, smoking tobacco is important for sustaining and nourishing life (Mooney 1900: 254–55), and smoking was an important aspect of public events that took place in Cherokee townhouses during the eighteenth century (Randolph 1983; Rodning 2014; Williams 1927). For the Cherokee and other peoples of Native North America, pipe smoking, and the smoke that trailed upward from the pipes that were containers for tobacco (and the ashes generated from burning it) was and is one means by which prayers were and are sent toward the sky (Blanton 2015; Godlaski 2013; Rafferty 2004; Rafferty and Mann 2004). These points do not in and of themselves demonstrate that ashes generated from smoking tobacco were powerful substances, but they are suggestive. From this perspective, it also seems likely that the smoke generated from the sacred fires kept in Cherokee townhouse hearths were similarly powerful in carrying prayers or other forms of offerings and communications from the earth to the sky. Material outcomes of these fires—and the fires that consumed abandoned stages of Cherokee townhouses—included ashes and embers. Those material outcomes of fire perhaps adopted and accumulated some of the same powers associated with fire itself.

As an outcome of fire and a substance created by it, ashes from fires associated with mounds, temples, townhouses, and similar settings in the Native American South, including Cherokee towns in the southern Appalachians, were materials that needed careful tending, handling, containment, and curation. I conclude that ashes were purposively embedded within the Cherokee landscape and emplaced within the townhouses and plazas that were the focal points of community life in Cherokee towns. I recommend further study of the roles of fire, smoke, ash, and burned materials as powerful forces and agents of cultural activity within the Cherokee landscape, past and present, and the ways in which Cherokee concepts and practices associated with fire and its transformative properties are related to antecedent cultural practices in prehistory.

Acknowledgments

Thanks to Barbara Roth and Charles Adams for the invitation to contribute to this book. I appreciate comments and guidance from Erin Nelson, Megan Kassabaum, Ben Steere, Maggie Spivey, Robert Hill, and Mark Yakich, and thanks to Steve Davis, Trawick Ward, and Bennie Keel for help with field records from excavations by the University of North Carolina at the Coweeta Creek site between 1965 and 1971. Thanks for support from several programs and departments at Tulane University, including the Committee for Research and the Provost's Office, the School of Liberal Arts Dean's Office, the Department of Anthropology, the Center for Archaeology, the New Orleans Center for the Gulf South, the Paul and Debra Gibbons Professorship, the Carol Lavin Bernick Faculty Grant Program, the ByWater Institute and A Studio in the Woods, and the Howard-Tilton Library. I dedicate this chapter to the memory of the late Jamie Chad Brandon, from the Arkansas Archeological Survey and the University of Arkansas, in honor of his unbridled enthusiasm for archaeology and for his colleagues and students in the field.

Christopher B. Rodning has an AB in anthropology from Harvard University and a PhD in anthropology from the University of North Carolina at Chapel Hill. His interests include the archaeology of landscape, monuments, architecture, culture contact and colonialism, and ritual and religion, with a particular focus on the archaeology of Native American peoples of the southeastern United States. He is author and coauthor of articles in *American Anthropologist*, *American Antiquity*, *Historical Archaeology*, *Southeastern Archaeology*, *North American Archaeologist*, and the *Journal of Archaeological Research*. He is professor of anthropology at Tulane University, New Orleans, Louisiana; the current secretary of the Southeastern Archaeological Conference; and the current editor of the *SAA Archaeological Record*.

References

Anderson, William L., Jane L. Brown, and Anne F. Rogers, eds. 2010. *The Payne-Butrick Papers*. Lincoln: University of Nebraska Press.
Beck, Robin A., Jr. 1997. "From Joara to Chiaha: Spanish Exploration of the Appalachian Summit Area, 1540–1568." *Southeastern Archaeology* 16: 162–69.
———. 2013. *Chiefdoms, Collapse, and Coalescence in the Early American South*. Cambridge: Cambridge University Press.
Blanton, Dennis B. 2015. *Mississippian Smoking Ritual in the Southern Appalachian Region*. Knoxville: University of Tennessee Press.
Brown, James A. 1979. "Charnel Houses and Mortuary Crypts: Disposal of the Dead in the Middle Woodland Period." In *Hopewell Archaeology: The Chillicothe Conference*, edited by David S. Brose and N'omi Greber, 211–19. Kent, OH: Kent State University Press.
Chapman, Jefferson. 1985. *Tellico Archaeology: Twelve Thousand Years of Native American History*. Report of Investigations 43. Knoxville: Department of Anthropology, University of Tennessee.
———. 2009. "Tellico Archaeology: Tracing Timberlake's Footsteps." In *Culture, Crisis, and Conflict: Cherokee British Relations, 1756–1765*, edited by Anne F. Rogers and Barbara R. Duncan, 45–61. Cherokee, NC: Museum of the Cherokee Indian Press.
Clay, R. Berle. 1998. "The Essential Features of Adena Ceremonialism and Their Implications." *Southeastern Archaeology* 17: 1–21.
Cobb, Charles R., and Eric Drake. 2008. "The Colour of Time: Head Pots and Temporal Convergences." *Cambridge Archaeological Journal* 18: 85–93.
Cobb, Charles R., and Bretton Giles. 2009. "War Is Shell: The Ideology and Embodiment of Mississippian Conflict." In *Warfare in Cultural Context: Practice, Agency, and the Archaeology of Violence*, edited by Axel Nielsen and William Walker, 84–108. Tucson: University of Arizona Press.
Cobb, Charles R., and Adam King. 2005. "Re-Inventing Mississippian Tradition at Etowah, Georgia." *Journal of Archaeological Method and Theory* 12: 167–92.
Coe, Joffre L. 1961. "Cherokee Archeology." In *Symposium on Cherokee and Iroquois Culture*, edited by William N. Fenton and John Gulick, 53–60. Bureau of American Ethnology Bulletin 180. Washington, DC: Smithsonian Institution.

Corkran, David H. 1953. "The Sacred Fire of the Cherokees." *Southern Indian Studies* 5: 21–26.

———. 1955. "Cherokee Sun and Fire Observances." *Southern Indian Studies* 7: 33–38.

Corkran, David H., ed. 1969. "A Small Postscript of the Ways and Manners of the Indians Called Cherokees." *Southern Indian Studies* 21: 1–49.

Creel, Darrell, and Roger Anyon. 2003. "New Perspectives on Mimbres Communal Pitstructures and Implications for Ritual and Cultural Developments." *American Antiquity* 68: 67–92.

———. 2007. "Burning Down the House: Ritual Architecture of the Mimbres Late Pithouse Period." In *Mimbres Lives and Landscapes*, edited by Margaret C. Nelson and Michelle Hegmon, 29–37. Santa Fe, NM: School for Advanced Research Press.

Creel, Darrell, Roger Anyon, and Barbara Roth. 2015. "Ritual Construction, Use, and Retirement of Mimbres Three Circle Phase Great Kivas." *Kiva* 81: 201–19.

Crown, Patricia L., and W. H. Wills. 2003. Modifying Pottery and Kivas at Chaco: Pentimento, Restoration, or Renewal? *American Antiquity* 68: 511–32.

Dickens, Roy S., Jr. 1967. "The Route of Rutherford's Expedition against the North Carolina Cherokees." *Southern Indian Studies* 19: 3–24.

———. 1976. *Cherokee Prehistory: The Pisgah Phase in the Appalachian Summit Region*. Knoxville: University of Tennessee Press.

———. 1978. "Mississippian Settlement Patterns in the Appalachian Summit Area: The Pisgah and Qualla Phases." In *Mississippian Settlement Patterns*, edited by Bruce D. Smith, 115–39. New York: Academic Press.

———. 1979. "The Origins and Development of Cherokee Culture." In *The Cherokee Indian Nation: A Troubled History*, edited by Duane H. King, 3–32. Knoxville: University of Tennessee Press.

———. 1986. "An Evolutionary-Ecological Interpretation of Cherokee Cultural Development." In *The Conference on Cherokee Prehistory*, edited by David G. Moore, 81–94. Swannanoa, NC: Warren Wilson College.

Duncan, Barbara R., and Brett H. Riggs. 2003. *Cherokee Heritage Trails Guidebook*. Chapel Hill: University of North Carolina Press.

Dye, David H. 2009. *War Paths, Peace Paths: An Archaeology of Cooperation and Conflict in Native Eastern North America*. Walnut Creek, CA: Alta Mira Press.

Gearing, Frederick O. 1958. "The Structural Poses of 18th Century Cherokee Villages." *American Anthropologist* 60: 1148–57.

———. 1962. *Priests and Warriors: Social Structures for Cherokee Politics in the 18th Century*. Memoirs 93. Menasha, WI: American Anthropological Association.

Godlaski, Theodore M. 2013. "Holy Smoke: Native American Use among Native American Tribes in North America." *Substance Use and Misuse* 48: 1–8.

Goodwin, Gary C. 1977. *Cherokees in Transition: A Study of Changing Culture and Environment Prior to 1775*. Department of Geography Research Paper 181. Chicago: University of Chicago.

Hally, David J. 1986. "The Cherokee Archaeology of Georgia." In *The Conference on Cherokee Prehistory*, edited by David G. Moore, 95–121. Swannanoa, NC: Warren Wilson College.

———. 2002. "'As Caves below Ground': Making Sense of Aboriginal House Form in the Protohistoric and Historic Southeast." In *Between Contact and Colonies: Archaeological Perspectives on the Protohistoric Southeast*, edited by Cameron B. Wesson and Mark A. Rees, 90–109. Tuscaloosa: University of Alabama Press.

———. 2007. "Mississippian Shell Gorgets in Regional Context." In *Southeastern Ceremonial Complex: Chronology, Content, Context*, edited by Adam King, 185–231. Tuscaloosa: University of Alabama Press.

———. 2008. *King: The Social Archaeology of a Late Mississippian Town in Northwestern Georgia*. Tuscaloosa: University of Alabama Press.

Hally, David J., and Hypatia Kelly. 1998. "The Nature of Mississippian Towns in Georgia: The King Site Example." In *Mississippian Towns and Sacred Spaces: Searching for an Architectural Grammar*, edited by R. Barry Lewis and Charles B. Stout, 49–63. Tuscaloosa: University of Alabama Press.

Hudson, Charles M. 1976. *The Southeastern Indians.* Knoxville: University of Tennessee Press.
———. 1986. "Some Thoughts on the Early Social History of the Cherokees." In *The Conference on Cherokee Prehistory*, edited by David G. Moore, 139–53. Swannanoa, NC: Warren Wilson College.
Kassabaum, Megan C., and Erin Stevens Nelson. 2016. "Standing Posts and Special Substances: Gathering and Ritual Deposition at Feltus (22Je500), Jefferson County, Mississippi." *Southeastern Archaeology* 35: 134–54.
Kay, Marvin K., and George Sabo. 2006. "Mortuary Ritual and Winter Solstice Imagery of the Harlan-Style Charnel House." *Southeastern Archaeology* 25: 29–47.
Keel, Bennie C. 1976. *Cherokee Archaeology: A Study of the Appalachian Summit.* Knoxville: University of Tennessee Press.
Keel, Bennie C., Brian J. Egloff, and Keith T. Egloff. 2002. "Reflections on the Coweeta Creek Mound and the Cherokee Project." *Southeastern Archaeology* 21: 49–53.
King, Adam. 2011. "Iconography of the Hightower Region of Eastern Tennessee and Northern Georgia." In *Visualizing the Sacred: Cosmic Visions, Regionalism, and Art of the Mississippian World*, edited by George E. Lankford, F. Kent Reilly III, and James F. Garber, 279–93. Austin: University of Texas Press.
King, Duane H., ed. 2007. *The Memoirs of Lieutenant Henry Timberlake: The Story of a Soldier, Adventurer, and Emissary to the Cherokees, 1756–1765.* Cherokee, NC: Museum of the Cherokee Indian Press.
Knight, Vernon J., Jr. 1986. "The Institutional Organization of Mississippian Religion." *American Antiquity* 51: 675–87.
———. 2006. "Symbolism of Mississippian Mounds." In *Powhatan's Mantle: Indians in the Colonial Southeast (Revised and Expanded Edition)*, edited by Peter H. Wood, Gregory A. Waselkov, and Tom Hatley, 421–34. Lincoln: University of Nebraska Press.
Krause, Richard A. 1996. "Observations on the Excavation of a Mississippi Mound." In *Mounds, Embankments, and Ceremonialism in the Midsouth*, edited by Robert C. Mainfort and Richard Walling, 54–63. Research Series 46. Fayetteville: Arkansas Archeological Survey.
Lankford, George E. 2007. "Some Cosmological Motifs in the Southeastern Ceremonial Complex." In *Ancient Object and Sacred Realms*, edited by F. Kent Reilly III and James F. Garber, 8–38. Austin: University of Texas Press.
———. 2011. "The Swirl-Cross and the Center." In *Visualizing the Sacred: Cosmic Visions, Regionalism, and Art of the Mississippian World*, edited by George E. Lankford, F. Kent Reilly III, and James F. Garber, 251–75. Austin: University of Texas Press.
Lewis, Thomas M. N., and Madeline D. Kneberg. 1946. *Hiwassee Island: An Archaeological Account of Four Tennessee Indian Peoples.* Knoxville: University of Tennessee Press,
Lewis, Thomas M. N., Madeline D. K. Lewis, and Lynne P. Sullivan, eds. 1995. *The Prehistory of the Chickamauga Basin.* Knoxville: University of Tennessee Press.
Mainfort, Robert C., Jr. 1989. "Adena Chiefdoms? Evidence from the Wright Mounds." *Midcontinental Journal of Archaeology* 14: 164–78.
———. 2013. *Pinson Mounds: Middle Woodland Ceremonialism in the Midsouth.* Fayetteville: University of Arkansas Press.
Mooney, James. 1889. "Cherokee Mound-Building." *American Anthropologist* 2: 167–71.
———. 1891. *The Sacred Formulas of the Cherokees.* Bureau of American Ethnology Annual Report 7: 301–98. Washington, DC: Smithsonian Institution.
———. 1900. *Myths of the Cherokee.* Bureau of American Ethnology Annual Report 19: 3–596. Washington, D.C.: Smithsonian Institution.
Moore, David G. 1986. "The Pisgah Phase: Cultural Continuity in the Appalachian Summit?" In *The Conference on Cherokee Prehistory*, edited by David G. Moore, 73–80. Swannanoa, NC: Warren Wilson College.
———. 2002a. *Catawba Valley Mississippian: Ceramics, Chronology, and Catawba Indians.* Tuscaloosa: University of Alabama Press.
———. 2002b. "Pisgah Phase Village Evolution at the Warren Wilson Site." In *The Archaeology of Native North Carolina: Papers in Honor of H. Trawick Ward*, edited by Jane M. Eastman,

Christopher B. Rodning, and Edmond A. Boudreaux III, 76–83. Special Publication 7. Biloxi, MS: Southeastern Archaeological Conference.

Muller, Jon. 1989. "The Southern Cult." In *The Southeastern Ceremonial Complex: Artifacts and Analysis*, edited by Patricia Galloway, 11–26. Lincoln: University of Nebraska Press.

———. 2007. "Prolegomena for the Analysis of the Southeastern Ceremonial Complex." In *Southeastern Ceremonial Complex: Chronology, Content, Context*, edited by Adam King, 15–37. Tuscaloosa: University of Alabama Press.

Nelson, Erin S. 2019. *Authority, Autonomy, and the Archaeology of a Mississippian Community*. Gainesville: University Press of Florida.

Nelson, Erin Stevens, and Megan C. Kassabaum. 2014. "Expanding Social Networks through Ritual Deposition: A Case Study from the Lower Mississippi Valley." *Archaeological Review from Cambridge* 29: 103–28.

Pursell, Corin C. 2004. Geographic Distribution and Symbolism of Colored Mound Architecture in the Mississippian Southeast. M.A. Thesis, Department of Anthropology, Southern Illinois University, Carbondale, IL.

Perttula, Timothy. 2009. "Extended Entranceway Structures in the Caddo Archaeological Area." *Southeastern Archaeology* 28: 27–42.

Perttula, Timothy, and Robert Rogers. 2007. "The Evolution of a Caddo Community in Northeastern Texas: The Oak Hill Village Site (41RK214), Rusk County, Texas." *American Antiquity* 72: 71–94.

Polhemus, Richard, ed. 1987. *The Toqua Site: A Late Mississippian Dallas Phase Town*. Department of Anthropology Report of Investigations 41. Knoxville: University of Tennessee.

Rafferty, Sean M. 2004. "'They Pass Their Lives in Smoke, and at Death Fall into the Fire': Smoking Pipes and Mortuary Ritual during the Early Woodland Period." In *Smoking and Culture: The Archaeology of Tobacco Pipes in Eastern North America*, edited by Sean M. Rafferty and Rob Mann, 1–42. Knoxville: University of Tennessee Press.

Rafferty, Sean M., and Rob Mann. 2004. "Introduction: Smoking Pipes and Culture." In *Smoking and Culture: The Archaeology of Tobacco Pipes in Eastern North America*, edited by Sean M. Rafferty and Rob Mann, xi–xx. Knoxville: University of Tennessee Press.

Randolph, J. Ralph. 1983. *British Travelers among the Southern Indians, 1600–1763*. Norman: University of Oklahoma Press.

Riggs, Brett H. 2008. "A Synthesis of Documentary and Archaeological Evidence for Early Eighteenth Century Cherokee Villages and Structures: Data for the Reconstruction of the Tsa-La-Gi Ancient Village, Cherokee Heritage Center, Park Hill, Oklahoma." Report on file. Chapel Hill: Research Laboratories of Archaeology, University of North Carolina.

Riggs, Brett H., and M. Scott Shumate. 2003. "Archaeological Testing at Kituhwa: 2001 Investigations at 31SW1, 31SW2, 31SW287, 31SW316, 31SW317, 31SW318, and 31SW320." Report on file. Cherokee, NC: Office of Cultural Resources, Eastern Band of Cherokee Indians.

Rodning, Christopher B. 2001a. "Mortuary Ritual and Gender Ideology in Protohistoric Southwestern North Carolina." In *Archaeological Studies of Gender in the Southeastern United States*, edited by Jane M. Eastman and Christopher B. Rodning, 77–100. Gainesville: University Press of Florida.

———. 2001b. "Architecture and Landscape in Late Prehistoric and Protohistoric Western North Carolina." In *Archaeology of the Appalachian Highlands*, edited by Lynne P. Sullivan and Susan C. Prezzano, 238–49. Knoxville: University of Tennessee Press.

———. 2002a. "The Townhouse at Coweeta Creek." *Southeastern Archaeology* 21: 10–20.

———. 2002b. "Reconstructing the Coalescence of Cherokee Communities in Southern Appalachia." In *The Transformation of the Southeastern Indians, 1540–1760*, edited by Robbie Ethridge and Charles Hudson, 155–75. Jackson: University Press of Mississippi.

———. 2002c. "William Bartram and the Archaeology of the Appalachian Summit." In *Between Contacts and Colonies: Archaeological Perspectives on the Protohistoric Southeast*, edited by Cameron B. Wesson and Mark A. Rees, 67–89. Tuscaloosa: University of Alabama Press.

———. 2007. "Building and Rebuilding Cherokee Houses and Townhouses in Southwestern North Carolina." In *The Durable House: House Society Models in Archaeology*, edited by Robin A. Beck, 464–84. Occasional Paper 35. Carbondale: Center for Archaeological Investigations, Southern Illinois University.

———. 2008. "Temporal Variation in Qualla Pottery at Coweeta Creek." *North Carolina Archaeology* 57: 1–49.

———. 2009a. "Mounds, Myths, and Cherokee Townhouses in Southwestern North Carolina." *American Antiquity* 74: 627–63.

———. 2009b. "Domestic Houses at Coweeta Creek." *Southeastern Archaeology* 28: 1–26.

———. 2010a. "Architectural Symbolism and Cherokee Townhouses." *Southeastern Archaeology* 29: 59–79.

———. 2010b. "European Trade Goods at Cherokee Settlements in Southwestern North Carolina." *North Carolina Archaeology* 59: 1–84.

———. 2011a. "Mortuary Practices, Gender Ideology, and the Cherokee Town at the Coweeta Creek Site." *Journal of Anthropological Archaeology* 30: 145–73.

———. 2011b. "Cherokee Townhouses: Architectural Adaptation to European Contact in the Southern Appalachians." *North American Archaeologist* 32: 131–90.

———. 2012. "Late Prehistoric and Protohistoric Shell Gorgets from Southwestern North Carolina." *Southeastern Archaeology* 31: 33–56.

———. 2013. "Architecture of Aggregation in the Southern Appalachians: Cherokee Townhouses." In *From Prehistoric Villages to Cities: Settlement Aggregation and Community Transformation*, edited by Jennifer Birch, 179–200. London: Routledge.

———. 2014. "Cherokee Towns and Calumet Ceremonialism in Eastern North America." *American Antiquity* 79: 425–43.

———. 2015a. *Center Places and Cherokee Towns: Archaeological Perspectives on Native American Architecture and Landscape in the Southern Appalachians*. Tuscaloosa: University of Alabama Press.

———. 2015b. "Native American Public Architecture in the Southern Appalachians. In *Archaeological Perspectives on the Southern Appalachians: A Multiscalar Approach*, edited by Ramie A. Gougeon and Maureen S. Meyers, 105–40. Knoxville: University of Tennessee Press.

———. 2018. "Cherokee Religion and European Contact in Southeastern North America." In *Religion and Politics in the Ancient Americas*, edited by Sarah Stacy Barber and Arthur Joyce, 75–97. London: Routledge.

Rodning, Christopher B., and David G. Moore. 2010. "South Appalachian Mississippian and Protohistoric Mortuary Practices in Southwestern North Carolina." *Southeastern Archaeology* 29: 80–100.

Rodning, Christopher B., and Amber M. VanDerwarker. 2002. "Revisiting Coweeta Creek: Reconstructing Ancient Cherokee Lifeways in Southwestern North Carolina." *Southeastern Archaeology* 21: 1–9.

Rogers, Anne F. 2009. "Archaeology at Cherokee Town Sites Visited by the Montgomery and Grant Expeditions." In *Culture, Crisis, and Conflict: Cherokee British Relations, 1756–1765*, edited by Anne F. Rogers and Barbara R. Duncan, 34–44. Cherokee, NC: Museum of the Cherokee Indian Press.

Schambach, Frank M. 1996. "Mounds, Embankments, and Ceremonialism in the Trans-Mississippi South." In *Mounds, Embankments, and Ceremonialism in the Midsouth*, edited by Robert C. Mainfort and Richard Walling, 36–43. Research Series 46. Fayetteville: Arkansas Archeological Survey.

Schroedl, Gerald F. 1986. "Toward an Explanation of Cherokee Origins in Eastern Tennessee." In *The Conference on Cherokee Prehistory*, edited by David G. Moore, 122–38. Swannanoa, NC: Warren Wilson College.

———. 1998. "Mississippian Towns in the Eastern Tennessee Valley." In *Mississippian Towns and Sacred Spaces: Searching for an Architectural Grammar*, edited by R. Barry Lewis and Charles B. Stout, 64–92. Tuscaloosa: University of Alabama Press.

———. 2000. "Cherokee Ethnohistory and Archaeology from 1540 to 1838." In *Indians of the Greater Southeast: Historical Archaeology and Ethnohistory*, edited by Bonnie G. McEwan, 204–41. Gainesville: University Press of Florida.

———. 2001. "Cherokee Archaeology since the 1970s." In *Archaeology of the Appalachian Highlands*, edited by Lynne P. Sullivan and Susan C. Prezzano, 278–97. Knoxville: University of Tennessee Press.

———. 2009. "Overhill Cherokee Architecture and Village Organization." In *Culture, Crisis, and Conflict: Cherokee British Relations, 1756–1765*, edited by Anne F. Rogers and Barbara R. Duncan, 62–82. Cherokee, NC: Museum of the Cherokee Indian Press.

Seeman, Mark F. 1979. "Feasting with the Dead: Ohio Hopewell Charnel House Ritual as a Context for Redistribution." In *Hopewell Archaeology: The Chillicothe Conference*, edited by David S. Brose and N'omi Greber, 39–46. Kent, OH: Kent State University Press.

Seeman, Mark F., and Frank Soday. 1980. "The Russell Brown Mounds: Three Hopewell Mounds in Ross County, Ohio." *Midcontinental Journal of Archaeology* 5: 73–116.

Shumate, M. Scott, Brett H. Riggs, and Larry R. Kimball. 2005. "The Alarka Farmstead Site: The Archaeology of a Mid–Seventeenth Century Cherokee Winter House/Summer House Complex." Report on file. Asheville, NC: United States Forest Service, National Forests in North Carolina.

Smith, Betty Anderson. 1979. "Distribution of Eighteenth-Century Cherokee Settlements." In *The Cherokee Indian Nation: A Troubled History*, edited by Duane H. King, 46–60. Knoxville: University of Tennessee Press.

Smith, Marvin T. 1989. "Early Historic Period Vestiges of the Southern Cult." In *The Southeastern Ceremonial Complex: Artifacts and Analysis*, edited by Patricia Galloway, 142–46. Lincoln: University of Nebraska Press.

Steere, Benjamin A. 2015. "Revisiting Platform Mounds and Townhouses in the Cherokee Heartland: A Collaborative Approach." *Southeastern Archaeology* 34: 196–219.

———. 2017. *The Archaeology of Houses and Households in the Native Southeast*. Tuscaloosa: University of Alabama Press.

Sullivan, Lynne P. 1987. "The Mouse Creek Phase Household." *Southeastern Archaeology* 6: 16–29.

———. 1995. "Mississippian Community and Household Organization in Eastern Tennessee." In *Mississippian Communities and Households*, edited by J. Daniel Rogers and Bruce D. Smith, 99–123. Tuscaloosa: University of Alabama Press.

———. 2007. "Shell Gorgets, Time, and the Southeastern Ceremonial Complex in Southeastern Tennessee." In *Southeastern Ceremonial Complex: Chronology, Content, Context*, edited by Adam King, 88–106. Tuscaloosa: University of Alabama Press.

———. 2018. "The Path to the Council House: The Development of Mississippian Communities in Southeast Tennessee." In *The Archaeology of Villages in Eastern North America*, edited by Jennifer Birch and Victor D. Thompson, 106–23. Gainesville: University Press of Florida.

Sullivan, Lynne P., and Christopher B. Rodning. 2001. "Gender, Tradition, and the Negotiation of Power Relationships in Southern Appalachian Chiefdoms." In *The Archaeology of Traditions: History and Agency before and after Columbus*, edited by Timothy R. Pauketat, 107–20. Gainesville, University Press of Florida.

———. 2011. "Residential Burial, Gender Roles, and Political Development in Late Prehistoric and Early Cherokee Cultures of the Southern Appalachians." In *Residential Burial: A Multi-Regional Exploration*, edited by Ron L. Adams and Stacie M. King, 79–97. Arlington, VA: Archeological Papers of the American Anthropological Association 20.

Trubitt, Mary Beth. 2009. "Burning and Burying Buildings: Exploring Variation in Caddo Architecture in Southwest Arkansas." *Southeastern Archaeology* 28: 233–47.

Walker, William H. 1995. "Ceremonial Trash?" In *Expanding Archaeology*, edited by James M. Skibo, William H. Walker, and Axel E. Nielsen, 66–79. Salt Lake City: University of Utah Press.

Walling, Richard, Robert C. Mainfort, Jr., and James R. Atkinson. 1991. "Radiocarbon Dates for the Bynum, Pharr, and Miller Sites, Northeast Mississippi." *Southeastern Archaeology* 10: 54–62.

Ward, H. Trawick, and R. P. Stephen Davis Jr. 1999. *Time Before History: The Archaeology of North Carolina*. Chapel Hill: University of North Carolina Press.

Waselkov, Gregory A., and Kathryn E. Holland Braund, eds. 1995. *William Bartram on the Southeastern Indians*. Lincoln: University of Nebraska Press.

Welch, Paul D. 2005. *Archaeology at Shiloh Indian Mounds, 1899–1999*. Tuscaloosa: University of Alabama Press.

Williams, Samuel Cole. 1928. *Early Travels in the Tennessee Country, 1540–1800*. Johnson City, TN: Watauga Press.

Williams, Samuel Cole, ed. 1927. *Lieutenant Henry Timberlake's Memoirs*. Johnson City, TN: Watauga Press.

———. 1930. *James Adair's History of the North American Indians*. Johnson City, TN: Watauga Press.

CHAPTER 9

Ash as an Agent of Transformation in Iroquoian Society

William Fox

Observations concerning Iroquois use of ash in ritual and domestic contexts have been recorded since the nineteenth century by ethnologists such as Schoolcraft (2002), Morgan (Tooker 1994) and Boyle (1898), while attempts to utilize ethnographic evidence, combined with the observations of seventeenth-century European visitors to the Great Lakes region, in the interpretation of the archaeological record have been practiced since the early twentieth century (i.e. Wintemberg 1908) using what Steward referred to as the "direct historical approach" (Baerreis 1961: 51). Early twentieth-century Ontario archaeologists studying Iroquoian sites were most interested in defining artifact manufacture and function, and rarely considered community social structure, and even more rarely "ideational culture" (Trigger 1978: 9). By mid-century, Ritchie had begun to explore archaeological evidence for Iroquoian ceremonialism on precontact Iroquoian sites in New York State (Ritchie 1947, 1950). Subsequently, he considered at some length the evocative evidence provided by grave goods from an early seventeenth-century Seneca Iroquois cemetery, as compared to ethnographic evidence of Seneca ceremonial events (Ritchie 1954: 63–69). Tooker likewise considered archaeological evidence of a medicine bundle from an early seventeenth-century Niagara Frontier Iroquois cemetery, in terms of ethnographically documented Iroquois ceremonialism (White 1967: 16).

While imagery on effigy pipes has generated efforts to correlate ethnological and historical documentation of Iroquois ideology with archaeological evidence (Mathews 1976), as has contextual evidence from cemeteries involving grave goods, little effort has been made to consider Iroquoian site structure or community patterns as these data may reflect ceremonial activities (Fox 1988). The latter can be ephemeral and, consequently, overlooked by archaeologists excavating sites in the Great Lakes region, where organic artifactual and structural evidence is normally lacking from the archaeological record (Fox 1997). The distribution of wood ash deposits on Iroquoian village sites has been considered almost exclusively in regard to hearth refuse disposal activities (Parker 1907: 480–90; Heidenreich et al. 1971: 207).

The Iroquois

In order to evaluate the validity of the direct historical approach to interpreting archaeological evidence of ceremonialism from early contact and, especially, precontact northern Iroquoian sites, it is important to understand the complexity of Indigenous political events in the Lower Great Lakes region during the one-hundred-year period from the mid-sixteenth century to the mid-seventeenth. The late sixteenth- to early seventeenth-century geographic distribution and character of Iroquoian communities in the Northeast has been the subject of numerous culture historical syntheses for over a century (Bradley 1987; Engelbrecht 2003; Fox 2015; Garrad 2014; Parmenter 2010; Schoolcraft 2002; Tooker 1967; Trigger 1987; Warrick 2008; Williamson 2012). These have been based on Indigenous testimony, early European documentation, and archaeological research. One of the most salient documents regarding the traditional territories of Northeastern Indigenous peoples in the early seventeenth century was only recently discovered in the British Admiralty Archives. The Taunton map appears to have been produced in 1641 by a French surveyor, Jean Bourdon, and provides the earliest surviving depiction of indigenous tribal locations in the Northeast (Heidenreich 1988) (figure 9.1).

This is an important document, as it improves the accuracy of Champlain's 1632 mapping of the Northern Iroquois (Biggar 1929), particularly the Ontario Iroquois who were dispersed and to a large extent adopted by the Five Nations Iroquois between 1648 and 1651. The victorious Five (later Six) Nations Iroquois, originally of upstate New York, were the subject of historical observations by Dutch and French settlers during the seventeenth century (Biggar 1929; Gehring and Starna 1988; Wrong 1939) and of ethnographic inquiry in the United States and Canada since the mid-nineteenth century (Boyle 1898; Schoolcraft 2002; Tooker 1994). Each of the latter studies has presented a different perspective and experience in their recording of Iroquois ritual, resulting in a considerable variability in specific detail (Fenton 1987: 338–39; Fox and Salzer 1999: 237–44; Tooker 1970: 48–82). That there was ceremonial variability between longhouses in Canada and in the United States during the nineteenth and twentieth centuries is perhaps not surprising, as it may

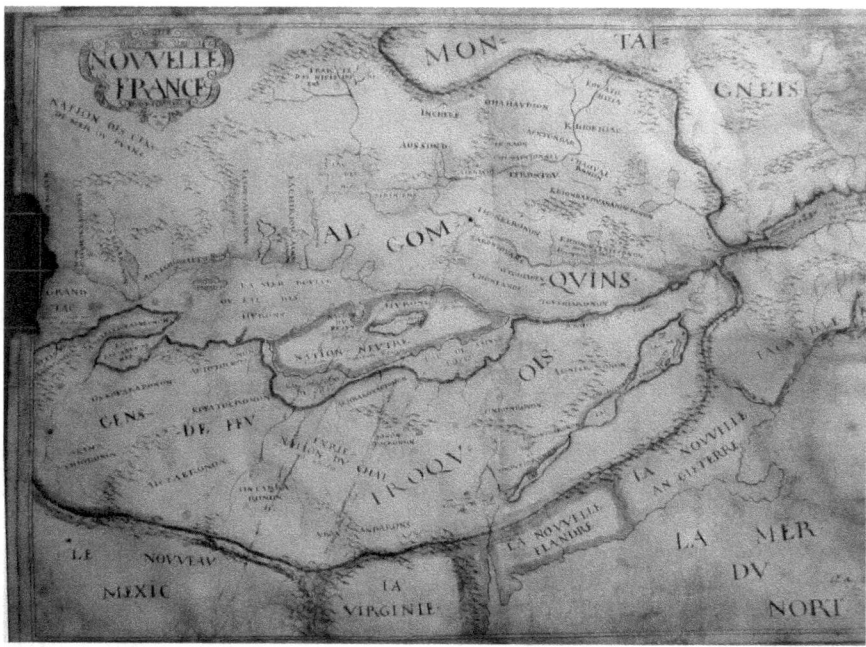

Figure 9.1. *The Novvelle France or Taunton map, describing predispersal tribal locations in the lower Great Lakes region and dating to ca. 1641. Photo by William Fox.*

reflect not so much the geographic separation of these communities as the late seventeenth-century coalescent nature of Iroquois society. Each tribe, and perhaps most of all the Seneca, was composed of a myriad of former nations adopted through the mid-seventeenth-century mourning wars, as reflected by Lalemant (Thwaites 1898: 45:207) in his *Relation* of 1659–60, where he observes:

> If any one should compute the number of pure-blooded Iroquois, he would have difficulty in finding more than twelve hundred of them in all the five Nations, since these are, for the most part, only aggregations of different tribes whom they have conquered,—as the Hurons; the Tionnontatehronnons, otherwise called the Tobacco Nation; the Atiwendaronk, called the Neutrals when they were still independent; the Riquehronnons, who are the Cat Nation; the Ontwagannhas, or Fire Nation; the Trakaehronnons, and others,—who, utter Foreigners although they are, form without doubt the largest and best part of the Iroquois.

The Iroquois had become an amalgam of Ontario Iroquoians, Central Algonquians, and the original New York population. This cultural diversity was not expressed socially in terms of changes in day-to-day life, including subsistence activities of these coalescent seventeenth-century communities; however, the same does not appear to have been the case concerning religious belief systems. Regarding Ontario Iroquoian influence on Five Nations Iroquois ritual, Fenton (1987: 67–69) wrestles with the fact that masking ceremonies, similar to those documented among the Seneca Iroquois False Face Society since the nineteenth century, were clearly recorded by the Jesuits among the Huron/Wendat prior to their dispersal in 1649. Further, evidence for an important False Face Society prop, the snapping turtle shell rattle as illustrated by Lewis Henry Morgan (Tooker 1994: 196), is absent from precontact archaeological sites in New York State; however, one specimen has been recovered from the ca. AD 1500 Lawson village in Ontario (Smith 1986: 5, fig. 2), occupied by the Neutral, a nation whom the Seneca adopted in such great numbers that they formed a substantial portion of two of their late seventeenth-century villages (Wright 1963: 57).

Hearths and Ash

The place of hearth ashes in Iroquoian society was both mundane and spiritual. Domestic hearths had been used for millennia for heating lodges and for the processing of foodstuffs, including corn or maize. The latter cultigen was one of the latest to arrive in the Northeast from the south some two thousand years ago (Hart et al. 2007), as evidenced by phytoliths preserved in carbonized residues adhering to ceramic vessels. Previously, carbonized kernels recovered from archaeological contexts had been used to argue for a later arrival, some fifteen hundred years ago (Birch and Williamson 2018: 90). However, the carbonized kernels likely represent fortuitous burning or new methods of processing, such as parching for later use. The latter is a significant event in the use of ash for cooking, as this ingredient has no place in the preparation of green corn meals. The use of mature or parched corn processed with ash to produce a basic corn soup (hulled corn soup) is recorded ethnographically among Indigenous peoples originally situated throughout eastern North America (Harrington 1908: 583; Hen-Toh 1957: 196, 202; Wright 1958: 158). The archaeological evidence for this cooking practice was recognized some thirty years ago on Ontario Iroquoian village sites (Fox 1989).

As a University of Toronto undergraduate, the author spent the better part of a summer on a crew excavating and recording a large segment of the Huron/Wendat north village at Cahiague (Emerson 1961; Tyyska 1969), the settlement where Champlain overwintered in 1615–16 (Heidenreich 2014; Manning et al. 2019) during his initial exploration of what is now southern Ontario (Biggar 1929). House after house displayed burnt orange patches running down the length of the central corridor, with small "ash pits" clustered around them (figure 9.2). Over succeeding

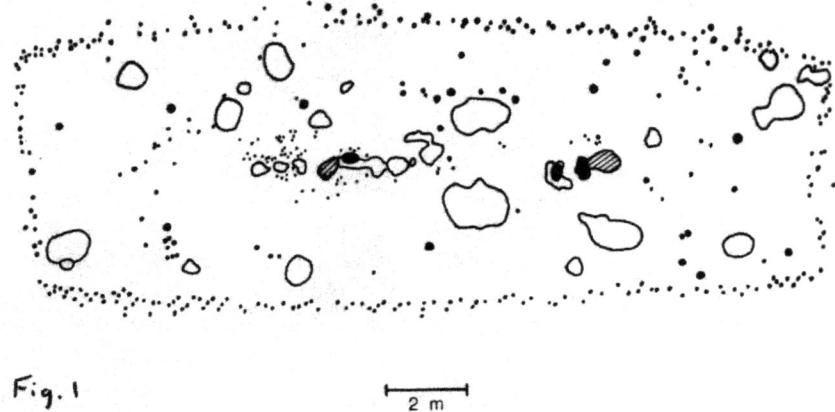

Fig. 1

Figure 9.2. *Floor plan of Cahiague North Village House 3. (Hatched features are hearths and black features are "ash pits"). Figure by William Fox.*

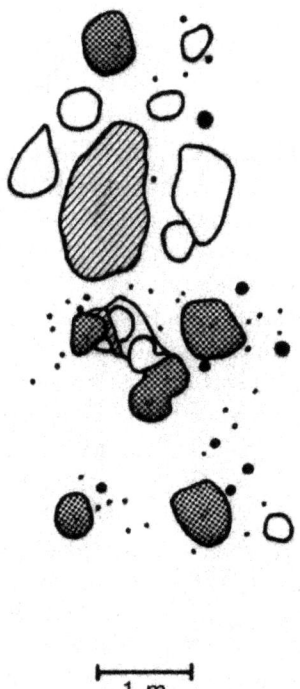

Figure 9.3. *Eleventh-century longhouse hearth complex (House 7, Elliott Village II). Figure by William Fox.*

years, the author mapped and excavated hundreds of such features at Ontario Iroquoian villages in southwestern Ontario such as the Early Iroquoian DeWaele (Fox 1976) and Calvert sites (Fox 1982), considering them to have "a predominately floor debris disposal function" (Fox 1976: 182) and to be "casual refuse pits," as referenced by Timmins (1997: 166).

Such hearth-side pits of ash have been documented as far back as a thousand years ago on Iroquoian villages in southern Ontario (Fox 1989: fig. 2; Pihl 1999: 18, 20, fig 4.1, appendix 1; Stothers 1977: 129–32) and continue as ubiquitous interior longhouse features into the early seventeenth century (Fox 1976: 182, fig. 9; Lennox 1984: 195; Timmins 1997: 166, 181, figs. 7.28, 7.34; Williamson 1985: 180, 199, figs. 14, 24; Wright and Anderson 1969: 14, fig. 2) (see figure 9.3). They are circular to oval in plan view, ranging from thirty to seventy centimeters in diameter, and are five to forty-five

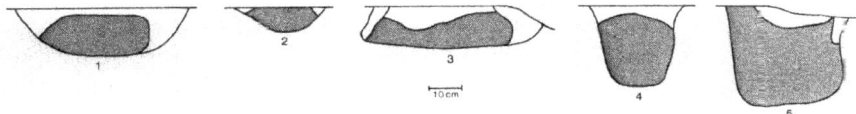

Figure 9.4. *Elliott Village "ash pit" profiles (stippled areas are ash fill). Figure by William Fox.*

centimeters in depth from the original floor surface. Profiles are basin- to bell-shaped, and many contain a central deposit of ash surrounded by gray-brown soil (see figure 9.4). While the ash content can be extremely variable, even within a single dwelling, those with a considerable quantity of ash often display an inverted cone profile almost as if the ash were poured into the pit. Artifacts are not abundant in such pure ash but occur in greater frequency in mixed ash and soil fills. The latter are exactly what one would expect in longhouse floor deposits.

Over the years, this longhouse feature pattern continued to confound the author along with a nagging question—why dig a hole in a longhouse floor to deposit debris that could be dumped steps away, outside the house in an adjacent midden? Certainly, the large in-house plant storage pits located away from the central corridor of these longhouse dwellings often displayed layered deposits containing abundant ash and artifacts, apparently dumped after these receptacles had been abandoned due to contamination. But these partially ash-filled pits had been excavated for a specific purpose other than waste disposal. The eureka moment occurred in the mid-1980s while preparing hulled-corn soup and adding baking soda, as directed by the Oneida reserve residents who had provided both the recipe and dried corn. The pale-yellow corn turned bright orange, as the hulls and skins separated and the kernels assumed the form of puffed wheat. A quick check of ethnographies by Harrington (1908: 583, 585), Parker (1968: 49, 69 and 73) and Waugh (1916: 90, 92) determined that the Iroquois used a weak lye solution made from "hard wood ashes and water" (Parker 1968: 69) to remove hulls and skins of boiling corn and pounded corn or hominy. Both Parker (1968: 51) and Waugh (1916: 63) describe ash sifter baskets, which presumably functioned to separate hearth wood ash from incidental hearth inclusions such as burnt artifacts and bone (Timmins 1997: 166) occurring in this desired cooking ingredient. Subsequently, Virginia Beaver of Six Nations reserve informed the author that hard maple wood was selected for the production of cooking ash and suggested that the ash pits were situated adjacent to the hearths "not only for ease of access, but also because this was the driest area of the longhouse floor" (Fox 1989: 17).

In addition to the use of cold ash as a cooking ingredient, ash in the hearth also played a role in the preparation of other corn dishes. Several traditional Iroquois dishes were cooked directly among the hearth ashes. Parker states that leaf cakes or tamales (leaf-wrapped green corn paste) can be boiled or baked in the hearth ashes (Parker 1968: 66). Scraped green corn could similarly be baked in leaves in the ashes, as could green corn on the cob in the husk (Parker 1968: 68). In all such cooking methods, the cobs or "cakes" were placed on the warm floor of the hearth, covered with cold ashes, and then covered with hot embers, which were used to ignite a hot fire. An important cooking implement for both boiled and baked corn recipes is a "hommony blade," which Morgan illustrated and explained was "used in every Indian household for making hominy, succotash, or soup, and for many other purposes." He further notes that they are "usually from three to four feet in length, and made from hard maple, or other tough wood" (Tooker 1994: 222). He illustrates two with ornately carved handles. Harrington (1908: 380, figs. 123, 127, and 128) refers to this implement as a "paddle, often used to move the loaves of corn bread when boiling and for stirring corn soup," and these paddles are "frequently elaborately carved." Such an implement may well have been and probably was used to move baked corn cakes and cobs from the ashes of the hearth. Similar paddles have a role in Iroquois rituals, such as the Midwinter Festival, where "stirring the ashes" is performed.

From the Mundane to the Sacred, but Always Spiritual

David Boyle, Ontario's first provincial archaeologist (Killan 1983: 180–86), spent considerable time on the Grand River Reserve (Six Nations) recording Iroquois ceremonies with the assistance of J. Brant-Sero as interpreter (Boyle 1898: 3). He wrote extensively on the "burning of the white dog" as part of the Midwinter Festival he attended at the Seneca longhouse in 1898, and reported that the day following "the Burning of the Dog, two runners appointed by the Old Men (Ro-dik-sten-ha) summon the people to stir or scatter ashes at the Longhouse the following day. On entering each house the runner himself scatters ashes, after which, addressing the heads of the household, he informs them that according to the wish of Niyoh (the Creator) they are to appear at the Longhouse the following day, and be sure to take the children with them" (Boyle 1898: 106–7).

The nighttime proceedings the following day began with a speech by a representative of the "Holder of the Heavens" (*Taronyawagon*), at the end of which he informed the members of the opposite moiety that a person had been appointed as master of ceremonies, who in turn appointed a leader of the "Paddle Party." Following the reply of the other moiety, he directed "two men representing the opposite sides of the Longhouse" to "hand newly made paddles to men, women and children of their respective gentes" (Boyle 1898: 108). Boyle then describes a march around the longhouse by the participants, attended by discharged guns "to attract or direct the attention of the real Taronyawagon." The master of ceremonies addressed the assembled group, stating that "the Great Spirit sitting above (sees) we have observed the ceremonies in praises and offerings of thanksgiving." The "tipping the paddle" song is sung, whereupon the paddle party leader states "this is all we are able to do" as he returns the paddles to the master of ceremonies (Boyle 1898:109). The opposite moiety does likewise until all present have "passed the fire" and the evening closes with a speech by the personification of *Taronyawagon*.

The second evening provides additional community members the opportunity to pass the fire and this part of the program is drawn to a close by the "last Paddle Party which is composed of chiefs, warriors and women representing the whole of the Longhouse" (Boyle 1898: 111). The *Taronyawagon* then speaks and confirms that the entire longhouse community has "passed once more at the fire built for Him" (Boyle 1898: 112), and the master of ceremonies speaks to close the proceedings, prior to the Big Feather Dance and Skin Dance.

Speck (1949: 53) describes a somewhat different "stirring ashes rite" at the Cayuga Sour Springs Longhouse on Six Nations reserve, which "marks the formal opening of the Midwinter Festival." Two fires were lit in the longhouse, representing the two moieties (Turtle and Wolf), and ten to twelve ceremonial "paddles" (often displaying burnt moiety animal emblems) were readied for distribution to each moiety's participants by the two "uncles" representing those moieties. Each of these uncles or chiefs takes "one of the ceremonial paddles and goes to the east fire, and then to the west fire," and they "stir the ashes in the fires, alternating four times between the two fires," singing stirring ashes songs (Speck 1949: 54). Speck (1949) states that the act stirs up or arouses the people, notifying them that the ceremony is about to begin. Attendees likewise circle their moiety fires, stirring them with paddles, and a speaker offers "thanks and supplication to the Great Spirit" before and after the public event of the first day. On the second day, the members of the moiety groups stir the ashes, and once completed, the two chiefs "stand up, go from fire to fire, and stir the ashes, thus signifying that the ceremony is being brought to a close" (Speck 1949: 55). A speaker and a singer acting for the Great Spirit thank the participants now circled around the fires, who then "stir the ashes at each fire twice. This performance is referred to as 'lifting up the paddles' and concludes the ceremony for the second day" (Speck 1949: 55).

Tooker (1970: 44) reports on the performance of this ceremony on the Tonawanda reserve in the 1950s and describes a considerably different program than that reported by Speck. The Tonawanda Seneca have two "uncles" representing the moieties; however, they travel from house to house to announce the New Year and "stir the ashes in the stove of each house." The uncles dress as "Big Heads" only at Tonawanda, and formerly dressed in buffalo robes bound with "ropes of braided corn husks" symbolizing "the union of the trophies of the hunt and the fruits of the harvest, men and women's subsistence activities respectively, in winter and summer," according to Fenton (1987: 63). Tooker (1970), in reference to Speck's description of the aforementioned Cayuga ceremony, suggests that the travel from house to house among the New York Seneca is due to the proximity of family residences to the longhouse on those reservations, as opposed to Six Nations where land allotment does not permit a similar settlement pattern. Certainly, the clustering of residences adjacent to the longhouse more closely reflects the structure of earlier Iroquoian villages (Fox 1988).

Taken as a whole and considering the range of activities and props utilized by various Iroquois communities, the stirring of the ashes seems to replicate the daily activity of preparing the morning meal—awaking the embers to restore the hearth for cooking, using an implement important in the preparation of boiled and baked corn foods. At a higher level of abstraction, the stirring of ashes may represent a "remnant of a New Fire rite" at the start of the New Year, as suggested by evidence collected by Fenton and Hewitt (Tooker 1970: 45). This proposal is supported by the *Taronyawagon* speech recorded by Boyle, above, describing a "fire built for Him" (the Creator). Tooker suggests that the New Fire rite was formerly "a winter solstice rite, one of whose purposes was to turn back the sun" (Tooker 1970: 83). She notes that such rituals throughout the Americas involved the "extinguishing of old fires and rekindling of new ones" as symbolized in the ash stirring, the "sacrifice of either a human or a dog," and that it "once included a war dance" (Tooker 1970: 84).

Curing Rituals

Beyond community-wide ceremonies, ash also functioned in curing rituals specific to individuals. Fenton (1987: 267) reports that the "False Faces participate in three kinds of ceremonies during the year," the most important being the cleansing of the village of disease in the spring and fall. The third activity, in conjunction with the Husk Faces (Boyle 1905: 58–59), is their role in the Midwinter Festival (see figure 9.5). In all three appearances, the blowing of ash on a household and, particularly, the sick

Figure 9.5. *Husk Face mask, produced by Yvonne Thomas, Wolf Clan Mohawk, at Six Nations, Ontario.*

in return for tobacco is an important component of their program of residential visitation, including traditional songs and dance. While the range of gestures and their symbolic meaning are complex, the following will focus on the use of ashes.

During the third day of the Tonawanda Seneca thanksgiving ceremony, the

> False Faces blow ashes on the person or persons who sponsored the dance. They rub their hands in the ashes and hot coals of the stove, place their hands on the person and blow, sending out a cloud of ashes. Various parts of the body are so

treated. The power of the False Faces is believed to be such that they are not burned while handling these hot coals. . . ." (Tooker 1970: 55)

Speaking of the Husk Faces, Tooker states that they have several rituals and "may ash individuals to cure them." During the evening of the sixth day, the False Faces ash each other after the tobacco invocation and continue "to ash each other" as they dance (Tooker 1970: 62). Later in the evening the False Faces and Husk Faces may continue to "ash some people in front of the men's stove." Similar ashing events are recorded for the Midwinter Festival and curing events at the Newtown, Coldspring, and Onondaga Longhouses in New York, and the Sour Springs and Onondaga Longhouses in Ontario (Tooker 1970: 66–82).

Clearly, wood ash (and embers) were considered "medicinal" in the context of curing by at least two Iroquois medicine societies. These medicines were applied to specific areas of a patient's body, presumably based on symptoms; however, the ash could be dispersed more widely through blowing. Considered in its context within the Midwinter Festival and a "new fire" ceremony, this material may have been seen to rejuvenate and cleanse an individual or diseased residence.

Ash in the Iroquoian Archaeological Record

The ethnographic information presented above as applied to Ontario Iroquoian archaeological evidence speaks to the importance of wood ash as a cooking ingredient for corn soup from a thousand years ago until the dispersal of these communities in the mid-seventeenth century. Similar community pattern evidence for ancestral Five Nations Iroquois groups is limited compared to Ontario, due to the small areas commonly exposed during archaeological investigations and the emphasis on artifact recovery. Engelbrecht (2003: 7), in his excellent Iroquois culture synthesis and overview, does not mention ash pits adjacent to hearths, but based on published community pattern data they appear to be present on the mid-thirteenth century Canandaigua or Sackett site (Hart 2000; Ritchie and Funk 1973: 215, fig. 22, feature 2), and may be present in House 1 on the ca. AD 1400 Onondaga Howlett Hill site (Tuck 1971: 78, fig. 4) and in House 1 on the sixteenth-century Mohawk Garoga site (Funk and Kuhn 2003: 87, fig. 45). The equivocal presence of these features in ancestral Five Nations Iroquois longhouses would appear to be more a question of identifying ash-filled pits as functionally separate from adjacent hearths, as opposed to their absence.

Archaeological evidence for intra-longhouse Ontario Iroquoian ritual activities can include obvious features, such as infant burials (Kapches 1976;

Fitzgerald 1979) or semi-subterranean sweat lodge facilities (MacDonald and Williamson 2001). However, identifying evidence for corporate ceremonial events can be more challenging (Fox 1988). The more subtle evidence of ash-stirring rites during a Midwinter ceremony or the ashing of individuals has yet to be identified in the archaeological record, but given the miniscule amount of airborne ash in the latter ritual activity, this is hardly surprising. Archaeological documentation concerning the presence of an unusually large and anciently disturbed hearth in the center of an eleventh-century Ontario Iroquoian longhouse, the longest in the village and containing artifactual and faunal evidence of ceremonial activities, is suggestive of Iroquois ash stirring rites recorded eight hundred years later.

As described above, wood ash served to connect the mundane to the sacred, to connect the act of food preparation to protection from spiritual disease. This life-giving, positive, and transformative capacity could be witnessed by community members through the result of ash addition to boiling dried corn and the production of a new, more palatable product. Thus, it seems that ash was seen to be a positive, transformative agent in the world of the Iroquois. It revitalized the individual and community, leading to the good life. It may even be that the white of the ash was metaphorically equivalent to the white of shell, as proposed by Hamell (1988: 205), representing "culturally valued states of physical, spiritual, and social well-being."

William (Bill) Fox has been involved in Ontario archaeology for over fifty years, often in close liaison with Indigenous communities. Additional research has been undertaken in the northeast United States, several European countries—most extensively in Cyprus—and most recently in Mongolia. He was employed by the Ontario government for nineteen years as a regional archaeologist in positions across the province, then as senior archaeologist for the province. Subsequently, he was hired by Parks Canada as chief of archaeology for the Prairie and Northern Region (Manitoba, Saskatchewan, Yukon, NWT [including Nunavut]). Today he continues his research as an adjunct professor at Trent University in Peterborough, Ontario.

References

Baerreis, D. A. 1961. "The Ethnohistoric Approach and Archaeology." *Ethnohistory* 8: 49–77.
Biggar, H. P. 1929. *The Works of Samuel de Champlain in Six Volumes*. Volume 3: *1615–1618*. Toronto: The Champlain Society.
Birch, J, and R. F. Williamson. 2018. "Initial Northern Iroquoian Coalescence." In *The Archaeology of Villages in Eastern North America*, edited by J. Birch and V. Thompson, 89–105. Gainesville: University of Florida Press.

Boyle, D. 1898. "The Pagan Iroquois." *Archaeological Report Ontario 1898, Being Part of the Report of the Minister of Education, Ontario*: 54–196.

———. 1905. "Husk False Faces." *Annual Archaeological Report 1904, Being Part of Appendix to the Report of the Minister of Education, Ontario*: 58–59.

Bradley, J. W. 1987. *Evolution of the Onondaga Iroquois*. New York: Syracuse University Press.

Emerson, J. N., ed. 1961. "Cahiague 1961." Manuscript in possession of the author. Toronto: Public Lecture Series, University of Toronto Field School.

Engelbrecht, W. 2003. *Iroquoia: The Development of a Native World*. New York: Syracuse University Press.

Fenton, W. N. 1987. *The False Faces of the Iroquois*. Norman: University of Oklahoma Press.

Fitzgerald, W. R. 1979. "The Hood Site: Longhouse Burials in an Historic Neutral Village." *Ontario Archaeology* 32: 43–60.

Fox, W. A. 1976. "The Central North Erie Shore." In *The Late Prehistory of the Lake Erie Drainage Basin: A 1972 Symposium Revised*, edited by D. S. Brose, 162–92. Cleveland, OH: Cleveland Museum of Natural History.

———. 1982. "The Calvert Village: Glen Meyer Community Patterns." *KEWA Newsletter of the London Chapter, Ontario Archaeological Society* 82: 5–9.

———. 1988. "The Elliott Village: Pit of the Dead." *KEWA Newsletter of the London Chapter, Ontario Archaeological Society* 88: 2–9.

———. 1989. "Add a Dash of Ash." *Profile Newsletter of the Toronto Chapter, Ontario Archaeological Society* 8: 16–19.

———. 1997. "Constructing Archaeological Expectations from Meskwaki Ritual." *Michigan Archaeologist* 43: 3–25.

———. 2015. "Ethnogenesis in the Lower Great Lakes and St. Lawrence Region." *Ontario Archaeology* 95: 21–32.

Fox, W. A., and R. J. Salzer. 1999. "Themes and Variations: Ideological Systems in the Great Lakes Region." In *Taming the Taxonomy: Toward A New Understanding of Great Lakes Archaeology*, edited by R. Williamson and C. Watts, 237–63. Toronto: Eastend Books.

Funk, R. E., and R. D. Kuhn. 2003. "Three Sixteenth-Century Mohawk Iroquois Village Sites." *New York State Museum Bulletin* 503. Albany, NY: The University of the State of New York, State Education Department.

Garrad, C. 2014. *Petun to Wyandot: The Ontario Petun from the Sixteenth Century*. Edited by J-L. Pilon and W. Fox. Mercury Series Archaeology Paper 174. Ottawa: Canadian Museum of History and University of Ottawa Press.

Gehring, C. T., and W. A. Starna. 1988. *A Journey into Mohawk and Oneida Country, 1634–1635, the Journal of Harmen Meyndertsz van den Bogaert*. Translated by C. T. Gehring and W. A. Starna. New York: Syracuse University Press.

Hamell, G. 1988. Life's Immortal Shell: Wampum Among the Iroquois. *Proceedings of the 1986 Shell Bead Conference Selected Papers*. Rochester: Rochester Museum and Science Center Research Records 20: 205.

Harrington, M. R. 1908. "Some Seneca Corn-Foods and Their Preparation." *American Anthropologist* 10: 575–90.

Hart, J. P. 2000. "New Dates from Classic New York Sites: Just How Old Are Those Longhouses?" *Northeast Anthropology* 60: 1–22.

Hart, J., H. Brumbach, and R. Lusteck. 2007. "Extending the Phytolith Evidence for Early Maize (*Zea mays* ssp. mays) and Squash (*Cucurbita* sp.) in Central New York." *American Antiquity* 72: 563–83.

Heidenreich, C. E. 1988. "An Analysis of the 17th Century Map 'NOVVELLE FRANCE.'" *Cartographica* 25: 67–111.

———. 2014. *Samuel de Champlain in Wendake: The Country of the Huron in Ontario, 1615–1616*. De Grassi Point: Oak Cottage Productions.

Heidenreich, C. E., A. Hill, D. Lapp, S. Navratil. 1971. "Soil and Environmental Analysis at the Robitaille Site." In *Palaeoecology and Ontario Prehistory*, edited by W. Hurley and C. Heidenreich, 179–237. Department of Anthropology Research Report 2. Toronto: University of Toronto.

Hen-Toh. 1957. "Mon-dah-min and the Redman's Old Uses of Corn as Food." *Chronicles of Oklahoma* 35: 194–203.

Kapches, M. 1976. "The Interment of Infants of the Ontario Iroquois." *Ontario Archaeology* 27: 29–39.

Killan, G. 1983. *David Boyle: From Artisan to Archaeologist.* Toronto: University of Toronto Press.

Lennox, P. A. 1984. *The Bogle I and II Sites: Historic Neutral Hamlets of the Northern Tier.* Mercury Series 121. Ottawa: National Museum of Man.

MacDonald, R. I., and R. F. Williamson. 2001. "Sweat Lodges and Solidarity: The Archaeology of the Hubbert Site." *Ontario Archaeology* 71: 29–78.

Manning, S., W. J. Birch, M. Conger, M. Dee, C. Griggs, and C. Hadden. 2019. "Contact-Era Chronology Building in Iroquoia: Age Estimates for Arendarhonon Sites and Implications for Identifying Champlain's Cahiagué." *American Antiquity* 84: 684–707.

Mathews, Z. P. 1976. "Huron Pipes and Iroquoian Shamanism." *Man in the Northeast* 12: 15–31.

Parker, A. C. 1907. *Excavations in an Erie Indian Village and Burial Site at Ripley, Chatauqua Co., N.Y. Being the Record of the State Museum Archaeological Expedition of 1906.* Museum Bulletin 117. Albany: New York State.

———. 1909. "Secret Medicine Societies of the Seneca." *American Anthropologist* 11: 161–85.

———. 1968. *Parker on the Iroquois: Book One—Iroquois Uses of Maize and other Plant Foods.* New York: Syracuse University Press.

Parmenter, J. 2010. *The Edge of the Woods.* East Lansing: Michigan State University Press.

Pihl, R., ed. 1999. *Turning the First Millennium: The Archaeology of the Holmedale Site (AgHb-191), A Princess Point Settlement on the Grand River.* Report on file. Toronto: Archaeological Services Incorporated.

Ritchie, W. A. 1947. "Archaeological Evidence for Ceremonialism in the Owasco Culture." *Researches and Transactions of the New York State Archaeological Association* 11: 55–75.

———. 1950. "Another Probable Case of Prehistoric Bear Ceremonialism in New York." *American Antiquity* 15: 247–49.

———. 1954. "Dutch Hollow, An Early Historic Period Seneca Site in Livingston County, New York." *Researches and Transactions of the New York State Archaeological Association* 13(1).

Ritchie, W. A., and R. E. Funk. 1973. *Aboriginal Settlement Patterns in the Northeast.* New York State Museum and Science Service Memoir 20. Albany: University of the State of New York.

Schoolcraft, H.R. 2002. *Notes on the Iroquois by Henry R. Schoolcraft.* East Lansing: Michigan State University Press.

Skinner, A. 1925. "Some Seneca Masks and their Uses." *Indian Notes* 2: 191–207.

Speck, F. G. 1949. *Midwinter Rites of the Cayuga Long House.* Philadelphia: University of Pennsylvania Press.

Smith, D. 1986. "Cylindrical Pits on the Lawson Site." *KEWA Newsletter of the London Chapter, Ontario Archaeological Society* 86: 3–7.

Stothers, D. M. 1977. *The Princess Point Complex.* Archaeological Survey of Canada Paper 58. Ottawa: National Museum of Man.

Thwaites, R. G., ed. 1898. *The Jesuit Relations and Allied Document.* Cleveland, OH: Burrows Brothers.

Timmins, P. A. 1997. *The Calvert Site: An Interpretive Framework for the Early Iroquoian Village.* Archaeological Survey of Canada Mercury Series Paper 156. Ottawa: Canadian Museum of Civilization.

Tooker, E. 1967. *An Ethnology of the Huron Indians 1615–1649.* Midland: Huronia Historical Development Council and Ontario Department of Education.

———. 1970. *The Iroquois Ceremonial of Midwinter.* New York: Syracuse University Press.

———. 1994. *Lewis Henry Morgan on Iroquois Material Culture.* Tucson: University of Arizona Press.

Trigger, B. G. 1978. "William J. Wintemberg: Iroquoian Archaeologist." In *Essays in Northeastern Anthropology in Memory of Marian E. White*, ed. W. Engelbrecht and D. Grayson, 5–21. Occasional Publications in Northeastern Anthropology 5.Rindge, NH: Franklin Pierce College.

———. 1987. *The Children of Aataentsic: A History of the Huron People to 1660*. Montreal: McGill-Queens University Press.

Tuck, J. A. 1971. *Onondaga Iroquois Prehistory, A Study in Settlement Archaeology*. New York: Syracuse University Press.

Tyyska, A. E. 1969. "Settlement Patterns at Cahiague." Manuscript on file. Toronto: Ontario Department of Records and Archives.

Warrick, G. 2008. *A Population History of the Huron-Petun, A.D. 500–1650*. New York: Cambridge University Press.

Waugh, F. W. 1916. *Iroquois Foods and Food Preparation*. Geological Survey Memoir 86. Ottawa: Canada Department of Mines.

White, M. E. 1967. "An Early Historic Niagara Frontier Iroquois Cemetery in Erie County, New York. Archaeology and Physical Anthropology of the Kleis Site." *Researches and Transactions of the New York State Archaeological Association* 16(1).

Williamson, R. F. 1985. "Glen Meyer: People in Transition." PhD diss., McGill University, Montreal, Quebec.

———. 2012. "What Will Be Has Always Been: The Past and Present of Northern Iroquoians." In *The Oxford Handbook of North American Archaeology*, edited by T. Pauketat, 273–84. New York: Oxford University Press.

Wintemberg, W. J. 1908. "The Use of Shells by the Ontario Indians." *Annual Archaeological Report, 1907: Being Part of Appendix to the Report of the Minister of Education, Ontario*: 38–90.

Wright, G. K. 1963. *The Neutral Indians: A Source Book*. Occasional Papers 4. Rochester: New York State Archaeological Association.

Wright, J. V., and J. E. Anderson. 1969. *The Bennett Site*. Bulletin 229. Ottawa: National Museums of Canada.

Wright, M. H. 1958. "American Indian Corn Dishes." *Chronicles of Oklahoma* 36: 155–66.

Wrong, G. M., ed. 1939. *Sagard's Long Journey to the Country of the Hurons*. Toronto: Publications of the Champlain Society.

Part II
ASH AND RITUAL

CHAPTER 10

Ashes to Ashes, Dust to Dust in Caddoan Mortuary Ritual

Marvin Kay

Introduction

A peculiar aspect of Caddoan mortuary ritual is the attention paid to sediments of varied textures and colors; among them ash. Ash was retained from deliberately burnt charnel houses. In one rendition, light-gray ash alternates in the superior, or upward, position with dense black clay or the black charcoal layer of a burnt thatch and cane roof and was leveled as a platform upon which mound construction proceeded. In other cases, this dichotomy is retained as small marker mounds, charnel pits, and prepared flattop mound surfaces.

In retrospect, ash's significance as a metaphor for life and regeneration is not to be trifled with. So, this chapter focuses on ash, what at first glance appears as a minor detail in Northern Caddoan platform mound archaeology, and expands on a central thesis: platform mound construction follows a simple, efficient symbolic grammar. It pays special attention to the process and products of burning and ritualized burial of charnel houses.

This study builds from earlier assessments (Bell 1972, 1984; Kay and Sabo 2006; Kay et al. 1989; Vogel et al. 2005; see also Sullivan and McKinnon 2013) about late prehistoric mound complexes in northwest Arkansas and east Oklahoma associated with the Northern Caddoan culture area of the Arkansas River Valley and to its north (figure 10.1). Most notable is Robert E. Bell's formative research at the Harlan site that defined the distinctive charnel houses and the internments of remains removed from them and secondarily buried in a separate mound. In ways complementary to Bell's research, Kay and Sabo (2006) reported on new excavation programs and, melding ethnohistory with archaeology, devel-

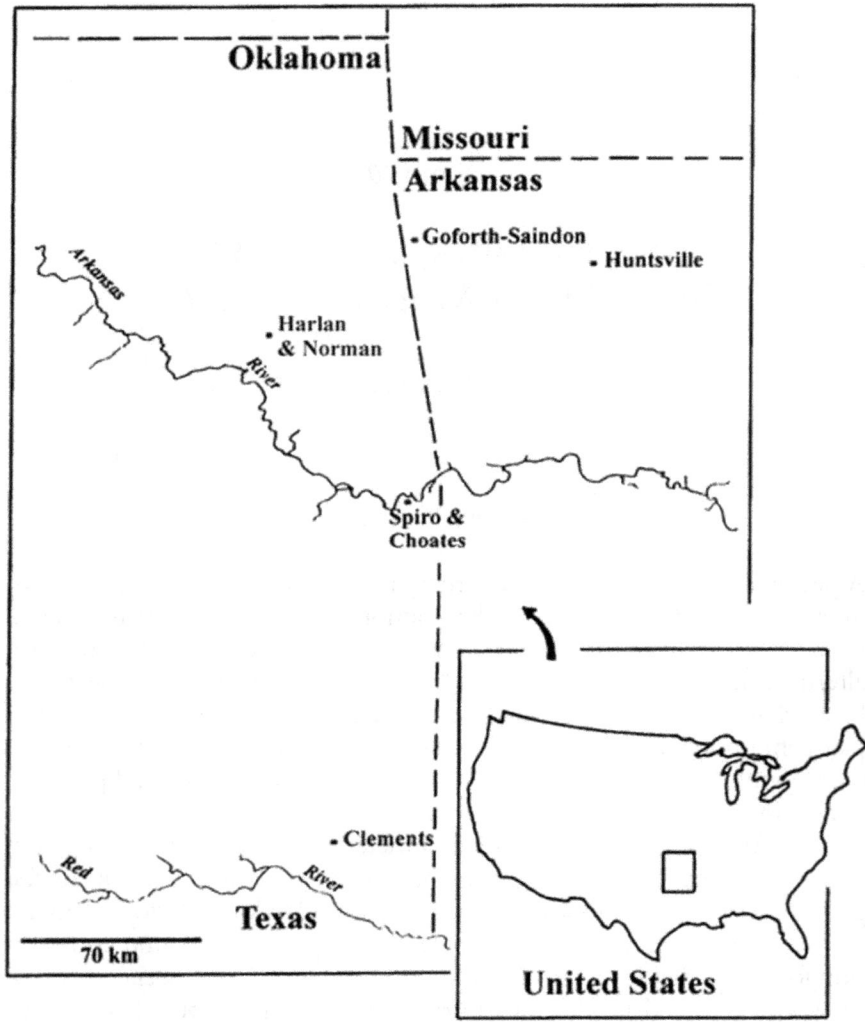

Figure 10.1. *Mound complexes in the study area. Harlan-style charnel houses are at Harlan, Goforth-Saindon, and Huntsville. Norman, Spiro/Coates, and Clements site investigations illustrate complementary platform mound constructions or derived charnel houses. Reprinted with permission of* Southeastern Archaeology *from Kay and Sabo 2006: 30, fig. 1.*

oped insights into their symbolic meaning and likely timing of the mortuary ritual coincident with the winter solstice sunset. These subjects are further surveyed here. Ash deposits and smoke billowing from burning buildings were seen as clues to cosmology. Yet as reconstructed from our writing (Kay and Sabo 2006: 40; Kay et al. 1989: 143), we treated ash as a self-evident if minor detail while exploring the larger Harlan-style charnel house mortuary program. The overall mortuary program lasted beyond the Harlan Phase, extended into the succeeding Norman Phase, and spanned in calibrated radiocarbon years an age of cal AD 1025–1281. Seventeenth-century and later ethnohistoric accounts further document aspects of mortuary programs derived in part from Harlan-style charnel houses (Kay and Sabo 2006: 32–34). In our opinion, the major insights of the ethnohistoric accounts associate death metaphors with the underground, or underworld, whereas souls live eternally in a house of death in the southwestern sky. Smoke from funeral fires serves as an *axis mundi* by which souls ascend from the middle world where people reside into the sky and the realm of life everlasting.

Ash has a prominent if easily overlooked role in the larger mortuary programs. To appreciate its heuristic value, one must review briefly the contexts in which ash is readily identified. Our excavations of two sites, Goforth-Saindon and Huntsville, revealed partial charnel house constructions near the base of platform mounds that are unmistakably similar—if not, dare we say, carbon copies—to the complete house excavations of the Harlan site. These were capped by later platform mound stages and distinctive small mounds atop these surfaces. Although the actual circumstances differ in these contexts, ash's symbolism remains constant. And that is the key to understanding. For my purposes here, I limit the descriptions to the evidence from Goforth-Saindon and draw broadly on how it reflects mortuary practices within the region.[1]

The mortuary program entailed ritually cleaned, paired rectangular charnel houses stacked one atop the other in shallow submound pits (figure 10.2).[2] Now devoid of material remains beyond exceedingly small, overlooked fragments of calcined bone, or cremains, one after the other was deliberately burned. The superior of the two also had a preserved, southwest-facing extended entryway passage with an elevated pedestal of clay at its throat (figure 10.3). Centered on the clay pedestal, a post blocked the entryway. After burning the second structure, its pyroclastic debris was leveled to that of the originating prepared mound platform surface. Construction of other, successive platform surfaces were separated by distinctive "marker" mounds whose fill alternated mostly between black clay and gray ash layers. These marker mounds were often truncated by other pit-digging episodes that did not intrude into an underlying platform surface. Thus, we infer that platform mound construction was done either by people knowledgeable about prior building activity or who simply dug out intervening matrices to judge where an earlier prepared surface lay so it could be avoided. Whether from superimposed charnel houses, marker mounds, or truncated pits, their alternating clay/ash layers are distinctive. They would have been obvious especially when viewed as truncated

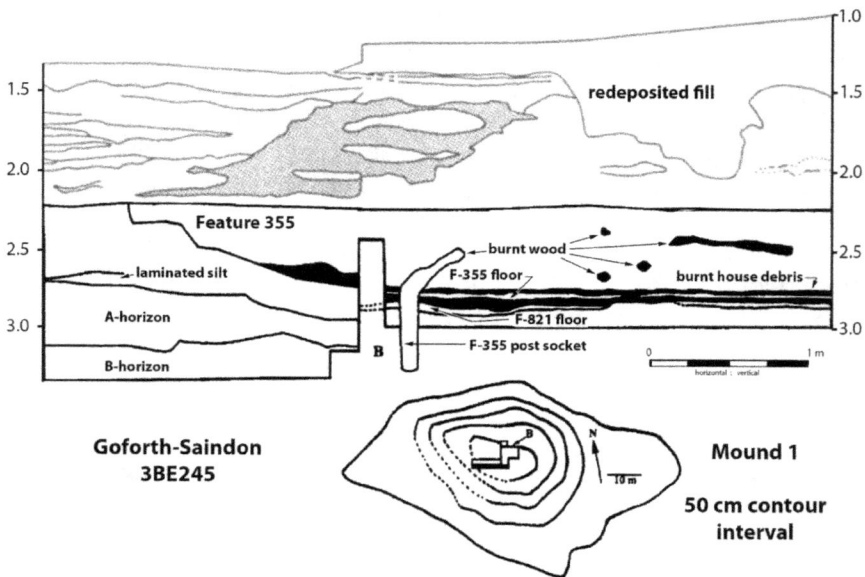

Figure 10.2. *Schematic vertical profile B of Goforth-Saindon Mound 1 excavation showing, in its earliest platform mound stage, submound pit (see laminated silt and "pinched" A-horizon that may distinguish the Feature 821 pit) and its two charnel houses (Features 355 and 821) beneath truncated pits with characteristic zebra-stripe fills in the intermediate platform mound stage. Directly beneath the redeposited fill is a final compound platform mound surface, the beginning of the final platform mound stage, at an excavation elevation between 1.0–1.5 meters below datum. Adapted from Kay, Sabo, and Merletti 1989: 139, fig. 44B, and Kay and Sabo 2006: 36, fig. 5, and with permission of* Oklahoma Archaeological Survey Studies in Oklahoma's Past *and* Southeastern Archaeology.

pit fill. And they go well beyond structural engineering requirements of mounding earth or layering it within a submound pit. Their characteristic "zebra-striped" quality cries out for meaning.

We are by no means the first archaeologists to be intrigued by zebra-striped mound fills from pits or marker mounds. The earliest descriptions of which we know are by a doyen of eastern North American archaeology, Joseph R. Caldwell, then of the Smithsonian Institution. His encounter in 1948 was during the salvage excavation of Mound I-1 and I-2, the largest conjoined mound and only surviving remnant of the Norman site. Norman is opposite from the Harlan site in what is now Fort Gibson Lake, a federal impoundment of Grand River in northeast Oklahoma that feeds into the Arkansas River. Caldwell's excavations were done in conjunction with Robert E. Bell, who saved Mound I-1 and I-2 from total destruction when the site was bulldozed for highway ramp fill for a bridge across the river. Later, in the 1970s, this excavation strat-

Ashes to Ashes, Dust to Dust

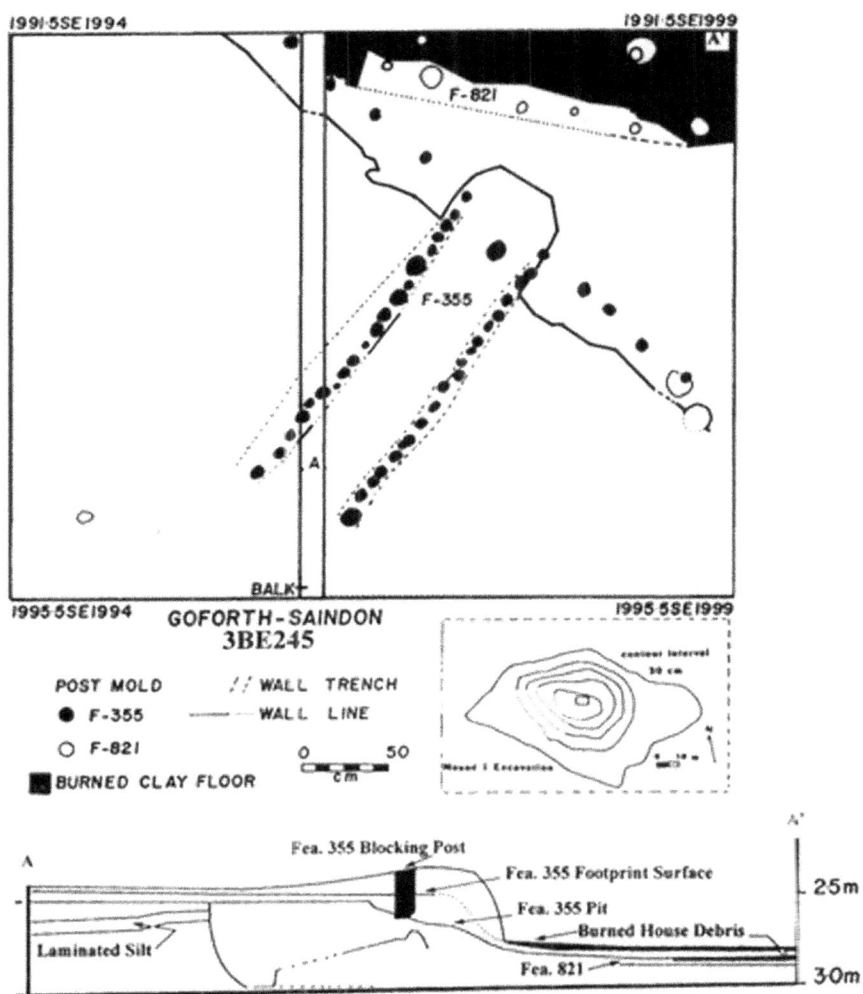

Figure 10.3. *Schematic views of excavated portions of charnel house Feature 355 overlying Feature 821 wall posts and carbonized roof debris on its fired clay floor. The house pit contains the floors and south walls of both structures. Feature 355 extended entryway was repaired with a new surface and clay pedestal added at its throat. This sealed the original entryway footprint surface. The entryway borders two post trenches whereas wall posts were in individual sockets. The blocking post is the entryway's last construction detail. Adapted with permission of* Southeastern Archaeology *from Kay and Sabo 2006: 35, fig. 4, and Kay and Sabo 2006: 38, fig. 8.*

egy produced similar mound construction details in the Caddo heartland of southwest Arkansas (Taormina 2015: 36–41). Caldwell's unpublished field notes and photographs on file at the Sam Noble Oklahoma Museum of Natural History, University of Oklahoma, describe them accurately as a "curious 'nongravitaic' arrangement in vertical areas" (as reported in Vogel et al. 2005: 38, 39, for Caldwell's original photographs of relevant stratigraphic details). As assessed by Vogel et al. (2005: 39), Caldwell's description applies to an area likely "somewhat east of the profiles revealed in 2000, and the pits revealed are likely some of the same ones" documented then. So, Caldwell undoubtedly recognized these features "as stratigraphic discontinuities [without understanding] what they were" (Vogel et al. 2005: 39).

Caldwell's description and those over a half century later now make perfect sense. Zebra-striped structures viewed whole might have looked like a mostly black clay conical mound with an occasional dusting of light-gray ash, assuming they were not vegetated initially. When cut into (see figure 10.2), their true character as either mound or pit fill would have the "curious 'nongravitaic' arrangement in vertical areas" of which Caldwell spoke. It is reasonable to assume the mound makers knew exactly the external appearance and internal structure of what they had created.

They had one other advantage that archaeology is uniquely suited to resolve: they knew *why* zebra striping was the mound fill of choice. As Kay and Sabo (2006: 30) argued, "The mortuary rituals and the cosmology they illuminate were intended to be preserved in ways that would have been intelligible to the actors themselves . . . [while] some aspects of structure and circumstance are identifiable still and provide cognitive insight." Indeed, the remarkable details preserved in these mounds were sculpted by capable hands, who might well qualify as the first Native archaeologists.

So, we face a true puzzle. Its solution is mostly, if not entirely, dependent on archaeological data, not ethnohistoric accounts. The latter complements as a "big picture" approximation, if at all (Wood 1990). But we need the fine details only archaeology provides. In making this assertion I follow well-established archaeological practice that addresses, if only in part, historical archives (Echo-Hawk 2000; Flannery and Marcus 1998; Silliman 2005).

Solving the Puzzle

To start, I begin with ash identification, then follow with the sequence of mound construction and deliberate burning of Goforth-Saindon charnel houses, and conclude with a review of vertical and horizontal platform mound staging. Other than the tangible aspects of mound fill, what we are really after is more process than product. For without a clear understanding of the process of mound makers and users, we will never understand the product. That is, we shall never understand why. Why, in particular, could I assert in the beginning that ash is the quintessential metaphor for life and regeneration? In coming full circle, I hope, we can achieve an inkling of the symbolic meaning—the grammar—underlying the cosmology that compelled both the Harlan-style charnel house mortuary program and its derivative structural elements of platform mound construction. The people repeatedly returned to a few essential and jealously guarded facts while sticking to a specified physical order of presentation.

Ash is easily traced to Mound 1 architecture at Goforth-Saindon and its Harlan-style charnel houses. Its earliest presence is with the superior charnel house, Feature 355, where it varies from secondary swirls of water-borne and sorted white ash around a burnt entryway trench (figure 10.4c) to a thick deposit of darker gray ash enveloping burnt wood beams on top of the thin deposit of black charcoal roof and wall debris (figure 10.4b) that collapsed onto the orange burnt clay floor (figures 10.2, 10.4a). These latter two deposits are in primary context that developed as the house burned and collapsed on itself. Sandwiched immediately beneath the clay floor is another black charcoal roof and wall debris zone

Figure 10.4. *Feature 355 charnel house excavation photographs. (a) The extended entryway above the orange burnt clay floor. The darker gray circular discoloration in the center of the clay pedestal is the blocking post mold. The white plaster jacket protects a charred wood beam. Note also on the left (north) wall the ash zone just above the floor. It was leveled out to conform with the original mound platform surface. (b) Thin zone of charcoal from collapse of interior walls and roof. (c) Left (west) entryway trench charred caps of posts above hollow voids that rotted out and comprised an oxygen-free zone (see a) where burning ceased. Note secondary white ash swirls within a fifty-centimeter grid square defined by lines of intersecting string. Photos by Marvin Kay.*

that fell onto the earlier orange burnt clay floor of charnel house Feature 821 (figures 10.2, 10.3), but without ash atop the charcoal roof debris zone. This layered intermingling of two superimposed zones of charred black superstructure debris and two underlying burnt clay house floors is all within roughly ten centimeters vertical thickness.

Let us now return to a point of difference between the two structures: the dark ash fill atop the superior structure. This ash deposit was leveled out to coincide with the prepared mound surface from which the Feature 355 house pit was dug (figure 10.2). Its origin is consistent with ash from the charnel house itself, probably from roof and wall thatch and an occasional wood beam. Other charred wood beams and wall posts are within its black charcoal roof and wall debris zone directly beneath the ash. So, the structural supports derived from interior walls and the roof. Indeed, one wall post had a bent or broken piece penetrating the ash (see F-355 post socket in figure 10.2).

Exactly what happened to the missing ash zone above the black charcoal roof and wall debris zone of the underlying Feature 821 charnel house is a mystery. It is inconceivable that a thick ash deposit did not form when the structure burned. That leaves the obvious inference of its deliberate, careful removal before erecting the superior charnel house Feature 355 and plastering its clay floor.

To sum up, the two charnel houses are mirror opposites. Their dialectical contrasts mark poles of a two-stage mortuary program. They were erected in separate pits—each symbols of the underworld and death—one atop the other while sharing similarly cleaned plastered clay floors. They were intentionally burned, and great care was taken to preserve the thin, burned roof and wall charcoal zone atop their floors. From that point on they differed radically in the sequence of deliberate destruction. The cleaned, inferior structure floor was carefully preserved and sealed beneath a black charcoal layer above which the lighter gray ash was stripped away. Its entryway was not apparent in our excavations. Judging from the complete charnel house excavations at Harlan, it would have been removed had it existed. The superior structure, however, had an entryway facing southwest; true also at Harlan and Huntsville and with implications for the winter solstice sunset timing of the mortuary ritual (see Kay and Sabo [2006] for the fully developed argument).

The clay pedestal and blocking post at its throat were added just before destruction by burning. Significantly, this addition changed the contours and slope of the entryway and access to the house pit's cleaned plastered clay floor. Now the entryway no longer descended gradually into the house pit but was instead elevated above it and dropped steeply into it. If only metaphorically, this changed access within and out of the house floor, because the entryway now was blocked physically by a post plus the vertical drop-off from the clay pedestal itself. One has to ask, why then burn the building unless doing so was instructive ritually? All of this was underneath ash mantled up from the collapsed superstructure as it burned. This was no accident. It was intended to protect the upper structure's architecture, even—actually, especially—in its burnt state and symbolically seal and protect this sacred spot to commemorate the dead.

This consecration left little to the imagination so there could be no doubt of its purpose and meaning. Moving from the larger details of charnel house architecture, they projected the metaphors of life and death into every aspect of construction and destruction of the paired building repositories.

Specifics identified for Stages 1 and 2 include:

- The charnel house pits are emblematic of death and portals to the underworld. At least the upper of the two originates, however, by cutting through a prepared, flat mound surface that signifies the middle world of the living.
- Within the pit, the collapsed building signifies death over life/regeneration.
- Smoke from the burnt buildings acts as an *axis mundi* by which spirits travel to the Upper World.
- The house pits were cleaned before deliberate burning, an inviolable death marker signified by the removal of the dead but leaving the burnt floors alone.

For Stage 2:

- Structure 2 was built on top of charred debris of the first structure, then cleaned and deliberately burned, thus repeating and adding to the imagery of the first charnel house, but with a twist.
- In the entryway one descends into death as one walks into the house pit.
- In walking or looking out the entryway, one faces southwest and life/regeneration.
- Prior to deliberate burning, the entryway surface was cleaned and replastered, and a clay pedestal was added.
- Then by emplacing a blocking post, followed by burning, sealing, and leveling, we now have ash as a life symbol and physically sculpted as a new (or renewed) surface for subsequent platform mound construction.

This last step resolves another enigma, the deliberate removal of ash from atop the first charnel house but only to where the charcoal zone begins.

In ridding the first building of its ash layer but leaving the underlying charcoal zone intact, we have a complementary practice to the destruction also of this structure's entryway. Each of these acts is symbolic of but one thing: death. The charcoal layer signifies death in both its color and material. Deliberate removal of the entryway is a death sign because the souls of the dead could not leave the house via its now-missing entryway. The collapse of burned roof and wall debris as a preserved charcoal zone quite literally seals the deal. The charnel house destruction by burning marks death reigning supreme over life in Stage 1.

That leads to a final question about both stages of the mortuary program: the clay plastered floors. Their oxidized orange color is due to house burning, so not necessarily a crucial detail beyond having been light colored if not orange originally. What is clear, however, is that the floors protected and sealed the house structures from the underlying pit basins. Their careful cleaning included replastering of worn areas. Viewed in this fashion, the clay plastered floors likely mean one thing only: life itself from which the dead were physically removed prior to cleaning and destruction in burning the buildings.

Adding these details together, it is clear that the two stages of the mortuary program head in opposite directions and reveal a sequential, ordered cosmology. In Stage 1, the paramount symbol expresses the struggle of death succeeding life, although both elements are present. Death in Stage 1 as signified by the house pit, the charcoal zone, and the missing entryway is the final piece of the process. The plastered clay floor blocks the pit surface and its portal to the underworld but then literally is buried by the charcoal zone of burnt building collapse.

In Stage 2, imagery meanings are the same, while also being embellished by other elements of mortuary practice that symbolically celebrate life and regeneration. The specifics are simple and must have been obvious to those privileged or steeped in the mythology. The key is the final acts that preserved the burnt building. Among the most obvious details are the entryway clay pedestal and its blocking post that paradoxically kept death at bay and also contained within the house pit. That is, death could not surmount the now steeply inclined step up the clay pedestal. Or if having done so, death could not pass beyond the blocking post. So neither the clay pedestal nor its blocking post pertain to death per se but rather are inviolable life markers. Next the intent was explicit: the entire burnt building (and, indeed, its underlying counterpart) were to be entombed, preserved, and memorialized within a thick ash layer. Its purpose was as much metaphorical as structural because, once flattened, the ash assumed the level of the platform surface from which the charnel house pit was dug. Thus, in leveling its upper surface, the ash became integral to the original platform surface and its understanding as a microcosm of the middle world of life itself.

Between this platform surface and the succeeding one about eighty centimeters above it are truncated pit features (figure 10.2) and at least one marker mound (figure 10.5) from the intermediate platform stage. Each contains zebra-striped fills as prime structural elements. These can now be seen for what they were. The truncated pits all extend near but not into the underlying platform surface and its paired, Harlan-style charnel houses. In this respect they connote the principal imagery of a new ritual cycle of charnel house pits. These do not intrude onto the earlier ones; and without necessarily adhering to earlier actual constructions or

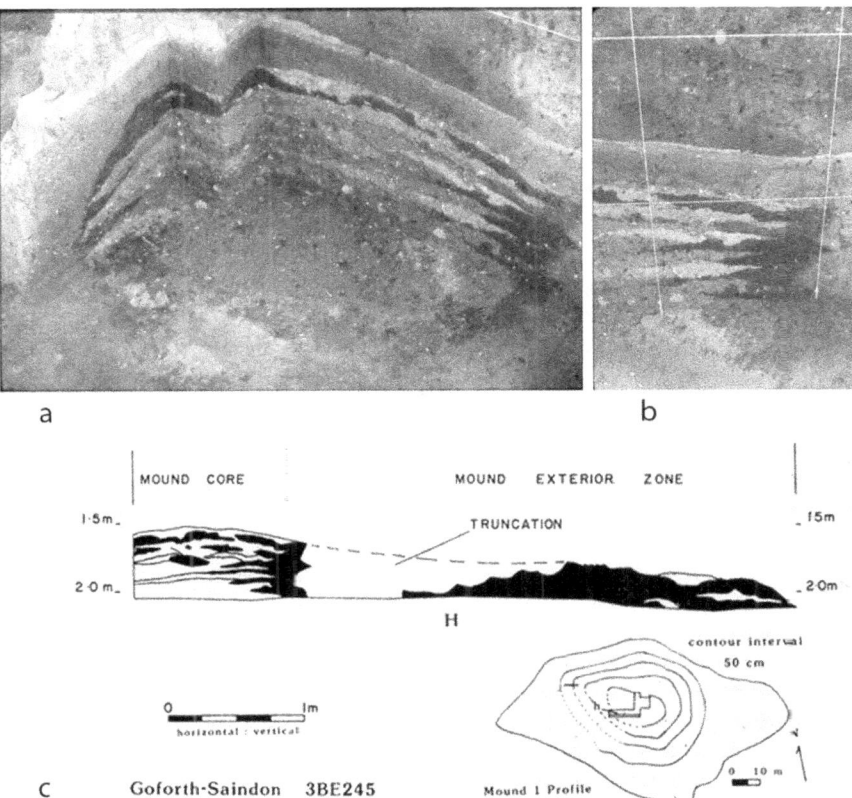

Figure 10.5. *Marker mound partially excavated. (a, b) Two views of the mound core and its truncated black clay beneath the next prepared mound platform surface. Note the ash is superior in the core area and similarly positioned in the mound exterior zone (c). The exterior zone is dominated by black clay. The platform surface is characteristic in its thick dark gray underlayer with a burnt upper surface of lighter oxidized orange color. This distinctive treatment likely has the same connotation as the dark charnel house pit beneath the burnt clay floor. Adapted from Kay, Sabo, and Merletti 1989: 145, fig. 47C line drawing, and with permission of* Oklahoma Archaeological Survey Studies in Oklahoma's Past.

ash usage. The marker mound is a more faithful rendition, however, in employing ash interlaced with black clay substituting for charcoal. Note the ash is superior in the core area and similarly positioned in the mound exterior zone (figure 10.5c). The exterior zone is dominated by black clay.

Figure 10.5 shows the order of zebra-striped ash-to-clay expressed in the marker mound core and its exterior zone. This repeats the metaphorical sequence of the superior charnel house from the original platform surface. The order in a more attenuated form is also apparent in the mound's overlying prepared compound platform surface. The implication is that the symbolic mortuary program grammar began with the Harlan-style charnel houses and persisted later in time, but stripped to its bare essentials. Among these are pairing light-colored and textured sediments when ash could not be found as readily or stood in place of oxidized, burnt clay floors. The connotation would have been as a broadly understood metaphor of the supremacy of life itself and regeneration. Charcoal and black clay fills appear as zones in burnt house layers or as the undersurface of prepared platform surfaces and signified the opposite metaphor of death. Regardless of their employment in either actual charnel house imagery or succeeding abstractions derived from it, the capping sediments all tend to consistently be light colored, if not ash.

Briefly put, these mounds are monuments that physically embody continuity in time and space of the meaning of life. The crucial timing appears to be at or just after the winter solstice sunset, when daylight begins to increase. They remain as powerful allegories of life and regeneration supplanting death. They offer hope to the grieving masses. Those who face death can be assured of immortality and life everlasting.

Marvin Kay is a dirt archaeologist with broad interests in sediments and geomorphology, processes of archaeological site formation, and reconstruction of primitive technologies and symbolism deduced from the archaeological record. Among his current projects are stone tool function of ancient agriculturalists in the Levant, Anatolia, and the Balkans; similar research of the Middle Stone Age in Ethiopia; and geomorphology and settlement at the late glacial to postglacial transition in the Plains and adjacent regions of North America.

Notes

1. Refer to Kay and Sabo (2006) for other pertinent examples and implications concerning footprints found in a sealed entryway surface, wood beam taxonomic identifications for Goforth-Saindon charnel house Feature 355.
2. If ethnohistoric accounts are a guide, then Caddoan houses lacked windows. Daylight illumination would have been from the mouth of the entryway.

References

Bell, Robert E. 1972. *The Harlan Site, Ck-6: A Prehistoric Mound Center in Cherokee County, Eastern Oklahoma*. Memoir 2. Norman: Oklahoma Anthropological Society.

———. 1984. "Arkansas Valley Caddoan: The Harlan Phase." In *Prehistory of Oklahoma*, edited by Robert E. Bell, 221–40. New York: Academic Press.

Echo-Hawk, Roger C. 2000. "Ancient History in the New World: Integrating Oral Tradition and the Archaeological Record." *American Antiquity* 65: 267–90.

Flannery, Kent V., and Joyce Marcus. 1998. "Cognitive Archaeology." In *Readers in Archaeological Theory: Post-processual and Cognitive Approaches*, edited by David S. Whitley, 35–48. London: Routledge.

Kay, Marvin, and George Sabo III. 2006. "Mortuary Ritual and Winter Solstice Imagery of the Harlan-Style Charnel House." *Southeastern Archaeology* 25: 29–47.

Kay, Marvin, George Sabo III, and Ralph J. Merletti. 1989. "Late Prehistoric Settlement Patterning: A View from Three Caddoan Civic Ceremonial Centers in Northwest Arkansas." In *Contributions to Spiro Archeology: Mound Excavations and Regional Perspectives*, edited by J. Daniel Rogers, Don G. Wyckoff, Dennis A. Peterson, 129–57. Studies in Oklahoma's Past 16. Norman: Oklahoma Archaeological Survey.

Silliman, Stephen W. 2005. "Culture Contact or Colonialism? Challenges in the Archaeology of Native North America." *American Antiquity* 70: 55–74.

Sullivan, Stephanie M., and Duncan P. McKinnon. 2013. "The Collins Site (3WA1): Exploring Architectural Variation in the Western Ozark Highlands." *Southeastern Archaeology* 32: 70–84.

Taormina, Kelsey. 2015. "An Architectural Analysis of Caddo Structures at the Ferguson Site (3HE63)." MA thesis, University of Arkansas Fayetteville.

Vogel, Gregory, Marvin Kay, and Louis Vogele Jr. 2005. "A Platform Mound at the Norman Site (34WG2), Eastern Oklahoma." *Southeastern Archaeology* 24: 28–45.

Wood, W. Raymond. 1990. "Ethnohistory and Historical Method." In *Archaeological Method and Theory*, edited by Michael B. Schiffer, 2:81–109. Tucson: University of Arizona Press.

CHAPTER 11

Ashes for Fertility

Cheryl Claassen

Introduction

Like other world cultures, American cultures had spirits and deities from within the realm of fire, earth, wind, and water. In Aztec theology, fire was embodied in two deities, one young and the other old, the Old Fire God being among the oldest deities in Mesoamerica. Old Man Fire lived at the center of the cosmos and in the center of every fire in the house and in shrines. He was the turquoise god and the North Star god, and the god of time. Cycles of time were marked with new fires, and each new house required a newly ignited fire drilled in the presence of old men. New fire ceremonies mandated that houses were swept; hearth stones discarded; and pestles, pottery, and idols broken, thrown away (into water), and replaced with new items. Food and drink were appropriate offerings to the house fire, as were odiferous herbs (López Luján 2005; Miller and Taube 1993).

Because the ashes that resulted from ritual fires and the remains of burnt offerings embodied the spirit honored, ashes were appropriately placed in community and personal sacred bundles, converted into paint, and even eaten, perhaps explaining the ash and charcoal in some Woodland period (twenty five hundred to three thousand years ago) fecal remains recovered in Mammoth/Salts Cave, Kentucky (Marquardt 1974). In some bundles, there were placed the ashes from which the people were created.

Red and black paint were derived from ashes. The Cherokee talk of the burning of the hated Stone Man, from whose ashes they gathered red paint (Hill 1997: 6). In the Aztec Creation story of the Fifth Sun, a god jumped into a dying bonfire to arise with his face covered in ashes. He became the moon. A jaguar leapt over this fire, which scorched his skin, creating the circular burn marks said to be the stars on the pelt (García 2015). No doubt reflecting the same story, the Winnebago believe that the spots on a bobcat as well as those on the fawn are also stars

(Dieterle 2005; Hall 1997). The Hunt God, Mixcoatl, chased a deer-goddess and killed her. When he burned her, the ashes flew back on his face. He became the god of the Milky Way. Darkened deity faces came to be called "star painting," and celestial objects in general were called "burned things." Stars were called "beings whose faces are covered in ash" (García 2015: 1). Numerous Aztec deities have black ashen eye masks conveying their residence in the ashy night sky as star deities (García 2015). The pair of statues found in a pit at the late prehistoric Etowah Mounds in Georgia each has such an eye mask.

Ashes also had medicinal properties. Cherokee medicine for whooping cough and worms was a strong ash made from green stalks of beans and other vegetables and water. This same medicine was swallowed before eating green corn (Witthoft 1949: 5n101). And let us not forget that mature maize kernels soaked in this mixture of ashes and water rendered a complete protein ("nixtamal"). We know this treated maize by the words "masa," "grits," and "polenta." One cure for dry breasts was to burn the mother's hair and have her eat the ashes (Mexica practice—Montellano 2004: 33). The ashes from human cremations were eaten by the Luiseño of California until recently, and eating cremains was once a widespread practice among Southwestern groups. The Luiseño believed they were ingesting the vital power of the dead (Furst 1977: 18).

As a new year marker, the rite of stirring ashes is and was performed at the Midwinter rites of the Sour Springs, Seneca and Onondaga peoples, in which the fire of every household was stirred in successive days by various visitors: the Bigheads and the two women who dressed them, then Four Faithkeepers, then two chiefs—all of these individuals were/are mature honored community members. Two Onondaga "Uncles," older men, put out and rekindle each household fire (Tooker 1970: 45, 67, 77, 270).

Eastern United States

It is the role of fire in purification, renewal, and transformation that I think brings us to some rock shelters of the Allegheny-Cumberland Plateau, Great Basin, and Colorado Plateau, shelters with incredible volumes of ash. I have argued that Newt Kash Shelter on Kentucky's Cumberland Plateau was a women's menstrual and birthing retreat place based on the materials present: bedrock mortar, medicinal plants, cradleboard, prepared plant fibers, cordage, textiles, and an infant burial (Claassen 2011). Subsequent review of rock shelters in the region led me to realize that I had ignored several other important categories of materials that were also key to this site function—sandals, bedding, shell spoons, and ash deposits. This expanded list led to a recognition of a dozen more retreat shelters on the Allegheny and Cumberland Plateaus (figure 11.1) in Kentucky and Ohio (e.g. Boston Ledges, Buzzard, Trace RS, Elyvar RS, Ash Cave, Overly, 33Ja13, 33Ho15—see Mills 1912).

Elsewhere I have addressed the role of these items and identified the new shelters. Shell spoons provide the requisite distinctive menstrual utensils, while shell is itself a fertility symbol (Claassen 2016). As for the sandals, the Below World or Underworld was the conceptual source of new life. The Mexica recognized feet as fertility symbols since feet are in touch with the Underworld, the source of future beings. The Dhegihan peoples of the Ozarks and Plains placed footprints in a cave that they imagined to be the vulva of First Woman, an entrance to the beneath world (Duncan and Diaz-Granados 2016). The rabbit is associated with the moon, and

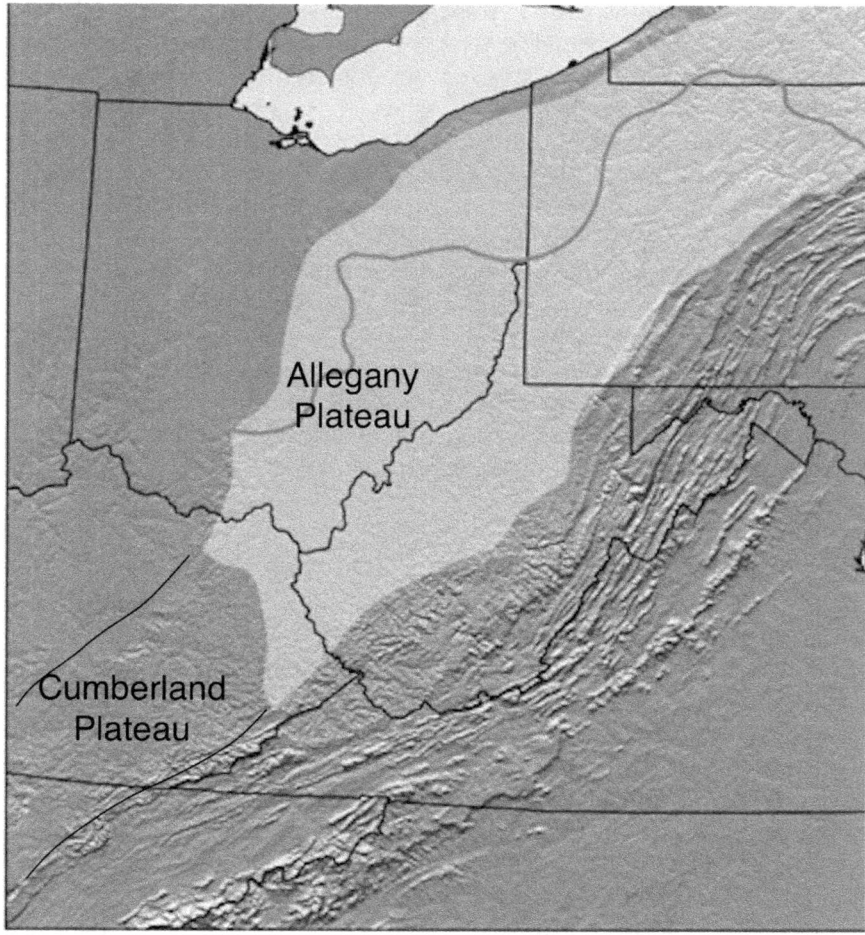

Figure 11.1. *Cumberland and Allegheny Plateaus. Wikimedia, CC BY-SA 2.5.*

the luck of the rabbit's foot is pregnancy. The sandal ceremony of the Winnebago clans presents new footwear to eleven different deities (Tooker 1979: 235). Sandals left in shelters, often worn out and unpaired, suggest a fertility offering, and the small shoe sizes of these sandals—children's and women's sizes—further seem to confirm this relevance (see Claassen 2016 for details). This shelter function seems to be no older than thirty-five hundred years in the East (even including the sandal offerings in Mammoth and Salts Cave, Kentucky), with the exception of much older sandals found in Arnold Research Cave, Missouri (Kuttruff et al. 1998).

The ash deposits in the few Early Woodland (two thousand to three thousand years ago) sites of Kentucky's Cumberland Plateau (figure 11.2; Red Eye, Little Ash Cave, Cave Fork Hill Cliff, Big Ash Rock House, Buckner Hollow, Great Rock House) and the Allegany Plateau of Ohio are remarkable for their volume and fineness, often earning them the name of "ash caves" (Funkhouser and Webb 1929, 1930). Details for these shelters are available in Claassen (2016). Ashes were removed from Ash Cave in Hocking County, Ohio, by the wagonload. There, ash was said to cover an area 200 feet (61 meters) by 30 feet (9.14 meters) and was 2.5 feet (0.76 meters) thick (Andrews 1877). Three feet (0.91 meters) of fine ash was removed from Buzzard Rock Shelter, Ohio, (33JA04) on Salt Creek, from an area 30 feet (9.14 meters) by 75 feet (22.9 meters) containing dozens

Figure 11.2 *Ash in Red-Eye Hollow. Reprinted from Funkhouser and Webb 1929: 46, with permission.*

of species of animals and four burials (Mills 1912). Newt Kash, Kentucky had an accumulation of ash 48 inches (1.22 meters) thick, and Red Eye shelter had up to 60 inches (1.52 meters) in places. Clay, and more often sand, was carried in and spread over the ashes to renew a surface.

What is the origin of this fine ash? And why would fine ash be more characteristic of women's shelters than others? I propose that we have here examples of burning related to renewal and medicine rites. Hill (1997) specified that Cherokee women danced around fires to provoke healing. "Women, wood, medicine, and healing all interwove in ritual" (Hill 1997: 13–14). It was/is customary for women completing their menses, birthing, or initiating into sodalities to discard old clothing. Dakota women deposit menstrual bundles in wild plum groves that are planted next to their "dwelling alone places" and subsequently "eliminate" those bundles before harvesting plums (LeBeau 2009). Predictable items to have accumulated in women's medicine shelters are clothing, moss, and grass menstrual bundles, moss baby diapers, moss and grass cradle padding, and old or soiled textiles. Fire is one way to cleanse the shelter, and these items would have generated fine ash when burned. Perhaps these blood and "filth" offerings were burned periodically both to make burnt offerings and to renew the shelter. Burning blood offerings is also characteristic of Maya practice (Miller and Taube 1993: 42).

Western United States

Although shelter used as a women's retreat seems to be uncommon and rather late in the eastern United States, women's shelters are abundant around the Great Basin and on the Colorado Plateau and occur early. Hundreds of shelters have sandals and textiles, grinding stones, awls, cordage, leather, skins, seeds, fauna, fur, and feces, indicating a range of activities, and some have ash lenses of note. Many of these sites with ash deposits are famous among archaeologists, such as Danger Cave (Jennings 1957) and Hogup Cave (Aikens 1970, Jennings 1978) in Utah.

Danger Cave, Utah

Excavations at Danger Cave in the 1950s yielded copious plant remains, textiles, and a projectile point sequence. Jennings refers to several layers as "dense ash beds" (figure 11.3), noting that most ash lenses and beds "represent burning of trash and litter in situ" (Jennings 1957: 58). In the second deepest component, DII (8,270–10,310 bp), he found "earths of various colors and many tons of ash, roof scalings, small rock fall fragments, guano and much vegetable material. In the central portion of the

Ashes for Fertility 191

Figure 11.3. *Danger Cave ash layer. Reprinted from Funkhouser and Webb 1929: 46, with permission.*

deposit, ash is the major component of this band averaging about 18" thick" (Jennings 1957: 58). If this band resulted from in situ burning, he puzzled, then where did the oxygen come from in this cave to feed such a massive burn at one time, and why was there faint layering within the ash zone? His answer (Jennings 1957: 64) reads as follows: "This huge ash bed results from oft-repeated fires of large amounts of some thin-spread, very fully combustible material (grasses and other small size fuel) here, and that the successive layers of ash insulated the scanty organic material underneath." The lack of guano on the surface of DII led Jennings to propose that a nearby lake had dried up. The final act of DII then was the burning of the organics.

The subsequent stratum, DIII, also had "many huge fires kindled—often repeated on the same spot" (Jennings 1957: 67). It, too, ended in an ash event. A pit was dug into the floor and then refilled with loose, fluffy ash. Stratum DIV, which began and ended with a spall layer, had "numerous extensive ash beds also burned in situ" (Jennings 1957: 71). A total of 568 pieces of milling stones was found throughout the cave, only 13 of which were more than 50 percent complete.

Hogup Cave, Utah

The south-facing, double-chambered Hogup Cave is located on the side of Hogup Mountain in the Great Salt Lake area. Excavations there sampled the profuse flora, fauna, and stone artifacts from what proved to be a seven-thousand-year sequence of deposits (Aikens 1970: 29–30). It is as famous as Danger Cave for the organics removed from its levels—particularly textiles and feces. Aikens remarks that

> man [*sic*] carried in hundreds of pounds of animal bone, hide, and hair, and literally tons and tons of vegetal matter—grasses . . . for seeds, rushes for weaving and bedding and many kinds of woody shrubs, presumably for fuel. Human fecal matter, too, is not insignificant in quantity. (Aikens 1970:11)

Three strata were particularly marked by ash content. Stratum 3, 6–10 inches thick (0.15–0.25 meters) with a date of 6020+/-380 bp (Aikens 1970: 28), was one of "widespread burning . . . that left its surface marked by a bed of fully oxidized white ash" (Aikens 1970: 14). Stratum 8, dated 3200+/-140 bp(?)(Aikens 1970: 29), was divided into upper and lower levels by "a bed of white ash," "the layer was burned over almost its entire extent. A hiatus in occupation subsequent to this event is suggested by the occurrence of a number of medium-sized roof spalls all lying on the burned surface" (Aikens 1970: 19). Stratum 14 with a date of 1210+/-100 bp (Aikens 1970: 29) had two burned areas. To the rear and center of the excavation was a great concentration of ash and charred material 6–8 feet (1.8–2.4 meters) in diameter and burned 5 feet (1.52 meters) deep. A second burned zone with a diameter of 3 feet (0.91 meters) and a depth of 14 inches (0.35 metres) was found.

In addition to the three strata with extensive ash, Aikens comments on numerous vegetal mats, or quids: "46 pads of shredded sagebrush bark and 3 of grass stems may have served as menstrual pads . . . the fibers are stuck together and matted rather tightly, as they might be if they had been impregnated with blood" (Aikens 1970: 119). These pads were found in nearly every level (two even escaped the burning in Stratum 3). Stratum 8 yielded 15 of these pads. Aikens (1970: 26) also mentions that there were areas of *Scirpus*, grasses and twigs 3–7 feet (0.91–2.1 meters) in extent that may have been sleeping or sitting areas and two possible "cradles," grass-lined pits set near fireplaces.

Conclusions

Ash-filled strata and ash-filled shelters signal a role in cultural use that is different from shelters lacking significant ash. I propose that this difference stems from their use as women's retreats and women's work party encampments. There are literally dozens of such shelters in the United states that beg the label "women's shelter" or "women's work camp." The tons of material found in Hogup and Danger Caves give me pause, however, in labeling these places medicine or retreat shelters. In that scenario, I think one or two women at a time would occupy the shelter, and their activities of plant fiber harvesting, cordage making, pickleweed processing, hide dehairing, etc., could not account for the quantity of remains, stressed by Aikens and Jennings as "tons" in weight. Instead, these western shelters and others in Utah, such as Old Man Cave, Bechan Cave, and Alvey Cave, and in Nevada, such as Lovelock Cave, Humboldt Cave, and Dust Devil Cave, seem to have been used by large work parties of women—some of whom were menstruating, some of whom were pregnant, some of whom were sickly—during the fall for pickleweed, bulrush, rabbit, and antelope hide processing activities. When these work parties vacated these caves, they purified them with fire, resulting in blood and filth "offerings" transformed into ash.

These sex-specific work party shelters typify early social organization in the vicinity of the ancient western lakes, with dates in the ninth and tenth millennia. This function for many shelters continued through the next nine thousand years. Many of these shelters have textiles, as well as unmatched or old sandals—which I believe were also left as fertility petitionings/offerings (see Claassen 2016 for details). While the typically small fragments of textiles may have derived from once-large items, *miniature* textile offerings, miniature looms, and miniature arrows are left by Wixarika women in rock shelters as thanksgiving and petitioning offerings (Schaefer 2002). Could we be finding large pieces of miniature offerings? Miniature bows were found in Danger Cave, as were tiny stone points (see Claassen 2017 for a discussion of lithic offering and stone fertility).

The women's shelters of the Cumberland Plateau in Kentucky and Ohio share, in many respects, the material culture categories in Hogup and Danger Caves and those of others mentioned here in the Great Basin and Colorado Plateau—the signs of industry such as fibrous material processing (bark, basket staves); cordage making; extensive nut or seed processing and probably dyeing; and special utensils (horn or shell), beds, cradles, awls, stone points, grinding equipment, and ash layers. Women of the two regions also shared a belief and a practice of burning for purification. Like the western shelters, the eastern shelters show strong seasonal use.

The so-called "ash caves" of the northern Cumberland and Allegheny Plateaus are intriguingly found in watersheds that drain to salt sources, and the shelters that surround Great Salt Lake clearly have salt association. There is reason here to recall the Aztec rites to Tlazolteotl, goddess of filth (including feces and garbage, "the old"), who was honored during their New Fire Ceremony, which has become the Busk in the Southeast (Hall 1997). Feces are often found in shelters with textiles or abundant organics perhaps indicating the honoring of a similar filth spirit. In addition to Tlazolteotl and a fertility goddess, a salt goddess Huixtocihuatl, elder sister of the rain spirits (Turpin 2011), was also honored at the same time in central Mexico. Several contenders for women's shelters in western Texas, Coahuila (Turpin 1997), and New Mexico (e.g. Pendejo Cave, High Rolls Cave) are also near salt. Taken as a set—feces, New Fire, and fertility practices—conducted in rock shelters near salt sources, there is good reason to suspect an ancient practice of honoring salt, filth, and fertility goddesses well into the past of North America. Turpin (2011) points out that in the Southwest, Salt Woman and Spider Woman are both earth deities and are apparently interchangeable, and she documents the place of fertility in the annual salt pilgrimage.

Fire purified and transformed matter and filth into celestial ash. Ashes could heal humans and transform sacred corn. That these ash beds in rock shelters are customarily associated with women's activities is easy to demonstrate. It may well be that ash and feces and salt are particularly associated with female spirits/deities in the period two thousand to ten thousand years ago as they were in later Mesoamerica cultures.

Cheryl Claassen received her PhD from Harvard in 1982 and has directed excavations in New York, Massachusetts, North Carolina, West Virginia, Tennessee, and Arkansas, as well as labs in Serbia and the Putnam Lab at Harvard. She has authored eleven books and many articles, typically on women, shells, rituals, and landscape.

References

Aikens, Melvin. 1970. *Hogup Cave*. Anthropological Papers 93. Salt Lake City: University of Utah Press.

Andrews, E. B. 1877. *Report on Exploration of Ash Cave in Benton Township, Hocking County, Ohio*. Harvard University Peabody Museum Reports 2: 48–50.

Claassen, Cheryl. 2011. "Rock Shelters as Women's Retreats." *American Antiquity* 76: 628–41.

———. 2016. "Rock Shelters, Boulders, and Bleeding Rocks: Uncovering Elements of Women's Ritual Landscape in the Midcontinent." In *Native American Landscapes: An Engendered Perspective*, edited by Cheryl Claassen, 3–34. Knoxville: University of Tennessee Press.

———. 2017. "Abundant Gifts of Stone and Bone." *Midcontinental Journal of Archaeology* 41: 274–94.

Dieterle, Richard. 2005. "Redhorn Panel Star Map." Retrieved 20 August 2017 from http://www.hotcakencyclopedia.com/ho.RedhornPanelStarMap.html.

Duncan, James, and Carol Diaz-Granados. 2016. "Rock Art, Gender, and the Dhegihan Landscape." In *Native American Landscapes: An Engendered Perspective*, edited by Cheryl Claassen, 86–108. Knoxville: University of Tennessee Press.

Funkhouser, William, and William Webb. 1929. *The So-Called Ash Caves in Lee County, Kentucky*. Department of Anthropology and Archaeology 1(2). Lexington: University of Kentucky.

———. 1930. *Rockshelters of Wolfe and Powell Counties, Kentucky*. Department of Anthropology and Archaeology 1(4). Lexington: University of Kentucky.

Furst, Peter. 1977. "The Roots and Continuities of Shamanism." In *Stones, Bones, and Skin Ritual and Shamanic Art*, edited by Anne T. Brodzky, Rose Danesewich, and Nick Johnson 1–28. Toronto: Society for Art Publications.

García, Elodie. 2015. "Color and Culture among the Aztecs, Part 2." Retrieved 3 Dec 2017 from http://mexicolore.co.uk/aztecs/home/colour-and-culture-among-the-aztecs-2.

Hall, Robert. 1997. *An Archaeology of the Soul: North American Indian Belief and Ritual*. Urbana: University of Illinois Press.

Hill, Sarah. 1997. *Weaving New Worlds: Southeastern Cherokee Women and Their Basketry*. Chapel Hill: University of North Carolina Press.

Jennings, Jesse. 1957. *Danger Cave*. University of Utah Anthropological Papers 27 and Society for American Archaeology Memoirs 14. Salt Lake City: University of Utah Press.

———. 1978. *Prehistory of Utah and the Eastern Great Basin*. University of Utah Anthropological Papers 98. Salt Lake City: University of Utah Press.

Kuttruff, Jenna, Gail DeHart, and Michael O'Brien. 1998. "7500 Years of Prehistoric Footwear from Arnold Research Cave, Missouri." *Science* 281(5373): 72–75.

LeBeau, Sebastian. 2009. "Reconstructing Lakota Ritual in the Landscape: Identification and Typing System for Traditional Cultural Property." PhD diss., University of Minnesota. Minneapolis.

López Luján, Leonardo. 2005. *The Offerings of the Templo Mayor of Tenochtitlan*. Albuquerque: University of New Mexico Press.

Marquardt, William. 1974. "A Statistical Analysis of Constituents in Human Paleofecal Specimens from Mammoth Cave." In *The Archaeology of Mammoth Cave*, edited by Patty Jo Watson, 193–202. New York: Academic Press.

Mills, William. 1912. "Archaeological Remains of Jackson County." *Ohio Archaeological and Historical Society Publications* 21: 175–215.

Montellano, Bernard Ortiz de. 2004. "Magia Medicinal Azteca." *Arqueología Mexicana* 12: 30–33.

Sassaman, Kenneth. 2010. *The Eastern Archaic Historicized*. Tuscaloosa: University of Alabama Press.

Schaefer, Sally. 2002. *To Think with a Good Heart*. Salt Lake City: University of Utah Press.

Tooker, Elisabeth. 1970. *The Iroquois Ceremonial of Midwinter*. New York: Syracuse University Press.

———. 1979. *Native North American Spirituality of the Eastern Woodlands*. New York: Paulist Press.

Turpin, Solvig. 1997. "Cradles, Cribs, and Mattresses: Prehistoric Sleeping Accommodations in the Chihuahuan Desert." *Journal of Big Bend Studies* 9: 1–16.

———. 2011. "Sex and the Salt Road: Interpretation of a West Texas Pictograph." *Plains Anthropologist* 56: 303–10.

CHAPTER 12

Ashes, Arrows, and Sorcerers

William H. Walker and Judy Berryman

Introduction

Ethnographies of Native peoples of the American Southwest consistently document perceptions that nonhuman objects, such as artifacts, architecture, plants, animals, rocks, minerals, clouds, rain, planets, and stars, possess animating powers analogous to those that enliven people (Bunzel 1992: 483). In the ethnographic record of the American Southwest, ash and projectile points offer protection against death and sickness caused by witchcraft and sorcery. As a result, people form social relationships with these nonhumans that necessarily defy pragmatic and scientific assumptions about how people interact with their tools, natural resources, and forces of nature. When we consider patterning in the life histories of these objects, including archaeological site formation processes, we need to take these relationships into account. For example, the interactions between people and buildings, arrow points and even ash shape the arc of these materials' lives, impacting how they enter the archaeological record.

Peoples of the American Southwest recognized that projectile points and ash possessed animate powers and used them accordingly (Bunzell 1992:490; Cushing 1920:617; Hill 1982: 125, 130, 314). Although archaeologists often assume points served for hunting or warfare and that ash is simply a byproduct of combustion, both possess more complex lives. Points find their way onto pueblo altars as life-giving powers (Fewkes 1899: plate XVIII, 267, plate XIX, 269; Voth 1901: plate XLIII, 77), and ash serves to protect life from other dangerous forces (Parsons 1916, 1996: 106; Stephen 1936: 97; Voth 1901: 107, 187, 196). Points bring users power and therefore can also serve as protective amulets, shielding their users from forces such as a newly created ceremonial building or the malevolent forces of witchcraft (e.g. Hodge 1890; Parsons 1996 [1939]: 332; Stephen 1936: 137). Considering these life histories, it should not surprise us that they can also enter the archaeological record for purposes related to these powers. We argue in this chapter that understanding such social relationships is the best way to explore deposits of arrow points, ash, and other artifacts in the burned rooms of many ancient Southwestern villages.

We begin with a discussion of object agency theory highlighting the benefits of behavioral archaeology's approach to the topic. Life histories, performance characteristics, and site formation process analyses all highlight ways to study patterning created by social relationships between people, ash, and arrows. In the synthetic model of inference (see Schiffer 1987: chap. 2) favored by behavioral archaeologists, the process of inferring unknown behaviors depends on establishing known correlations between people and things by using ethnographic and experimental sources.

In the second section of this chapter, we review ethnographic examples of the use of arrow points and ash. We build on the assumption that earlier ritual interactions in an object's life history tend to correlate and influence similar interactions later in their lives, including their use in discard activities. Ethnographic evidence demonstrates that fire imparts or inscribes ash with purifying power that can cure and retard malevolent forces (Parsons 1996 [1939]: 106–7, 183–84, 392; Robbins et al. 1916: 29; Stephen 1936: 371, 386, 458; see also Adler, chapter 5). Similarly, lightning animates arrow and spear points, giving the dual power to kill and provide protection from killers (Parsons 1996 [1939]: 106, 332–33). Southwestern Native peoples like many nonwestern peoples assumed that witches and related malevolent forces acted as the primary source of death. Therefore, they developed ritual technologies to address these dangers. We argue that a critical but often overlooked part of that technology involves site closure and the processing of homes and communities when people move. After abandonment, witches can still act from a distance on objects a person once touched. Thus, houses, tools, and human remains in a site all become vulnerable. Therefore, in the final section we explore the ritual processing that occurred to thwart such dangers.

We illustrate our discussion with a case study of Cottonwood Spring Pueblo (LA 175), a late prehistoric El Paso phase (AD 1300–1450) pueblo community covering an area approximately one square kilometer on the western flanks of the San Andres Mountains in southern New Mexico. This community includes four El Paso–phase pueblos designated Loci A, B, D, and E, and an Early Dona Aña–phase (AD 1000–1150) village. We concentrate on Area A, an adobe pueblo with approximately two hundred rooms. All rooms so far reveal closure processes involving burning and purposely placed floor assemblages that include projectile points, shell beads, turquoise, shaft straighteners, and a few sherds and flakes. These do not resemble household assemblages. Instead, they are ritual deposits placed in an effort to harness the powers associated with these objects (Walker 1995, 1998, 2001). Such processes are often overlooked because archaeologists assume they are looking for rare, "nonutilitarian" artifacts rather than useful everyday artifacts (e.g. ash, arrow points) animated by spiritual powers (Walker 1995). We contend that the perceived powers to purify and protect these objects were the reason they were deposited with the closure of the pueblo.

Animacy and Artifact Agency

In the 1990s through the early 2000s, social theory in archaeology focused on applying practice and agency studies of Bourdieu (1977), Giddens (1979), Sahlins (1976, 1981), and others interested in bridging the often larger-scale questions about society and its relationship to its social actors (e.g. Conkey and Gero 1997; Dobres and Hoffman 1994; Dobres and Robb 2000; Pauketat 2001; Whiteley 2002). Growing out of this attention to practice, the causal questions about human actors morphed into questions about the causal powers of objects (e.g. Gell 1992; Latour 1993). After all, material culture is the most obvious attribute of the human species. When people act, they always employ some form of object; therefore, it became interesting to consider how objects, like people, contribute to the structure of society.

In his science and technology studies, Latour used the term *actant* for nonhuman things. He devised a theoretical framework focusing on the networks of interactors (human and non) to reframe causal understandings of human activity. Alfred Gell (1998) elaborated a theory of artifact agency in *Art and Agency: An Anthropological Theory*, focusing on how pieces of art, like other fabricated objects, play causal roles in activity, beginning with their construction and continuing during their life histories in societies (see also Gell 1992). Although he used art, particularly paintings, as a foil to illustrate his approach, this is a more universal theory, and some of the best examples derive from classic ethnographic contexts such as the making of idols.

Schiffer and Miller (1999) approach the issue from the perspective of building a communication theory where artifacts play a central role. Like Gell they recognized that the interaction between maker and made is a two-sided equation where both as interactors contribute to the creation of the activity and its outcomes. They argue that this process can be modeled as either a behavioral interaction where the analyst partitions the causal contributions of both interactors or alternatively as a communication process where the analyst models an exchange of information. In the communication analysis, causal questions revolve around how the interactors receive, send, and emit information. Despite different terminology and bibliographies, Schiffer and Miller's communication model and Gell's agency theory mirror each other closely. In both, artifacts play a critical role in the transmission of information between people and things, contributing causally to the forward motion of activities. Equally important, both approaches take the critical step of focusing on the reception of information rather than the sending of it. This allows them to more easily identify material traces of information flow through the indirect measure of the receiver's (or in the case of Gell, "patients"') actions. While one can observe senders and model their action, one cannot assume that what they sent was received. The receiver's actions offer a more accurate approach. Focusing on receivers and artifacts moves both approaches away from more common communication theory. This is not a coincidence but a consequence of recognizing that material objects (artifacts, architecture, natural things and forces) count in the flow of human actions.

Given that things are not sentient (from a scientific point of view), they have often been assumed as not causal. However, when we recognize that they have causal consequences, then we can see that receivers make sense given their interactions with objects. Indeed, both approaches introduce multiple roles for people and things, where things cause reactions in people and vice versa. For Schiffer and Miller (1999), all interactors (people and things) can send and receive information as well as serve in the role of "emitters." Emitters receive information from senders and then broadcast that information to other receivers. Schiffer and Miller (1999) call this the three-body model to emphasize the critical importance that artifacts play as "emitters." However, artifacts can also serve as senders of information and receivers, as can people. Finally, this behavioral approach combines two other successful archaeological models, the synthetic model of underlying archaeological site formation processes (Schiffer 1987) and performance characteristic analysis associated with the study of artifact function (Schiffer and Skibo 1987).

Subsequent archaeological theory wove various combinations of these perspectives into Americanist and European archaeology (e.g. Knappett and Malafouris 2008; Mills and Walker 2008; Olsen 2010; Webmoor and Whitmore 2008). Although these scholars did not imagine that objects were sentient beings like people, they did imagine that other people saw them as such. Archaeologists also recognized that even without anthropomorphizing them, nonhuman objects can causally hinder and enhance activities affecting how they happen. These theoretical innovations continue to meet resistance from quarters who can only accept human actors as the causal drivers of activity. In a recent edited volume about materiality, for example, Van Dyke (2015: 20) declared that "the authors in the volume remain firmly and unapologetically 'anthropocentric' in the sense that we are anthropologists ultimately interested in the relevance of our work for human beings, not objects."

Practice theory opened the door for reconsidering the dichotomies between mind and body, thought and action, but those same dichotomies also underlie the divisions between people and objects in the analysis of human activity. As Webmoor and Whitmore (2008: 57) put it in their discussion of Meskell and Preucel's use of "dialectic" as a mediator between the social and the material of technology,

> The problem is that, despite hoping to move beyond, never mind transcend or resolve, "impermeable worlds," Meskell and Preucel are still taken in by the enchantment of the social and the modernist priority of humans as the locus of action sanctioning it. . . . Deploying the term "dialectic," we suggest, is not the correct trench to be digging in if we are to excavate underneath these divides.

Anthropocentrism ironically is modern and the vehicle that continues to promote cartesian dualism that masks the importance of the causal consequences of material objects in human behavior. As a result, archaeologists miss the critical effects of Native American animism, which is the opposite of anthropocentricism.

Ash and Arrows in the American Southwest

If we turn to the ethnographic record of the Pueblo cultures of the American Southwest, then it is clear that ash and arrow points cleanse and dis-charm materials (often people) put in danger through contact with spiritual powers (Parsons 1996 [1939]). This same cleansing power also allows them to perform as prophylactics against potential encounters with such forces, particularly witches. Buildings and many artifacts such as ceramics, projectile points, and ground stone become animated in the process of their construction and use. As Mindeleff (1891) demonstrates in his studies of Pueblo architecture, the rituals involved in the construction of kivas animate them, leading to their naming and use as power-filled places. With respect to ash and arrow points, archaeologists often imagine these tools in pragmatic terms. Ash is often viewed as detritus at the end of the life history of other objects and not as something with its own uses and performance properties. Points serve as the tips of projectiles such as atlatl darts or arrows used to kill either people or animals. To the degree that uses and recycling during their life histories come to mind (e.g. knives or drills respectively), these uses typically involve performance characteristics such as ease of penetration, or clean cutting, associated with their primary projectile uses (but see Sedig 2010, 2014). While power to thwart witchcraft, ease of purification, or dis-charming power do not immediately spring to mind for most scholars, within Pueblo people's logic these performances derive from the underlying power that inhabits ash and arrows.

Prophylactic

Ash offers a universal protective force. Hopi place ashes on their faces to protect them from the dead and other dangers during the month of December (Parsons 1996 [1939]: 463, 504). Newborn children after a period of seclusion at Hopi, Zuni, Laguna, and other pueblos will also be rubbed with ash prior to taking them outside for the first time (Stevenson 1901–2: 881). At Zia Pueblo the mother rubs herself with ashes for this event (Parsons 1996 [1939]:463). Zia fire society men make medicine by wetting charcoal in their mouths. At Zuni Pueblo a doctor who has previously been snakebitten must protect his young patient by smearing ash on them. To protect houses, ashes will be placed at thresholds such as doors and windows (Parsons 1996 [1939]: 106). Ash, like cornmeal, can also define a sacred space for ceremony (Stevenson 1901–2: 399–400). Confrontations with power such as the hunting of witches or combating sickness caused by witches is dangerous work. Eastern Pueblo doctors, therefore, will rub themselves with ash as a form of armor (Parsons 1920: 118–22; 1996 [1939]: 710–13).

Projectile points have similar protective powers and appear in oral traditions as sacred weapons. Warrior Twins used them to slay water monsters and other dangerous beings (Parsons 1996 [1939]: 1043). Like many people around the world, pueblo oral traditions describe arrow points and other stone tools as created by lightning strikes (Skeat 1912). As such, they ascribe the animacy of points to the power of lightning. Points therefore can be used to kill, or harnessed to protect their owner. Parsons describes this lightning power in protecting children: "The Arrowpoint that has been fastened to the Acoma infant's cradle board is hung around his neck when he leaves his cradle of lightning-riven wood" (Parsons 1996 [1939]: 332; White 1929–30: 134–35). The cradle, like the point itself, holds the power of lightning.

In the past it was common for adults to also wear arrow points as protective amulets. Women at Isleta, Laguna, and San Juan wear them around their waists. Laguna war priests wear them in leather bags tied about their necks (White 1929–30). Similar to ashes in times of fear at night, one can also carry a point in the mouth as protection. Scalp takers at Zia and Zuni also carry points in the mouth to protect them from the power of those they have killed (Parsons 1996 [1939]: 332). Arrow points find their way onto Pueblo altars where they become associated with lightning and power.

Fewkes (1899) illustrates two exceptional examples from the Tewa Hopi village of Hano. Arrow points figure prominently on Winter Solstice altars in association with lightning extenders, drawn images of lightning, the great serpent, and mountain lion paws. For the Zuni and many others, arrow points derive their power from lightning. As Cushing (1883: 10) notes in his discussion of Zuni Fetishes.

> Although fashioned by man, it [arrow point] is regarded as originally the gift or "flesh" of lightning, as made by the power of, and rendered more effective by these connections with the dread element; pursuant of which idea, the zig zag of lightning marks are added to the shafts of arrows.

This arrow power can protect the boundary between the living and the dead (Parsons 1996 [1939]: 106). At Taos, pueblo points are used to draw a protective line around graves, and at Isleta, points are passed over the walls of the deceased's home to cleanse it (Parsons 1996 [1939]: 332).

Purification

Similar to antibiotics, one turns to ash to disinfect or perhaps dis-charm after contact with an unclean substance, or to use prophylactically if one anticipates such contact. Voth (1903a: 348) used the Hopi word "nav-ochiwa" to describe the ash cleansing procedure at the end of the snake antelope ceremony when participants sing a cleansing song and throw ashes through the hatch of the kiva and, when the song ends, rub themselves with it to remove any other dangers (see also Parsons 1996 [1939]: 458–59, 668–69; Voth 1901: 109, 1903b: 44). Parsons (1996 [1939]: 183) notes that Yukioma, a Hopi leader of the anti-American faction at Hotevilla, explained that he had the power to arrest or stop enemies by blowing ashes at them. He gained this power from the god Masaw, lord of death and fire. In another dis-charming act, when a Hopi katsina dancer removes his mask, he waves it around his head with a pinch of ash to avoid sores, bad eyes, serious illness, and dreams of the katsina (Parsons 1996 [1939]: 458; Stephen 1936: 371, 386). Zunis will also use ashes to exorcize dangerous power (Stevenson 1901-2: 492). A Tewa priest will dis-charm himself with ash when constructing a new set of altar objects. A Hopi priestess wishing to give children some peaches from a Marau altar must rub them first with ash to cleanse them of power (Stephen 1936: 881).

Arrow points also empower other artifacts and architecture. The Acoma reenactment of an ancient battle with katsinas titled "Kachinas Are Going to Fight Us" illustrates both the power to kill and to protect embedded in the logic of arrow power and by extension many empowered objects.

Before the battle, the war society chiefs walk the town, pushing their arrow points into the walls of all the houses to give them strength. The allied katsina similarly touch the walls with their wooden staffs. During the battle, the attacking katsinas are killed and revived by the touch of the war chief's arrow points and then killed again. The war chiefs also use the points to heal scouts castrated during the battle (White 1929–30: 88–94). These ethnographic examples in sum document the many ways that "both ashes and arrow points are used in separating a person from a dangerous influence" (Parsons 1996 [1939]: 106).

Cottonwood LA 175: Ash, Charcoal, and Arrow Points

The Cottonwood Spring Pueblo (LA 175) is on a large drainage on the western flanks of the San Andres Mountains in southwest New Mexico. The area has several El Paso Phase (AD 1300–1450) pueblos that have been designated as Areas A, B, D, and E. Area C is a hilltop shrine, and Area F is an Early Doña Aña–phase (AD 1000–1150) pueblo that preceded the later El Paso–phase aggregation (figure 12.1). LA 175 contains some of the largest Jornada Mogollon pueblos in the area and has been previously investigated by several scholars (Browning 1991; Chapman 1926; Kemrer 2010; Lekson and Rorex 1987; Yeo n.d.).

The fieldwork completed by New Mexico State University (NMSU) has focused on Areas A and E. To date NMSU has exposed and/or excavated approximately twenty-two rooms in six loci across Area A and twelve rooms in Area E (Walker et al. 2018). A range of cultural materials have been recovered, including projectile points, various minerals, shell, and beads in those rooms, and these seem to be purposeful inclusions during abandonment rituals (see Hedquist 2016; Roth and Schriever 2015; Whalen 2013). All of these rooms exhibit evidence of burning (figure 12.2).

Further, there are a series of rooms (1–10) in Locus 2 in the north end of Area A that were placed over a larger room that was burned earlier, creating a particularly rich sequence of ritual deposits (Corl 2014). The pattern of room burning and the inclusion of projectile points in the fill, roof fall, adobe melt and floor in Room 3 seem to correspond to similar processes across the site that are particularly intense in the rooms built in this part of Area A (figure 2.3). In general, rooms in this locus contain higher frequencies of points, minerals (i.e. ochre, selenite, chrysocolla), marine shell (i.e. olivella beads, worked *Glycymeris*, shell tinklers, drilled abalone), polishing stones, quartz crystals, and other materials. These artifacts were compared with the distribution of broken ceramics and flakes to

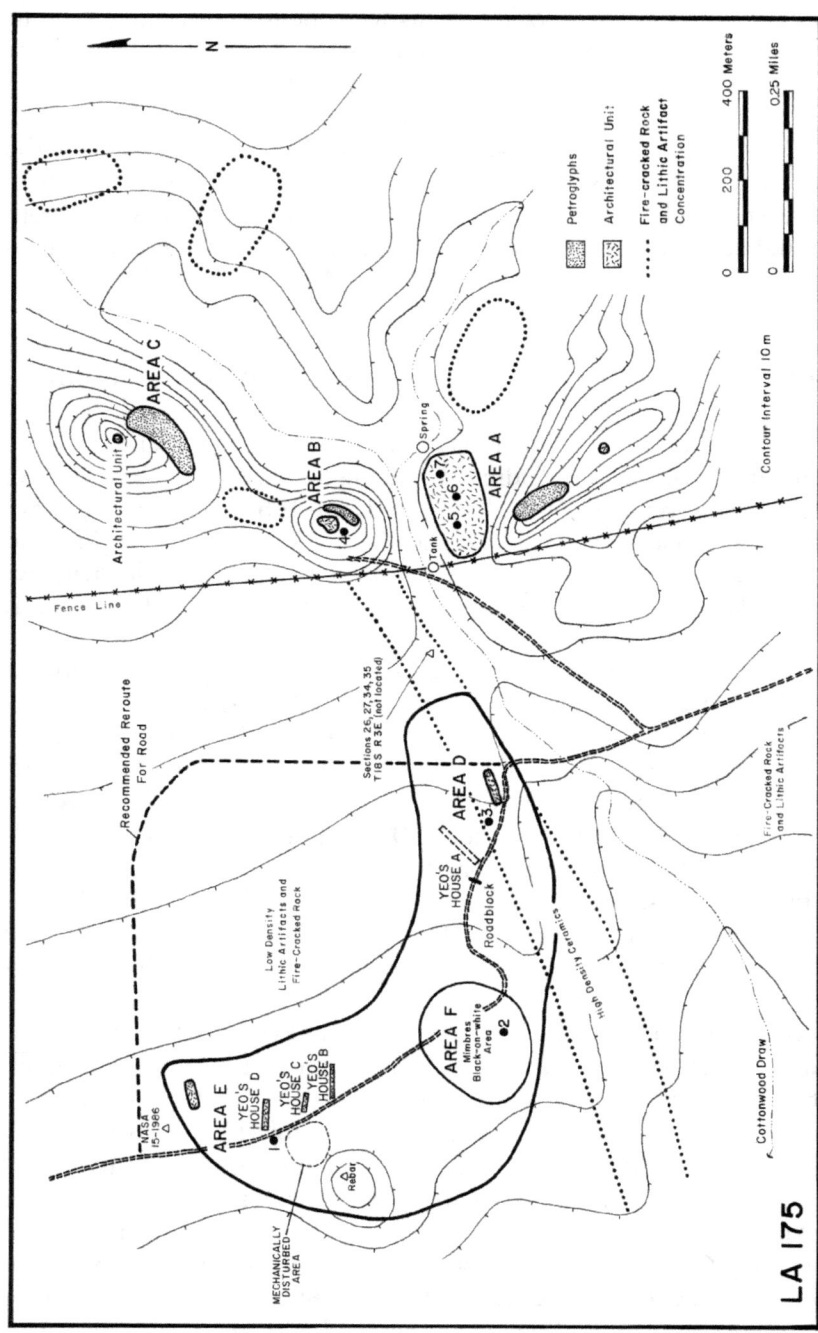

Figure 12.1. *Cottonwood Spring Pueblo, Areas A through F (Lekson and Rorex 1987: HSR Report, p. 10, fig. 3). Created by the Human Systems Research.*

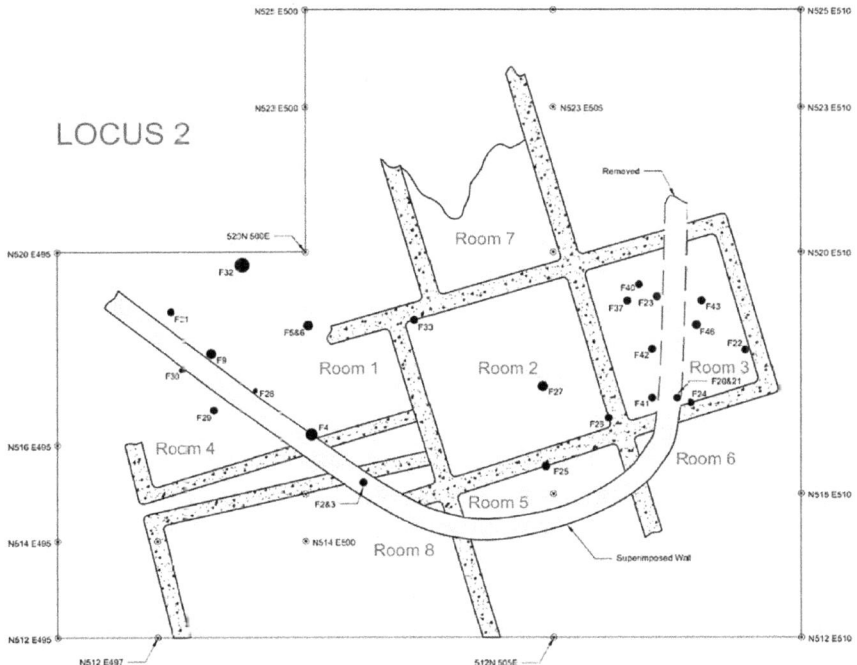

Figure 12.2. *Cottonwood Spring Pueblo, Area A, Locus 2. Created by the authors*

determine if there was a particular artifact type that was recovered mostly within a floor and/or roof fall context.

Ash lenses occur on most floors, albeit to date we are not able to distinguish whether they resulted from the burning of roof materials alone or were also added to the deposits before the burning. We suspect the placement was intentional in some cases (see Walker 2000). Ash is also ubiquitous in an extramural midden, and lenses of ash occur in the wall

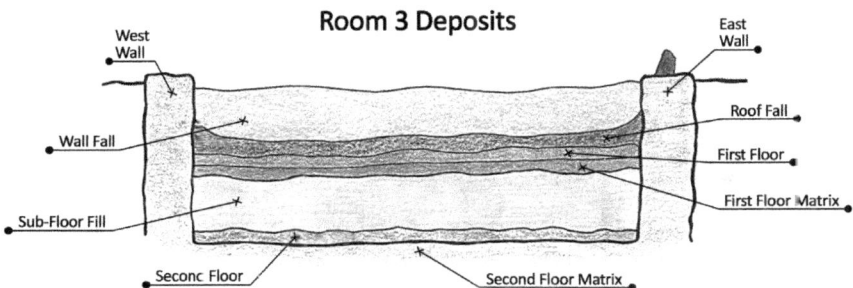

Figure 12.3. *Illustration of deposit sequence in Room 3 (Corl 2014: 185, fig. 3). Created by Kristin Corl, used with permission.*

fall and roofing of several rooms. Thus far, ninety-seven projectile points have been recovered from Locus A: thirty-four from the floor or between floors; twenty-one within the loose wind-blown sands above the pueblo rooms; seventeen in the midden; eighteen in the roof fall; and seven in generalized adobe melt (figure 12.4).

The projectile points ranged from Archaic to Formative/Protohistoric, with Cottonwood and Pueblo Side-Notched the dominant styles. Seventeen of the points lacked distinctive markers and were classed as indeterminate. Eight of the points are larger atlatl projectiles that were collected and curated by the Cottonwood people. Tularosa Corner-Notched date to an earlier pithouse period (AD 250–650) and the other to Middle and Late Archaic contexts (Carlsbad, Gypsum, Maljamar, Pandale, San Pedro, and Ventana Side-Notched). At Ventana Cave, Haury (1975) found a fourteenth-century Hohokam burial with a necklace composed of two Late Archaic San Pedro points. Similarly, these Archaic points at Cottonwood were curated and then deposited at a much later time in pueblo room floor, adobe melt, and surface contexts. Half of these points occur in Locus 2 deposits on the north end of the site above a presumed large ceremonial room. Locus 2 accounts for almost half of the recovered projectile points from the site, with seventeen recovered from Room 3 alone (table 12.1).

Discussion

What do we make of these patterns of abandonment/burning, ash, and projectile points scattered across deposits of the site? Are these events the

Figure 12.4. *Sample of projectile points collected from Cottonwood Spring Pueblo (A: Durango; B: Pueblo Side-Notched; C: Side-Notched; D: Maljamar; E: Bull Creek; F: Cottonwood Triangular; G: Awatovi Side-Notched). Created by the authors.*

Table 12.1. *Projectile Point Distribution at Cottonwood Spring Pueblo Area A*

Projectile Point Type	Area A					
	Locus 1	Locus 2	Locus 3	Locus 4	Locus 5	Total
Awatovi	1			1		2
Black Mesa	1					1
Bull Creek	1	7	1			9
Carlsbad		1				1
Cottonwood	7	10	4	8		29
Durango				1		1
Gypsum		1				1
Indeterminate	3	8	5	1		17
Maljamar				1		1
Pandale		1				1
Pueblo Side Notch	6	12	6	3		27
San Pedro		1	1			2
Snaketown	1					1
Temporale				1		1
Tularosa	2					2
Ventana					1	1
Total	22	41	17	16	1	97

results of violence, ritual abandonment of rooms, accidental fires, or other processes (Walker 1996)?

In planned and gradual abandonment, most valuable items will be moved to the new settlement location. Additionally, during the terminal stages of abandonment, artifacts and materials that normally would have been collected or cleaned and deposited as secondary refuse tend to be left as primary refuse (Miller et al. 2009: 10–14). Decisions involving the types, sizes, and weights of objects left behind during a planned change in residence depend upon several factors, including the time the occupants have to prepare for the move, the distance to be traveled, and whether they intend to return (Lightfoot 1993; Varien 1999). When little or no de facto refuse is found on the floor or cached below the floor of a structure, it may generally be assumed that useful items were removed during abandonment, and therefore the abandonment was planned and gradual and return was not anticipated (Schlanger and Wilshusen 1993; Varien 1999). Conversely, if large quantities of de facto floor items are encountered, it may be that the items were left behind because abandonment was unplanned, the residential move involved a large distance, or nearby conflict broke out. In situations of catastrophic or unplanned abandonment, many items of value, including whole and unbroken items, will be left in place.

The presence of large wooden construction elements, ceramic vessels, stored foods, and so forth may be indicators of unplanned or catastrophic abandonment. The rooms examined at Cottonwood Pueblo contain very little de facto or primary refuse. Thousands of sherds have been recovered, but only one whole ceramic vessel (Room 300) has been found on any of these floors. Indeed, except for crystals, shell ornaments, bone tools, turquoise, ochre, and polishing stones, the floor assemblages are relatively sparse. The rooms appear to have been cleaned out prior to burning. Until recently we would likely try to square this pattern with some pragmatic story that avoided the idea that there was any purposefulness to these patterns. Instead rooms would have burned accidently, and the projectile points were simply lost or forgotten during the move. Alternatively, some might argue that the rooms were burned in battle and the points lost in the fray. Context in these rooms mitigates against these interpretations.

Instead, points, ash, and other objects seem placed there as part of the closure process. Given that fire and points (arrow, spear, hand axe) are the oldest of technologies emerging in tandem with the evolution of our modern biological forms, they likely possess many deep-seated animate powers for many cultures. In the Americas it seems that Paleoindian points can enter the record through ritual discard (Frison et al. 2018). This makes sense given the ritualized nature of many hunting activities, as Morrow (2016: 63–64), has noted:

> From the acquisition of stone and other raw materials to the culturally specified manufacture of tools and object, to the location, propitiation, sharing, and tasting of prey, to the maintenance and refurbishment of needed equipment, the hunting of animals by Paleoindians consisted of activities or ritualizations that comprised a successful strategy

The challenge is to see the richer world of uses in ash and arrow points.

Conclusion

In summary, ash and projectile points protect people from the dangers of ceremonial power and its more hostile uses by witches and other malevolent beings. We can imagine that abandoning pueblos can create dangers. They are places intimately associated with peoples' lives, spirits of ancestors, and other sources of power. The buildings and any objects left behind would be vulnerable to attack by those intent on using these materials through contagious magic for harm. Rendering these buildings into charcoal and ash and placing projectile points within these rooms would have hardened them against such trespass. Alternatively, if these places had been tainted by witchcraft or other bad events that contributed to the abandonment, then burning them would purify the place and take away those dangers.

William Walker is professor of anthropology in the Department of Anthropology at New Mexico State University. He received his MA and PhD in anthropology at the University of Arizona. Walker works primarily in the North American Southwest, but has participated in excavation and survey in the Southern Andes (Argentina and Bolivia) as well as in the North American Northeast. He specializes in the study of prehistoric ritual, including ritual site formation processes, ritual violence, performance characteristic analysis of rock art, and religious responses to climate change.

Judy Berryman is affiliated faculty in anthropology in the Department of Anthropology at New Mexico State University. She received her training at San Diego State University (master's) and University of California, Riverside (PhD). She has over thirty-six years of experience in cultural resource management within the Southwest and California. Her research interests include history and prehistory, with extensive field and archival research. Dr. Berryman has taught at the University of California, San Marcos; the University of Nevada, Reno; and recently at New Mexico State University, Las Cruces.

References

Bourdieu, Pierre. 1977. *Outline of a Theory of Practice*. Translated by Richard Nice. Cambridge Studies in Social Anthropology 16. Cambridge: Cambridge University Press.
Browning, Cody. 1991. "El Paso Phase Structural Sites in the Southern San Andreas Mountains, New Mexico." *Jornada Mogollon Archaeology: Collected Papers from the Fifth and Sixth Jornada Mogollon Conferences*, edited by M. S. Duran and P. H. Beckett, 17–33. Las Cruces, NM: Coas Publishing and Research and Human Systems Research.
Bunzel, Ruth L. 1992. *Zuni Ceremonialism*. Albuquerque: University of New Mexico.
Chapman, Kenneth M. 1926. "An Archaeological Site in the Jornada del Muerto." *El Palacio* 20: 118–22.
Conkey, Margaret W., and Joan M. Gero. 1997. "Programme to Practice: Gender and Feminism in Archaeology." *Annual Review of Anthropology* 26: 411–37.
Corl, Kristin. 2014. "A Case Study of Burning in the Jornada Mogollon at Cottonwood Spring Pueblo: In *Collected Papers from the 18th Biennial Mogollon Archaeological Conference*, edited by Lonnie Ludeman, 181–91. Las Cruces: New Mexico State University.
Cushing, Frank. 1883. *Zuni Fetishes*. In Bureau of American Ethnology Annual Report 2: 3–45. Washington, DC: Smithsonian Institution.
———. 1920. *Zuñi Breadstuff*. Museum of the American Indian, Indian Notes and Monographs 8. New York: Heye Foundation.

Dobres, Marcia-Anne, and Christopher R. Hoffman. 1994. "Social Agency and the Dynamics of Prehistoric Technology." *Journal of Archaeological Method and Theory* 1: 211–58.

Dobres, Marcia-Anne, and John E. Robb, eds. 2000. *Agency in Archaeology*. New York: Psychology Press.

Fewkes, Jesse Walter. 1899. "The Winter Solstice Altars at Hano Pueblo." *American Anthropologist* 1: 251–76.

Frison, George, George M. Zeimens, Spencer R. Pelton, Danny N. Walker, Dennis J. Stanford, and Marcel Kornfeld. 2018. "Further Insights into Paleoindian Use of the Powars II Red Ochre Quarry (48PL330), Wyoming." *American Antiquity* 83: 1–20.

Gell, A. 1992. "The Technology of Enchantment and the Enchantment of Technology." In *Anthropology, Art, and Aesthetics*, edited by J. Coote and A. Shelton, 40–66. Oxford: Clarendon Press.

———. 1998. *Art and Agency: Anthropological Theory*. Oxford: Clarendon Press.

Giddens, Anthony. 1979. *Central Problems in Social Theory: Action, Structure and Contradiction in Social Analysis*. Berkeley: University of California Press.

Haury, Emil. 1975. *The Stratigraphy and Archaeology of Ventana Cave, Arizona*. Tucson: University of Arizona Press.

Hedquist, Saul L. 2016. "Ritual Practice and Exchange in the Late Prehispanic Western Pueblo Region: Insights from the Distribution and Deposition of Turquoise at Homol'ovi I." *Kiva* 82: 209–31.

Hill, W. W., ed. 1982. *An Ethnography of Santa Clara Pueblo, New Mexico*. Albuquerque: University of New Mexico Press.

Hodge, F. W. 1890. "A Zuni Foot-Race." *American Anthropologist* 3: 227–31.

Kemrer, Meade. 2010. "Archaeological Studies in the LA 175 Cottonwood Site, Dona Ana County, New Mexico." USDA-ARS Jornada Experimental Range Interim Report 1. New Mexico: New Mexico State University.

Knappett, Carl, and Lambros Malafouris, eds. 2008. *Material Agency: Towards a Non-anthropocentric Approach*. New York: Springer Science & Business Media.

Latour, Bruno. 1993. *We Have Never Been Modern*. Translated by C. Porter. Cambridge, MA: Harvard University Press.

Lekson, Stephen, and Alex Rorex. 1987. "The Cottonwood Spring and Indian Tank Sites, Dona Ana County, New Mexico." Report 8634. Las Cruces, NM: Human Systems Research.

Lightfoot, R. R. 1993. "Abandonment Processes in Prehistoric Pueblos." In *The Abandonment of Settlements and Regions: Ethnoarchaeological and Archaeological Approaches*, edited by C. M. Cameron and S. A. Tomka, 165–77. Cambridge: Cambridge University Press.

Mills, Barbara J., and William H. Walker, eds. 2008. *Memory Work: Archaeologies of Material Practices*. Santa Fe, NM: School for Advanced Research Press.

Miller, Myles, Nancy Kenmotsu, and Melnda Landreth, eds. 2009. "Significance and Research Standards for Prehistoric Archaeological Sites at Fort Bliss: A Design for the Evaluation, Management, and Treatment of Cultural Resources." Historic and Natural Resources Report 05-16. Fort Bliss, TX: Environmental Division, Fort Bliss Garrison Command.

Mindeleff, Victor. 1891. *A Study of Pueblo Architecture: Tusayan and Cibola*. Bureau of American Ethnology 8th Annual Report. Washington, DC: Smithsonian Institution.

Morrow, Juliet E. 2016. "Evidence for Paleoindian Spirituality and Ritual Behavior: Large Thin Bifaces and Other Sacred Objects from Clovis and Other Late Pleistocene–Early Holocene Cultural Contexts." In *Research, Preservation, Communication: Honoring Thomas J. Green on His Retirement from the Arkansas Archaeological Survey*, edited by Mary Beth Trubitt, 18–65. Research Series 67. Fayetteville: Arkansas Archaeological Survey.

Olsen, Bjørnar. 2010. *In Defense of Things: Archaeology and the Ontology of Objects*. Lanham, MD: Rowman Altamira.

Parsons, Elsie C. 1916. "A Few Zuni Death Beliefs and Practices." *American Anthropologist* 18: 245–56.

———. 1920. *Notes on Ceremonialism at Laguna*. Anthropological Papers 19(14). New York: American Museum of Natural History.

———. 1996 [1939]. *Pueblo Indian Religion*. 2 vols. Lincoln: University of Nebraska Press.
Pauketat, Timothy R. 2001. "Practice and History in Archaeology: An Emerging Paradigm." *Anthropological Theory* 1: 73–98.
Robbins, W. W., J. P. Harrington, and B. Freire-Marreco. 1916. *Ethnobotany of the Tewa Indians*. Bureau of American Ethnology Bulletin 55. Washington DC: Smithsonian Institution.
Roth, Barbara J., and Bernard Schriever. 2015. "Pithouse Retirement and Dedication in the Mimbres Mogollon Region of Southwestern New Mexico." *Kiva* 81: 179–200.
Sahlins, Marshall. 1976. *Culture and Practical Reason*. Chicago: University of Chicago Press
———. 1981. *Historical Metaphors and Mythical Realities: Structure in the Early History of the Sandwich Islands Kingdom*. Ann Arbor: University of Michigan Press.
Schiffer, Michael B. 1987. *Formation Processes of the Archaeological Record*. Albuquerque University of New Mexico Press.
Schiffer, Michael B., and A. R. Miller. 1999. *The Material Life of Human Beings: Artifacts, Behavior, and Communication*. London: Routledge.
Schiffer, Michael B., and James M. Skibo. 1987. "Theory and Experiment in the Study of Technological Change." *Current Anthropology* 28: 595–622.
Schlanger, S. H., and R. H. Wilshusen. 1993. "Local Abandonments and Regional Conditions in the North American Southwest." In *Abandonment of Settlements and Regions: Ethnoarcheological and Archaeological Approaches*, edited by C. M. Cameron and S. A. Tomka, 85–98. Cambridge: Cambridge University Press.
Sedig, Jakob. W. 2010. "Getting to the Point: An Examination of Projectile Point Use in the Northern American Southwest, AD 900–1300." Master's thesis, University of Colorado, Boulder.
———. 2014. "An Analysis of Non-utilitarian Stone Point Function in the US Southwest." *Journal of Anthropological Archaeology* 34: 120–32.
Skeat, Walter W. 1912. "Snakestones and Stone Thunderbolts as Subjects for Systematic Investigation." *Folklore* 23: 23–80.
Stephen, Alexander M. 1936. *Hopi Journal*. Edited by E. C. Parsons. Contributions to Anthropology 23. New York: Columbia University.
Stevenson, Matilida. 1901–2. *The Zuni Indians*. Bureau of American Ethnology 23rd Annual Report. Washington, DC: Smithsonian Institution.
Van Dyke, Ruth, ed. 2015. *Practicing Materiality*. Tucson: University of Arizona Press.
Varien, M. D. 1999. *Sedentism and Mobility in a Social Landscape: Mesa Verde and Beyond*. Tucson: University of Arizona Press.
Voth, H. R. 1901. *The Oraibi Powamu Ceremony*. Field Columbian Museum 61, Anthropological Series 3(2). Chicago: Field Museum of Natural History.
———. 1903a. *The Oraibi Summer Snake Ceremony*. Field Columbian Museum 83, Anthropological Series 3(4). Chicago: Field Museum of Natural History.
———. 1903b. *The Oraibi Oa'qöl Ceremony*. Field Columbian Museum 84, Anthropological Series 3(1). Chicago: Field Museum of Natural History.
Walker, William H. 1995. "Ceremonial Trash?" In *Expanding Archaeology*, edited by J. Skibo, W. Walker, and A. Neilson, 67–79. Salt Lake City: University of Utah Press.
———. 1996. "Ritual Deposits: Another Perspective." In *River of Change: Prehistory of the Middle Little Colorado River Valley, Arizona*, edited by E. C. Adams, 75–91. Arizona State Museum Archaeological Series 185. Tucson: University of Arizona.
———. 1998. "Where Are the Witches of Prehistory?" *Journal of Archaeological Method and Theory* 5: 245–308.
———. 2000. "Stratigraphy and Practical Reason." *American Anthropologist* 104: 159–77.
———. 2001. "Ritual Technology in an Extra-natural World." In *Anthropological Perspectives on Technology*, edited by M. B. Schiffer, 87–106. New World Studies Series 5. Dragoon, AZ: Amerind Foundation.
Walker, William, Stanley Berryman, Judy Berryman. 2018. "New Mexico State University Field School: Cottonwood Spring (LA 175) Summary of Field Results 2012–2018." Report on file. Las Cruces, NM: New Mexico State University.

Webmoor, T., and C. L. Witmore. 2008. "Things Are Us! A Commentary on Human/Things Relations under the Banner of a 'Social' Archaeology." *Norwegian Archaeological Review* 41: 53–70.

Whalen, Michael E. 2013. "Wealth, Status, Ritual, and Marine Shell at Casas Grandes, Chihuahua, Mexico." *American Antiquity* 78: 624–39.

White, Leslie. 1929. *The Acoma Indians*. Bureau of American Anthropology 47th Annual Report. Washington DC: Smithsonian Institution.

Whiteley, Peter M. 2002. "Archaeology and Oral Tradition: The Scientific Importance of Dialogue." *American Antiquity* 67: 405–15.

Yeo, Herbert. n.d. "Notes on the Cottonwood Wash." Santa Fe, NM: Laboratory of Anthropology.

CHAPTER 13

Divine Food and Fiery Covenants
The Significance of Ash in Ancient Maya Religion

James L. Fitzsimmons

Introduction

Fire was an important element of religious life in ancient Mesoamerica. Mesoamerican peoples viewed fire as a source of heat and life, light and power (Tiesler and Scherer 2018). As a result, they used fire not only to purify but also to vivify places (Stuart 1998). The Classic Maya, for example, used fire to terminate, prepare, and regenerate built spaces. They brought fire into houses, temples, and tombs; they opened, purified, and closed these spaces, leaving behind burned layers and deposits of ash (Mock 1998). Indeed, there are ash deposits across Mesoamerica, from cremains to burned incense, that mirror the findings elsewhere in this volume. In a basic sense, most peoples of ancient Mesoamerica viewed fire as a generative, destructive, and transformative agent, like the peoples of the American Southwest (chapters 1 through 5) or the Cherokee of southern Appalachia (Rodning, chapter 8).

Likewise, many peoples of ancient Mesoamerica performed fiery rituals to protect themselves. They did so in a variety of contexts, particularly during burial rites. However, they were (usually) not protecting themselves from malevolent creatures like the witches of Cottonwood Spring Pueblo (Walker and Berryman, chapter 12) or the "others" of the northern Rio Grande (Adler, chapter 5).[1] They were protecting themselves from the wrath of their gods and ancestors who, if not properly venerated, might wreak havoc upon their lives, their agricultural fields, or their kingdoms. Most Mesoamerican peoples believed in a kind of mutual obligation or covenant between living people and supernatural beings. Scholarship on that covenant stems primarily from Classic (AD 250–900) and Postclassic (AD 900–1500) sources (e.g. Hunt 1977; López Austin

1984; Monaghan 1995, 2000; Houston, Stuart, and Taube 2006; Fitzsimmons 2009; Fitzsimmons and Shimada 2011; Scherer and Houston 2018; Tiesler and Scherer 2018), particularly for the Postclassic K'iche', K'ekchi', and Tzotzil Maya of southern Mesoamerica, the elites of lowland Classic Maya civilization, and for the Postclassic Mixtecs and Aztecs of Oaxaca and Central Mexico, respectively. That covenant was not only the reason for veneration but also the rationale for human mortality: the general theme was that the two sides, living people and supernatural beings, suffered (and even died) for each other so that fundamentals like agriculture, time, or civilization could function normally (Monaghan 2000) (figure 13.1).

Figure 13.1. *Map of Maya area. Created by James L. Fitzsimmons.*

Much like the living, Mesoamerican gods and ancestors needed people to take care of them. Gods and ancestors were potent, knowledgeable, and ever-present, but they were also dangerous. They had needs that, if ignored, could have catastrophic results for the living. Some, given physical form as effigies, needed to be clothed. Most needed to be fed. As a result, one might say that Mesoamerican peoples were preoccupied with keeping supernatural beings happy. However, proper care of supernatural beings all but ensured that humans would be prosperous, happy, and healthy. Consequently, reciprocity defined the relationship between human beings and the supernatural throughout ancient Mesoamerica. The peoples of ancient Mesoamerica performed fiery rituals, in part, to create and affirm covenants with divine beings. This chapter explores one aspect of the covenant among the Classic Maya, involving divine food, and provides a fresh perspective on the fiery remains of that covenant in Maya sacrificial and mortuary behaviors: ash.

Food for the Gods

In the first millennium AD, many of the most complex, ancient kingdoms in Mesoamerica were in the Maya area, a region roughly stretching east to west from the Mexican state of Chiapas to western Honduras. The heart of this complexity was in the central part of that zone known as the southern Maya lowlands. More than six million people lived there in the Late Classic (AD 600–900), most of them ruled by fiercely belligerent, independent monarchs.[2] The elites of this era used sophisticated calendrical, mathematical, and astronomical systems, created sculptures, and commissioned extensive architectural projects. They mobilized their people to build networks of roads, temple complexes, hierarchical settlement patterns, sweat lodges (sweat baths), and other public works. Perhaps most importantly, they wrote about their exploits in hieroglyphic form, carving historical and mythological narratives for posterity in stone. They painted hieroglyphs on pottery, cut words into bone, and shaped sentences in stucco. As a result, Maya archaeologists have had the privilege of finding not only material but also written evidence for the foundation, development, and eventual collapse of the southern lowlands in the nineteenth century. To be sure, that evidence—written by and for the ruling elite—is not without bias. However, it provides us with intellectual currents and religious ideas that would otherwise be inaccessible. Advances in hieroglyphic decipherment, coupled with the steady growth of archaeological data from projects both old and new, have enabled Maya archaeologists to ask and explore a variety of difficult social, political, and religious questions.

For the present chapter, we might ask and explore a number of difficult questions. For example, what does a god eat? As Stephen Houston (2018), David Stuart (1998), and Karl Taube (1993) have noted, supernatural creatures and gods—particularly those associated with death and darkness—ate food that living people considered "repellent." They delighted in "a hearty offering of human hands, feet, skulls, and eyeballs arranged neatly into bowls; in short, all the offal and scrapings of the butcher's abattoir" (Houston, Stuart, and Taube 2006: 123). Throughout ancient Mesoamerica, gods preferred to eat humans. The choicest part was, not surprisingly, the heart: human hearts, particularly those belonging to war captives, abound in the sculpture and pottery of Classic and Postclassic Mesoamerica. One can find images of supernatural creatures, cavorting with plates of human hearts, across cultures ranging from Central Mexico to Honduras. For the Classic and Postclassic Maya, the god most often associated with heart consumption was the Sun God. Images, words, or allusions to his preferred food appear across a wide range of contexts, from Classic Copan in the east to Postclassic Coba in the south. There are examples of him eating hearts at Postclassic Chichen Itza and in the Dresden Codex (Houston, Stuart, and Taube 2006: 122–24). His penchant for hearts even played out in royal names and titles, including the name of a rather unlucky king of Sa'aal (the modern archaeological site of Naranjo, Guatemala) in the early seventh century: K'uxaj Chan K'ihnich, or "Sun God is Eating Hearts in the Sky" (Tokovinine 2007: 19). Nevertheless, the Sun God was by no means alone in eating hearts or other human body parts. Although some gods, particularly those associated with hummingbirds, drank chocolate or ate flowers, nectar, incense, or even music (Culbert 1993: fig. 84; Houston, Stuart, and Taube 2006: 123), many gods ate human flesh.

In the Classic Maya worldview, human beings were part of a cycle of consumption. There was not a food chain per se, so plants to animals, animals to humans, and humans to gods, but a symmetrical cycle where everything ate everything else: gods ate humans, humans ate gods (particularly the god of corn, known as the Maize God in the literature), plants ate humans, and so forth. All beings had to participate in that food cycle, without exception. However, one might defer one's own consumption with a proxy, or *k'ex* sacrifice (Carlsen and Prechtel 1997; Houston, Stuart, and Taube 2006: 127; Hunt 1977: 89; Love 1989; Monaghan 2000: 37; Scherer 2015: 144–45; Taube 1994). During the Late Classic (AD 600–900), there were many types of precious goods offered as proxies to the gods. These included sumptuary goods, war captives, and, in the western Maya lowlands as well as Belize, foreign infants or children (see Scherer 2015: 153). Such was the rationale for human sacrifice in the southern Maya lowlands.

As a foodstuff for the gods, human flesh overlapped conceptually with two basic and less repugnant comestibles. The first of these was maize. The Classic Maya, like their colonial period and modern descendants, saw themselves as people of corn. This is an important idea because it implies a special relationship between the Maya and their landscape, suggesting a parallel between the agricultural cycle and the human experience. The ancient Maya carved overt as well as subtle references to this on stelae, where rulers portrayed themselves as embodiments of the Maize God or described their children as *ch'ok*, or "maize sprouts" (e.g., see Fitzsimmons 2009; Houston 2018). Miller and Taube (1991) have suggested a pervasive, rather extreme form of maize mimicry by the Classic Maya; they have suggested that the predominant form of cranial modification used by the Maya, tabular erect, derives from an attempt to mimic the elongated form of a maize cob. Subsequent works have even compared thick hair of the Maize God to corn silk or otherwise drawn parallels between human bodies, vegetation, and the Maize God (e.g., see Braakhuis 2009, 2014; Houston, Stuart, and Taube 2006; Just 2009; Quenon and LeFort 1997; Taube 2009). The best evidence for pairing the human and maize cycles, however, comes from the use of maize iconography on monuments and within burials: human heads sprout as ears from maize plants, funerary temples flower with corn, and artifacts portray the dead as vegetation (Fitzsimmons 2009). As a result, when gods ate humans they were, in a sense, eating maize.

The second conceptual overlap bridges the choicest food of the gods, the human heart, and a ubiquitous foodstuff in the Maya area today: the tamale. As Houston, Stuart, and Taube (2006: 122–27) have noted, there are visual and contextual overlaps between tamales and hearts on Maya ceramics, as well as between the types of dishes and serving vessels used to hold them for humans and gods, respectively. They have drawn some basic, physical parallels between the two objects as well: they characterize both as having "meaty innards surrounded by 'doughy' fat" (2006: 123). Conceptually, both were made of corn. Indeed, the tamale (not the tortilla) was the chief way to eat corn for the ancient Maya (Evans and Webster 2001: 277), so it is no wonder that these conceptual overlaps were in place. Maya gods and humans were just eating "corn" in its most available form.

How does a god eat? Mesoamerican gods consumed precious goods, including people, in a variety of ways. Not surprisingly, earth gods tended to eat buried things. Indeed, for many Mesoamerican peoples, the earth was not only a place of life but also a place of death. It was the source of human mortality and the origin point for many a covenant between the living and the dead. For example, as observed by Alfredo López Austin in his seminal book, *The Human Body and Ideology* (1984), the Postclassic Aztecs of Central Mexico saw mortality as an acquired attribute. For them, mortality was stigma acquired during maize consumption: ingesting maize was a way of consuming death and incorporating death into the body.[3] By eating maize, people brought what was born of the earth, of the realm of death, into their bodies. A quote from modern Nahuatl (the language of the Aztecs), from San Miguel Tzinacapan in Puebla, Mexico, echoes this sentiment: "We eat from the earth/because of this the Earth eats us." (Knab 1979: 130).

Similar ideas existed among the ancient Maya, who viewed gods of the earth as consuming both honored (buried dead) and dishonored (sacrificed war captives) dead. The important distinction between the two was that the dishonored dead were so much unwilling flesh. Dishonored, defeated captives, if sacrificed (not all were), became fertilizer for the victors. The victors (probably) did not sow defeated captives into agricultural fields. Instead, they installed them into the built environment of a Maya city (Houston, Stuart, and Taube 2006: 223–26). Given that the ancient Maya considered nearly every aspect of that environment to be potentially animate, with the capacity to live, die, or house a soul, defeated captives were literally food for architecture. When the Maya installed a person in a building, they were feeding it or even giving it a soul (Fitzsimmons 2009). As a result, gods and earthbound supernatural creatures often fed on people directly. However, they could also receive their food ethereally. Both earthbound and celestial creatures, including the various Mesoamerican solar gods, consumed ethereal fare. Such fare might consist of fragrances or music, but it most often included burnt offerings (Houston, Stuart, and Taube 2006: 126). In these instances, the flames, the smoke, and the objects themselves were important.

For most Mesoamerican peoples, flames, as well as the heat produced by them, were animate forces signifying strength and vitality. People generally believed that gods and particularly powerful people, such as kings, housed immense heat as well (Tiesler and Scherer 2018). For example, the Classic Maya word *k'uh* ("god" or "divine essence") was part of every royal title and inherently connected to heat. *K'uh* was a term linked to vitalizing energy, a kind of hot, fiery essence that coursed through the blood (Houston and Stuart 2001: 55). Whereas rulers possessed *k'uh* in abundance, often tracing their lineages to specific divine beings, gods were *k'uh* incarnate. For these beings, fiery food was only natural.

The ancient Maya attracted gods with nourishment as well as combustibles that reflected godly qualities. They believed that burning sumptuary goods, war captives, and other precious objects produced smells that were not only pleasing to gods but also similar to godly breath (see, e.g., Grube 2000: 96–100; Houston, Stuart, and Taube 2006: 126; Scherer and Houston 2018). The idea was that because gods ate precious things, their breath smelled like precious things, so burning precious things would attract divine beings.[4] One can find similar rationales among many peoples of Mesoamerica, past and present, from the Aztecs of Central Mexico to the contemporary Lacandon Maya (Chávez Balderas 2018; McGee 1990: 49; Palka 2018). Smoke was a primary medium through which Maya gods, and Mesoamerican gods more generally, consumed their offerings. They appeared in the smoke and ate their fill.

Those materials offered to the flames, whether they were sumptuary goods or people, eventually reduced to ashes and charred remains. When Maya archaeologists view those remains, many of us see dedication or termination deposits, much like our counterparts elsewhere in Mesoamerica. We seek to reconstruct what the Maya offered and why they offered it, at that specific time and place; we see fire as transformative, as a means to destroy and to transport offerings to other places (Tiesler and Scherer 2018). These are worthy concerns, but we might also view those ashes as if they were the remains of a meal. When we find burnt goods or human remains, particularly those bearing contextual or symbolic signs of sacrifice to godly beings, we might think about how the Maya would have viewed the ashes. Perhaps some might have thought "a god has eaten here."

Food for the Ancestors

Gods were not the only creatures who required sustenance in Maya cosmology. Supernaturals abound throughout the corpus of Maya art, some of whom blur the lines between spirits and gods proper. Apart from gods, perhaps the hungriest creatures of all were ancestors. One might draw a line between royal or noble ancestors and everyone else, in that the Maya often deified them. Such individuals might be reborn as aspects of the Sun God, the Maize God, or other rather "generic" deities. For example, the Late Classic rulers of the site of Yaxchilan usually depicted deceased royal men and women inside solar or lunar cartouches emanating sunlight or moonlight like normal celestial bodies. At Palenque, deified individuals seemed to embody more local entities, such as the patron gods of the kingdom, known in the literature as the Palenque Triad (Fitzsimmons 2009).

At the same time, many royal or noble ancestors retained their individual qualities, apparently choosing the form of a god, an ancestor, or a hybrid of the two depending upon the context in which they appeared. Such creatures, reborn as deities, ate food that was repellent to the general population: as gods proper, they ate people as well as inedible sumptuary goods. Theoretically, they continued to eat maize, albeit in a human form that—barring occasional, if poorly attested, instances of ritual cannibalism—living Maya did not consume (Houston, Stuart, and Taube 2006: 122). As gods, royal ancestors consumed celestial foods that were both familiar to, and different from, those consumed by the living.

Apart from deified rulers and their immediate families, however, it is very difficult to make the case that other deceased individuals enjoyed hearts or other repellent foods (symbolic or otherwise) in Maya religion, largely because the sources we draw upon for this kind of information were produced for a small group of people. We do know that ancient Maya (nonroyal) elites and commoners venerated their own ancestors on a broad scale, however, performing rites for lineage ancestors throughout the Classic and Postclassic periods.[5] Nevertheless, as Patricia McAnany has noted, the practice of ancestor veneration and the rituals surrounding it were not extended equally to all members of society but employed preferentially when particularly important or influential members of a lineage died (1995: 11). In other words, not everyone could become an ancestor in Maya society. Likewise, not everyone regarded as an ancestor remained so for all time. Ancestors only remained important if people remembered them: people needed to maintain or reinvent the memories of their honored dead in order to keep them relevant. Most Classic Maya kingdoms, for example, gave birth to people who aggressively campaigned for their legacies, as well as to situations where those legacies were intentionally destroyed. Kings often minimized, forgot, or ignored unfortunate ancestors, favoring newer, more powerful ones (Fitzsimmons 2009).[6] There is every reason to suppose that similar dynamics existed among commoners whose fortunes, after all, were even more precarious than those of their royal counterparts. Most of the details on these changing relationships are lost, but, presumably, "new" ancestors created fresh, superseding covenants with the living and ate the food once allocated to their forgotten predecessors.

We might reason that the quantity, quality, and character of food for elite and commoner ancestors was different from the food enjoyed by deceased kings and exalted nobles. Indeed, some of the sumptuary goods burned by kings were socially restricted items (particularly jade). However, everything we know about Precolumbian ancestor veneration suggests that elite and common ancestors ate abstract foods that overlapped with foods for gods; across time, space, and class, Mesoamerican peoples burned paper, blood, incense, and/or rubber for their dead. We can find basic, shared ideas about burning materials for ancestors from the Maya area to Central Mexico for most of the Precolumbian era. We can find these ideas during the Late Postclassic in northwestern and western Mexico too.[7] Often, the peoples of ancient Mesoamerica burned bundles of different goods (including incense), leaving ash deposits behind inside and outside their temples, houses, and burials.

Incense was particularly important for the ancient Maya, featuring heavily in Maya ritual and mortuary behavior (see, e.g., Houston, Stuart, and Taube 2006: 125). The type of incense used (and still in use) by the Maya was copal, a pine resin that, when burned, produces thick, black smoke as well as a sweet aroma. In Maya religion, copal was the prime substitute for human blood and, when modeled as such, the human heart. As Allen Christenson (2003: 133) has pointed out, most contemporary Mayan languages use the same word for "blood" and "tree sap," the raw material that forms copal incense. Indeed, copal still figures heavily in Maya religiosity.

The sixteenth-century K'iche' Popol Vuh, with antecedents in Maya painting and sculpture stretching back to the Late Preclassic (400 BC–AD 250), provides a clue as to why copal acquired so much importance in the Maya area. Filled with creation myths, one tale (now familiar to Mayanists) from this text explicitly involves copal. The story takes place at a time before the gods create humans, when supernatural beings walked the surface of the earth as well as above and beneath it. One such being, Lady Blood, becomes pregnant through supernatural means. Though not a death goddess herself, she is the daughter of one of the lords (gods) of death. Shamed by her pregnancy, her father demands her death, charging some of his subordinates to bring him her heart. When the subordinates find Lady Blood, they take pity on her and fashion a heart out of copal. They take that false heart to the lords of death and burn it, but instead of realizing it is copal, the death gods rejoice at the smell and believe the heart is genuine. Their failure to recognize the ruse plays into larger themes in the Popol Vuh, chief among them being the triumph of life and fecundity over death (see, e.g., Christenson 2003: 129–34; Fitzsimmons 2009: 52; Schele and Miller 1986: 267; Scherer 2015: 23–24).

Why do the sixteenth-century death gods fall for this (admittedly) simple ruse? They fall for it because alone, of all the Maya gods, their breath is not sweet. Their essence is not pleasant and fragrant, but anal and foul. For the K'iche' Maya, the realm of death was an awful, smelly, frightening place filled with gods bearing equally foul (personified disease or injury) names like Flying Scab, Pus Demon, and Bloody Teeth (Christenson 2003: 161–62). The death gods of the Classic and Postclassic periods were just as foul, if not more so, than their K'iche' analogues; when they appear on Maya ceramics, stucco, or other media, they are universally terrifying, rotting creatures. Indeed, the purpose of many elite (and probably commoner) mortuary rituals during the Precolumbian era was to help the dead escape these beings, to help them be reborn or apotheosize into ancestors living in paradisiacal places (see, e.g., Coe 1978; Fitzsimmons 2009; Quenon and LeFort 1997; Schele and Miller 1986; Scherer 2015; Taube 1993). The reason why the K'iche' death gods fell for the copal ruse was because it was sweet, the stuff of celestial gods. It was the opposite of foul breath; copal was god breath, evoking the essence of something that was not a death god (in this case, Blood Woman). A similar dynamic probably existed in Precolumbian times, where the celestial scent of copal was set in opposition to the stench of death and decay.

As noted above, incense was one of the primary foods burned for ancestors as well as for gods. For the Precolumbian and modern Maya, copal is divine or supernatural food (see, e.g., McGee 1990: 49; Palka 2018). The ancient Maya burned copal, played music, and provided other fragrances to ancestors not only to feed them but also to attract their presence (Houston, Stuart, and Taube 2006: 125–26). As we have seen for Maya gods, smoke was the primary medium through which ancestors consumed food. If incense was the breath of celestial gods, it was also the breath of ancestors. At the site of Palenque, for example, the connection between breath and ancestors was explicit: the stone markers on the terraces of the Temple of the Cross, bearing the names of dead courtiers, pair with anthropomorphic incense burners that literally breathe copal smoke from their nostrils (Easby and Scott 1970: plate 175; Houston, Stuart, and Taube 2006: 126; Schele and Mathews 1979: plates 281 and 282).[8] As such, when we find burnt incense and the ashes accompanying it in mortuary contexts, we might think about how the Maya would have viewed them. They probably had stories like the aforementioned one from the Popol Vuh in mind; they burned copal and other sumptuary goods in mortuary contexts, in part, to oppose death and to attract ancestors with celestial breath and divine food. Perhaps some of them looked at the ashes and thought, "An ancestor has breathed here."

With copal, what we have is a multivocal symbol that is both divine food and divine exhalation, a means of attracting and representing supernatural beings that conceptually brings the attributes and desires of gods and ancestors together. We might view many, if not most, of the combustibles offered to these beings in a similar way. Many of the ash deposits we find across Maya sites, from incense burners to ancestral shrines to burials, are thus (supernatural) food remains as well as the remains of ancient attempts to attract gods and ancestors. Maya archaeologists can often (rightfully) describe these remains in terms of dedication or termination rituals (see, e.g., Mock 1998), but such terms concentrate on the "why" and the "when" of ritual; why were these materials burned here and when were they burned? Seeing ashes as the remains of food or breath explores the "what," specifically what the ancient Maya hoped was actually happening during a dedication or a termination ritual.

A Covenant Maintained

However, we should not view ashes (of humans, sumptuary goods, or otherwise) solely as byproducts of Maya ritual or divine consumption. As both archaeologists and ethnographers have noted cross-culturally, rituals are opportunities for identity and social memory to be constructed, tested, and renegotiated (see, e.g., Bell 2009; Stevenson 2015). Mortuary and sacrificial rituals are particularly rich opportunities for this behavior (see, e.g., Bloch 1971; Chesson 2001; Gillespie 2001; Metcalf and Huntington 1991; O'Shea 1984). For the ancient Maya, one of the most spectacular such rituals is known as tomb reentry. This was the widespread lowland tradition of (1) removing capstones or other masonry elements in burials; (2) modifying the grave furniture and skeleton, often through such activities as the burning of incense or the removal of bones; (3) sealing the burial, either permanently or temporarily with removable stones; and (4) writing about it or illustrating it on public monuments. Fire was a key element of tomb reentry, with incense, torches, or both lit inside or just outside the burial chamber. Sometimes people entered these tombs multiple times or even kept the access points open.[9] This resulted in the partial cremation or blackening of artifacts and skeletal remains or the production of copious ash deposits inside or outside the burial (Fitzsimmons 1998, 2006, 2009; Scherer 2015).

Rituals like tomb reentry unequivocally fall into termination or dedication categories for most Maya archaeologists (see, e.g., Mock 1998; Fitzsimmons 2009; Freidel 1989; Scherer 2015; Stuart 1998). In light of the present discussion, they also involve ancestors arriving and consuming food, drawn by the sweet smells released during the burning of precious goods. However, they also involved people leaving behind proof of religious observances in the form of ash. In cases where the Maya repeatedly entered the same tomb or visited the same mortuary shrine, ashes provided tangible proof that the ancestors had been there. They had eaten at this location! They had breathed upon this place! Barring knowledge of a major calamity in the past, the ashes also provided proof that the ancestors were happy.

As a result, the ash that we find in such a deposit and (all too often) consign to backfill was not only a byproduct of penitent behavior but also a testament to it. When the ancient Maya entered the tombs of their ancestors or burned successions of hearts in godly shrines, they saw proof that someone had previously fed a divine being. They got confirmation that divine beings had visited these places and breathed upon them, that someone had maintained the covenant between human beings and the divine. Then they added to that proof with ash of their own. We might imagine the people lighting these fires, desperately hoping that they had satisfied the terms of the covenant with their gods and their ancestors. Perhaps we should look to the ash deposits here and in other parts of Mesoamerica, from the fires built for burials to dedicatory fires for houses, temples, and mortuary shrines, and think about how the people who made these deposits viewed the piles of ashes they left behind: had they offered enough?

James L. Fitzsimmons is professor of anthropology at Middlebury College. His research interests include the anthropology of death, the rise of complex societies in ancient Mesoamerica, and the origins of writing. He has directed or worked on a variety of archaeological projects in Belize, Guatemala, Honduras, and the United States. He is the author or editor of five books, including *Death and the Classic Maya Kings* and *Living with the Dead: Mortuary Ritual in Mesoamerica*. He is currently writing about a failed imperial experiment in the Classic Maya (AD 250–900) lowlands as well as the people responsible for it.

Notes

1. The Classic Maya did believe in witches. They may have punished those accused of witchcraft with dismemberment (see Lucero and Gibbs 2007).
2. See Estrada-Belli and others in Clynes 2018 at https://news.nationalgeographic.com/2018/02/maya-laser-lidar-guatemala-pacunam/. A recent LiDAR survey has drastically altered population estimates for the Maya area. We used to believe that there were several million people in all the Maya lowlands, but current estimates range from anywhere from ten to fifteen million. The southern lowlands would have seen a greater share of the population, but the northern lowlands had several densely occupied cities during the Late Classic. For examples, see Hutson (2016).
3. Participating in sexual activity was another way of bringing death into the body. This was less about what Monaghan (2000) calls the "phagiohierarchical" life cycle and (probably) more about souls and potential soul loss. Colonial Nahuatl describes knowing *in teuhtli, in tlazolli* "the dust, the filth" of sex as a willing surrender of oneself to the things of the earth, but the idea that one could lose a soul (or a part of it) during sex seems to be a Precolumbian concept. The implication here is that people, if they were able to refuse the earth, would live forever. The Postclassic Aztecs viewed young children who had not tasted corn, for example, differently than those who had: "[They] were the ones who never knew, who never made the acquaintance of dust, of filth . . . they become green stones, they become precious turquoise, they become bracelets" (Florentine Codex [VI, 115] translation by López Austin in 1984: 314). Instead of reaching Mictlan they go to Tonacacuauhtitlan to await a second birth, nursed under the branches of a world tree. Fernandez de Oviedo and Gonzalo Valdes (1851–55) cite an alternative view for the Nicaraos of Nicaragua, who believed that children who died before eating corn would resuscitate and return to the earth as men. See also Fitzsimmons (2009).
4. The smells associated with burning bodies or parts are not as recognized in the academic literature as equivalent to godly breath as, for example, incense. However, the ancient Maya freely burned the two together. Conceptually, there is considerable overlap between all forms of burned, sacrificial offerings and godly breath. Jade, for example, is ubiquitous as godly breath in Maya sculpture and on Maya ceramics, but also features in burnt offerings. Incense

and hearts clearly overlap in the Popol Vuh too (q.v.). See Houston, Stuart, and Taube 2006: 127: fig. 3.23.
5. The term "commoner" is somewhat problematic, but it appears in broad use throughout the literature. The "common people" made up anywhere between 90 and 98 percent of the population at a given Classic Maya city, for example. For scholarship on the behavior of "commoners" and definitions thereof in Maya society, see Chase and Chase (1992); Giddens (1974: 4); Houston and Stuart (2001); Inomata (2001a, 2001b, 2004); Lohse and Valdez (2004); and Marcus (1983).
6. A classic example of minimizing behavior comes from Palenque, where the dead K'inich Janaab Pakal had outsized influence for decades. He was clearly at the top of the ancestral hierarchy for many years, even superseding his own (deceased) children at times. As for forgetting, one can find good examples at Naranjo or Seibal, where kings intentionally highlight certain ancestors to the detriment of what were once, presumably, other prominent ancestors. For more examples of this behavior, see Martin and Grube (2008).
7. Spiked and "frying pan" incense burners are used in mortuary ritual at Postclassic Ixtapa, on the Pacific Coast. See Mountjoy (2000: 98). In the Tarascan heartland, layers of ash occasionally accompany burials too. There is burned incense as well. See Pollard (1993); Pollard and Cahue (1999: 275); Núñez et al. (2010: 300); and Seler (2000: 209).
8. Some of these burners are deified ancestors and appear godly, but others are more human in aspect. See Rands and Rands (1959).
9. Perhaps the best-known example of this occurs at Palenque, where the Maya built a staircase to the tomb of K'ihnich Janaab' Pakal and kept it open for a time, before sealing it permanently (see Ruz Lhuillier 1958 for details).

References

Bell, Catherine. 2009. *Ritual Theory, Ritual Practice*. Oxford: Oxford University Press.
Bloch, Maurice. 1971. *Placing the Dead: Tombs, Ancestral Villages, and Kinship Organization in Madagascar*. London: Seminar Press.
Braakhuis, H. E. M. 2009. "The Tonsured Maize God and Chicome-Xochitl as Maize Bringers and Culture Heroes: A Gulf Coast Perspective." *Wayeb Notes* 32: 1–26.
———. 2014. "Challenging the Lightnings: San Bartolo's West Wall Mural and the Maize Hero Myth." *Wayeb Notes* 46:131–142.
Carlsen, Robert S., and Martin Prechtel. 1997. "The Flowering of the Dead." In *The War for the Heart and Soul of a Highland Maya Town*, edited by Robert S. Carlsen, 47–67. Austin: University of Texas Press.
Chase, Diane Z., and Arlen F. Chase, eds. 1992. *Mesoamerican Elites: An Archaeological Assessment*. Norman: University of Oklahoma Press.
Chávez Balderas, Ximena. 2018. "Fire, Transformation, and Bone Relics: Cremated Remains at the Templo Mayor of Tenochtitlan." In *Smoke, Flames, and the Human Body in Mesoamerican Ritual Practice*, edited by Vera Tiesler and Andrew Scherer, 379–410. Cambridge, MA: Harvard University Press.
Chesson, Meredith, ed. 2001. *Social Memory, Identity, and Death: Anthropological Perspectives on Mortuary Rituals*. Archaeological Papers 10. Washington, DC: American Anthropological Association.
Christenson, Allen J. 2003. *Popol Vuh: The Sacred Book of the Maya*. Norman: University of Oklahoma Press.
Clynes, Tom. 2018. "Laser Scans Reveal Maya 'Megalopolis' below Guatemalan Jungle." *National Geographic*. Retrieved 10 June 2019 from https://news.nationalgeographic.com/2018/02/maya-laser-lidar-guatemala-pacunam/.
Coe, Michael D. 1978. *Lords of the Underworld*. Princeton, NJ: Princeton University Press.

Culbert, T. Patrick. 1993. *The Ceramics of Tikal: Vessels from the Burials, Caches, and Problematical Deposits*. Tikal Report 25(A). Philadelphia: University Museum, University of Pennsylvania.

Easby, Elizabeth K., and John P. Scott. 1970. *Before Cortés: Sculpture of Middle America, A Centennial Exhibition at the Metropolitan Museum of Art, from September 30, 1970, through January 3, 1971*. New York: Metropolitan Museum of Art.

Evans, Susan Toby, and David L. Webster, eds. 2001. *Archaeology of Ancient Mexico and Central America: An Encyclopedia*. New York: Garland Publishing.

Fitzsimmons, James L. 1998. "Classic Maya Mortuary Anniversaries at Piedras Negras, Guatemala." *Ancient Mesoamerica* 9: 271–78.

———. 2006. "Tomb Re-entry among the Classic Maya: Archaeology and Epigraphy in Mortuary Ceremonialism." In *Jaws of the Underworld: Life, Death, and Rebirth among the Ancient Maya*, edited by Pierre R. Colas, Geneviève LeFort, and Bodil Liljefors Persson, 35–42. Acta Mesoamericana 16. Möckmühl: Verlag Anton Saurwein.

———. 2009. *Death and the Classic Maya Kings*. Austin: University of Texas Press.

Fitzsimmons, James L., and Izumi Shimada, eds. 2011. *Living with the Dead: Mortuary Ritual in Mesoamerica*. Tucson: University of Arizona Press.

Freidel, David. 1989. "Dead Kings and Living Temples: Dedication and Termination Rituals among Ancient Maya." In *Word and Image in Maya Culture*, ed. William F. Hanks and Don S. Rice, 233–43. Salt Lake City: University of Utah Press.

Giddens, Anthony. 1974. "Elites in the British Class Structure." In *Elites and Power in British Society*, edited by P. Stanworth and A. Giddens, 1–21. London: Cambridge University Press.

Gillespie, Susan D. 2001. "Personhood, Agency, and Mortuary Ritual: A Case Study from the Ancient Maya." *Journal of Anthropological Archaeology* 20: 73–112.

Grube, Nikolai. 2000. "Fire Rituals in the Context of Classic Maya Initial Series." In *The Sacred and the Profane: Architecture and Identity in the Maya Lowlands*, edited by Pierre Robert Colas, Kai Delvendahl, Marcus Kuhnert, and Annette Schubart, 91–109. Acta Mesoamericana 10. Markt Schwaben: Verlag Anton Saurwein.

Houston, Stephen D. 2018. *The Gifted Passage: Young Men in Classic Maya Art and Text*. New Haven, CT: Yale University Press.

Houston, Stephen D., and David Stuart. 2001. "Peopling the Classic Maya Court." In *Royal Courts of the Ancient Maya*, edited by Takeshi Inomata and Stephen D. Houston, 1:54–83. Boulder, CO: Westview Press.

Houston, Stephen D., David Stuart, and Karl Taube. 2006. *The Memory of Bones: Body, Being, and Experience among the Classic Maya*. Austin: University of Texas Press.

Hunt, Eva. 1977. *The Transformation of the Hummingbird: Cultural Roots of a Zinacantan Mythical Poem*. Ithaca, NY: Cornell University Press.

Hutson, Scott R. 2016. *The Ancient Urban Maya: Neighborhoods, Inequality, and Built Form*. Gainesville: University Press of Florida.

Inomata, Takeshi. 2001a. "The Power and Ideology of Artistic Creation: Elite Craft Specialists in Classic Maya Society." *Current Anthropology* 42: 321–49.

———. 2001b. "King's People: Classic Maya Courtiers in a Comparative Perspective." In *Royal Courts of the Ancient Maya*, edited by Takeshi Inomata and Stephen D. Houston, 1:27–53. Boulder, CO: Westview Press.

———. 2004. "The Spatial Mobility of Non-elite Populations in Classic Maya Society and Its Political Implications." In *Ancient Maya Commoners*, edited by Jon C. Lohse and Fred Valdez Jr., 175–96. Austin: University of Texas Press.

Just, Bryan. 2009. "Mysteries of the Maya Maize God." *Record of the Art Museum* 68: 2–15.

Knab, Tim. 1979. "Talocan Talmanic: Supernatural Beings of the Sierra de Puebla." *Actes du 42nd Congrès International des Amèricanistes* 6: 127–36. Paris: Congrès du Centenaire.

Lohse, Jon C., and Fred Valdez, Jr. 2004. "Examining Ancient Maya Commoners Anew." In *Ancient Maya Commoners*, edited by Jon C. Lohse and Fred Valdez Jr., 1–23. Austin: University of Texas Press.

López Austin, Alfredo. 1984. *The Human Body and Ideology: Concepts of the Ancient Nahuas*. Vol 1. Translated by Thelma Ortiz de Montellano and Bernard Ortiz de Montellano. Salt Lake City: University of Utah Press.
Love, Bruce. 1989. "Yucatec Sacred Breads through Time." In *Word and Image in Maya Culture: Explorations in Language, Writing, and Representations*, edited by William F. Hanks and Don S. Rice, 336–50. Salt Lake City: University of Utah Press.
Lucero, Lisa, and Sherry Gibbs. 2007. "The Creation and Sacrifice of Witches in Classic Maya Society." In *New Perspectives on Human Sacrifice and Ritual Body Treatments in Ancient Maya Society*, edited by Vera Tiesler and Andrea Cucina, 45–73. New York: Springer Press.
Marcus, Joyce. 1983. "Lowland Maya Archaeology at the Crossroads." *American Antiquity* 48: 454–88.
Martin, Simon, and Nikolai Grube. 2008. *Chronicle of the Maya Kings and Queens*. London: Thames and Hudson.
McAnany, Patricia A. 1995. *Living with the Ancestors: Kinship and Kingship in Ancient Maya Society*. Austin: University of Texas Press.
McGee, R. Jon. 1990. *Life, Ritual, and Religion among the Lacandon Maya*. Belmont, CA: Wadsworth.
Metcalf, Peter, and Richard Huntington. 1991. *Celebrations of Death: The Anthropology of Mortuary Ritual*. Cambridge: Cambridge University Press.
Miller, Mary, and Karl Taube. 1991. *The Gods and Symbols of Ancient Mexico and the Maya*. London: Thames and Hudson.
Mock, Shirley B. 1998. "Preface." In *The Sowing and the Dawning: Termination, Dedication, and Transformation in the Archaeological and Ethnographic Record of Mesoamerica*, edited by Shirley B. Mock, 3–18. Albuquerque: University of New Mexico Press.
Monaghan, John D. 1995. *The Covenants with Earth and Rain: Exchange, Sacrifice, and Revelation in Mixtec Society*. Norman: University of Oklahoma Press.
———. 2000. "Theology and History in the Study of Mesoamerican Religions." In *Handbook of Middle American Indians, Supplement 6: Ethnology*, edited by John D. Monaghan and Barbara W. Edmonson, 24–49. Austin: University of Texas Press.
Mountjoy, Joseph. 2000. "Prehispanic Cultural Development along the Southern Coast of West Mexico." In *Greater Mesoamerica*, edited by Michael S. Foster and Shirley Gorenstein, 81–106. Salt Lake City: University of Utah Press.
Núñez Enríquez, Luis Fernando, and Roberto Martínez González. 2010. "Prácticas Funerarias Mexicas y Purepecha: El Problema de la Confrontación entre Datos Ethnohistóricos y Arqueológicos." *Ancient Mesoamerica* 21: 283–308.
O'Shea, John. 1984. *Mortuary Variability: An Archaeological Investigation*. New York: Academic Press.
de Oviedo, Fernandez, and Gonzalo Valdes. 1851–55. *Historia General y Natural de las Indias, Islas y Tierra-Firme del Mar Océano*. Vol. 11. Asunción del Paraguay: Editoria Guaranía.
Palka, Joel W. 2018. "Where There's Fire There's Smoke: Lacandon Maya Burning Rites and Cremation Symbolism." In *Smoke, Flames, and the Human Body in Mesoamerican Ritual Practice*, edited by Vera Tiesler and Andrew Scherer, 287–320. Cambridge, MA: Harvard University Press.
Pollard, Helen. 1993. *Taríacuri's Legacy: The Prehispanic Tarascan State*. Norman: University of Oklahoma Press.
Pollard, Helen, and Laura Cahue. 1999. "Mortuary Patterns of Regional Elites in the Lake Patzcuaro Basin of Western Mexico." *Latin American Antiquity* 10: 259–80.
Quenon, Michel, and Geneviève LeFort. 1997. "Rebirth and Resurrection in Maize God Iconography." In *Maya Vase Book*, edited by Justin Kerr, 5:884–902. New York: Kerr Associates.
Rands, Robert L., and Barbara C. Rands. 1959. "The Incensario Complex of Palenque, Chiapas." *American Antiquity* 25: 225–36.
Ruz Lhuillier, Alberto. 1958 "Exploraciones Arqueológicas en Palenque 1953–1956." *INAH Anales* 10: 69–299.

Schele, Linda, and Peter Mathews. 1979. *The Bodega of Palenque, Chiapas, Mexico*. Washington, DC: Dumbarton Oaks.

Schele, Linda, and Mary Miller. 1986. *The Blood of Kings: Dynasty and Ritual in Maya Art*. Fort Worth, TX: Kimbell Art Museum.

Scherer, Andrew. 2015. *Mortuary Landscapes of the Classic Maya*. Austin: University of Texas Press.

Scherer, Andrew, and Stephen D. Houston. 2018. "Blood, Fire, Death: Covenants and Crises among the Classic Maya." In *Smoke, Flames, and the Human Body in Mesoamerican Ritual Practice*, edited by Vera Tiesler and Andrew Scherer, 109–50. Cambridge, MA: Harvard University Press.

Seler, Eduard. 2000. "Los Antiguos Habitantes de Michoacán." In *La Relación de Michoacán*, edited by Moisés Franco Mendoza, 139–234. Zamora: Colegio de Michoacán.

Stevenson, Barry. 2015. *Ritual: A Very Short Introduction*. Oxford: Oxford University Press.

Stuart, David. 1998. "'The Fire Enters His House': Architecture and Ritual in Classic Maya Texts." In *Function and Meaning in Maya Architecture*, edited by T. Inomata and S. D. Houston, 373–425. Washington, DC: Dumbarton Oaks.

Taube, Karl. 1993. *Aztec and Maya Myths*. Austin: University of Texas Press.

———. 1994. "The Birth Vase: Natal Imagery in Ancient Maya Ritual." In *The Maya Vase Book: A Corpus of Rollout Photographs of Maya Vases*, edited by Barbara Kerr, 4:650–85. New York: Kerr Associates.

———. 2009. "The Maya Maize God and the Mythic Origins of Dance." In *The Maya and Their Sacred Narratives: Text and Context in Maya Mythologies*, edited by Geneviève Le Fort, Raphael Gardiol, Sebastian Matteo, and Christophe Helmke, 41–52. Acta Mesoamericana 20. Möckmühl: Verlag Anton Saurwein.

Tiesler, Vera, and Andrew Scherer. 2018. "Introducing Smoke, Flames, and the Body in Mesoamerican Ritual Practice." In *Smoke, Flames, and the Human Body in Mesoamerican Ritual Practice*, edited by Vera Tiesler and Andrew Scherer, 1–28. Cambridge, MA: Harvard University Press.

Tokovinine, Alexandre. 2007. "Stela 45 of Naranjo and the Early Classic Lords of Sa'aal." *The PARI Journal* 7: 1–14.

Afterword

Tammy Stone

Archaeologists have long looked at archaeological remains (features, artifacts, and ecofacts) as the rubbish left behind when a site, or a portion of a site, ceases to be used. We have correctly spent a great deal of our time thinking about ways deposits accumulate, borrowing heavily from geology and physical geography to understand how stratigraphic profiles form and can be analyzed (see McAnany and Hodder 2009 for a history). We know that deposits and their archaeological contexts can be impacted by natural and cultural transformation processes (Schiffer 1976, 1987). These studies have resulted in continuing emphasis on the analysis of primary versus secondary context to understand the strength of our data sets (Schiffer, Riggs, and Reid 2017), as well as the analysis of midden accumulation rates and mixing to study shifts in house placement and use in long-term occupations (Lightfoot 1993; Varien and Mills 1997) Early work on the social processes that produced the remains concentrated on decision-making tied to the abandonment process, including the length of time to prepare for the move, distance of the move, transport cost, anticipation of return (Cameron and Tomka 1993; Stevenson 1982), as well as recycling and scavenging behavior (Cameron 1999; Rothschild and Dublin 1994).

These are important studies and have provided a powerful set of tools for interpretation of archaeological remains. More recently, studies of deposits and stratigraphy have expanded to include concepts of social practice, social memory, meaning, and transformation of meaning of place and material for the people who created the deposits. Considerable research in this area has centered on daily practice (Creese 2012; Hodder and Cessford 2004), bodily movement (Amerlinck 2001; Stone 2015, 2016; Tilley 1994), and dedication and ritual closure of domestic and ritual spaces (Creel 2010; Creel and Anyon 2003; Lightfoot 1993; Walker 2002).

These changes in our understanding of archaeological deposits have occurred within a broader theoretical shift. This shift has been aided by increasing consultation with descendent populations, as well as new ways of doing ethnographic and ethnoarchaeological research. These approaches have brought home the fact that meaning is complex, fluid, and contextually based (Hodder 1982, 1986). Our methodological and theoretical tools for understanding the fluid nature of creating meaning by past groups have grown considerably in the last twenty years. This volume is situated within this movement and is an important contribution to this line of research.

Methodologically, we have developed sophisticated approaches to interpreting stratigraphic remains on both the micro and macro scale (Creese 2012; Hodder and Cessford 2005; McAnany and Hodder 2009; Roth and Baustian 2015). These approaches come under a broader tactic that concentrates on the biography of places and things. By understanding the construction, use, destruction, and rebirth cycles of architectural structures, we can see meaning and social memory being created and manipulated (Bailey 1990; Eriksen 2016; Gerritsen 1999; Stone 2015; Waddington 2014). Social action related to architectural structures can challenge or reify meaning and social memory; it can change and create new meanings. Similarly, artifacts have life histories that are tied not only to change in use (Barton 1990) but also to changes in meaning (Jervis 2014).

The transformative nature of fire, the subject of this volume, falls within this tradition. Destruction of items, buildings, and bodies (i.e., cremation) through fire is ritually imbued and socially important (Creel 2010; Walker 2002) to those participating in the social action and to subsequent generations. The form of burned deposits changes, but its importance, ritual power, and meaning carry on. The deposits become part of a socially meaningful place and confirm additional meaning on that space. These places continue to be used, lived in, and interpreted, and the burned remains are part of that process. For example, the ritual landscape surrounding Stonehenge, with its wooden and stone circles, avenues, barrows, and ash pits incorporate ash from bonfires, cremations, and feasting as important actions of renewal and continued creation of meaning (Parker Pearson et al. 2006). For example, the eastern banks of the Avon River stretching from Dunnington Walls to the Avenue leading to Stonehenge are lines of ash pits. These pits were filled with wood ash from a single event, occasionally including artifacts. The volume of the ash deposit indicates massive bonfires, a considerable investment in a ritual activity given that the area had been deforested and the logs involved had to be imported from some distance. The careful saving of the ashes in the pits indicate continuing importance and ritual significance of the fires and ash.

In North America, the closing of Great Kivas (ritual structures) by communities along the Mimbres River in the American Southwest provides another example. The ritual closing of Great Kivas is a planned activity, following the same pattern throughout the area (Creel 2010; Creel and Anyon 2004). First, ritual items are placed on the floors of the Great Kiva, then the roof is burned at a high temperature directly on the floor. After the fire, the walls are toppled in, covering the resulting ash, and the main support post pulled. The ritual closing of the Great Kiva is witnessed by members of the community as well as seen and experienced by members of other communities in the region through the smoke plume (Creel 2010).

For both of these examples, the social action and use of fire create local and regional meaning and social memory. The current volume is a welcome addition to this tradition. The case studies are theoretically sophisticated and centered within the common theme of the transformative nature of fire: fire sanctifies and purifies; it destroys and leads to rebirth. The resulting ash has ritual power, and its deposition is the result of social action. The case studies employ careful methodologies to explore these deposits, and their conclusions are based on sound and well-grounded data. The combination of solid methodology and sophisticated theory places the works in this volume within the broader movement of understanding social action and meaning in archaeology and provide a path that researchers can follow in other areas as research in this area continues in the future.

References

Amerlinck, Mari-Jose. 2001. *Architectural Anthropology*. Westport, CT: Bergin and Grave.
Bailey, Douglass W. 1990. "The Living House: Signifying Continuity." In *The Social Archaeology of Houses*, edited by Ross Samson, 19–48. Edinburgh: Edinburgh University Press.
Barton, C. Michael. 1990. "Beyond Style and Function: A View from the Middle Paleolithic." *American Anthropologist* 92: 57–72.
Cameron, Catherine M. 1999. *Hopi Dwellings: Architecture at Orayvi*. Tucson: University of Arizona Press.
Cameron, Catherine M., and Steven A. Tomka. 1993. *Abandonment of Settlements and Regions*. Cambridge: Cambridge University Press.
Creel, Darrell. 2010. "Burning Down the House: Ritual Architecture of the Mimbres Late Pithouse Period." In *Mimbres Lives and Landscapes*, edited by Margaret C. Nelson and Michelle Hegmon, 29–37. Santa Fe, NM: School of Advanced Research Press.
Creel, Darrel, and Roger Anyon. 2004. "New Interpretations of Mimbres Public Architecture and Space: Implications for Culture Change." *American Antiquity* 68: 67–92.
Creese, John L. 2012. "The Domestication of Personhood: A View from the Northern Iroquoian Longhouse." *Cambridge Archaeological Journal* 22: 365–86.
Eriksen, Marianne H. 2016. "Commemorating Dwelling: The Death and Burial of Houses in Iron and Viking Age Scandinavia." *European Journal of Archaeology* 19: 477–96.
Gerritsen, Fokke. 1999. "To Build and to Abandon: The Cultural Biography of Late Prehistoric Houses and Farmsteads in the Southern Netherlands." *Archaeological Dialogues* 6: 78–97.
Hodder, Ian. 1982. *Symbols in Action: Ethnoarchaeological Studies of Material Culture*. Cambridge: Cambridge University Press

———. 1986. *Reading the Past: Current Approaches and Interpretation in Archaeology.* Cambridge: Cambridge University Press.

Hodder, Ian, and Craig Cessford. 2004. "Daily Practice and Social Memory at Catalhoyuk." *American Antiquity* 69: 17–40.

Jervis, Ben. 2014. "Pots as Things: Value, Meaning and Medieval Pottery in Relational Perspective." In *The Chiming of Crack'd Bells: Recent Approaches to the Study of Artefacts in Archaeology,* edited by Paul Blinkhorn and Christopher Cumberpatch, 3–16. Oxford: BAR International Series 2677.

Lightfoot, Ricky R. 1993. "Abandonment and Processes in Prehistoric Pueblos." In *Abandonment of Settlements and Regions,* edited by Catherine M. Cameron and Steven A. Tomka, 165–77. Cambridge: Cambridge University Press.

McAnany, Patricia, and Ian Hodder. 2009. "Thinking about Stratigraphic Sequence in Social Terms." *Archaeological Dialogue* 16:1–22.

Parker Pearson, Mike, Josh Pollard, Colin Richards, Julian Thomas, Christopher Tilley, Kate Welham, Umberto Albarella. 2006. "Materializing Stonehenge: The Stonehenge Riverside Project and New Discoveries." *Journal of Material Culture* 11: 227–61.

Roth, Barbara, and Katheryn M. Baustian. 2015. "Kin Groups and Social Power at the Harris Site, Southwestern New Mexico." *American Antiquity* 80: 451–71.

Rothschild, Nan, and Susan Dublin. 1994. "Deep Trash: A Tale of Two Middens." In *Exploring Social, Political and Economic Organization in the Zuni Region,* edited by Todd L. Howell and Tammy Stone, 91–100. Anthropological Research Paper 46. Tempe: Arizona State University.

Schiffer, Michael B. 1976. *Behavioral Archaeology.* New York: Academic Press.

———. 1987. *Formation Processes of the Archaeological Record.* Salt Lake City: University of Utah Press.

Schiffer, Michael B., Charles Riggs, and J. Jefferson Reid. 2017. *The Strong Case Approach in Behavioral Archaeology.* Salt Lake City: University of Utah Press.

Stevenson, Marc G. 1982. "Toward an Understanding of Site Abandonment Behavior: Evidence from Historic Mining Camps in the Southwest Yukon." *Journal of Anthropological Archaeology* 1: 237–65.

Stone, Tammy. 2015. *Migration and Ethnicity in Middle-Range Societies, a View from the Southwest.* Salt Lake City: University of Utah Press.

———. 2016. "Organizational Variability in Early Aggregated Communities in Middle-Range Societies: An Example from the Kayenta Region of the American Southwest." *American Antiquity* 81: 58–73.

Tilley, Christopher. 1994. *A Phenomenology Landscape, Places, Paths and Monuments.* Oxford: Berg.

Varien, Mark D., and Barbara Mills. 1997. "Accumulation Research: Problems and Prospects for Estimating Site Occupation Span." *Journal of Archaeological Method and Theory* 4: 141–91.

Waddington, Kate. 2014. "The Biography of a Settlement: An Analysis of Middle Iron Age Deposits and Houses at Howe, Orkney." *Archaeological Journal* 171: 61–96.

Walker, William H. 2002. "Stratigraphy and Practical Reason." *American Anthropologist* 104: 159–77.

Index

abandonment, 229; of ash-filled hearths, 22–23; burning and, 97–98; house closure and, 23–24; planned and gradual, 206–8. *See also* closure
Acoma, 47, 70; "Kachinas Are Going to Fight Us," 202–3
Adena culture: ceremonialism, 147
agency, 2, 5–7, 41, 114; of houses, 23–24; of nonhuman objects, 136, 198–200; social systems and, 58–59
Albert Porter Pueblo, 54
Allegheny-Cumberland Plateau: caves and rock shelters in, 187–88, 189–90, 193–94
altars: Pueblo, 201–2
American Bottom region, 115–16; ash deposits in, 117–18, 119–25(table), 126–28; burned buildings in, 113, 128–29, 130
ancestors, 4, 213; feeding, 4, 48, 70, 215, 219–21, 222; protection of, 89, 91
Ancestral Puebloans, 7, 76. *See also* Hopi; Mesa Verde region; northern Rio Grande region
animacy, 218; of Mimbres houses, 23–24; of nonhuman objects, 136, 196, 197, 198–200
Ani'-Suwa'lï, 139
anthropocentrism, 199–200
antlers, deer, 87, 88
architecture: cleansing, 113; social production of, 58–59
Argentina: house closure in, 97–98

Arnold Research Cave: sandal offerings, 189
arrow points, 37; power of, 9, 200–203
artifacts, 41, 87; life histories of, 58, 230; in Mesa Verde hearths, 51–55; broken, 36, 37
"ash boys," "Ash Youths," 70, 82
ash caves, 189–90; and salt, 193–94
ash cones: Homol'ovi I, 67–68
ash-filled hearths: Mesa Verde region, 47, 58; Mimbres, 16, 18, 22–23, 25–26; at Pot Creek and Picuris pueblos, 87, 90
ash deposits, 5, 222; at Brandy's Pueblo, 34–35; at Caddoan sites, 174, 180; at Cahokian sites, 113, 117–18, 119–25(table), 126–28, 130; at Danger Cave, 190–91; in Homol'ovi Settlement Clusters, 66–68
ash emplacements: in Cherokee towns, 138, 145, 148; in Mississippian sites, 146–47
ash lenses: at Cottonwood Spring Pueblo, 203, 204(fig.), 205–6
ash piles: Pueblo use of, 2, 87
ash pits: in Iroquoian longhouses, 159–61; in Pot Creek kivas, 87; in Stonehenge area, 230
ash zones: American Bottom sites, 118, 127
awls, bone, 87, 88
axes mundi: smoke as, 137, 175, 181
Aztecs, 218, 224n3; deities, 186, 187, 193–94

bears: in Mimbres sites, 18–19
Beaver, Virginia, 161
behavioral archaeology: and object agency theory, 197
Bell, Robert E., 176
Big Ash Rock House, 189
birds: in Mesa Verde hearths, 56, 57
birthing retreats, 187; material traits associated with, 188–89
blocking posts: in Caddoan charnel houses, 179(fig.), 181, 182
blood: offerings of, 9, 190, 193
blowing ashes: by False Faces, 164–66; by Hopi, 202
blue-green minerals, 69, 70. *See also* turquoise
bodies: ash on, 82, 90
bone, 55; at Bridge River site, 102, 104, 105–6, 108; in Cahokian mounds, 127–28
Boyle, David, 162
Brandy's Pueblo (AZ P:3:114 [ASM]), 30–31, 32(fig.), 40; artifacts from, 36–37, 41; ash-covered surfaces at, 34–35; structure of, 33–34; walls in, 35–36
Brant-Sero, J., 162
Bridge River site, 94–95, 108; bone at, 105–6; description of, 99–101; roof deposits, 102–7
British Columbia: housepit villages in, 8, 94–95, 99–101
Buckner Hollow, 189
buildings: burial and rebuilding of, 144; construction of, 200; feeding, 218. *See also by type*
bundles, bundling, 2, 186; in Cahokian religious politics, 113, 114–15, 117, 130, 131
burials, 9, 40, 69, 144, 173, 190; Mesoamerican, 213, 223; Mimbres, 19, 24–25, 26–27; at Pot Creek Pueblo, 85–87, 90
burning, 4, 7, 8, 19, 38, 41, 47, 49, 62, 87, 113, 162, 230; American Bottom sites, 117, 128–29; blood and filth offerings, 190, 193; Caddoan charnel houses, 174, 180–81; Cottonwood Spring Pueblo, 197–98, 203, 205; experimental, 50–51; of faunal remains, 55, 56, 57; in Maya burial ritual, 223–24; mid-Fraser River houses, 94, 96–98, 102, 104–7; persistence of, 39–40; of precious goods, 218–19; as protection, 76–77
"burning of the white dog" ceremony, 162
burnt offerings, 186, 218, 224–25n4; as food for ancestors, 220–21; incense as, 221–22; in Maya tombs, 223–24
Busk, 194
Buzzard Rock Shelter, 189–90

Caddoans: charnel houses, 9, 177, 181–82; marker mounds, 183–84; mortuary program, 173–76
Cahiague North Village, 159, 160(fig.)
Cahokia, 8, 116; ash deposits in, 118, 126, 127; religious politics, 113, 114–15, 117; burning in, 128–29
Caldwell, Joseph R.: and Norman site, 176–77
Calvert site, 160
Canandaigua site, 166
Çatalhöyük, 97
Cave Fork Hill Cliff, 189
caves, 9, 186; ash in, 189–90, 193; as women's retreats, 190–92. *See also* rock shelters
Cayuga, 162; Sour Springs Longhouse, 163, 166, 187
celestial ash, 194
Central Algonquians, 158
ceramics, 41, 87; at Brandy's Pueblo, 34, 36–37; corrugated, 31, 33; Homol'ovi, 64–65; in Mesa Verde hearths, 51, 52(table), 53–54; in Mimbres ritual deposits, 16, 20, 21, 24, 26
ceremonialism, 83; Iroquois, 156, 157–58, 159, 162–64, 166–67
charnel houses, 9, 147, 173, 174(fig.), 177; dismantling and construction

Index

of, 181–82; superimposed, 175, 179–80
Cherokee, 8, 136–37, 186, 187, 190; townhouses, 137–46; pipe smoking, 147–48
Chevelon Pueblo, 33, 64, 65
Chichen Itza, 216
childbirth, 9, 62
children, 217, 224n3; protection of, 82, 89, 201
Cibola Whiteware, 36
Circle Post Monument (Cahokia), 126
Classic Maya, 214, 220, 224n1; feeding supernaturals, 216–17
Classic Mimbres period, 15, 26; Elk Ridge site, 20–22
clay, 190; black, 9, 178; in Caddoan charnel houses, 173, 179(fig.), 181, 182, 184
cleansing, 2, 6, 70, 91, 182, 193; projectile points used in, 200–201
closure, 4, 5–6, 7; at Cottonwood Spring Pueblo, 197–98, 207–8; house burning, 97–98, 108; Homol'ovi structures, 33, 66; at Hopi, 37; of Mimbres houses, 16, 17, 18–24, 25–26; persistence of practices, 39–40; projectile points in, 208–9
Coahuila, 194
Coba, 216
Cochiti Witch Kiva (Picuris), 89–90
Coldspring Longhouse, 166
Coles Creek culture, 147
Colorado Plateau: rock shelters, 187, 190
colors, color symbolism, 4, 5, 6; Pueblo, 70–71
communication theory: artifacts in, 198–99
conflict: pueblo burning, 38, 39
consumption: of ash, 186; of cremains, 187; of humans, 216–17; of offerings, 218–19
contamination: spiritual, 40, 41, 62
cooking practices, 80; Iroquois, 159, 161–62, 164, 166
copal: Maya use of, 221–22

Copan, 216
Copper site: ash and bone at, 127, 128
corn, 37, 62, 117, 187, 217, 218; in Iroquois sites, 159, 161–62; nixtamalization of, 130–31. *See also* hulled-corn soup
Cothrun's Kiva site (AZ P:12:277[ASM]), 39
cottontails: in Mesa Verde hearths, 56, 57
cottonwood (*Populus* sp.): ash from, 37, 90
Cottonwood Spring Pueblo (LA 175), 197–98; abandonment of, 207–8; ash lenses at, 203, 204(fig.), 205; projectile points at, 206, 208–9
covenants: between living and supernatural beings, 213–14
Cowee, 141
Coweeta Creek site: structure of, 141–42; townhouse at, 142–46
cremains, 175, 187
Creswell Pueblo (AZ J:14:282[ASM]), 38–39
cross-cultural surveys: associations in, 78–80
cross-in-circle motifs, 136
Crow Canyon Archaeological Center Research Database, 48–49, 56
Cumberland Plateau: ash caves, 193–94; caves and rock shelters, 187–88, 189–90
curing rituals, 9; Iroquois, 164–65, 167

Dakota: menstrual bundles, 190
Danger Cave, 193; as women's shelter, 190–91
death, 40, 224n3; earth gods and, 218; Maya gods and, 221–22; and structure burning, 4, 96, 98
decommissioning, 49; of ancestral Hopi structures, 39, 40; of hearths, 51–55, 59; Pot Creek kivas, 87–89; of structures, 47–48
deities: fire, 186. *See also* gods; supernaturals
demarcation: ash lines, 47
descendent populations: consultation with, 229–30

De-Waele site, 160
Dhegihan peoples, 188
Diné (Navajo), 40, 71, 81(table), 84, 98
Direct Historical Approach: in Iroquoian archaeology, 156, 157
dis-charming powers, 202; arrow points, 200–201
ditches: in downtown Cahokia precinct, 16
Dresden Codex, 216
Dunnington Walls, 230

Early Iroquoian sites, 160
Early Pithouse period (Mimbres), 22
Early Woodland period, 189
earth: in Cherokee townhouses, 140–41
earth lodges: Pawnee, 98
earth ovens: Range site, 126
East St. Louis precinct, 115, 126, 127
effigies: feeding, 215
elites: Maya, 214, 215
Elk Ridge, 20–22, 26, 27
embers: in cleansing, 70
emitters: nonhuman objects as, 199
ethnographic data, 26, 197; cross-cultural associations, 78–80; on Iroquois, 157–58; US Southwest, 77–78, 80–81, 84–85
Etowah Mounds, 187
exorcism, 2, 202
extended families: and Mimbres houses, 22, 24–25
eye masks, 187

faces: ash on, 82
False Face Society, 159; blowing ashes, 164–66
faunal remains, 51; Bridge River site, 102, 104, 105–6, 108; Buzzard Rock Shelter, 190; in Mesa Verde hearths, 55–57; in Pot Creek kivas, 87–88
feasting: and ritual deposits, 16
feces, 186, 192, 194
feeding: ancestors, 4, 48, 70, 215, 219–21
feet: as fertility symbol, 188
fertility, 188–89, 193, 194

Fifth Sun (Aztec), 186
filth, 9; offerings of, 190, 193, 194
fire, 1, 2, 4, 8, 47, 49, 71, 96, 113, 186, 194, 197, 213; Cherokee views of, 136, 137, 139–41; as cleansing, 91, 190; and *Itiwana* ceremony, 70; as transformational, 40–41, 81, 117, 147
firekeepers: Cherokee, 139–40, 145
fire society: Acoma, 47, 70; Zia, 201
First Woman (Dhegihan), 188
Five Nations Iroquois, 157, 159, 166
floors: in Caddoan charnel houses, 182; and roof sequences, 94–95
floor vaults: decommissioning of, 48
food, 4, 47, 186; for ancestors, 219–21; Iroquois preparation of, 159, 161–62, 164, 166, 167; for Mesoamerican deities, 216–18; recipes, 80
footprints: ancestral Hopi sites, 37; in caves, 188
forgetting: purposeful, 40, 41
French Broad River: Cherokee towns on, 138–39
fuel woods: experimental burning of, 50–51; Mesa Verde region, 48; Pot Creek kivas, 87, 88
funerary rituals: Tewa, 84. *See also* mortuary rituals
Fur Trade period: Bridge River site, 100, 101

Galaz site, 25
Galton's problem, 78
Garoga site, 166
Gell, Alfred: on agency, 198, 199
gender, 6, 9, 41. *See also* women's retreats
ghosts: protection from, 82, 84
Glycymeris shell: in Little Colorado River Valley, 34–35; in Mimbres sites, 24
gods: Maya Death, 221–22; food for, 216–18
Goforth-Saindon site, 174(fig.), 175; mounds, 176(fig.), 178, 179–80
Grand River Reserve (Six Nations): ceremonialism, 162–64

graywares: in Mesa Verde hearths, 51, 52(table), 53–54
Great Basin, 9, 83, 84–85, 187, 190–91, 193
"Great Kiva" (Pot Creek Pueblo), 90–91
great kivas, 39; Mimbres, 15–16, 17, 20, 230–31
Great Lakes region, 157. *See also* Lower Great Lakes
Great Rock House, 189
ground stone: in termination activities, 54–55

Hano, 202
Harlan site, 173, 176, 180
Harris site, 22, 26; agency of houses as, 23–24; burials at, 25, 27; great kiva at, 15–16; pithouse ritual closure at, 19–20
hatch covers: in Mesa Verde hearths, 54–55
Havasupai: use of ash, 81(table), 84
hawks: as dedicatory offerings, 57
healing, 82, 83, 85, 91; Cherokee, 187, 190
hearths, 4, 58; in American Bottom, 118, 127; ash accumulation rates, 49–51; ash-filled, 16, 18, 22–23, 25–26, 87, 90; Cherokee, 138, 141–42, 144; decommissioning of, 45, 59; feeding, 48, 70; in longhouses, 159–61, 162; in Mesa Verde region, 7, 51–57; sealing, 47, 88–89
hearts: as food for gods, 216, 217
hogans: avoidance of, 40, 84
Hogup Cave, 192, 193
hominy: preparation of, 161, 162
Homol'ovi I (AZ J:14:3[SM]), 63, 64; ash and turquoise at, 68–69, 71; ash cones at, 67–68; turquoise at, 62, 65–67
Homol'ovi Settlement Cluster (HSC), 30, 38, 40, 63; ash deposits at, 67–68; chronology, 64–65
Homol'ovi II, 38, 64, 65
Hopewell sites: mortuary practices, 147

Hopi, 4, 41, 63, 81(table), 82, 83, 84, 201, 202; ancestral, 30–33, 37; New Fire Ceremony, 5, 47, 62
Hotevilla, 202
Hough's Great Kiva (AZ P:16:112[ASM]), 39
households: extended family, 22; social memory, 41
housepit villages: Bridge River site, 8, 94–95, 96, 100–101, 102–8
houses: agency of, 23–24; closure of, 16, 17, 18–20, 26, 39–40, 97–98; as sociopolitical entities, 107–8. *See also* charnel houses; housepit villages; pithouses
Howlett Hill site, 166
HRAF. *See* Human Relations Area Files
HSC. *See* Homol'ovi Settlement Cluster
Huixtocihuatl, 194
hulled-corn soup, 159, 161, 162, 166
Human Relations Area Files (HRAF): Collection of Ethnography, 77–80
humans: consumption of, 216–17, 219–20; and supernatural beings, 213–14
Hunt God (Mixcoatl), 187
Huntsville site, 174(fig.), 175, 180
Huron/Wendat, 159
Husk Faces, 164, 165(fig.), 166

illness, 83, 89, 201; healing, 82, 91, 167
incense: Maya use of, 221–22, 225nn7, 8
infants, 82, 90, 201
initiation ceremonies: Zuni, 83
Iroquois, 9; ceremonialism, 157–58, 162–64; coalescence of, 158–59; curing rituals, 164–66; ethnographic and archaeological data, 156–57, 166–67; food preparation, 161–62
Isleta: projectile points as amulets, 201
Itiwana ceremony, 70

Jeddito Yellow Ware: and Homol'ovi chronology, 64–65
Joara, 139

Jornada Mogollon, 203. *See also* Cottonwood Spring Pueblo
juniper (*Juniperus* sp.): ash from, 37, 48

"Kachinas Are Going to Fight Us," 202–3
Kâsdu'yĭ, 138
katsina religion, 64; Acoma, 202–3
Keatley Creek site, 108
K'ekchi' Maya, 214
k'ex sacrifice, 216
K'iche' Maya, 214, 221
Kituhwa, 139, 141
kivas: 49, 200; decommissioning of, 39, 41–42, 48; hearths in, 7, 45; material culture in, 51–55; natural decomposition of, 89–91; ritual retirement of, 15–16
Kunnermann Mound (Cahokia), 127
K'uxaj chan K'ihnich (Sun God is Eating Hearts in the Sky), 216

Lacandon Maya, 219
Lady Blood, 221
La Gila Encantada, 22
Laguna, 201
Lake Roberts Vista (LRV), 26; architecture at, 17–19; pithouses at, 18–19
land tenure, 19, 22
La Rinconada: house closure in, 97–98
Late Classic period (Maya), 215
Late Classic period (Mimbres), 21
Late Pithouse period (Mimbres), 15, 17, 19, 21, 22, 26
Late Preclassic (Maya): copal use, 221
Late Woodland period, 118; burned buildings, 128–29; mounds, 147
Lawson village, 159
Ledford Island site, 145–46
lightning, 197, 201, 202
lithic debitage: Bridge River site, 102
Little Ash Cave, 189
Little Colorado River valley: Homol'ovi Settlement Cluster, 30–31
"living" spaces: protection of, 76
Longe, Alexander: on Cherokee life, 137, 138

longhouses, 9, 157–58; ceremonialism in, 162–64; 166–67; hearth & ash pit complexes, 159–61
LRV. *See* Lake Roberts Vista
Luiseño: cremain consumption, 187

maize. *See* corn
Maize God, 216, 217, 219
malevolent spirits: protection from, 81–83
mammals: in Mesa Verde hearths, 55–56, 57
Mammoth/Salts Cave, 186, 189
Marakwet tribe, 2
Marau altar, 202
Marge site, 126, 129
marker mounds, 175; Caddoan, 173, 176, 183–84
marker posts: in Cahokia and East St. Louis precincts, 126, 127
Masaw, 202
masking ceremonies: Iroquoian, 159
material culture: dangerous, 62; and hearth decommissioning, 45, 51–55, 58. *See also* artifacts; nonhuman objects; objects
materiality: anthropocentrism of, 199–200
Maya, 9, 213, 214, 215, 224–25nn2, 4–6; feeding ancestors, 219–20; feeding supernaturals, 216–19; tomb reentry, 223–24, 225n9; use of incense, 221–22
mealing structures, 67
medicine, 187, 190
menstruation, 9; material traits associated with, 188–89, 190; retreats, 187
Mesa Verde region, 7, 45, 46(fig.), 48; faunal remains in hearths, 55–57; material culture in hearths, 51–55
Mesoamerica, 9–10, 186; fire in, 213–14. *See also* Maya
Mexica: on fertility symbols, 188
Middle Cherokee towns, 141
Mid-Fraser Canyon, 8; Bridge River site in, 94–95, 102–7; house burning in, 96–97

Midwinter Festival (Seneca), 162; False Faces, 164–66; stirring ashes ritual, 163, 187
Milky Way, 187
Mimbres region: ash-filled hearths in, 22–23, 25–26; burials, 24–25, 26–27; structure closure ritual, 7, 15–16, 17, 18–22, 230–31
mimicry: maize, 217
miniature objects, 21, 193
Mississippian period, 126; burning and ash deposits in, 128–29, 130, 146–47; fire in, 136
Mississippian tradition, 113; bundling, 114–15
Mixcoatl, 187
Mohawk: Garoga site, 166
monuments: Caddoan mounds as, 184
Mooney, James, 137; on townhouses, 139–41
Moorhead phase: ash deposits, 127–28, 130
Morrison site, 118
mortality: as acquired attribute, 218
mortuary rituals, 9, 84; Caddoan, 173, 175–78, 181–82; Maya, 221–22; Northern Rio Grande, 85–87; Pot Creek Pueblo, 91–92
Mother Towns (Cherokee), 139
mounds: in American Bottom sites, 126, 127, 128, 129–30; Caddoan, 173, 174(fig.), 178, 179–80, 183–84; and Cherokee townhouses, 139–40; Late Woodland, 147
"Mounds and the Constant Fire, The," 139
mourning wars: Iroquois, 158
Multi-kiva (MK) site (AZ P:3:112[ASM]), 30, 38, 41
Murdock Mound (Cahokia), 127

Nahuatl: turquoise use, 71
NAN Ranch, 20, 25
Naranjo (Sa'aal), 216, 225n6
Navajo, 40, 71, 81(table), 84, 98
Neolithic period: structure burning, 6, 97
Nequassee, 139, 141

Neutral (Iroquois nation), 159
New Fire Ceremony: Aztec, 194; Hopi, 5, 47, 62; Iroquois, 164, 187
Newt Kash Shelter, 187, 190
Newtown Longhouse, 166
nixtamal, nixtamalization, 130–31, 187
nonhuman objects: agency and animacy of, 198–200; social relationships with, 196–97
Norman site, 174(fig.), 176–78
Northern Caddoan culture: mortuary rituals, 173–74
Northern Rio Grande region, 8, 76; kivas, 87–89; mortuary contexts, 85–87
Northwest Coast: house abandonment and reconstruction, 98
Nuvatukya'ovi (San Francisco Peaks), 63

object agency theory, 197
objects, 6, 45, 47; dedicatory, 16, 57, 58. *See also* artifacts; nonhuman objects
offerings, 70, 117, 186, 189; blood and filth, 190, 193; Mesoamerican burned, 220–21; supernatural consumption of, 218–19
Old Fire God, 186
Onondaga: Howlett Hill site, 165
Onondaga Longhouse, 166, 187
Ontario Iroquois, 157, 158; longhouse hearth complexes, 159–61
Ozarks: caves and rock shelters, 188

Paddle Party, 163
paddles: in Iroquoian ceremonialism, 162, 163
paint: from ash, 186
Palenque, 219, 222, 225nn6, 8
palisade: at Cahokia, 115, 126
parching: corn kernels, 159
Pawnee: earth lodge disassembly and rebuilding, 98
Picuris Pueblo, 76, 85; unburned kivas at, 89–90
piiki bread, 62
pipe smoking: Cherokee, 148–49

pithouses, 96; agency of, 23–24; ash-filled pits in, 22–23; hearths in, 45, 49; Mimbres, 7, 15, 17, 18–20, 26; replica, 50–51; roof burning, 98–99. *See also* housepits
pits, 16; in American Bottom sites, 118, 126, 128
plants: burned for ash, 37, 48, 87, 88
platform mounds: Caddoan, 173, 175, 183
Popol Vuh: copal use, 221, 222
Postclasic period (Mesoamerica), 214, 216
Pot Creek Pueblo, 76; kiva decommissioning, 87–89; mortuary contexts, 85–87, 91–92; unburned kivas at, 90–91
pottery. *See* ceramics
Pottery Hill (AZ P:12:12[ASM]), 39
practice theory, 200
precious goods: burning of, 218–19; as food for gods, 216, 217–18
projectile points, 9, 87, 196, 206; in closure rituals, 208–9; Mimbres ritual use of, 16, 24; Pueblo symbolism of, 200–203
protection, 5, 6, 9, 26, 62; burning and ash as, 41, 70, 76–77; from malevolent spirits, 81–83; projectile points and, 16, 196, 201–2; from underworld, 88–89; from violence, 83–84
public architecture: Cahokia and East St. Louis, 115, 118, 126
Puebloans, 2, 37; color symbolism, 70–71; fire as transformational, 40–41; projectile point symbolism, 200–203; turquoise use, 61–62
pueblos: Mimbres, 7, 15, 17, 20–22; purposeful destruction of, 35–36
Pulcher site, 118
purification, 5, 9, 37, 62, 96, 197; projectile points, 202–3; Puebloan practices, 40, 61, 71–72; of rock shelters, 192, 193

rabbits: in Mesa Verde hearths, 56, 57; symbology of, 188–89

Range site: ash deposits at, 118, 126, 127, 128; mound deposits, 129–30
Rattlesnake Point: cultural turquoise at, 70
Red-Eye Hollow (Red Eye shelter), 189, 190
refuse pits: ash in, 129
renewal, 5–6, 7, 9, 21, 47, 62; Pueblo use of, 61, 71–72
replastering: in Caddoan charnel houses, 182
ritual paraphernalia: burning of, 62
Rock Art Ranch, 30
rock shelters, 9: ash deposits in, 189–90, 192–93; and salt, 193–94; as women's work party camps, 187–89, 190–92. *See also* caves
rodents: in hearth contents, 55–56
roofs, 16, 47; Bridge River site, 102–7; burned, 8, 94–95, 96–99
Room 822 (Pot Creek Pueblo), 90
Russell site, 128

Sa'aal (Naranjo), 216, 225n6
Sackett site, 166
sacrifices, 41, 69; human, 216–17, 218
sagebrush (*Artemisia* sp.): ash from, 37, 48; in decommissioned kivas, 87, 88
salt: and rock shelters, 193–94
Salt Woman, 194
sanctification, 83, 84
sandals, 188, 189, 193
Sand Prairie phase, 130
San Francisco phase (Mimbres), 17, 19, 24
San Juan pueblo, 201
San Miguel Tzinacapan, 218
Santa Clara pueblo, 82
scalp takers: Zia and Zuni, 201
Seneca, 156, 158; Midwinter Festival, 162–63, 187; Thanksgiving ceremony, 165–66
shell artifacts, 24, 188; Cherokee, 140, 144; in Little Colorado River Valley, 34–35
Shields Pueblo, 54
Siberia: pithouses in, 98

sipapus: decommissioning of, 48
Six Nations: ceremonialism, 162–64
Skeenah Creek, 138
Skeona, 138, 146
smoke, 8, 9, 96, 108, 114, 174, 219, 222; as *axis mundi*, 175, 181; in Cherokee tradition, 136, 137, 139, 147–48
smudge fires, 96; St'át'imc society, 107, 108
snapping turtle shell rattles, 159
social memory, 6, 37, 41, 223, 229, 230, 231; Homol'ovi rituals, 67–68
social relationships: with nonhuman objects, 196–97
solstice ceremonies: Acoma, 47, 70; Zuni, 2, 70
sorcery, 9, 82
Sour Springs Longhouse, 163, 166, 187
space(s), 62, 76; demarcation and protection of, 47, 70; opening and closing of, 9–10
Spider Woman, 194
"Spirit Defenders of Nikwasi, The," 139
spirits: protection from malevolent, 81–83
stars: origins as, 186–87
St'át'imc tradition, 96, 98; smudge burning, 107, 108
Stirling phase: ash deposits, 126, 127, 130
stirring ashes rites (Iroquoian), 163–64, 187
Stonehenge area: burned deposits, 230
Stone Man, 186
stone tools: in Cahokian offerings, 117
stratigraphy, 229, 230; Caddoan mounds, 176, 177(fig.), 178, 183; Caddoan charnel houses, 179–80; Danger Cave, 190–91; Hogup Cave, 192
structures, 8, 15, 67; intentional burning of, 4, 39–40. *See also by type*
submound deposits: East St. Louis and Cahokian, 126
Sun God, 216, 219
supernatural beings, 215, 219; covenants with, 213–14

Swarts Ruin, 25
sweat lodges: American Bottom, 127
symbolic grammar: Caddoan, 173

Talpa Phase, 85, 86, 89
Taos Pueblo, 85, 87
Taronyawagon (Holder of the Heaven): Midwinter ceremonies, 162, 163, 164
Taunton map, 157, 158(fig.)
Terminal Late Woodland period, 115, 129; ash deposits, 119, 126
termination events, 58; fire and ash in, 47, 51, 114; in Mesa Verde region, 49–50, 54–55
Tewa pueblos, 81(table), 84; "ash boys/Ash Youths," 70, 82
textiles: in rock shelters, 192, 193, 194
thanksgiving ceremony: Tonawanda Seneca, 165–66
Thompson (Nlaka'pamux) people, 96, 98
Three Circle phase, 16, 17, 25
Tiwa, 85; ritual use of ash, 90, 91–92
Tlazolteotl, 193–94
tobacco: sacredness of, 147–48
tomb reentry: Maya, 223–24, 225n9
Tonawanda Reserve: stirring ashes ritual, 164; thanksgiving ceremony, 165–66
townhouses: ashes and fire in, 138, 139–41; Coweeta Creek site, 142–46; smoke from, 137
transformation, 2, 5, 8, 9, 229; ash and fire in, 4, 40–41, 114, 117; burning and, 7, 49, 81
transitions, 77, 85
"trapping": with ash, 47
truncated pits: clay/ash layers in, 175–76
turquoise, 7–8, 24; at Homol'ovi I, 65–69, 71; Pueblo use of, 61–62, 63, 70
Tzotzil Maya: covenants with supernaturals, 214

uktena, 140, 144
underworld: kivas and, 88–89

Unta'kiyatsti'yĭ, 138
Upper Lillooet (St'át'imc) tradition, 96, 98; smudge burning, 107, 108

Ventana Cave, 206
vessels, 47, 54; at Brandy's Pueblo, 36–37; Mimbres killed, 24, 26
villages: closure of, 38, 39, 40
violence: protection from, 83–84
vitality: Pueblo, 71–72

walls: purposeful destruction of, 35–36, 38, 41
war captives, 216, 218
warfare: house burning, 98, 99; protection from, 83–84; and village closure, 38, 39
War Gods, 84
Warrior Twins, 201
Washausen site, 118
water symbolism: cottonwood and, 90
Winnebago clans: footwear, 189
winter ceremonies: Iroquois, 162–64; Zuni, 2, 70
winter solstice: and Caddoan charnel houses, 180
witchcraft, witches, 197, 224n1; defense against, 2, 9, 62, 82, 83, 85, 89, 91, 196, 201
women's retreats, 194; rock shelters as, 187–88, 193
Woodland period: ash consumption, 186. *See also* Late Woodland period
work parties: women's encampments, 190–91, 192, 193

Yaxchilan, 219
Yazoo Basin, 147
Yukioma, 202

Zia: use of ash, 81(table), 201
Zuni, 26, 48, 81(table), 201; sanctification, 83, 84; winter ceremonies, 2, 70

www.ingramcontent.com/pod-product-compliance
Lightning Source LLC
Chambersburg PA
CBHW051535020426
42333CB00016B/1945